Beyond Justice

AGNES HELLER

Basil Blackwell

Copyright © Agnes Heller, represented by EULAMA, Rome, 1987

First published 1987
First published in paperback 1989
Reprinted 1991

Basil Blackwell Ltd
108 Cowley Road, Oxford, OX4 1JF, UK

Basil Blackwell Inc.
3 Cambridge Center
Cambridge, MA 02142, USA

British Library Cataloguing in Publication Data

Heller, Agnes
  Beyond Justice.
  1. Justice (Philosophy)
  I. Title
  179   B105.J87
  ISBN 0–631–15206–7
  ISBN 0–631–17081 2 (Pbk)

Library of Congress Cataloging in Publication Data
Heller, Agnes
  Beyond justice.
  Bibliography: p.
  Includes index.
  1. Justice. I. Title
  JC578.H45 1987   320'.01'1   86–26825
  ISBN 0–631–15206–7
  ISBN 0–631–17081 2 (pbk.)

Typeset in 10½ on 12pt Sabon
by Columns of Reading
Printed in Great Britain by
Athenaeum Press Ltd, Newcastle upon Tyne.

Contents

Preface

The title of this book, *Beyond Justice*, sums up both the subject matter of the book and the standpoint from which it is discussed. The subject I examine is, of course, the question of justice. The inclusion of the word 'beyond' in the title indicates the position I have adopted, and this is reflected in three distinct, though inter-connected, aspects of the argument contained in the book. These can be summarized as follows. First, I present a critique of certain theoretical assumptions underlying both traditional and modern notions of justice. Secondly, I argue that all claims to justice are rooted in certain values other than justice itself – namely, in 'freedom' and 'life'. Finally, I argue that, while justice may well be a precondition of the good life, the good life is something beyond justice.

The book consists of two analytical chapters, two historical chapters and two chapters which address the normative grounding of justice. The analytical chapters clarify the meaning of the concept of 'justice' and discuss how the concept is used, by actors in social and political conflicts. The historical chapters contain the *critique* of the *philosophical* concepts of justice, ancient and modern. In the last two chapters, which address the normative grounding of justice in the contemporary world, I seek to make a case for combining formalistic and substantive approaches to the question of justice. The analytical, historical and normative chapters have each required a different style of argumentation, yet no one chapter is more important than any other as far as the theoretical argument of the book as a whole is concerned.

In pre-modern times political philosophy, social philosophy and moral philosophy were not yet divided; in modern times they are clearly separated. The problem of justice lies precisely at the point where these three branches of philosophy meet. The value and virtue of justice is a focal point in all three of them. In addressing this problem, I have not intended to write a work of political philosophy, social philosophy or moral philosophy. Rather, I have sought to shed light on a question which serves as a point of contact for all three.

At the request of the publishers, the original manuscript has been abridged. A chapter on just judgement has been omitted, along with two shorter sections (one on righteousness and another on Mandeville and Kierkegaard). The remaining chapters, though abbreviated, remain largely unchanged.

I should like here to express my gratitude to the Australian Research Grant Committee for their generous financial help during the period of writing this book. I should also like to thank Brett Lockwood, who edited my English with great care and devotion; Julian Triado for his work on checking the abbreviated version; and the administrative staff of the Department of Sociology, La Trobe University, for their conscientious typing of the manuscript.

The University of Wisconsin at Madison invited me in November 1984 to give a series of lectures based on the chapters on distributive and retributive justice. The lively discussions which followed each session aided me in the revision of the manuscript. I wish to express my gratitude to the Department of Sociology collectively, and personally to Eric O. Wright and Ivan Szelenyi; to the members of other departments, as well as to those students who attended the seminars and whose remarks were often very illuminating. I was also invited by the University of Barcelona to participate in a conference held in Santander in August 1984 and benefited greatly from being able to read three chapters of the book there. I wish to express my gratitude and appreciation to all participants in the discussion at the conference, and in particular to Victoria Camps for her interesting and substantial remarks, to which she added in our subsequent correspondence concerning the book as a whole. I should also like to thank Professor Arthur Jakobson (Cardozo Law School, New York) for his perceptive criticism of the section on retributive justice, which was presented on a seminar in the New School for Social Research in October 1984.

To my friend and husband, Ferenc Fehér, I cannot adequately express my thanks within the framework of a formal acknowledgement. My work was as much his concern as mine. He discussed the chapters with me, he criticized them, made me rethink certain important questions and also gave me a good deal of technical assistance with the manuscript. I thank him not only for his support but also for his good judgement.

Agnes Heller

1

The Formal Concept
of Justice

The formal (or static) concept of justice is formal (or static) in that (a) it is so *defined* as to encompass the common properties of all types of justice, and, as a result, (b) it is abstracted not only from all normative content, criteria and procedures of justice, but from the (finite) ideal types as well, which are reasonably construed via different combinations of content, criteria and procedures. Chaim Perelman, in his book *The Idea of Justice*, on which I rely heavily at this initial stage of my analysis, uses the term 'formal justice' in what I should call a misleading way. Weber introduced a particular definition of 'formal' justice in his theoretical discourse, in contradistinction to substantive concepts. He meant thereby the formalization of just procedure, a relatively modern type of justice emerging with the rationalization of legal authority, and I see no compelling reason to dismiss the Weberian definition or replace it with any other. Formal justice is thus one kind (or type) of justice. However, the formal concept of justice contains the common features of *all* kinds of justice, be it 'formal' or 'substantive'. It is not the kind of justice it refers to that is formal, but the concept. The formal concept of justice implies, then, a far higher level of abstraction than the concept of 'formal justice'.

Being born into any society and any social group means that members of this particular society and social group must learn about and practise the norms and rules of that particular society and social group. This is the process called 'socialization'. Normally, different sets of norms and rules apply to different groups of people (one fundamental division being that between men and women). Accordingly, learning about and practising norms and rules is tantamount to two distinct sets of behaviour. On the one hand it means knowing, practising and expecting a certain set of norms and rules; on the other it means knowing and expecting, but not practising the same set of norms and rules – in other words, ingroup and outgroup behaviour. The norms and rules regulating the actions of outgroup members have to be known, and the observance of these norms and rules is expected. However, the practice oriented towards the outgroup is regulated not by the norms and rules of this group, but by those of the ingroup. Within an ingroup, expectation and action (speech acts included) are symmetrical: I do in relation to you exactly what I expect you to do in relation to me, for the simple reason that we are both supposed to observe exactly the same norms and rules. By contrast, in relations between ingroup and outgroup, both expectation and action (speech acts included) are asymmetrical: I expect you to do something different from what I do, for the simple reason that we are supposed to observe different norms and rules, or, at least, different ones in addition to common ones. This is obviously a simplified model. Social relations are far more complex than this even when they occur in a so-called 'primitive' milieu. But this simple schema is an ideal point of departure for the establishment of a preliminary, formal concept of justice.

Theories of justice conditioned by the view that justice must be explained in terms of the 'equality–inequality' dichotomy depart, as a rule, from the Aristotelian dictum that being just means treating equals equally and unequals unequally. However, this dictum (or reference) is normally analysed out of its original context, dislocated from the complete Aristotelian conception, where it did make sense. Aristotle never believed that two persons could be each other's equals. Rather, in criticizing Plato's *Republic* (in the *Politics*) he emphatically argued the contrary. In contrast to Aristotle, those who have established a theory of justice based on the principle that equality means treating equals equally and unequals unequally really do intend that people who *are in fact equal* should be treated equally, and that those who *are in fact unequal* should be treated unequally. But what does it really mean that two persons are equals, or, for that matter, unequals? People obviously differ from one another and each and every person is *unique*. On what ground, then, can we compare them? Human beings cannot be quantified (at least, not without a significant residue considerably impairing the value of such quantification), so it would be more than ridiculous for one to establish the equation $A = B = C$, etc., or similarly to establish that $A > B > C$. An obvious objection to this is that the statement 'equals should be treated equally and unequals unequally' refers not to A and B as wholes but to one aspect of A and one aspect of B – for instance, stating that A, B and C are girls or are persons all eighteen years of age. But the mere fact that A, B and C are *equally* girls or equally persons eighteen years old does not make them equals as girls or as eighteen-year-olds, *unless* there are certain norms and rules which apply to *all* girls or to all eighteen-year-olds. To be 'equally such and such' means that we *share* certain characteristics. Indeed, even if we all are singular human beings we do share certain properties with other human beings, and, again, we share certain essential properties with each and every human being. However, Rousseau was clearly aware of how little these shared properties have to do with social equality or inequality, unless they are *created*, or at least *reinforced*, by social norms and rules. Everyday users of language may identify the adverb 'equally' with the noun 'one's equal' if a social order is taken for granted as quasi-natural (where only those who are one's equals are treated equally). This not being the case, even everyday language-users tend to arrive at the standpoint from which I began this discussion – that equality and inequality are normatively constituted. In other words, if the *same* norms and rules apply to a cluster of people, we refer to the members of this cluster as *equals*. If *different* norms and rules apply to two clusters of people and the asymmetry of the pertinent behaviour of the members of the two clusters towards each other is constant, we refer to the relation of the members of the two clusters as *unequal* and to the members themselves as (each other's) *unequals*. If A, B, C are free citizens and D, E, F are not, the norms and rules of free citizenry apply to A, B, C and do not apply to D, E, F. As far as citizenship is concerned, A, B and C are equal with one another (are each other's equals), and D, E, F are, again, equal with one another, but they are unequal with A, B, C (members of the different groups). *Social* equality and inequality is not an ontological given; it is constituted by the application of distinct sets of norms and rules. Conversely, distinct sets of norms and rules constitute social inequality only if the following conditions prevail: (a) a strict division obtains between the sameness of knowledge, action and expectation within the ingroup, and the difference between knowledge and expectation on the one hand, and action on the other hand, in relation to the outgroup; (b) the asymmetry is constant.

Let me disregard for the time being the relation between various social clusters, and talk only about a single social cluster, where the same norms and rules apply to every member of this cluster. But even where every member must observe the norms and follow the rules, they can observe and follow them with different degrees of intensity and consistency. The infringement of norms and rules can be regarded as a sin, crime, offence or blunder according to the gravity of transgression of failure to comply. Norms and rules themselves provide the standards for the establishment of merits and demerits (in moral or other forms of excellence). Comparing persons according to their merits and demerits – which is, after all, a most common form of doing justice and injustice – is a procedure that can hardly be understood in terms of the dichotomy 'equality–inequality', not even within the framework of a modern, highly technical and formalized legal system. If both A and B are sentenced to six years imprisonment, there is no reason to assume either that A and B are alike, or that their respective crimes are alike. Speaking of merit, if A, B, and C are awarded the Nobel Prize, it is presumed that all three excel in something, but it is not presumed that they excel in the same thing or that they are 'alike' in their excellence.

Perelman offers three definitions of the formal concept of justice, or, to use his phrase, of 'formal or abstract' justice. This concept is supposed to be 'a principle of action in accordance with which beings of one and the same essential category must be treated in the same way'; and, further, it means 'applying one rule to all members of an essential category' and 'observing a rule which lays down the obligation to treat in a certain way all persons who belong to a given category'.[1] These definitions serve as my own starting-points as well, with certain modifications. Perelman's definitions might create the impression that there are certain pre-existing essential categories (or clusters) to which the same rules should then apply. But in my view it is precisely the application of the same norms and rules to a certain cluster of people that *constitutes* that very cluster, and *not* the other way round.

Further, I shall not use the term 'rule' (or 'rules') alone, but shall speak of '*norms and* rules'. To my mind it is wrong to assert that all social regulations assume a rule character, even if this is widely held in sociology or modern philosophies. Rules can only be followed in a single and definite way. If rule Y applies to case X, there can be doubt whether X is the case: there can be no doubt, however, concerning the ways and modes of following rule Y *if* X is the case. If X is the case, rule Y has to be followed without deliberation and reflection, and there is only one way to follow this rule. Norms, on the other hand, are different in nature. There are *concrete* and *abstract* norms. Concrete norms are rule-like, abstract norms are not: for example, the virtue of 'acting with civility' is an abstract norm, whilst norms which require that we treat a visitor in a particular manner are concrete. Though related, they are clearly different. Abstract norms enjoin us to act always in a certain manner; concrete norms tell us *how* to act in particular situations. However, while concrete norms are rule-like in nature, they are not rules. How strongly they enjoin compliance depends on their proximity to abstract norms. The observance of norms is not exhausted by following rules – at least, not in a complex society or 'essential category'. This holds true for the simplest game situation as well. During a soccer match, the referee is only concerned with the rules; there can be no doubt whatsoever in his mind whether or not – in the case of fault – the rules prescribe a free kick against the offending party. On the other hand it is not his business whether a player is showing dedication or just idling around during the match. However, the latter is one of the main concerns for both coach and fellow players, utmost personal dedication being one of the norms (and not a rule) of the game. And, given that social life is not a game situation and cannot be adequately characterized in any game theory, the use of the term 'rule' instead of 'norms and rules' inhibits the understanding of its complexity.

My redefinition of the formal concept of justice is as follows: the formal concept of justice means the consistent and continuous application of the same norms and rules to each and every member of the social cluster to which the norms and rules apply.

This definition sounds tautological, but it is not (nor is Perelman's). The formal concept of justice is the *maxim* of justice; the consequence of non-observance is self-contradiction. But it is far from easy to act, judge and distribute without manoeuvring ourselves, time and time again, into such a self-contradiction.

There are two distinct ways of deviating from acting, judging and distributing under the guidance of the maxim of justice. This happens, first, if the norms and rules are not applied to the members of the particular social cluster to which they ought to be applied (if other norms and rules are applied), and secondly, if the application of the norms and rules which should be – and indeed are – applied is inconsistent or discontinuous (discontinuity being a special case of inconsistency). Observing the maxim in the first way poses more complex *theoretical* problems than observing it in the second way, particularly when it comes to applying *norms*. Even if we normally know which norms apply to which cluster, deciding whether a person should be treated according to one norm or another can present a serious problem if the person belongs in at least two *different* clusters. At this juncture moral conflicts may arise; for instance, as to whether the person who committed a particular crime is mentally ill or sane. Obviously, the decision made on this question entails different forms of reaction to the crime, and the risk of coming to a wrong decision, of passing a wrong judgement, is quite obvious. Normally, more than one norm applies to members of social clusters, which raises the question of which (for instance, which merit or demerit) should be given priority. Further, one can be lenient or strict in a greater or lesser degree in the application of the same norms to each and every member of the cluster to which they apply. What are the limits of rigorousness and liberalism if the proper norms and rules are applied? There are no general answers to these problems, but they indicate in their being that the formal concept of justice is indeed a maxim.

The maxim that the same norms and rules should apply to each and every member of a social cluster constituting that cluster regulates two, relatively distinct, kinds of action, speech acts included. The individual A who belongs to cluster X must himself observe the norms and follow the rules, and his interaction with all other members of cluster X *should depend* on *whether they* have observed the same norms or followed the same rules, and if so, to what extent. Even though these two factors are regulatively interwoven, *inconsistency* may appear in applying norms and rules if one factor is more constitutive than the other. People tend to judge others harshly for deeds they themselves have committed, and this is certainly unjust, even if they make these judgements about others consistently. Eventually, the obverse can be the case as well: severity in self-judgement, lenience in the judgement of others. If this inconsistent judge judges others consistently, we might say that he is unjust to himself, but normally we do not call him an unjust person.

Let me demonstrate the formal concept of justice by a very simple example. A rule exists that every student who achieves 340 marks in his or her High School Certificate (HSC) should be admitted to the law school of any university. This rule establishes the cluster of students who have indeed achieved at least 340 marks. Yet such a rule does not make the students 'alike', not even in respect of their mental excellence. But, irrespective of their remaining personal differences, all are *equalized* by the rule, because it applies to all of them. Therefore, should any one student with 340 points or more not be admitted to the law school of a university, we have a case of injustice. There cannot be the slightest doubt about this conclusion, for the cluster in question was constituted by a rule (not a norm). As mentioned, if we apply a rule, we merely have to determine whether X is the case. If it is, then Y should be done, and it can only be done in one way (in our case, if at least 340 points 'is the case', the student gains admittance to any law school).

The cluster of students constituted by the rule in question is a *result cluster*, in that it results from a previous *procedure*. We can term a procedure just or unjust (from the perspective of the formal concept of justice) if the norms and rules of a procedure constitute a social cluster. In our example, the cluster previous to the result cluster consists of all students who sit their HSC, and sitting their HSC means following rules and observing norms related to 'sitting for the HSC'. (In this respect, the minimum number of subjects a student must take is a rule, and so it can only be observed in one way.) On the other hand, preparing for the HSC is a norm, not a rule: different students do it in different ways and with different degrees of commitment. However, the procedure for HSC constitutes not one but two clusters (ingroup–outgroup): one cluster which meets the standards set externally, the other verifying whether the members of the ingroup have indeed met the externally set standards (the marking teachers).

Under further scrutiny, three conclusions can be drawn from our simple model.

1 The formal concept of justice applies to *procedure* as well. Or, more precisely, a procedure can only be termed just or unjust if the formal concept of justice applies. There is *no specific* procedural justice as contrasted to the formal concept of justice. However, one specification has to be made. If rule or norm Y applies to case X, we must first ascertain whether X is indeed the case before applying the rule (norm). Prior to the emergence of modern formal justice (which is now termed 'formal' in the narrower sense of the word), procedures were admitted or eventually invented to establish the *facts* (for instance, innocence or guilt); procedures to which the formal concept of justice was *not* applied. In this vein, the procedure invented by Solomon to determine the real mother of a child cannot be brought under the heading of the formal concept of justice, whilst his final decision, after having ascertained the truth, obviously can. This and similar idiosyncratic procedures are still with us, even if they do not operate in the legal domain.

2 The application of the same norms and rules to each and every member of a cluster to which the norms and rules in question apply is, together with consistency in application, a *moral imperative*, even if the norms and rules themselves are not of a moral nature. Conversely, making exceptions in the application of these norms and rules is a moral offence, even if the subject matter is not of moral provenance. So an unjust act is morally wrong in itself, irrespective of whether marking, judging, comparing, or distributing has anything to do with the morals of those marking, judging and distributing, or with the morals of

those towards whom we act or to whom we distribute.

3   It was not just for simplicity's sake that I took the norms and rules for granted. Clearly, they can be questioned. The norms and rules constituting a social cluster can be declared unjust, or the procedure itself may be declared unjust, even if the norms and rules in question are consistently applied to each and every member of the cluster. How and when they can and should be declared unjust will be discussed in chapter 3. Yet, by declaring either the norms and rules or the procedure unjust, we already form in our mind (in communication with certain others) the *idea* of different norms and rules which have the *telos*, or at least the potential, to constitute social clusters different from existing ones. But even in this 'ideally existing' cluster the same norms and rules should apply to each and every member of the cluster. One cannot criticize existing norms and rules rationally without proposing alternative ones, or at least an alternative procedure for establishing social clusters. Thus the formal concept of justice itself is not tested and queried, even if norms and rules are.

THE VIRTUE OF JUSTICE AND THE FORMAL CONCEPT OF JUSTICE

Viewed from the standpoint of static justice, *judgement* is passed on *merit* and *excellence* and their respective opposites. Except when we keep our judgement to ourselves, all judgements are actions. They are speech acts, and often include acts other than speech acts. Scolding and praising are speech acts; punishing and rewarding include acts other than mere speech acts. The speech act of judging may have a perlocutionary and an illocutionary power, or it may have only the latter. If one turns to the person one scolds or praises, the perlocutionary power of judgement is intended; the case of public scolding and praising is similar, even if the person in question is absent. Privately undertaken acts of judgement in the absence of the person on whom judgement is passed can only have an illocutionary power. But, whatever power these speech acts have, all judgements passed on merit and excellence imply either scolding or praising or both, if only implicitly. Further, all judgements imply ranking and/or comparing from the standpoint of norms and rules the persons upon whom judgement is passed. Not even judgements about another person's taste or mode of dress are exceptions. If there are no norms and rules concerning proper taste or modes of dress for members of a social cluster, judgement is neither just nor unjust (it is precisely in this vacuum that we may say that personal taste is not open to discussion). Obviously, not all forms of ranking and comparing are related to justice, only those passed on persons according to social norms and rules.

Judgements passed on merit and excellence can be viewed as acts of distribution. Praising or scolding means distributing honour and shame. If such speech acts are followed by direct actions, it is punishment or reward that is being distributed. This usually happens via the distribution or redistribution of 'social positions' or material goods. Whether kings distribute lands according to the loyalty of their vassals, or authorities of a liberal state distribute promotion on the basis of excellence, being just means observing the norms and rules and applying them consistently. Consequently, one can be unjust in two ways. First, one can apply to the members of a social cluster norms and rules other than those that should be applied to them. If this happens, one will normally be regarded as unjust by the members of the cluster, even if these norms have been applied consistently to each and every member of the cluster. Secondly, one can inconsistently and discontinuously apply the norms which do apply.

Moreover, there are two kinds of inconsistency. First, there is inconsistency in comparing and ranking *persons*, applying norms and rules to some but not to others (the exception could be one person), being more severe to some, more lenient to others. Inconsistency of this kind is normally attributed to personal motivations, such as liking or disliking, vested interest, passions and the like. Secondly, one can be inconsistent in comparing *groups*. The distinction between a group and a social cluster is constituted by the norms and rules themselves. In so far as the same norms and rules apply to different groups of persons, those groups belong to the same cluster and the members of them must be judged by common norms and rules. If one judges one severely and another leniently, when the same X (action, form of behaviour or forbearance) applies to both, this is unjust. This inconsistency is called the application of *double standards*. It is attributed to social (and occasionally ideological) *bias*. Of course, if two groups do not belong to the same social cluster (being constituted by different norms and rules), then, if we apply different standards to the members of the respective groups, we are not guilty of applying double standards because we have applied the proper (because different) rules to these clusters, and we have done so consistently in accordance with the formal concept of justice. Distinguishing between different and double standards is of the highest importance. If, for example, excellence is the only accepted norm and rule in selecting people for certain positions (without provisos and further conditions), anyone who consistently prefers males to females applies a double standard. However, there can be provisos and conditions built into the norms and rules themselves, such as preventing criminals from exercising their civil rights. This is a very simple case because it concerns a rule and not a norm (or norms). However, if at least two different norms can apply to a situation, one must have priority. In the United States the debate is still continuing on how to apply the norm of excellence in conjunction with another norm (that of historical equity) in order to rectify previous discriminations against disadvantaged groups (blacks, chicanos, women); there are several different general guidelines and opinions as to how to make a just decision and how to apply the second norm without infringing the first. Even so, irrespective of these guidelines, people making the concrete decisions have been forced to decide, at least in the more complex cases, in favour of one norm as against another. In this and all similar cases each and every concrete decision has to be justified. To follow the argument of Marcus Singer,[2] we can say that the generalization principle fails in such a situation (we cannot act as *everyone* should act in a similar situation), and consequently the justification principle has to be applied. We have to justify why we have acted (decided, judged, distributed) in a particular way in a particular case. Although we have dealt only with the problem of inconsistency in the treatment of members of different groups, if this inconsistency is built into the norms themselves then the same can be said of the inconsistent treatment of persons under the same conditions. The only exception to this is judgement as a mere illocutionary act, where different norms can be applied simultaneously without contradiction. But, if we act towards persons (punishing, rewarding, distributing, or anything else) in a context where two norms apply, and we prefer to apply one norm rather than the other (which is inevitable), we are again obliged to *justify* our action through having recourse to a norm which applies to all members of the social cluster to which the person so treated belongs.

   The allegory of justice is the blindfolded woman holding up the scales of balance. Eventually, she may also hold a sword. This is the typical graphic representation of the formal concept of justice. The allegory of justice as depicted by Giotto in the chapel of Arena is, however, a representation of the dynamic concept of justice, not of static justice. Justice appers here as a queen holding a statue in both hands, the angel of war and the angel of peace, the latter being heavier than the former. And the figure is not blindfolded; her eyes look forward, into the future.

It is the allegory of the formal concept of justice to which we restrict our discussion here. The deity is blindfolded for very good reasons: she *must not* see *whose* acts are going to be weighed. Justice must be impersonal and impartial. It must not be influenced by liking or disliking, passion or interest, nor should it be influenced by charity, pity or goodness of heart. These latter stipulations are just as important as the former. If ten people are sentenced to death in accordance with the requirements of certain norms and rules, those who are moved by pity and rescue even one of them are unjust. This is so whether those who make the exception do so because the person is a friend or relative or because they are moved by the natural dignity of his behaviour in the face of impending execution. Clemency and mercy are only just if practised according to norms and rules. Deeds motivated by the most sublime feelings can be unjust. Being just is a *cold virtue*, sometimes even a cruel one. How mild or how cruel it actually is depends on the *norms and rules themselves*, but this problem cannot be addressed in a discussion of the formal concept of justice.[3] The Romans, both with their maxim of *fiat justitia pereat mundus* ('let justice be done though the world perish'), and with their heroes Brutus, who killed his son, and the second Brutus, who killed Julius Caesar, his stepfather, represent the epitome of unflinching impartiality. But even in other times, such as ours, when mercy and forgiveness are part of the normative system of personal interaction (if not in the legal system), justice still preserves its chillness, this quality which sometimes borders on cruelty. Every teacher who ever failed a student, every parent who ever punished a child, every person who ever ranked, graded, distributed and judged (and we all have), has felt the coldness and even the cruelty of justice. *Fiat justitia* is an unconditional imperative of the formal concept of justice, even if the qualification *pereat mundus* need not be appended to it.

Still speaking from the standpoint of the formal concept of justice, persons can be called just if they consistently and continuously apply norms and rules to each and every member of any social cluster to which those norms and rules apply. '*Any* social cluster' is an important qualification. A just father can yet be an unjust friend. Anyone who applies double standards in any respect is an unjust person, even if he so acts consistently and continuously. A just person must be just overall; it is not acceptable to be just in one respect and unjust in another. Cold as this virtue might be, it is a major virtue all the same. The legitimacy, the validity of *any* system of norms and rules depends on whether the members of a given society practise this virtue and to what extent. Generally speaking, as long as the system of norms and rules is legitimized, the members of this society will on average be more just than unjust. Injustice is the exception and justice is the rule. Were it otherwise, no system of norms and rules could operate, for they simply do not exist outside the sphere of their application. As a rule, people are not 'just overall' (they are not just persons), but they are basically just in all areas in which their personal interest, passion, liking, disliking and bias do not make them act otherwise.

I have mentioned several human qualities that make a person just. All are encompassed in the notion of *impartiality*. Impartiality is the precondition of objectivity in human affairs. We must be detached from our personal likings or dislikings and our vested interests to establish in a given situation 'what the case is'. I emphasize here that impartiality in our judgements presupposes partiality for our norms and rules. Fanaticism and justice do not exclude one another, unless norms exclude fanaticism. Members of religious or political groups can be extremely fanatic. Partiality for their *own* norms and rules can reach the level where no minor deviation from any norm is tolerated. Yet they can be just in that they censure or punish equally or proportionally and with the utmost consistency. However, partiality for our own norms and rules distorts our judgements of people who do not share them, for it excludes even relative *impartiality* in our judgements of norms and rules. People tend to judge members of another culture by their own standards, which is the extreme opposite of the application of double standards, but does not occur less frequently. Religiously, politically or ideologically underpinned or overdetermined norms are usually not open to any kind of relativization. If such norms happen to shape social clusters within a common social milieu, and the members of these clusters judge members of other clusters by their own norms, the outcome may be blatant injustice, even if those norms are applied consistently and continuously. How those who are 'just overall' (within their ingroup) can be 'unjust overall' (in judging members of a group with different norms and of a different persuasion) is a problem I can only outline here, not discuss.

Being just (in the sense of the formal concept of justice) is the result of practice. One has to learn the habit of being just. 'Impartiality' does not imply that one cannot pursue interests, cannot like some and dislike others, cannot be passionate, jealous and envious, cannot have a 'good heart'. It simply means applying the same norms and rules consistently *irrespective* of personal interest and emotional involvement (warm and positive or otherwise). It is generally presumed that highly emotional people are less capable of practising justice. So most societies provide the opportunity for such people to 'put things right' before they consider them liable to punishment; this may take the form of self-humiliation, asking for forgiveness and the like. If such a gesture is accepted then the 'balance of justice' is restored. These and similar habits and incidents 'teach' people to be just rather than unjust, in the first instance simply to avoid further humiliations. Self-humiliation, asking for pardon or forgiveness, can restore a social hierarchy and authority relationships, but only if the person asking forgiveness belongs to a hierarchically lower social cluster than the person able to grant it.

Apart from the virtue of (qualified) impartiality, just practice requires practical wisdom, a kind of *phronesis*, to use Aristotle's terminology. One has to know the facts, the circumstances, the persons, to make a proper judgement, to act properly or distribute justly. If, during a famine, foodstuffs in short supply are to be distributed, one must know if hidden reserves exist, and who has them, in order to distribute justly. A judge must establish the facts before passing verdict. In most cases not all the relevant facts are known, but there is a threshold to knowledge below which just action or judgement can only occur through luck or intuition. Knowledge is a prerequisite for the application of both norms and rules, but phronesis (practical wisdom) is normally activated only in the former case, for here the question of the *method* of application arises. Incidentally, however, *phronesis* might serve as the vehicle for finding out what the case really is. Stories about wise rulers meeting their people in disguise are illustrations of practical wisdom as the ability to unveil the facts on the grounds of which just judgement can then be passed.

No person can be just in all of his or her actions, judgements, acts of distribution, even if this person is basically just. At times the available knowledge is below the threshold level, action is still necessary, and intuition fails. Further, if norms are to be applied, and different norms can be applied to a given situation, there is no single just action that can be called upon, but only several approximately just ones. Being just means covering a certain area, not illuminating a single point. Genuinely just persons are nearly always aware of the approximative character of justice. Should they accidentally commit an injustice because of ignorance, incorrect assessment, the false character of available information (if they are deceived), they will rectify it by passing just judgement on themselves and asking for forgiveness from the offended.[4]

From the perspective of static justice, three major sources of social conflict may arise:

1 the inconsistent application of norms and rules pertaining to a social position;
2 an attempt to alter the width of the social cluster to which certain norms and rules apply;
3 asymmetry of ingroups and outgroups.

At this stage the process by which norms and rules themselves are tested cannot be discussed, and neither can the social conflicts arising therefrom.

(1) We have already seen that norms and rules constitute social clusters (in Perelman's terminology, 'essential categories'), and that they have to be applied consistently and continuously to every member of the social cluster to which they relate. This fact stabilizes *expectations*, as well as establishing a *relative* causal nexus between an action and its consequences. By 'relative causal nexus' I mean a strong *probability*. In our actions we can usually rely upon a strong probability. If I interact with people who are obliged, according to the norms and rules, to keep their promises, I can expect them to keep their promises. In the same vein, if I interact with an outgroup wherein 'keeping a promise' does not belong to the norms and rules – where, for example, cheating, deceiving and lying are accepted behavioural forms – I cannot expect that any promises will be kept. Of course, we can be disappointed in our expectations even in the former situation, for injustice can never be excluded as a *possibility*. The relation between the probability of expectation fulfilled and the possibility of expectation disappointed is variable, and depends on several factors. As a rough estimate one could say that the probability is very high in respect of the application of rules, less so in respect of the application of norms. But since people are just rather than unjust if their interests, passions and biases do not dictate otherwise, the relation between expectation fulfilled and expectation disappointed is always that of probability–possibility.

One situation exists in which this network of expectation breaks down. This happens when there is someone (or more than one person) to whom *no norm or rule applies*. Persons with no norms and rules applied to them can choose (though they do not necessarily do so) not to apply any norms and rules to members of any social cluster, but to act according to the maxim *sic volo, sic jubeo* ('as I wish, so I command'). These people are *tyrants*. A tyrant not only excludes himself from the application of certain norms and rules; he regards himself as a person to whom they do not apply at all. Tyranny is the state of *absolute injustice*. In this situation all expectations break down. The relative causal nexus between acting in a certain manner and the consequences of this action is replaced by mere possibility and conjecture. One has no idea whether any promise will be kept; one cannot know whether any rule will be applied. Observing the law does not make it more probable that one will not be executed or imprisoned; at best, there is only a possibility of this. In the state of absolute injustice, 'reading the tyrant's mind' is usually substituted for observing norms and rules.

Absolute injustice can be total or partial. It is total if the tyrant controls the whole of society, and partial if he controls a distinct social cluster (in which case we must speak of tyrants in the plural). Stalin's Russia is a good example of the first. In Stalin's time all expectations broke down. The relative causal nexus between acts and the consequences of acts disappeared. Slavery is a good example of the second, if – *and only if* – slaveholders are not obliged to observe certain norms and rules in the treatment of their slaves (as they indeed were in the ancient Greek city states). In the case of slavery (except if implemented in the state of total injustice), norms and rules apply to society, to all 'free' clusters of society, but not to slaves. It is always indicative of the nature of a society whether it tolerates or even encourages absolute injustice in the form of partial injustice. (Total injustice can be endured, but never encouraged, by any society.) There were, and still are, societies encouraging absolute injustice *within the family*. The tyranny of the paterfamilias is a typical form of partial absolute injustice.

The state of absolute injustice (total or partial) is the hotbed of hate, resentment and, occasionally, social conflict. Such conflict can assume violent forms. With total absolute injusice it often ends with the gesture of tyrannicide (if the tyrant does not die naturally). But the end result of this conflict, whatever form it takes, is the reinstatement (or creation) of the validity of norms and rules that were not applied in the state of absolute injustice. This ensures again the relative predictability of human action.

(2) Social conflicts may emerge because of an attempt to *widen* or *narrow down* social clusters to which certain norms and rules

apply. Again, the validity of the norms and rules is not queried. What is questioned is the exclusion of certain groups from, or the inclusion of certain groups in, a particular social cluster. I am of course alluding here to conflicts fought to the slogan of *equality* or *inequality*. I stated at the outset that both equality and inequality are created by norms and rules. People are *made* equal by *creating* a cluster through the application of a certain set of norms and rules: alternatively, people are *made* unequal by applying different norms and rules to the members in another cluster. If the same norms and rules apply to each and every member of an entire society (regardless of the social groups to which these members belong), these norms and rules make *everyone equal* from the standpoint of the norms and rules in question. 'Narrowing down' or 'widening' the clusters to which the same norms and rules apply are only two aspects of the same procedure. 'Equalization' (in other words, the widening of the application of the same norms and rules to social clusters) can take three distinct forms. First, norms and rules applied to an 'upper cluster' may be applied to the 'middle' and eventually also to the 'lower' cluster (aristocracy, oligarchy and democracy in ancient Athens). Secondly, norms and rules hitherto applied only to the middle, and then to the lower cluster, may be applied to the upper cluster (the paying of taxes extended to the nobility, a form of financial equalization). Thirdly, norms and rules that hitherto have been applied only to the lowest cluster may be extended to the whole of society (for example, that no one should have property). Social conflicts related to these three clusters usually go hand in hand with testing and changing the norms and rules themselves; but this problem cannot be addressed from the viewpoint of the formal concept of justice.

The social struggle *for the right to be different* is another form in which the issue of *equality* is raised. Let me refer back to the problem briefly mentioned a short while back: if norms are religiously, politically or ideologically underpinned or overdetermined, the ingroup judges the members of another group with its own, and not with *their* own, norms and rules. The struggle for the recognition of the *difference* of a normative system is a struggle for equality, for what is being sought is equal recognition. The contest concerns the pluralism of value systems and the recognition of this pluralism, restricted (for instance, to two value systems) or general. The struggle for the general recognition of pluralism appears only at the dawn of modernity, and cannot be dealt with (at least *in toto*) in the context of social conflicts viewed from the perspective of the formal concept of justice. But the struggle for the recognition of a restricted pluralism can. If two systems of norms and rules are equally taken for granted by the members of respective clusters, one does not need to test the validity of either by granting at least limited recognition to both. Even though before the emergence of modernity this and similar forms of mutual recognition were usually only temporal, and non-recognition could be either reinvoked or reversed (previous outgroups imposing their norms on previous ingroups), social conflicts occurred repeatedly over this issue.

(3) If different sets of norms and rules apply to two clusters of people within the same milieu or life world, and the asymmetry of the members of the two clusters is constant, the relation of the members of the two clusters is socially unequal. This is the social constellation that comes first to mind in connection with the dictum that unequals should be treated unequally. Of course, there are other kinds of inequality; for instance, inequality in merit or excellence. The Aristotelian idea of *proportionality* refers precisely to this kind of inequality. Proportionality in action, judgement and distribution presupposes the existence of a common yardstick (a common set of norms and rules) for measuring merit or excellence. The imperative of proportionality (another name for the principle of consistency) is valid in the treatment of people who are each other's social equals. Proportionality should be effective among equals. This is the idea underlying Aristotle's discussion of commodity exchange. In his view, if two kinds of commodities are exchanged, there must be one common (equal) standard with which to establish the proper proportion. And Aristotle is only highly consistent when he comes to the conclusion that it is *convention*, certain norms and rules of economy, that applies to each and every *person* who performs any kind of labour to produce commodities. Equality is to be understood here, just as everywhere else, in the sense that the same norms and rules apply to each and every member of the cluster, and proportionality is established by the yardstick of this norm by which one measures different forms and acts of labour.

What happens if no common norm or rule applies to two social clusters? Here the imperative of proportionality becomes absolutely meaningless, because respective members cannot be compared. In Aristotle, one in fact cannot compare 'proportionally' the action of a free man with the action of a slave, the merit of a free man with the merit of a woman, the merit of a father with that of his son, a minor. One can compare the merits of free men only with those of other free men, the merits of women only with those of other women, the excellence of slaves only with that of other slaves. The moment we compare all of them, we declare thereby that men and women, masters and slaves, adults and minor in fact belong to the same cluster; or at least we do so in one important respect, in that there are certain norms and rules which apply to all of them.

Asymmetry, or social hierarchy among various clusters or 'essential categories' of people, implies, however, something above and beyond the social division of norms and rules. We should remember the ancient dictum that to be just means to *treat* equals equally, and unequals unequally. The question implicitly raised here is this: who can *treat* whom equally or unequally? Equals can treat their equals, those in higher social positions can treat those in lower social positions, but those in lower social positions can never treat people in higher social positions, either equally or unequally or proportionately. Under the conditions of an all-embracing social hierarchy, both being just and being unjust are prerogatives allotted to the repositories of social authority. The 'God-anointed king' can be just or unjust with his subjects, but his subjects cannot be either just or unjust with him (except when he is a mere *primus inter pares*), only loyal or disloyal, faithful or treacherous. Similarly, a paterfamilias can be just or unjust with his wife, but the converse *cannot* hold: his wife can only be obedient or disobedient, good or bad, faithful or unfaithful, and the like. The master refers to *faithful* servants, *obedient* slaves, never *just* ones; or, if he does, he has in mind servants and slaves who are just to their fellow servants and and fellow slaves. Gods can be just and unjust; the 'living God' can only be just. Creatures, on the other hand, can transgress or sin against gods or God, but they cannot be unjust either with them or Him. Not only is vengeance mine, but judgement is as well – these are the words of a consistent God.

One could object to all this that, if the members of a hierarchically higher cluster can be just or unjust to everyone belonging to a lower cluster, the members of this lower cluster can pass at least one judgement on the members of this higher cluster. They can say the following; that X (a member of a higher cluster) treated us justly (or unjustly). This is clearly possible. But the gist of the matter is that members of the hierarchically higher cluster cannot be treated by the members of the lower cluster either justly or unjustly. Members of the lower cluster cannot confer anything upon the members of a higher cluster, neither wealth, nor position, nor honour. Even, if they pass judgements on the members of a higher cluster, this judgement is meaningless to the latter because it bears no authority. They do not feel honoured by a complimentary opinion, and they are not ashamed if blamed. Whether right or wrong in these judgements of their hierarchical superiors, hierarchical inferiors cannot *do* them either justice or injustice, at least not in any direct way. But even the indirect way is *seeking* justice rather than doing justice, in that it is *supplication* submitted to an authority *superior*, or at least equal in standing, to the member of the hierarchically higher cluster. This authority can, then, lend an ear to the *grievance* of the members of the lower cluster (if he wishes to do so) and rectify injustice.

Hierarchical relations thus imply two kinds of inequalities:

i inequalities which are due to the mere existence of 'lower' and 'higher' social clusters to which different sets of norms and rules apply;
ii inequalities due to the fact that the members of a lower cluster cannot treat the members of a higher one either justly or unjustly.

If (ii) is the case, (i) is necessarily the case. If (i) is the case, (ii) is not necessarily the case.

If there are no common norms and rules at all for two clusters of people in a hierarchical interactive situation, (i) and (ii) both hold. If there exist some common norms and rules, but the *set* of norms and rules differs (and it must, otherwise we could not speak of two social clusters), then (i) is certainly the case, but (ii) is not, as there exists, or at least virtually exists, a *common standard* for measuring the actions and behaviour of people belonging to two hierarchically ordered clusters. One could roughly say that, if the hierarchical relation in question is a relation of *personal dependence*, (ii) is normally the case, even if there are some shared (common) norms and rules. If, however, the hierarchical relation is not a relation of personal dependence, and if (but only if) certain norms and rules apply to *both* clusters in question, then, even though (i) is still the case, (ii) is usually not the case.

Several social conflicts can emerge, in connection with the formal concept of justice, from the hierarchical (asymmetrical) relation of social clusters. In static societies, where norms and rules themselves are normally taken for granted, and the question of their justness or unjustness is not yet raised, almost all social conflict can be intelligible from the perspective of the formal concept of justice, and almost all springs from, or is interrelated with, the hierarchical (asymmetrical) relation of social clusters.

Those who cannot commit either justice or injustice in relation to the members of a higher social cluster must take the norms and rules for granted (otherwise they could commit both justice and injustice). Social conflicts can often become personalized, and here norms and rules remain unaffected; the tax-collector, not the tax system, is the target of hostility. In such cases it is anger and not indignation that fuels a conflict that may swell into rebellion. Anger and supplication are not mutually exclusive. Justice is done if the particular offender is dismissed or disciplined by the higher authority, and the members of the higher cluster properly observe *their norms* in interactions with members of the lower cluster.

Conflicts may occur around the *transformation* of personal dependence into a relationship of social hierarchy. At this juncture, a most important social category, that of the rights of the members of a lower cluster, makes its appearance. There is still an enormous difference between the situation where the members of the higher cluster must observe norms in their behaviour towards the members of the lower, and the members of the lower cluster can *expect* them to do so, and the situation where the member of the lower cluster have established rights, perhaps different from those of the higher cluster, but rights none the less. The difference can be summed up as follows. First, references to rights are substituted for supplication. Secondly, where rights exist, obligations exist as well, and it is a duty to describe what the obligations consist of. Accordingly, where members of a lower cluster 'have' certain rights, the enactment of justice or injustice can be *relatively reciprocal*. Sometimes the gaining of certain 'rights' does not change the norms and rules at all. But it does change the relationship between the members of the higher and lower clusters, for the members of the lower cluster can to some extent commit justice or injustice in relation to the members of the higher cluster.

Conflicts can also aim at the transformation of personal dependence into social hierarchy in such a primary relationship as marriage. Even if a woman is 'treated well' by her husband, the phrase infers that she has no rights: she is being acted upon, she cannot act upon her husband. She has duties to perform, and failure to carry them out is not injustice but disobedience. If the husband treats her badly and infringes his own norm of 'treating a wife well', the only channel of redress available to the wife is her father or brother (an equal authority), who may achieve justice for her where she cannot achieve justice for herself. If, however, she has certain rights (and obligations), justice and/or injustice can be relatively reciprocal, as under Roman law. But the complete transformation of personal dependence into a hier-archical relation is never possible in marriage, because the relationship is irrevocably personal. This is why social conflict cannot stop short of lifting the 'cluster barriers' between the sexes; that is, stop short of applying exactly the same norms and rules to both men and women.

THE RULES OF STATIC JUSTICE

Studies of justice often refer to the 'golden rule', the shorthand of formal justice. 'I do unto you what I expect you to do unto me' is indeed a rule, and a formal one. It tells me that I *should* do unto you what I expect you to do unto me, but it leaves open the question of *what* exactly it is that I should do.

The golden rule can be interpreted in the following way: 'I do unto you *the same* as I expect you to do unto me.' Although this is not the only interpretation and the only way to observe this rule, it can be stated that the golden rule applies only to those interactions where the rule can be precisely so interpreted. In short, the golden rule only applies to symmetrical relations, never to asymmetrical ones. Let me recall the preliminary definition of the formal concept of justice: the norms and rules applying to a social cluster should be applied to each and every member of this cluster. The golden rule advises us *how* to act in order to observe static justice. If the norms and rules should apply to every member of the social cluster, they apply to any A, or any B of that cluster. Thus A should act *in the same way* unto B as B should act unto A: I (A) expect B to observe the norms and rules in acting unto me, therefore I (A) should observe the norms and rules in acting unto him.

The presumption that the golden rule has the status of an unrestricted generality is to be attributed to the Jewish–Christian tradition, under which at least some norms, and fairly abstract norms at that – to begin with, the Ten Commandments – were to be applied to everyone. In other words, there were (abstract) norms valid for everyone, regardless of the social cluster to which they

belonged. In principle, every A had to observe the commandments
of the Lord in interaction with every B, and could expect every B to
do exactly the same. Yet it is common knowledge that even abstract
norms were concretized and interpreted in different ways within the
sets of norms and rules pertaining to different social clusters.
Observing the presumed generality of the golden rule was the case of
supererogation. The universalization of certain values and the
subsequent dismantling of the social division in moral norms along
the lines of stratification had to occur before the golden rule could
become a universal *regulative* idea, no longer restricted to the
observance of a few common norms. As such, it functions not as a
rule but as the idea of a rule.

To sum up: the golden rule can orient us in all our actions only if
human relations are symmetrical – that is, if our interactions are
those of *social equals*, though not equals in merit or excellence. As
we already know, if the same norms and rules apply to each, any
member must be treated *proportionately* (according to merit and
excellence), where proportionality presupposes social equality (the
common yardstick). Viewed from this angle, various formulae
involving the complete or restricted application of the golden rule
have to be distinguished.

(1) I do unto you *the same* as I expect you to do unto me.

This is the formula of absolute reciprocity. Equality is
presupposed, but not proportionality. ('I help you in your need: I
expect to be helped by you in my need'.)

(2) I do unto you what you deserve; I expect you to do the same
thing unto me *if* I deserve it.

This formula does not imply that I expect you to do the *same*
thing unto me as I do unto you. When I express my gratitude for
something you have done I do not expect you to express gratitude
to me, unless I have done something of equal merit. Proportionality is taken into consideration.

(3) I do unto you what you deserve; you *should* do the same
thing unto me *if* I deserve it.

Again, this formula does not imply that I expect you to do the
same thing unto me that I do unto you. But it differs from
formula 2, for I do not *expect* you to do the same thing unto me.
This is the formula applied in the case of just punishment. I do
not expect to do something that deserves punishment. But I can
punish only to the extent that others should punish me if I
deserved it. Proportionality is taken into consideration.

But if we turn to the discussion a *asymmetrical* human relations, we shall immediately see that none of these formulae for the golden rule applies to them. The master cannot tell the slave or the servant, the lord the serf, the husband the wife, 'I feed you well and I expect you to feed me well.' Or, conversely, the slave, the servant, the wife cannot say to the master, the lord or the husband, 'I serve you faithfully and I expect you to do the same.' The master cannot tell the slave, 'I do unto you what you deserve. I expect you to do the same thing unto me if I deserve it.' In fact, the golden rule turns out to be completely nonsensical if we apply it to asymmetrical human relations.

This, however, does not mean that there are no abstract rules of justice to be applied to asymmetrical social–personal relations. Normally, the set of norms and rules of higher clusters includes norms for action and behaviour in relation to the members of lower clusters, and *vice versa*. Of course, there are exceptions, and we have referred to them in our brief discussion of *tyranny*. In tyranny, there is no justice at all, and there are no rules of abstract justice either.

The rules of abstract justice in asymmetrical relations (which are far from golden) are the following.

(i) I do X unto you; I expect you to do Y unto me.

It is in this sense that Confucius' definition of reciprocity, 'What you do not want done to yourself, do not do to others' is interpreted in *The Doctrine of the Mean* (XIII 3f.): 'To serve my father, as I would require my son to serve me. . .; to serve my prince, as I would require my minister to serve me. . .; to serve my elder brother, as I would require my younger brother to serve me. . .; to set the example in behaving to a friend, as I would require him to behave to me.'[5] The doctrine makes a strong distinction between asymmetrical and symmetrical reciprocity. Asymmetrical reciprocity is emphasized by the use of the verb 'I serve', symmetrical by the use of the verb 'I behave'.

This general formula implies that I *do* such because I *am* what I am, and I expect you to do such because you are what you are. (Supreme authority, God, says, 'I am what I am.') Thus, 'I command, you obey' ('I do X unto you; I expect you to do Y unto me') implies that I *am* a commanding officer, you are a private; I am your husband, you are my wife, and so on.

This is the formula of *asymmetric reciprocity*. It is asymmetrical because X and Y are not interchangeable. But it must include reciprocity, provided that the members of the higher cluster can be *both* just and unjust to the members of the lower cluster, as we have assumed. As a result, the formula 'I do unto you; I expect you to do unto me' can be read as follows: 'I have spent my whole life in your service; I expect you not to let me starve in my old age.' This is a matter of justice, because the servant can expect that in all probability he will be fed in his old age if he spends his working life in his master's service.

(ii) I do X unto you as you deserve. You *should* do Y unto me, for I deserve it (because I did X unto you).

This can only be applied by members of the higher cluster to the members of the lower. 'I liberated you from slavery, for you were faithful, and now you should be faithful to me because I liberated you.'

(iii) I do X unto you, which is due to you; I expect you to do Y unto me because I have done what was due.

For instance: 'I followed you through all adversities; I expect you to be kind to me because I . . . .'

(iv) I do unto you something you deserve; you should accept it.

The formula applied in respect of just punishment is not reciprocal; not even analogic reciprocity can be fathomed in it; at least not from the perspective of the formal concept of justice. And, given that the rules of justice, all formulae included, are but the rules of *static* justice (those of the formal concept of justice), we must terminate our discussion at this point.

THE IDEAS OF JUSTICE FROM THE PERSPECTIVE OF THE FORMAL CONCEPT OF JUSTICE

Perelman enumerates the following ideas of justice:

1 To each the same thing.
2 To each according to his merits.
3 To each according to his works.
4 To each according to his needs.
5 To each according to his rank.
6 To each according to his legal entitlement.

Nicholas Rescher[6] lists the following possible ideas of *distributive* justice:

1 As equals (except possibly in the case of certain 'negative' distributions such as punishment).

2   According to their needs.
3   According to their ability.
4   According to their efforts and sacrifices.
5   According to their actual productive contribution.
6   According to the requirements of common good or public interest, or the welfare of mankind, or the greater good of the greater number.
7   According to a valuation of their socially useful services in terms of their scarcity in the essentially economic terms of supply and demand.

Ideas (*alias* principles) of justice can be discussed at two levels: as constitutive or as regulative ideas. In discussing the constitutive use of ideas, we have in mind a use in which the ideas actually prescribe the norms of proportionality. For example, the ideas involved in saying 'to each according to his merits, works, rank' prescribe the ways of establishing proportionality, whereas the idea 'to each the same thing' disallows proportionality of any kind. In discussing regulative ideas, one has in mind philosophies, social theories or ideologies which suggest the acceptance of one or two all-embracing ideas that would prescribe methods of establishing proportionality in order to *make* society *just*. As yet, such ideas do not concern us, because they raise the issue of the 'just society' (an issue I shall address in chapter 5). Here, I restrict my discussion to the ideas of justice as constitutive ideas.

The ideas of justice mediate between the *substance* of justice – that is to say, the concrete norms and rules applying to each and every member of a social cluster – and the *criteria* of justice: that is, the values on which justice is based, which are always values other than justice. For example, the idea 'to each according to his merits' leaves wide open the question of *what merit* we have in mind, what kinds of actions are considered meritorious, and what kinds are not. All sorts of values, such as the good of the state, the salvation of the soul, fraternity and efficiency, can be mediated by the idea 'to each according to his merits'. 'What merit really is' will be different in all these cases.

Perelman starts his discussions with the remark that the ideas of justice he lists are irreconcilable. He later solves the problem of irreconcilability by the introduction of the formal concept of justice, which encompasses all ideas of justice and to which I too subscribe. Indeed, in introducing the formal concept of justice he discovered the *maxim* of justice, reconsidering all ideas from the viewpoint of this maxim. In the main, I shall follow this example. But I wish to emphasize that the ideas are irreconcilable only if they are supposed to regulate or constitute the *same* social or human relationship, for they can be easily reconciled if they are supposed to regulate or constitute different social or human relations (or the same relations from a different viewpoint). As constitutive ideas, all of them have actually regulated human intercourse simultaneously. Should we even have in mind the regulative use of ideas (whereby one idea is supposed to be all-encompassing in order to establish the 'just' or 'the good' society), the simultaneous application of different ideas is not excluded. Moreover, I have never heard it suggested that any of these ideas should apply *exclusively* to any society, real or imaginary. For example, the ideas 'to each the same thing' and 'to each according to needs' were (and are) suggested as ideas of *distributive* justice, and this alone. The first concerns an egalitarian society, the second the ideal of a society beyond justice. Whatever our opinion of these ideas might be, they restrict the application of the idea of justice to the distribution of material *wealth* (and occasionally of other kinds of wealth). When, for example, Marx distinguished between the so-called 'first' and 'second' stages of communism in his *Critique of the Gotha Programme*, seeking the acceptance in the first stage of the principle 'to each according to his work', and in the second that of 'to each according to his needs', he was clearly referring to the distribution of material wealth. Perelman struggles with self-created ghosts when he writes as follows about the idea 'to each the same thing':

According to this conception, all the people taken into account must be treated in the same ways, without regard to any of their distinguishing particularities. Young or old, well or sick, rich or poor, virtuous or criminal, aristocrat or boor, white or black, guilty or innocent – it is just that all should be treated in the same way, without any discrimination or differentiation. In popular imagery the perfectly just being is death, which touches every man on the shoulder regardless of any of his privileges.[7]

But is there such a thing as an all-encompassing idea of justice regulating all social relations? To my knowledge there is not. At the same time, it can be safely stated that the idea (or principle) to 'each the same thing' appears as one regulative idea of justice (among many) in several different social relations, legal justice being perhaps the most important. Of course, it has its obvious limitations. For example, Rescher realized (even if he mentions it only in an aside) that the idea 'to each the same thing' cannot be rationally applied at all in the situation he calls 'negative distribution' (punishment).

Put properly, the problem we are facing is as follows. Although different ideas of justice apply to all (real or imaginary) societies, there are always *dominating* ideas of justice, as well as restricted ones (of greater or lesser degree). Indeed, certain dominating ideas may exclude the validity and application of certain other ideas operative in a society as a *whole*. Other dominating ideas can relegate lesser ideas to a subordinate position, to particular realms, or may allocate only a corrective function to them, though without eliminating them.

Even though I believe that Perelman fought against logical possibilities and not genuine conceptions, I shall follow in his footsteps by further analysing the idea 'to each the same thing'. Let us imagine that the same norms and rules apply to all humankind, and thus must be applied to every human being. Here, *all* human beings would have exactly the same rights and obligations. The principle would then be 'to each the same'. Application of the idea 'to each the same' would not exclude application of the idea 'to each according to his merits' or 'to each according to his excellence', because different people could live up to more or less the same norms, and could be judged accordingly (proportionately); but it would certainly exclude application of the principle 'to each according to his rank', which implies the exclusivity of certain rights and obligations. There are numerous possible and actual interpretations of the idea 'to each the same thing', but even the most egalitarian of them (which recommends equality in the distribution of material goods) is far from nonsensical, as much as I disagree with it.

In fact, we always operate with the principle 'to each the same thing', even if it is far from being the dominating idea. At this point we may recall the example of the High School Certificate. According to its charter, everyone obtaining more than 340 marks is eligible to enter the law school of any university. The principle 'to each the same thing' is applied, then, in this case. If women struggle for equal wages for equal work, their struggle is guided not by the idea 'to each according to her work', but by the idea 'to each the same thing'. They believe that exactly the *same* norms and rules should apply to their work as to the work of men; that the yardstick by which the idea 'to each according to his/her work' is measured should be exactly the same for both sexes. Moreover – this already follows from the Aristotelian interpretation of equal proportionality – the idea 'to each according to his merit' (or demerit) cannot be applied except in conjunction with the idea 'to each the same thing'. If people should be punished *in proportion* to the crimes they commit, two persons who commit exactly the same crime should suffer the same type and amount of punishment, whether black or white, rich or poor, sick or well, aristocrat or boor, young or old, to repeat Perelman's examples. In other words, the idea 'to each the same thing' applies.

This brief discussion of ideas illustrates by way of example my initial thesis that no idea of justice can be exclusive, that the various ideas are in fact not all irreconcilable, whilst at the same time certain ideas are indeed irreconcilable with certain others. If we analysed the other ideas listed by Perelman we should reach exactly the same conclusions. I should mention here that I am only discussing Perelman's list because Rescher's list is more haphazard and also fairly inconsistent. Rescher confuses the criteria of justice (values) with the ideas of justice. In point 6 he lists the following ideas: 'According to the requirements of common good or public interest, or the welfare of mankind, or the greater good of the greater number'. However, these are (mostly utilitarian) criteria of justice, not ideas of justice. In point 7 he simply defines the *content* of an idea of justice: 'According to a valuation of their socially useful services', where 'socially useful services' stands for 'merits' or 'works'. It is only in points 1, 3, 4 and 5 that he enumerates ideas proper, if in a fairly confused way. In point 3 he mentions 'According to their merit', and in point 4 'According to their efforts and sacrifices', and does so as if these were two distinct ideas, although 'effort' and 'sacrifice' are really only two sub-cases of merit. These inconsistencies make it better to work from Perelman's list.

It should be noted that in my analysis of the formal concept of justice it sufficed to operate with Perelman's ideas 1, 2, 3 and 5. In discussing asymmetrical relations, I referred to the idea 'to each according to his rank' (5); in discussing symmetrical relations I referred to the ideas 'to each according to his merits' (2) and 'to each according to his excellence' (3),[8] and finally to the idea 'to each the same thing' (1). For very good reasons, I did not discuss either the idea 'to each according to his needs' (4), which also figures in Rescher's list, or the idea 'to each according to his legal entitlement' (6).

The idea 'to each according to his rank' *is* operative in *every* hierarchical society. The ideas 'to each according to his merit', 'to each according to his excellence' and 'to each the same thing' *can* be operative in any society, real or imaginary. If norms and rules apply at all (*any* norms and rules), these three ideas apply as well. Given that we cannot imagine the existence of any society that does not recognize the validity of at least a few norms and rules, neither can we imagine a society in which these three ideas of justice do not apply, regardless of which is dominant. Nevertheless, should we imagine such a society, it will be *beyond justice*, a society having neither justice nor injustice. I shall return to this problem in chapter 5. For the time being it will suffice to bear in mind that, if we mention justice in universal terms, we speak of the application of exactly these three ideas of justice.

Thus the ideas 'to each the same thing', 'to each according to his merits', 'to each according to his excellence' are the *universal* ideas of justice. 'To each according to his rank' is a *general* idea of justice operative in every hierarchical society.

'To each according to his legal entitlement' is neither a universal nor a general idea. To 'have' a 'legal entitlement' there must exist, apart from an ethical–normative structure, a legal system, which is not always the case. Also, in almost all pre-modern societies, 'legal entitlement' was identical with *rank*, the reward for excellence. In modern societies, at least in democratic states (and in all democratic theories), the 'rights of man and citizen' have been established, and so 'to each according to legal entitlement' is *identical* with 'to each the same thing'. As a result, the idea 'to each according to his legal entitlement' can only be conceived of as a *restricted* idea applied to *distributive justice*, and based on property ownership. The acceptance of a restricted idea of justice while advocating universal ideas of justice caused a lot of theoretical trouble to those philosophers aware of the inconsistency this involved. This is why Locke made excessive efforts to prove that property results from work (excellence), and that the idea 'to each according to his legal entitlement' is only an example (sub-case) of the application of the idea 'to each according to his excellence (works)'. All theorists who have challenged the right of inheritance have wanted to eliminate the idea 'to each according to his legal entitlement' as applied to property by suggesting that such legal entitlement (to property) should be the *reward for excellence and merit alone*. For this to occur, 'property' would have to be shifted from the context 'according to' to the context 'to each . . .'

Before discussing the idea 'to each according to his needs', which in my view is *not* an idea of justice, I should like to mention an idea of justice which has not appeared in either list scrutinized so far. It is easy to grasp the reasons for its absence: first, it can never become the dominating idea of justice; and, second, in Perelman's view it is identical with the idea 'to each according to his needs', which he did list. This idea is 'to each what is due to him by virtue of being a member of a social cluster or essential category'. If charity is a social norm, those belonging to the cluster 'starving people' should be provided with food irrespective of their merit and excellence.

However, this does not mean or imply that we provide them with food 'according to their needs', only that we feed them because they 'are in need'. (I analyse this example because Perelman used it to illustrate the relevance of the idea 'to each according to his needs'.) It depends on the norms and rules of a society whether life itself has a claim (irrespective of social rank, merit or excellence), though of course it often has. Certain cultures have developed norms to be applied to foreigners and members of an outgroup, and these define precisely what is due to such people. At this point the Old Testament comes to mind: if you do not gather the crops from the margin of your field, but leave something for the alien as well, you simply 'give them a chance'. Once again, if the enemy's children are spared, it would be strange to claim that this is due to the idea 'to each according to his needs'. In other words, the relevant idea of justice here is not 'to each according to his needs', but 'to each what is due to him' (by virtue of being the member of a particular cluster, because of a socially acknowledged norm). If proper education is due to the children of a particular stratum, and a child from this milieu is brought up in ignorance, he can justifiably accuse his parents of *injustice*; this is part of a well-known tale from Shakespeare. It could be stated that this idea of justice is only a sub-case of the idea 'to each the same thing', but this is not generally true, even if the two principles can occasionally overlap in practice. The norm that all sick people should be treated does not imply that all must get the *same* treatment ('the same thing'). This would be ludicrous. Nor does educating all the children of a family mean education in the same thing; similarly, charity does not entail the distribution of equal amounts of food of identical quality. Of course, Perelman was not misguided when he applied the idea 'to each according to his needs' to at least one of the above-mentioned cases: food, life, good education, medical treatment – all of these are indeed needs. All the examples of the application of the idea 'to each what is due to him by virtue of being a member of a social cluster or essential category' have something to do with needs, whereas the examples of the application of the principle 'to each the same thing' have not, with the exception of the example concerning human rights, where the application of the principles overlap.

   Perelman was aware that the idea 'to each according to his needs', as it stands, is not an idea of justice. Instead, he suggested a restricted version of the idea: 'to each according to his *essential* needs'. However, the crux of the matter is that we simply cannot divide needs into 'essential' and 'inessential' ones, as Perelman himself admits elsewhere. Apart from mere drive reduction, there is nothing naturally 'essential' in needs, and even the objects of drive reduction are socially patterned. Food is essential for human living, but what kind of food is considered essential is an entirely different matter. Systems of needs are shaped by the norms and rules (the values) of each and every society, and thus different systems of needs are *allocated* to different social clusters. The systems of needs allocated to a social cluster are *recognized needs*. It is generally presupposed that members of a social cluster 'have' needs which are allocated to them by the norms and rules. Thus the needs recognized as 'essential' needs of each and every member of a social cluster are precisely those that have been allocated to the very cluster to which they belong. It depends on the norms and rules as to which needs are considered 'essential' and which not. If, for example, 'good education' is allocated by the norms and rules to the members of the social cluster 'nobility', the need for good education is allocated also to the sons of noble families, and so any father who keeps his sons in ignorance is unjust, for he withholds the satisfaction of a recognized need. If the normative system of a society recognizes life as a value (which is far from always being the case), then the need for mere survival is recognized as well, and the allocation of food to those in need is meant as the satisfaction of an 'essential need', and is therefore a just act.

This why I believe that even the restricted version of 'to each according to his needs' – that is, 'to each according to his essential needs' – is inconclusive, for it involves a naturalistic fallacy. And so I would replace it with the idea 'to each what is due to him by virtue of being a member of a social cluster or essential category', which in my view formulates clearly the crux of the matter. The norms and rules themselves define here what is due to someone by virtue of being a member of a social cluster or essential category, and, if someone does not receive the material and/or spiritual goods or the proper means due to him, injustice has taken place. Finally, it should be clear why I have augmented 'social cluster' with 'essential category'. There are essential categories which are not connected with any social clusters. An example of this is that 'medical treatment is due to sick persons'. Further, 'essential categories' can be distinguished within the same social cluster; for example, the sons of a nobleman all belong to the same social cluster, but the first, second and third son, because they may belong to entirely different 'essential categories', may receive very different forms of education, as history attests.

However, individual systems of needs are very rarely, if at all, completely identical with the system of social needs allocated to each and every member of a social cluster or essential category. Usually, socially allocated needs define the framework in which personal systems of needs may evolve. That which is due to me or those like me regulates my aspirations, excites my fantasy or keeps it under tight control. Yet the particular system of individual needs varies from person to person. No norm or rule can completely shape the system of needs; in other words, no norms and rules can possibly apply to the ever-existing systems of individual needs. Moreover, norms and rules have a *levelling*-function. Their character includes abstraction from the concrete system of needs which we can call *individual* as against *social* needs. Since individual and social needs almost never completely coincide, and no norm or rule applies to the former, justice stops short of the *singularity* of the person. Individual structures of needs are the *limits to justice*. Of course, an idea pertaining to individual needs can, in principle, be formulated and brought close to the form of the ideas of justice. For instance, it can be said, 'to each according to his singularity'. But this idea would no longer be an idea of justice. Singularity is by definition beyond comparison and ranking, and without the latter there is no justice. Grasping singularity is an interminable task. One can state that in general judgement is passed on the finite, not the infinite, a constellation clearly grasped by all religious concepts of justice. The French proverb *tout comprendre, c'est tout pardonner* is perhaps morally suspect, but it certainly conveys an important message. To comprehend everything is an infinite task, and a full understanding of even a single action of a single person may involve an infinite number of interpretations and reinterpretations. As a result, if one intends to understand everything, one can neither forgive nor condemn. Still, judgement is passed via the application of norms and rules, and one should understand only so much of a person's action as to allow the application of the proper norms in this process of judgement (by comparing the action in question to the actions of other people).

So far I have briefly argued that the idea 'to each according to his needs' is *not* an idea of justice. The reader must bear in mind that here we are dealing with ideas of justice in their capacity of *constitutive* and not *regulative* ideas. Though this is only a preliminary discussion, some further qualifications should be made. Even if a typology of singular needs is not possible (for they *are* singular, and so cannot be typified), a typology of *relations* between singular systems of needs and various sets of norms and rules can be constructed. The attempt I shall make at this is nothing more or less than that: it is an attempt, and does not lay claim to being a complete explanation.

(1) At least in cultures such as our own, there are moral norms which are *not* norms of justice because they do not apply to every member of a cluster. Apart from certain others (which do not need to be discussed here), these are the norms that apply to *personal relations, qua* personal relations. The norm of satisfying the needs of others stands out among them as the most important: in other words, goodness (or 'goodness of heart'). If a friend or someone we love says, 'I need you', the answer is, 'Here I am.' If that person says, 'I need this', the answer is, 'Here you are.' The person who says, 'I need you' or 'I need this and this', is not obliged to argue on behalf of his need or for this 'something'. Anyway, needs cannot be argued for. Rather, the converse is true: it is the one who has been addressed but has rejected the appeal who has to argue on behalf of his non-action. The justification principle elaborated by Marcus Singer applies also in this case.[9] Justification must take recourse to norms other than the norms we fail to observe. Thus I can justify my refusal to satisfy the needs of others by pointing out that the satisfaction of the need in question would infringe certain norms or values, including the value of justice. If the norm is that sick persons should be treated, then every sick person should be treated. This is a matter of justice from the viewpoint of the idea 'to each what is due to him by virtue of belonging to a social cluster or an essential category'. But a person watching over a sick friend day and night does not practise 'justice'; he does not satisfy a social, but rather an individual, need. While he is indeed acting to satisfy the need of his friend ('I need you' – 'Here I am'), this and similar acts cannot be subsumed under the idea 'to each according to his needs', for no society can 'provide' people with good friends. Not even the following formulation is possible: each friend of a sick person must attend the latter day and night. This formulation is not possible because, for a start, some sick people often prefer to be left alone. The satisfaction of personal–singular needs is one of the most sublime virtues, but because of this it is beyond justice.

(2) By allocating certain social needs, at the same time normative systems 'outlaw' some others. They can do this in a relative and in an absolute sense.

Needs are 'outlawed' relatively if social clusters are hierarchical and the relation between their members is asymmetrical. Consequently, needs that are socially allocated to the members of a higher cluster can only become individual in respect of the members of the lower clusters. Education is not 'due' to a serf, and so his claim to education is not considered *just*.

Needs are 'outlawed' absolutely, and must remain purely individual, if they are unrecognized by norms and rules whatever social cluster their 'bearers' might belong to. What I have in mind is not 'repression' in general, which is too broad a problem to be discussed here, but a phenomenon which can be illustrated by the following example. Politicians normally feel the need for power; that is why they choose politics as a profession. However, in a democratic body politic they have only limited power, and their individual need for unlimited power is outlawed. This need cannot even be expressed in the form of a just claim, so long as the prevailing social conditions (political democracy) remain.

(3) Even if the idea 'to each according to his needs' is not an idea of justice, it can still be applied as a *corrective* idea of justice, as an idea of *equity*. Whichever idea of justice should be applied in a given action, those who are ranking and comparing, acting, judging and distributing can take into consideration the *singularity* of each and every person, and first of all the singular system of needs of the persons in question, though this can occur *only to a degree*. This degree is determined and prescribed by the norms themselves, whereas, in the case of the application of rules, equity is out of the question. Equity, as corrective justice, can modify judgement, action and distribution and decrease the rigidity of norm application. None the less, the same norms and rules as otherwise establish the particular idea of justice prevailing here have to be applied *without* extreme rigidity. Corrective justice is thus a sub-case of justice, as Aristotle correctly claimed. If one considers the singularity of persons in grading, ranking, acting, judging and distributing through *violating* the norms of justice, one cannot be either just or equitable (though one can still be good). However, equity is usually conditional, whereas justice is always unconditional.

It should also be remembered that the idea 'to each according to his needs', as an idea of equity (corrective justice), does not entail the application of this idea in full. Only those types of needs are considered which are absolutely relevant from the perspective of the application of a norm (normally there is only one such need). Further, 'to each according to his needs', as the principle of equity, very rarely includes the satisfaction of needs; rather it urges the provision of means for the satisfaction of certain needs. Also, there are needs requiring satisfaction to which neither justice nor equity applies, such as the need for love.

THE FORMAL CONCEPT OF JUSTICE AND 'HUMANKIND'

Contemporary political action is not confined to one country or one culture, nor even to several countries or cultures. 'World history', once a construct of philosophies of history and applied 'to all times', has become the reality of our time. Different cultures (thus different histories) not only share the same planet; they also share the fate of this globe. When we mention 'humankind' we have this undeniable fact in mind. 'Humankind' is defined as the 'sum total of human beings who inhabit our globe'.

Since the dawn of modernity, philosophies have taken excessive pains to discover the *common elements* of all existing the possible human cultures. The notion 'culture' itself is a product of this inquiry. 'Common elements' must not only be factually and verifiably common; they must indicate the 'essence' of the human species as well. They must include propensities other than the merely visible. These essential features, which are attributed to all human beings (in all human cultures), are called *human universals*. When referring to humankind, we may have these human universals in mind, or at least we have one of them in mind. We can refer to humankind as '*Homo sapiens*, by virtue of X', where X stands for any human universal. (The scientific category *Homo sapiens* was also coined in modern times, and it has no meaning at all without combining this seemingly purely 'anatomical' notion with at least one human universal.)

From the viewpoint of values, human universals are construed as interpretations of certain empirical facts. True enough, a form of evaluation is also involved in the definition of humankind as 'the sum total of human beings who inhabit our globe'. However, to operate with a slightly modified Kantian categorical framework, 'humankind' defined as 'the sum total of human beings who inhabit our globe' is a merely empirical concept, whereas defined in terms of 'human universals' it is not an empirical concept, even if the definition involves recourse to interpreted empirical facts. 'Humankind' understood in this way is rather a theoretical idea in which values are embedded. The merely empirical definition of humankind is not binding, for the imperative 'As a member of humankind, you should act such' does not follow from the assertion that you share the globe with members of the same species. Yet not even the definition of humankind through human universals is morally binding. Whether 'work' or 'language' or 'division of labour' figures as such a universal, it fails to provide us with any moral imperative.

Even so, those who promoted the ideas of 'freedom' or 'reason' to the rank of human universals were not simply offering a theory; they were proposing a moral commitment as well. The rediscovery and reinterpretation of 'natural law' bears witness to this commitment. The recognition of a certain kind of 'natural law' (the secularized divine law) which must not be infringed by any positive law includes a practical commitment, at least in a negative sense. No other human universals offer this much. But even 'natural law' has serious flaws, the most severe being that (as Croce pointed out) *it does not exist*. In order to be committed to 'freedom' and 'reason', if only in a negative sense, one must first *choose* the idea of natural law, which by definition means that one can reject it as well (it is precisely in this sense that natural law does not 'exist'). Secondly, even if there are many who interpret 'natural law' as a moral commitment (for instance, in the following form: 'As a member of humankind you should respect the freedom and the reason of all human beings and should act such that they can make proper use of them'), this commitment does not directly *follow* from the theory of natural law (as a human universal). What does directly follow from the theoretical statement is the claim, 'As a member of humankind I am born free and endowed with reason; I have the right to make use of my freedom and reason.'

The notion 'humankind' can also be defined by *substantive goals*. Evolutionist philosophies of history normally establish such substantive goals. Thus 'humankind' is not the sum total of persons who inhabit our globe, even when defined as all born free, equally endowed with reason and conscience, but is history itself, progressing towards the state of freedom and/or reason. 'The greatest happiness of the greatest number' is also a substantive goal, though this utilitarian creed is based on the assumption that 'every human being strives for happiness'. Understanding humankind as history, and from the perspective of its end result, implies a commitment to act in harmony with the substantive goal. However, what a happy, free or rational humankind looks like is a matter of decision. Thus different interpretations of this end result carry different commitments, and often conflicting ones. Further, if the essence of humankind is an end state, the problem of the means to this end state must be raised. Action, judgement and distribution in the present are mere means to this end, and must be assessed through the substantive result they are supposed to promote. The universal claim of any action is therefore only indirect, never direct, and as such is not practical but merely pragmatic. Almost all kinds of actions can be rationalized in their capacity as means to the substantive goal.

Today, all political actors pay lip service to humankind. We all act 'on behalf of humankind', and we undertake many different things in this service. We may have entirely different interpretations of 'humankind' in mind: eventually, even the three interpretations of 'humankind' can merge. It is generally held that acting 'on behalf of humankind' is just. Hence, from the viewpoint of the actors, every action is considered just, for all actors rationalize their actions as 'on behalf of humankind'. But the crux of the matter is that 'acting on behalf' is neither a definition nor an idea of justice; in fact is has nothing to do with justice. 'To act on behalf of X' can be both just and unjust.

Of course, very different things are done in the name of humankind. In the last half century, certain acts have met with the full approval of our moral sense, our sense of justice, but certain other acts have met with our full disapproval as immoral and unjust. But, even in relation to the former, it would only cause confusion if we tried to apply the formal concept of justice to the actions in question.

I feel free to disregard here those actions committed in the name of 'humankind' and 'justice' which meet with the disapproval of our moral sense and sense of justice. They are so numerous and widely known that they need no further comment. I intend rather to address an action which has met with the full approval of a general sense of justice. The Nuremberg Trials is an appropriate example for this purpose.

Clearly, the Nuremberg Trials were conducted on the basis of *natural law*; if they had not been, the notion of 'crimes against humankind' would make no sense whatsoever. Humankind has no common positive legal system, so one can infringe international legal agreements, but it is not possible to infringe the (postive) law of humankind. Such a notion presupposes that all members of the human species are born with certain inalienable rights, the most fundamental of which is the *right to life*. The violation of this 'right of nature' is the infringement of the supreme law, and those who have violated it have committed a crime against humankind, even if they act under the command and the authority of national and positive systems of law. Even those who do not generally subscribe to the theory of natural law feel that the verdict handed down in this trial was just in the most sublime meaning of the word, and did not represent merely the revenge of the victors over the vanquished (as Göring suggested in a remark on the moral status of the trial).

We feel it; we are aware of it; we are committed to it. But we cannot explain it.

Let us stipulate for a moment that 'the right to life' and 'the right to liberty' are *in fact* the rights of every human being. This would mean that we are all subject to the authority of the same norm. If the right to life and to liberty constitute the social cluster 'humankind', then every member of this cluster should be treated in accordance with these rights, and everyone should respect the life and liberty of all others ('to each the same'). Everyone who violates this norm must be punished, and in proportion to the severity of his offence ('to each according to his offence').

This norm exists as a regulative, but unfortunately not as a constitutive idea. There is *in fact* no such norm. One judge presiding at the Nuremberg Trials was guilty of crimes similar to those he was sitting in judgement upon (crimes against life, against liberty).[10] Similar crimes have been committed a hundred times since and have remained unpunished. Through the Nuremberg Trials, humankind established a representative exception, but not a rule. We cannot explain why the judgement was just, even if we feel and know that it was just. In the verdict, the claim had been raised that humankind should become a social cluster, that it should become something which it is not. And it is still not a social cluster.

As has been mentioned, all representative political actors, whatever interests they may pursue, pay lip service to 'humankind'. Everything is done 'for the best of humankind', 'on behalf of humankind', 'in the interest of humankind'. This reference to humankind is almost empty, just as the reference to God was almost empty once, for it bestows a blessing upon good and evil deeds alike. In all ways, the simile is but approximative: the laws of God are valid for the members of the religious group which seeks His blessing, whereas one can refer to humankind in any of its above-mentioned interpretations, among which only the theory of 'natural law' can constitute certain (if only virtual) binding norms. Thus the reference to humankind is emptier than the reference to God. It sounds sacrilegious to say that we act 'for the best of God', 'on behalf of God', and in particular 'in the interest of God'. However, one can still act 'for God's sake', for so to act means, first and foremost, to observe His commandments. One can claim to act 'for the sake of humankind' only if one observes 'commandments' that are binding for the human species. But no such 'commandments' (norms) are recognized by empirical humankind, by the 'sum total of human beings who inhabit our globe'. And so after this detour we still come back to Kant: there is an unbridgeable gap between empirical humankind and the idea of humankind.

We reproach one another for applying double standards in our judgements in general, and in our judgements of political actions and actors in particular. If identical acts of oppression and violence are committed in countries with different political institutions or cultural traditions, and X denounces these acts as 'horrible' in one case and justifies them as 'appropriate measures' in another, we accuse X of having and practising double standards.

The notion 'double standard' carries the meaning 'unjust', but why? According to the formal concept of justice, which is the all-encompassing concept of justice, if the same norms and rules apply to a social cluster, the same norms should be applied to every member of the cluster. 'Double standards' can be defined as follows: certain common norms apply to two groups of people that make them, even though they remain members of distinct groups, members of the same social cluster: nevertheless, we apply different norms to these two groups. The application of double standards is unjust because it contradicts the formal concept of justice. But to apply *different standards to entirely different social clusters* is by no means unjust. This is expressed in the Latin dictum *quod licet Iovi, non licet bovi* ('What is permitted to Jove, is not permitted to an Ox'). Thus if we indignantly reproach X for applying double standards, we must first inquire whether the notion 'double standard' makes sense at all in the case under scrutiny. And we come to the extremely disquieting conclusion that what we so indignantly reject in certain actions and patterns of behaviour is the application not of double standards but of *different standards*, for the simple reason that humankind is not a social cluster. There are no common norms and rules that apply to all human beings irrespective of their culture, and so there is no common yardstick for comparing and ranking human actions, not even a single yardstick recognized as unconditionally valid by each and every member of humankind.

At this point, our sense of justice will protest that we do have such a yardstick, namely *humankind*. But which humankind? History as *telos* can certainly not serve in this capacity; neither can the empirical notion of humankind or human universals. The only human universals capable of providing us with an answer (life, freedom, reason) can be chosen only within the framework of a theory of natural law, a theory we can accept as well as reject, and which, once accepted, is only conditionally binding. But our sense of justice continues to protest. This protest cannot be accounted for in terms of the formal concept of justice, for it transcends the latter's sphere of competence. In chapter 3 I shall return to this problem of the 'sense of justice', but it must be stated here that, whenever this 'sense of justice' makes its voice heard, it heralds the claim for new norms and thus new social clusters, and this is why it does not contradict the formal concept of justice, even though it transcends its sphere of competence. The sense of justice protests against the application of 'double standards', although it is indeed confronted with the application of different standards. It is exactly this sense of justice which transforms the different standards into 'double standards'. In so doing, our sense of justice raises the claim that humankind should become a social cluster, that humankind should be the essential cluster, that at least a few common norms and rules should apply to all cultures and all members of *Homo sapiens*, that there should be a common yardstick for comparison and ranking. The sense of justice which tranforms different standards into 'double standards' (in that it perceives double standards where ostensibly there are only different ones), implies a new notion of humankind, not identical with the empirical or the teleological–substantive concept of humankind, or with the definition of humankind through 'universals' alone. 'Humankind' as the essential human cluster constituted by certain common norms and rules is a concept of humankind which can only be conceived of as binding. For, if certain common norms constitute humankind, these very norms are valid for all human beings and should be applied to all members of humankind, and all members of humankind should apply them equally. And, further, to apply these norms to cases to which they should be applied is just, whilst not to apply them is unjust; to apply them consistently is just, whilst to be inconsistent in this application is unjust. 'Humankind' as the essential social cluster is the unity of empirical humankind and the idea of humankind. It is empirical humankind because it encompasses the sum total of human beings who inhabit our globe. It is also the idea of humankind because membership of the essential social cluster is constituted by universal and binding norms. The norms which constitute the essential cluster cannot be both chosen and rejected; they can only be observed or infringed. Everyone is obliged to observe the common norm and to apply it to everyone else (to every human being) continuously and consistently. There is a common yardstick for comparison and grading; the formal concept of justice is validated.

The sense of justice which induces us to denounce the application of different standards as 'double standards', and therefore as unjust, cannot be accounted for but as the expression of the will to construe humankind as the essential social cluster.

Logical as it may sound, this solution leaves several doubts in mind. And these doubts stem from the same quarter as gave birth to the most reasonable, even though still unsatisfactory, idea of humankind – the area of human universals. What we have in mind here is the human universal of 'culture', which can be interpreted in the spirit of *extreme cultural relativism.*

In what follows, I shall argue that extreme cultural relativism contradicts the claim of the sense of justice. If we accepted extreme cultural relativism, we could no longer denounce the application of double standards. Extreme cultural relativism can make its appearance equally in *Geistesgeschichte*, in cultural hermeneutics and in straightforward positivism, though I cannot deal here with their respective specific features. It suffices to enumerate the basic tenets of such relativism.

Let us assume that all values, opinions, world views, patterns of actions and beliefs are so many prejudices, all relative to the time and space in which they are held. In any given period, including the present, there are several distinct coexisting cultures, each with its own values, opinions, world views and patterns of actions, all taken for granted as 'beliefs'. Each is different from every other; there is no way to compare them. Yet it is not only cultures as wholes that cannot be ranked. There is not a single action pattern or custom of a particular culture that can be compared with any single and functionally equivalent action pattern of another culture. This is for the simple reason that all action patterns are embedded in their respective cultures as wholes. The same belief which is true and the same action which is right within the tradition of one particular culture may be false and wrong within the tradition of another. We cannot even raise the question of whether one action pattern is more correct (or better) than another, because there is *no common standard* by which an evaluation can be made. Whenever we carry out a ranking of any kind, whenever we apply common standards in judging the same action performed by people of different cultural backgrounds, we do so from the position of our own particular culture, from the standpoint of values and standards of measurement that we take for granted. Thus we superimpose our prejudices on other cultures. The application of double or even multiple standards is more just than the application of common standards to all cultures. Those operating with double or multiple standards simply place themselves within the patterns of cultural traditions different from their own. They identify with the different cultural traditions and understand (interpret) their own heritage as an alien system of prejudices.

The logic of argumentation here is obviously fallacious. And the problem it raises, but does not solve, is undoubtedly real. Let us first analyse the logical fallacy and then proceed to the problem itself. Anyone who states that all cultures are *unique*, and that we cannot compare or rank various cultures from any common viewpoint – moreover, anyone who holds that this is true not only about cultures as wholes, but also about all particular beliefs and patterns of action inherent in each and every culture – raises *in uno actu* a claim to truth and a claim to right (good) judgement. The claim is that the proposition 'All cultures are unique and cannot be either compared or ranked by any standards' is true, and that the norm 'Do not compare or rank cultures by any common standards because they are unique' is right. However, in so far as someone claims that this proposition is true and this norm is right, *a comparison of various cultures has already taken place.* For the following should at least be acknowledged by implication. All cultures being unique and equal, in the sense that every one of them contains true opinions and right norms (in that the norms and opinions prevalent in them are regarded there as true and right), those cultures holding the opinion that all cultures are unique and equal and claiming the norm that, as a result, they should not be compared or ranked are superior to those others not sharing such an opinion, for the simple reason that they claim *one more* true opinion and right norm than all other cultures. Given that Western culture is one of the very few cultures which at least permit the raising of such claims, it is *not* equal in value with all other cultures, but is superior, at least as far as *one* norm and opinion is concerned. The end result, then, is a highly ethnocentric proposition which shows the inner vulnerability of the entire model. However, there is more to be said on the matter than just outlining this (ineliminable) inconsistency.

Let me divide the argumentation of extreme cultural relativism into (1) statements of facts, and (2) imperatives or recommendations.

(1) It is a statement beyond reasonable doubt that human cultures are different and that each of them is unique. And, though not all critics of extreme cultural relativism would go along with me, I also accept the further proposal that unique cultures as *wholes* cannot be either ranked or compared. Whenever cultures are in fact graded or ranked in this way, ranking is performed by the standards of *one* culture among many, and the normative system of the assessing culture is taken for granted and recognized as the 'true' and the 'right' one, or at

least the 'advanced one', in contrast to the baseness and imperfection, eventually the 'primitiveness', of the assessed cultures. What is now called 'ethnocentrism' is the *natural attitude* of all cultures towards alien ones. Philosophies of history are only highly sophisticated and streamlined versions of this 'natural attitude'.

Extreme cultural relativism deduces its imperative from this statement of fact. To deduce an 'ought' sentence from an 'is' sentence is, in my view, a legitimate procedure. The gist of the matter in this case, however, is that the imperative deduced from the statement of fact does not follow from the facts which have been established.

(2) It indeed follows from the statement that all cultures are unique that they ought to be understood in their uniqueness. However, the imperative that they ought not to be ranked, compared or graded at all does *not* follow from the above assertion. Let us briefly analyse an analogous case. All individuals are unique. One can never fully understand individuals. The process of their understanding is in principle infinite, and the patterns of their interpretations are also in principle infinite. But comparing and ranking individuals has very little, if anything, to do with their uniqueness. One compares individuals by applying norms to particular actions and performances using the norm as a yardstick to grade and compare with. Of course, there is a difference between the uniqueness of individuals and the uniqueness of cultures because cultures are systems of norms and rules. But, if humankind were the overarching (essential) human cluster, there would be at least one norm shared by each and every culture. Cultures would not cease to be unique, but they could and should be compared by the standard of the very norm they share. Thus the recognition of the uniqueness of all culture, on the one hand, and the possibility of comparing certain patterns of various cultures, on the other hand, do not exclude each other in principle. What is excluded, however, is comparing, ranking and grading cultures as *wholes*, because the uniqueness of each and every culture consists of the specificity of norms, rules and action patterns unshared with any other culture.

The sense of justice protests against extreme cultural relativism. If different and unique cultures cannot be compared, ranked or graded in any way at all, there is no justice, and accusing anyone of the use of 'double standards' is simply meaningless, null and void. But the same sense of justice does not protest against moderate cultural relativism. If I state that animism has its proper place in culture X but is an aberration in culture Y, no one's sense of justice will protest. The objection could still be made that I am wrong, even that I am a poor judge in such matters, but it would not be that I apply double standards and so am unjust. The sense of justice indicates, therefore, that 'something' should be compared, but *not* that everything should be compared. If the sense of justice expresses the will that humankind should become the 'overarching (essential) cluster', and if the same sense of justice demands that something, but not everything, should be compared, then the 'good' that this will aims at allows for a plurality of 'goods' – of normative systems and value systems – within the limits of the shared 'good'. But what is this 'shared good' at which the sense of justice aims?

It is not necessary to take recourse to a hypothetical situation of choosing 'under the veil of ignorance' in order to discover which cases we must apply a common standard to if we intend to live up to the normative demands of the sense of justice. Nor is it necessary to make statements of history (of the past, present and future), nor even to identify the so-called 'universals' of the human species. It suffices to drop our anchor in the present age and to cast a glance at contemporary historical consciousness, to interpret the empirical evidence disclosed by this historical consciousness.

Let me ask the simplest of questions: when, and in which cases, do people accuse each other of applying 'double standards'? When, and in which cases, does our sense of justice denounce the application of different standards as unjust? This happens *exclusively* when we judge or assess acts of domination, coercion, force and violence. If people are imprisoned, tortured, killed, humiliated, even discriminated against, within particular cultures, it is then, and only then, that the sense of justice enjoins us to apply exactly the same standards to all of them. Whether women wear veils or miniskirts is a matter of particular (unique) cultural taste. However, should they be *forced* to wear veils, it ceases to be a matter of 'cultural uniqueness' and becomes a matter of coercion or force.

The claim for a common standard is a claim for grading and comparing. The sense of justice, while transforming different standards into double standards, not only demands the application of the same standards in the assessment of actions and behavioural patterns and systemic constraints which involve domination, coercion, force or violence, but calls for cultures to be compared and ranked from the viewpoint of these standards as well.

The *postulate* raised by the sense of justice is a decrease in domination, coercion, force and violence. All those protesting against the application of double standards *must* compare, rank and grade different cultures with the guidance of this postulate. Obviously, all cultures contain domination or coercion or force or violence in one or another way and to a certain degree. One particular culture will score higher in a certain aspect and lower in another when it is compared to other cultures according to a common standard. And cultures with a lower overall level of domination, coercion, force and violence will score higher than those in which the level of these constituents is higher.

The procedure described above is just and can be accounted for by the formal concept of justice. According to the latter, the norms and rules which constitute a social cluster have to be applied consistently and continuously to each and every member of the cluster. Members of the cluster have to be ranked and compared by using the common norms and rules as standards for ranking and comparing. But on what grounds do we compare various cultures, if humankind is not a social cluster? And indeed it is not.

Here we return to our starting-point: the sense of justice expresses the will to constitute humankind as the overarching (essential) cluster. All those not applying double standards in their judgements act *as if* humankind were the overarching (essential) cluster. Although I have now returned to my point of departure, I have done so at a different level. First I came to the conclusion that the sense of justice expresses the will that certain norms, or at least one norm, should be common for all humankind, for all cultures: the norm of constituting humankind as the essential cluster. Now we know something above and beyond this: we know which kind of norms (or norm) should constitute humankind as the overarching (essential) cluster. Since our sense of justice warns against the application of double standards only if acts or patterns of domination, coercion, force and violence are to be judged or assessed, the common norms of humankind as an essential cluster should be such that their observance would minimize domination, coercion, force and violence in every unique culture. There can be different norms of this kind. Kant has already formulated the most sublime and the most abstract of them all: men should not be used as mere means by other men.

Humankind does not consist of single individuals who can enter into a social contract, real or virtual, under the veil of ignorance or otherwise. Humankind consists of various cultures and various histories. Individuals are socialized into different cultures and are part of different histories according to different traditions. There is something precious, as well as something abominable, in all of them.

Only cultures, not individuals, can enter into a 'contract', symbolically speaking, by accepting a few common norms, in particular the one which enjoins us to respect the life and liberty of all its members and the members of all 'outgroups'. If we speak of humankind as 'the sum total of human beings who inhabit our globe', we only obscure the fact that we are talking about the sum total of human cultures.

This circumstance does not draw its importance from the speculation about the possibility or desirability of a 'social contract' in the version hinted at above. Rather, its importance is that we cannot be *just* without facing it, here and now. The gist of the matter is that, even if we apply a few common standards to all cultures, then, if an action or systemic pattern includes domination, coercion, the use of force and violence, we cannot compare *individual actors* of different cultures by this common standard alone. Nor can we rank them according to their merits or shortcomings by applying *only* these common standards, even if they in fact apply – that is to say, in cases of force, violence and the like. It is a matter of the gravest concern how far the ban on the application of 'double standards' should regulate our comparison of individuals and in which cases. Without offering a foolproof recipe, I think that the Weberian 'ethics of responsibility' can serve as a guideline for such a decision. One could say that, in political actions proper, a common standard should apply to individual actors as well, and it stands to reason why. World history, once a construct of philosophies of history, has become a reality in our time. Whatever happens in one corner of the globe can have, and more often than not does have, fateful *consequences* for the lives of the denizens of every culture, every country. Since political action proper influences – in whatever culture it might take place – the lives of the denizens of each and every contemporary culture, the consequences of any political action proper transcend the limits of the culture in the framework of which it has taken place. Political actors cannot be assessed by the standards of their own respective cultures alone, but should also be assessed by the standards of those cultures which bear the consequences of their actions. However, if we assessed a political actor by applying a standard of any other culture but his own, the judgement would be unjust, since we should be applying norms and rules to a member of social cluster in which those norms were not valid. And should we assess a political actor by applying *all* standards of the empirically coexisting cultures, we could not reach agreement in our assessment. The only way to be just in our judgement is to apply to the actions of the political actors proper the norms which do not yet constitute humankind as the overarching (essential) cluster. Respect for life and liberty qualifies for universal normative use. Political actors can and should be compared on the grounds of their respect or disrespect for the lives and liberties of all people, their own included. In saying this, I only reaffirm the claim to a moderate cultural relativism. Only those actions including domination, coercion, force and violence should be ranked or compared at all. Political actions proper include at least one of these alternatives to a greater or lesser extent; and it is precisely this 'greater' or 'lesser' extent that provides a firm yardstick to compare and rank individual political actors.

To sum up my argument: extreme cultural relativism contradicts our sense of justice. If we accepted extreme cultural relativism, we could not protest against the use of 'double standards'. In this case, we either could not raise the claim to just judgement and action at all, or we should have to accept ethnocentric assessments as just. And the sense of justice does exist, for we denounce the application of 'double standards' as unjust. An obvious objection to this would be that, although we reject the use of 'double standards', we certainly apply them all the time. Political adversaries accuse each other of using double standards, but they are not apprehensive about their own use of them. This sad fact is, however, does not refute the assertion, 'The sense of justice exists.' The same thing or something similar happens whatever norms ought to be applied to each and every member of a social cluster. It is always easier in every respect to judge others justly than to judge ourselves. The second possible objection is more serious. One can argue that there is a certain concept of humankind that defines the latter through some substantive ends, and that this concept itself excludes justice and encourages the application of different standards from the viewpoint of the *substantive end*. This is undeniably true. However, it only proves that the sense of justice is not general, not that it does not exist. The will that humankind should be the overarching (essential) cluster to which certain norms should apply, and that these norms should enjoin us to respect the lives and liberties of all human beings, no matter what their culture, does exist, but not every human being shares this will. If all did, humankind would already, in fact, be the overarching (essential) cluster. For humankind to become this, humans of all political affiliations must share this will, and this is clearly a very difficult goal to achieve. But, even so, we can and should act as if they did share this will. Regardless of how other people act, we ourselves should not apply double standards.

2

The Ethico-Political Concept
of Justice

The idea that the good should be happy because they are worthy of happiness and that the wicked should be unhappy because they are unworthy of happiness is the foundation of the *ethical concept of justice*. A world order in which the good are in fact happy and the wicked unhappy is thus the *idea of a just world order* from the perspective of the ethical concept of justice.

Not all kinds of ethical concepts of justice imply a political concept of justice. Instead of claiming that the good *should* be happy, one can assert that the good are indeed happy, or that they will be. One can state that 'goodness is its own reward'. If it is, and if, correspondingly, wickedness is its own punishment, then good people are happy and wicked people are unhappy in every social and political order.

Not all ethico-political concepts of justice project a socio-political order where all norms are moral. Just the contrary: the absolute utopia is the exception rather than the rule. What all adherents of this concept claim is the establishment of a political order where the observance of a system of heterogeneous norms and rules does not necessitate the infringement of moral ones. Finally, what has to be considered as morally good, virtuous or meritorious is normally defined in conjunction with the image of the political order projected as 'just'. The diversity of definitions of 'goodness' (and happiness) is consonant with the plurality of the ethico-political concepts of justice.

Indeed, in order to stand firmly by an ethico-political concept of justice, one *must know* what 'goodness' or 'virtue' is. We do not know whether the good are happy or unhappy if we are not aware of *who* the good persons are. The good and the virtuous are good and virtuous because they observe certain *moral norms* still valid within the unjust social order.

If someone speaks of 'just' people in relation to the formal concept of justice, and someone else does so in relation to the ethico-political concept of justice, they are not referring to the same quality or virtue. Even in his time, Aristotle was aware of the polysemic character of the notion 'justice' (*dikaiosune*). Obviously, when the Talmud states that there are always thirty-six 'just' persons in the world, 'just' in this context does not stand for a readiness consistently and continuously to apply the prevailing norms and rules to each and every member of a given social cluster, but for something above and beyond this.

In what follows I shall refer to the ethical concept of justice as 'righteousness'. A person is righteous if he or she observes moral norms irrespective of social sanctions.

Actions of the righteous person were often believed to be 'ends in themselves'. Given that all actions are related to an end, or, more precisely, to an end which affirms the action, this explanation seemed to be the only relevant one that made sense of the most 'sublime' way of life. However, the attitude 'I have a good conscience and I am not concerned that the world may perish' is definitely not that of the righteous person, and has no explanation in the theory which holds that righteousness is 'an end in itself'. Briefly to set forth my own theory on this matter, a righteous action is related to an end outside the action itself, and this end must be self-affirmative. There can be two different ways of affirming righteous actions. The righteous person can will that everyone else should be righteous; in other words, that everyone should observe moral norms irrespective of social sanctions. This would be a self-contradictory end, for, if everyone observed moral norms irrespective of social sanctions, there would be no one left to apply social sanctions, meaning that there would be no social sanctions at all, and so it would not be possible for anyone to act irrespective of such sanctions. The righteous person can also will that *all* social norms should be moral ones, which would amount to the absolute coincidence of social and internal sanctions. This also implies the disappearance of social sanctions, and the disappearance of the righteous person (who acts irrespective of social sanctions). Thus the end implicit in all righteous actions is the establishment of a *totally moral world* where the choice between good and evil can no longer be made.

If the objective of the righteous person is self-contradictory, it seems that we must fall back on the theory in terms of which a righteous act is simply an 'end in itself' and only makes sense as such. If the end of any action is self-affirmative, the righteous person cannot have the will to a world without righteousness. But, if the righteous person wills that every person should be righteous or that every social norm should be a moral norm, she or he cannot will that people should be righteous. However, this antinomy can be solved as follows: the good end implicit in the righteous act is not the totally moral world but the *best possible moral world*. In a best possible moral world not everyone is righteous and not all norms are moral. No norms set sanctions against the righteous, but several norms and rules put a premium on non-moral qualities and administer sanctions in the absence of such qualities. In a best possible moral world, those who are worthy of happiness can be happy, but so can those who are unworthy of happiness. Consequently, 'true happiness' and 'happiness of opinion' do not completely coincide. Whether the best possible moral world is *indeed* possible is a question of no interest. Of interest is only the idea that the best possible moral world can be seen, without any logical self-contradiction, as the intrinsic end of all righteous actions.

Let us imagine for a moment that all norms and rules constitute social clusters (in other words, that there are no interclusteral norms and rules at all). In this case, all norms and rules apply exclusively to the members of one or another cluster. Different norms and rules can have a different normative power. Some can be optative, others imperative. Since all norms and rules constitute social clusters, all of them are intrinsically interwoven, and observing them means observing *all of them*. That is to say, all social norms are simultaneously more or less ethical norms. This is normally the case in small tribal societies. Even the increasing distinction between pragmatic and practical rules and norms is only an insufficient precondition of the distinction between social and moral ones. This is the case if the all-encompassing and primary idea of justice is 'to each according to his rank'. One set of norms and rules constitutes one rank; another set constitute another rank. All norms and rules which constitute a single rank constitute the way of life of the members of this rank. Members of all ranks are measured and judged on the grounds of their norms and rules. The sum total of the norms and rules of the highest cluster is the model of supreme ethical behaviour; it constitutes supreme ethical behaviour. The members of lower clusters cannot be morally supreme; indeed, it would be a challenge to the ethical world order if they intended to be. *The distinction between moral and social norms can only be made if there are moral norms and rules which do not constitute a social cluster, but are interclusteral.* The dividing-line between justice and righteousness comes at this point.

The notion of 'interclusteral norms' (moral norms proper) needs further specification. They can be norms of an 'ideal cluster' (in Durkheim's terminology, an 'ideal community') capable of being juxtaposed to the norms and rules of real social clusters. Here, the distinction between interclusteral and intraclusteral norms is relative. For example, landlords, serfs and burghers were equally supposed to belong to the same ideal cluster, that of Christianity, which itself was further confronted with other (pagan) real and ideal clusters.[1] Whichever cluster a person belonged to, he or she could choose to observe the norms of the ideal cluster instead of the norms and rules of his or her own real cluster. In chapter 1 I referred to the social conflict (viewed from the perspective of the formal concept of justice) which occurs if social actors aim at widening or narrowing down a cluster to which certain norms and rules apply. The very existence of interclusteral norms constituting an ideal cluster serves to justify the social objective of changing the widths of the real clusters. The notion 'social contract', and that of 'society' as distinct from the 'state', served as a powerful lever (and justification) for such a widening or enfranchizing in the development towards universal suffrage.

Yet different interclusteral norms may be of entirely different provenance. There exists a great variety of moral norms which, upon assuming interclusteral validity, cannot constitute any social cluster, real or ideal. Let me refer to a norm which has become extraordinarily fashionable in contemporary moral discourse, that of 'keeping a promise'. If 'keeping a promise' is a norm as such, it cannot constitute a social cluster. The norm can constitute a cluster only if it is specified in the following way: 'The members of cluster A should promise to do or give *a* and *b* to the members of the same cluster, and should promise to give or to do *c* and *d* to the members of cluster B, and all these promises should be kept.'

However, the norm 'to keep a promise' is valid and relevant as an interclusteral norm. If I promise you my friendship, I should keep that promise, and the same thing applies if I promise to lend you a hand, to continue my studies, to care for your children, or to stop drinking. But I cannot postulate that every member of a social cluster should do the same. I cannot even postulate this much: all who can mend dresses, should promise to mend dresses for others. Keeping the promise as such is a norm which regulates *personal* relations. However, norms of justice demand that certain promises should be made, and certain others should not, and that those which should be made should also be kept, for this is just. Norms and rules which constitute social clusters leave many possibilities for promise-making of a type neither enjoined nor prohibited. And these promises should be kept. If I do not keep them, I infringe the norm of 'keeping a promise'; but, from the standpoint of the formal concept of justice, I am not unjust thereby. Ordinary language-users make this distinction quite correctly. If someone promises to do something according to a norm or rule of justice (for example, 'I am going to distribute the food equally among the needy') and later goes back on his word (does not distribute it equally), ordinary language-users will call him unjust. But, even if the failure to keep promises (for example, in personal relations) has nothing to do with the virtue of 'being just', it may have much to do with the moral quality of 'righteousness'. Indeed, a righteous person keeps his promises, be they mere trifles or things of great importance. A righteous person is 'as good as his word'; one can *rely* on him.

All interclusteral norms, be they norms of an 'ideal cluster' or norms of a personal relationship, are, or at least can be, observed by the righteous person. The infringement of certain interclusteral norms does not entail social sanctions at all. To flatter someone for gain does not entail social sanctions, nor does promising help and then going back on one's word, nor does the affectation of emotions (insincerity in general), or thriftiness, vanity or envy, provided that the norms and rules of the social cluster in question are not infringed. But the opposite may often be the case as well. If a man promises to marry a woman below his social level and keeps his promise, in certain social clusters his act does entail social sanctions. If one fails to flatter, one may be disowned (Cordelia is a famous case in point). If one offers haven to the politically persecuted, the act does entail social sanctions. And unfortunately it often happens that, in a face-to-face interaction with a social authority, sincerity too invokes social sanctions. We now know that to be righteous means observing norms irrespective of social sanctions – which, of course, does not mean that the righteous never observe norms the infringement of which entails social sanctions. However, the righteous observe such norms for their own sake, not because their infringement entails social sanctions.

My analysis of 'righteousness' adds nothing new to the concept of righteousness. In presenting my case, I have tried to follow a tradition dating back 3,000 years, more or less. The proviso 'more or less' refers to changes in the interclusteral norms themselves that the righteous person was supposed to observe. Yet what is astonishing is not the presence of variable elements in interclusteral normative systems, but the predominance of the constant ones. Kant's suggestion that there is no 'progress' in morality seems to be well founded, although one can add, 'except for the emergence of morality itself'.

The concept of righteousness is the concept of morality, and it is an absolutist concept in that it is *unconditional*. The acts and the conduct of righteous persons imply that their end is the best possible moral world. We do not know whether the best possible moral world is actually attainable, just as we do know that this question is of absolutely no relevance from the standpoint of morality. But the same question is very relevant to the ethico-political concept of justice.

The ethical facet of the ethico-political concept of justice (the ethical concept of justice) takes the position of righteousness. But the political (social) facet of the same concept addresses conditional, not unconditional, acts. By 'conditional' acts I mean political acts of legislation (in the broad sense of the word). Moral legislation and political legislation presuppose one another. Political legislation, in contrast to moral legislation, can be cognizant of the possible. Whilst from the viewpoint of righteousness it is irrelevant whether the best possible moral world is possible at all, the question of possibility is raised in any complete ethico-political concept of justice. The crucial question to be raised here, and solved, concerns the type of political legislation that is needed for the best possible moral world to be established. If the creator of an ethico-political concept of justice concludes that no political legislation can establish the best possible moral world (for this is impossible), he or she will legislate for the second-best possible moral world, or simply a 'better' moral world. Plato pondered the second-best possible moral world after designing the 'best possible'. On the other hand, certain ethico-political concepts of justice (mainly – but not exclusively – religious ones) stuck to the image of an absolute moral world, to the absolutist idea of the impossible. And I do mean impossible. The possibility of an absolute moral world can only be maintained if we hope for an anthropological revolution or for divine grace. All the same, I still think it reasonable and acceptable to aim at legislating for the best possible moral world, even as for the 'second-best', or at least a better one.

THE EMERGENCE OF THE ETHICO-POLITICAL CONCEPT OF JUSTICE

As Bloch once aptly remarked, one has to break a limit in order to recognize it as a limit. This is particularly true of the ethico-political concept of justice. This concept is initially formulated not as an affirmation but as a negation of negation – moreover, as a double negation of negation. The world is regarded as *unjust*, as the very negation of justice, and this negation of justice must itself be negated. The existing justice is considered to be double-edged: men are unjust because they are corrupt and wicked, rather than righteous, and society (or the body politic) is unjust because it puts a premium on wickedness and allows the righteous to be trampled upon and to perish. Negation must therefore be double-edged as well: a new man of righteousness and a new city of justice should be posited. The reality of wickedness and injustice is to be unmasked as mere appearance, as foolishness, as untruth, whereas the imagined world of righteousness and justice should shine in the light of essence, wisdom and truth. It is because of the double character of the negation of negation that we can speak of the *ethico-political* concept of justice. Condemnation is called up and directed at not only the particular offenders but also the society that promotes them. However, the injustice of society or the body politic does not acquit individual offenders. There is a tension between the ethical and the socio-political aspects of the ethico-political concept of justice, a tension eliminable only in religion and philosophy. But can it really be eliminated? In what follows I shall give a brief account of the first religious and philosophical attempts at solving the problem. I shall show that the first religious solution culminates in the *paradox of faith*, while the first philosophical solution culminates in the *paradox of reason*.

I shall exemplify the religious solution via the prophetic idea of justice, the philosophical solution via the philosophy of Plato. It will be seen that the paradox of faith invokes philosophy and that the paradox of reason invokes religion. I shall not discuss as a whole either the message of the prophets of Israel or the Platonian philosophy. Rather, it is the two attitudes they demonstrate that interest me: two attitudes treated as symbols because they represent all other attempts to solve this same problem. The prophets and Plato alike can be interpreted from the vantage point of their respective historical situation. They share the historical consciousness of their own time and culture. But the symbolic attitude they express is timeless; to be more precise, it is transhistorical, for they raise the deepest and most vexing issues of our *historicity*.

The prophetic idea of justice and the paradox of faith

A. J. Heschel writes as follows about justice:

> The two key terms are *tsedakah* (*tsedek*) and *mishpat*. The word *mishpat* means the judgment given by the *shofet* (judge); hence the word can mean justice, norm, ordinance, legal right, law. The word *tsedakah* may be rendered by 'righteousness'. While legality and righteousness are not identical, they must always coincide. . . . Righteousness goes beyond justice. Justice is strict and exact, giving each person his due. Righteousness implies benevolence, kindness, generosity. . . . Justice may be legal; righteousness is associated with a burning compassion for the oppressed. . . . It would be wrong to assume that there was a dichotomy of *mishpat* and kindness. . . . Justice dies when dehumanized, no matter how exactly it may be exercised. . . . The logic of justice may seem impersonal, yet the concern for justice is an act of love.[2]

The formal concept of justice is thus interpreted *within* the framework of the ethico-political concept of justice. Righteousness is the supreme form of being just, and the *tsaddik*, the righteous man, is the most just of all. Justice and benevolence are not two separate virtues (which is how they are viewed – via Hume – in modern times) but one virtue, for the simple reason that partiality for those who suffer is encompassed in justice as righteousness. The sufferers constitute a social cluster to which the norms of benevolence, of help, of partiality, apply. The prophets enumerate these clusters frequently: the widows, the orphans, the poor. If someone fails to show partiality to those who suffer (if he is not righteous), he violates abstract justice.

Yet what is most perplexing is that the act of mercy too belongs to justice as righteousness. Shakespeare, a latecomer to the ethical concept of justice, understood this perfectly well. Hamlet says to Polonius, 'Use every man after his desert, and who should escape whipping? Use them after your own honour and dignity: the less they deserve the more merit is in your bounty' (*Hamlet*, II.ii). For the prophets, it is God who sets the example: 'Therefore the Lord is waiting to be gracious to you; – Therefore He exalts Himself to show *mercy* to you. For the Lord is a God of *justice*' (Isaiah 30:18).[3] Mercy, however, cannot be accounted for within the framework of the formal concept of justice. If we are merciful to everyone then no offence will be punished, and we fail to treat people according to their deserts, as the formal concept of justice enjoins us to do. If we are merciful to some, but not all, then, unless we are observing a concrete norm which recommends mercy in such and such a case, we are infringing formal justice. If mercy, as a general virtue, is

included in justice as righteousness, the formal concept and the
ethical concept of justice are torn apart. This is why the prophets are
so uneasy about including mercy in divine justice.

When the prophets raise their voices against injustice, they mean
by this term *both* wickedness and injustice. (Unless otherwise
indicated, biblical quotations in this section are from the *New
American Bible*.)

> ... they sell the just man for silver,
> and the poor man for a pair of sandals.
> They trample the heads of the weak
> into the dust of the earth,
> and force the lowly out of the way. . . .
>   (Amos 2:6–7)

> Yes, I know how many are your crimes,
> how grievous your sins:
> Oppressing the just, accepting bribes,
> repelling the needy at the gate!
> Therefore the prudent man is silent at this time,
> for it is an evil time.
>   (Amos 5:12–13)

> Woe to him who builds a city by bloodshed,
> and establishes a town by wickedness!
>   (Habakkuk 2:12)

> Woe to those who enact unjust statutes,
> and who write oppressive decrees,
> Depriving the needy of judgment
> And robbing my people's poor of their rights.
>   (Isaiah 10:1–2)

What should men do?

> But if you would offer me holocausts,
> then let justice surge like water,
> and goodness like an unfailing stream.
>   (Amos 5:22)

> Seek justice,
> Undo oppression;
> Defend the fatherless,
> Plead for the widow.
>   (Isaiah 1:17)[4]

And the judgement will be this:

Yes, days are coming, says the Lord God
when I will send famine upon the land:
Not a famine of bread, or thirst for water,
but for hearing the word of the Lord.
Then shall they wander from sea to sea
and rove from the north to the east
In search of the word of the Lord
But they shall not find it.
    (Amos 8:11–12)

Woe to you, destroyer,
Who yourself have not been destroyed;
You treacherous one,
With whom none has dealt treacherously!
You will be destroyed.
When you have made an end of dealing treacherously,
You will be dealt with treacherously.
    (Isaiah 33:1)[5]

I will turn my hand against you,
And refine your dross in the furnace
removing all your alloy.
I will restore your judges as at first,
and your counselors as in the beginning;
After that you shall be called
city of justice, faithful city.
Zion shall be redeemed by judgment,
and her repentant ones by justice. [!]
    (Isaiah 1:25–7)

He shall judge between the nations,
and impose terms on many peoples.
They shall beat their swords into plowshares
and their spears into pruning hooks;
Our nation shall not raise the sword against another,
nor shall they train for war again.
    (Isaiah 2:4)

    This entire edifice is built on faith. But this faith is not irrational: it is the faith of knowledge and wisdom. Knowledge is threefold. It includes knowledge of the norms and commandments of God, knowledge of the world (of the fact that the commandments are not kept, and of how and why they are infringed) and, finally, knowledge of God as just judge. One 'walks with God' on the ground of this knowledge, which is atemporal. Wisdom, unlike knowledge, is temporalized. In general, it includes the distinction between appearance and essence; in particular, the distinction between the appearance of the presence and the essence of the future. As Amos said, the prudent man is silent in this time because it is an evil time. And, as Isaiah said, woe to those (in the future) who create unjust statutes (now). That which will happen should be contrasted with that which happens now. There is a dialectical relationships between knowledge and wisdom. And it is exactly this dialectical relationship that makes the prophetic concept of justice an ethico-political concept of justice *par excellence*.

The world so emphatically denounced by the prophets is a world where injustice is both committed and suffered and where evil is strong and goodness weak, for evil makes men strong and powerful, while goodness fosters weakness, and silences the righteous. Nothing in this conception points toward the philosophical idea that the virtuous are happy, even in dark times. Those whose faith is like rock know that they walk with God, but this is not the happiness Plato and Aristotle attribute to the virtuous. How can the virtuous be happy if they see – and they do see – the weak being trampled 'into the dust of the earth'? How can they be happy if they see (and they do) that cities are 'built by bloodshed'? Righteousness has not the slightest, not even the most subtle utilitarian foundation. However, in spite of the absence of a promise of happiness, the prophetic concept of justice already includes the Platonian idea that the worst act is to commit injustice without having suffered injustice: 'Woe to you . . . treacherous one, with whom none has dealt treacherously!'

The motive of happiness can be absent precisely because the wisdom of 'temporalized' divine justice is present. However, divine justice does not contain even subtle utilitarian connotations. No hereafter is promised where all will be judged by their merits or demerits. Justice will be done on earth, and it will be done to peoples. People whose cities have been built by bloodshed will be destroyed, as will people who sell the just man for silver and the poor man for a pair of sandals. The righteous person is neither happy, nor buys other worldly happiness. Being righteous is simply a contribution to the redemption of his people. But the righteous cannot know whether their people will be saved, because they cannot know whether others will offer God 'holocausts'. This is beyond knowledge. What is not beyond knowledge is simply the following: that, if there is redemption, my righteousness contributes to it. Acts of righteousness are thus performed in the view of the absolute moral world, where 'justice surge[s] like water, and goodness like an unfailing stream'.

The prophetic idea of justice is based on wisdom about divine justice. Whatever my fate, justice will be done: this is the kind of wisdom to which righteousness pertains. Righteousness is an end in itself, yet it implies an end outside the action, not for the actor but for the whole – for 'my' people, and, incidentally, for all people (the emphasis on the latter is particularly strong in Isaiah). Accordingly, a good conscience is not only an 'end in itself', but also the vessel carrying the promise of a righteous future.

All non-utilitarian aspects of the prophetic ethico-political concept of justice are grounded on faith. Faith is supported on three pillars.

1 I must believe that moral norms are God's commandments. I can neither test nor query them. Knowledge is the knowledge of God's commandments. Each and every deflection from these commandments, every flirtation with alien gods, with their norms and customs, is sin. No comparison may be made, no reasoning permitted. Faith and knowledge coincide.

2 I must believe that God sees both everything that I do and that everyone else does. My righteousness may contribute to the possible redemption of my people only because God *sees* that I am righteous. If I fight oppression, defend the helpless, plead for the widow, God's eyes rest on me. He appreciates me even if no one else does, loves me even if no one else does.

3 I must believe that people such as I will be redeemed when God judges nations, that people such as I will inhabit 'the city of justice, the faithful city'. I must be aware that I am a part of the whole (of my people, of humanity), as well as that the fate of the whole depends on individuals and their righteousness, on people such as I.

The prophetic idea of justice is based on faith, which is the coalescence of knowledge and wisdom. This coincidence (or coalescence) of knowledge and wisdom is, however, extremely fragile: it tends to break down. Once someone actually reflects on the prophetic idea of justice, this disassociation occurs immediately, and we arrive at the paradox of the ethico-political concept of justice based on faith.

As mentioned, the idea of the merciful God leads to a paradox. The righteous man is merciful because God commands mercy, because God is merciful. However, if God is merciful and if justice includes mercy, God can extend redemption to those who have led a wicked life, provided they repent. But, if God can pardon the wicked (on the condition of repentance), one's righteousness (throughout the whole of life, as Aristotle would later say) is not *conditio sine qua non* of redemption. One could thus walk the path of the wicked because righteousness would not be seen by God as a necessary element of the just judgement. Nineveh was wicked, yet it escaped punishment from God because its inhabitants had finally turned to the right path. If God is merciful, my righteousness can only be an end in itself, nothing else. One would then be righteous (if one chose to be) for the sake of righteousness, not for the sake of one's people, not for the sake of the future, perhaps not even for the sake of God. Righteousness would be a matter of conscience alone. But, if I reach this conclusion, my righteousness is no longer based on faith, but becomes philosophical, for I shall be righteous irrespective of God's ways.

This paradox is the outcome of the problematization of wisdom. But an even more puzzling paradox stems from the problematization of knowledge. Listen to Habakkuk:

> How long, O Lord? I cry for help
> *but you do not listen!*
> I cry out to you, 'Violence'
> *but you do not intervene. . . .*
> (1:2; emphasis added)

> Too pure are your eyes to look upon evil,
> and the sight of misery you cannot endure,
> Why, then, do you gaze on the *faithless in silence*
> while the wicked man devours
> one more just than himself?
> (1:13; emphasis added)

> Look over the nations and see,
> *and be utterly amazed!*
> For a work is being done in your days
> *that you would not have believed, were it told.*
> (1:5; emphasis added)

The eternal paradox of faith, which ever since has been either explained or explained away, is formulated here for the first time. Why does God not listen? Why does He not intervene? Why does He gaze on the faithless in silence? In asking these questions, Habakkuk does not query divine justice, but queries our knowledge of God. When Habakkuk asks, 'Why does God not listen?' he assumes that we have no answer to the question because we do not know Him. We simply do not know God's ways. The prophet implores God to look over the nations. But does He not see everything anyway? Is God really the God we know Him to be?

What if God's eyes were too pure to look on misery? What if God instead turned His eyes away from His world? What if our faith turned out to be faith in the unknown? What if judgement and knowledge coincided, and knowledge preceded judgement? ('But the earth shall be filled with the knowledge of the Lord's glory as water covers the sea' – Habakkuk 2:14.) Clearly, the theme of the *deus absconditus* has been intoned here; and this theme unfolds with the utmost radicalism in the book of Job.

The story of Job begins with the wager between Satan and God. The substance of the wager is identical with the substance of the argument between Trasymachos and Socrates. Satan contends that Job is righteous and God-fearing *because* he enjoys the rewards of recognition and well-being, whilst God insists that he would still be righteous and God-fearing in the most adverse circumstances. Being in the sphere of religion, the issue cannot be settled by argument, only by the wager; the good man himself must prove or disprove the worth of righteousness. Satan says, 'now put forth your hand and touch anything that he has, and surely he will blaspheme you to your face' (Job: 1:11). And God puts forth His hand, and they see – the unshakable force of pure conscience.

This step already constitutes a paradox. The God that men know loses the wager, for Job indeed blasphemes that God, and in so doing Job goes against his whole world. The friends who represent religious common sense (or, in Platonian terms, religious *opinion*), and who believe that common knowledge is true knowledge, insist in turn that Job must be a sinner, otherwise God would not have moved against him. God is just, they know; He cannot punish the innocent. Where there is such suffering, there must be guilt. But Job is stubborn in defending his righteousness. His conscience is pure. He is not guilty, whatever God does. He does not query his own righteousness, but rather his knowledge of God. 'It is all one, therefore I say: Both the innocent and wicked he destroys' (9:22). As Buber writes, 'And if it is so, it is not proper to walk in His ways. In spite of this Job's faith in justice is not broken down. But he is no longer able to have *single faith* in God and in justice. His faith in justice is no longer covered by God's righteousness. He believes now in justice in spite of believing in God, and he believes in God in spite of believing in justice.'[6] Thus Job believes that man should be righteous even if God is not. Eliphaz, one of the friends, raises the question, 'Can a man be righteous as against God?' (4:17). And Job answers, 'Even that God would decide to crush me, that he would put forth his hand and cut me off! Then I should still have consolation and could exult through unremitting pain, because *I*

have not transgressed the commands of the Holy One' (6:9–10).
And when Zophar asks, 'Can you penetrate the designs of God?
Dare you vie with the perfection of the Almighty?' (11:7), Job
answers as follows: 'What you know, I also know; I fall not short of
you. But I would speak with the Almighty; *I wish to reason with
God*' (13:2–3). And he repeats these words in his last plea: 'This is
my final plea; let the Almighty answer me' (31:37).

There are further ramifications to Job's claim and plea. First, his
plea itself is a claim. He does not understand himself as subject to
God's wishes; he wants to know the truth, the whole truth, beyond
the knowledge of faith. His righteousness itself is the rock
substantiating his claim. He raises the claim to hear God's *reasons*;
he wants to *reason* with God. He does not accept knowledge not
based on reasons. The hidden God is not rational. But the true God,
the God of truth, must be rational: he must listen to the righteous
man, to his reasons, and give a rational answer to those reasons.
Truth cannot be hidden, it must be spoken, and it must be spoken as
reason. Only reason can plea for the justice of injustice. The
religious concept of ethico-political justice raises the claim to a
philosophical truth. And Job gets his truth.

'Who is this that obscures divine plans with words of ignorance?'
asks the Lord (33:2). Job, who wanted to know the truth, was being
ignorant, because he did not understand the essence of divine justice.
To quote Buber again, 'The creation of the world is justice, not a
recompensing and compensating justice, but a distributing, a giving
justice. God the Creator bestows upon each what belongs to him,
upon each thing a being, insofar as He allows it to become entirely
itself . . . divine justice . . . gives to everyone what he is.'[7] Divine
justice is thus not of a punishing and rewarding nature, as people
believe in their folly, a folly they take for knowledge. That each
creature may become 'fully itself' is what divine justice is all about.

God wins the wager with Satan, even though Job did blaspheme.
But Job blasphemed the God of appearance, not the God of essence.
The God of essence was hidden from his eyes, and in that sense he
was ignorant: Job did not know Him. But he acted as if he had
known Him. Because Job was stubborn in his righteousness, because
he knew himself from his own deeds, because he never believed that
he was guilty, because he had no ear for his friends' plea, because he
did not accept that he had been justly punished by God, because he
blasphemed the God who supposedly punishes the wicked and
rewards the righteous, this God of appearance – this is why Job,
even in his ignorance, knew more than the others about the hidden
God, the God of essence. To be righteous – this and nothing else

makes man 'fully himself'. The Creator gives everyone what he is. Job stuck to his righteousness, stuck to what he really was, and by doing this he acted according to esssential divine justice. This is why God says to these friends at the end of the poem, 'For you have not spoken rightly concerning me, as has my servant Job' (42:8).

But what if this God of essence neither punishes the wicked nor rewards the righteous? What if His justice is distributive? – if it means that each creature may become fully itself. Then right and wrong are fully the doing of the creature, and the right is done for the sake of goodness, for the sake of one's human destination; it is done to become truly what one is. No city of justice is promised to the righteous, for he is no longer the vessel of promise, no longer in time. Man becomes his own destiny. Heaven will not help him, will not obstruct him. Creation becomes of the past, or, more precisely, of the everlasting, where man has his share. Man can become what he is destined to be. He can become righteous, or he can fall short of his being in his guilt and wickedness. But God will remain silent. Habakkuk's question is thus answered: God will neither listen, nor intervene; He will gaze on the faithless in silence. To echo the words of Leibniz, He created the best possible world, still a world of injustice, but one where righteousness is always possible, since man can indeed become what he is, can become fully himself.

In the book of Job, the *ethico-political* concept of justice is broken down. Without the promise of the 'city of justice' the political component of the concept disappears; the ethical aspect, and it alone, remains. Let us recall Hamlet here: 'Use them after your own *honour* and *dignity*'. What place is left here for faith? One does not need faith in creation to act according to honour and dignity. Moreover, the myth of creation as the myth of distributive justice is not religious but philosophical. Ours is the best possible world, and there is no hereafter. But, if this is so, God is like the gods of Epicur, and the religious heaven is empty. Job pleads with God no longer; he has understood His essence, and this is why he becomes a stoic.

Still, the book of Job is not yet about the philosophical concept of justice: rather it contains the paradox of the religious concept. For, at the end of the tale, Job is restored to health, wealth and happiness. God is what He says He is not; God does what He says He does not do. He rewards Job for his righteousness – moreover, for having 'spoken rightly' about Him. Job spoke rightly in saying that the 'honest and wicked he exterminates', but God restores the honest, and thus expresses His essence through his appearance. God can be both the essence and the appearance. God gave his reasons to Job and Job understood them well, but the reasons do not bind

God. He does as He chooses. He is *irrational*. We cannot know His ways. He remains *deus absconditus*. And Habakkuk's questions remain, in the end, unanswered. They never will be. We do not know, but we can still believe and hope.

The philosophical idea of justice and the paradox of reason

The biblical tradition has quietly shaped many centuries of Plato reception, and it remains an unconscious current even today. By 'biblical tradition' I do not mean Christian reception alone. In *The Philosophy of Plato* Alfarabi wrote the following,

When he [Plato] . . . looked around him, it became evident to him that it is complete injustice and extreme evil; these grave evils – and they are extremely grave – would not slacken or vanish so long as the cities continued as they were; another city ought to be founded which is different from those cities [and] in which . . . there would be true justice and all the goods that are truly good.[8]

Many scholarly books still sum up the Platonian idea of justice as embodied and realized in the 'just city', where each group (each caste) does its own work. What is missed in this is both the complexity of Plato's argument and the perplexing *modernity* of his approach. In what follows I shall argue that to the same extent as the notion of divine justice concluded in the paradox of faith, the notion of man-made justice concludes in the paradox of reason, and that Plato elaborated this paradox in full.

The book of Job begins with the wager between Satan and God. A brief narrative follows (the narrative of what happened to Job) in which the subject of the wager does not act. The book concludes with another brief narrative, where again the subject of the wager does not act (the restoration of Job). The action proper takes place in the form of argumentation. It is in the speech acts, in the dialogues – first between Job and the friends, later between Job and God – that the problem of justice and righteousness is raised and solved, even if the paradoxical nature of the solution (the paradox of faith) is apparent in the final narrative.

There is also a wager in both the Platonian dialogues (*Gorgias* and *The Republic*) that address the problem of how righteousness is possible within the framework of pure philosophical reason. And here the wager is to the same extent one between good and evil. But, since this is the medium of philosophy and not of religion, the repositories of both good and evil are humans, and the only means of winning the wager is rational argument. The paradox of reason is not narrated, for it is embedded in the argument itself. Briefly, it comprises the following: in philosophy, only rational argument can win the wager against evil. However, rational argumentation cannot win the wager because no rational argumentation can prove that it is better to suffer injustice that to commit injustice. But this is not the whole paradox. If it were, we should be dealing not with a paradox but simply with the argumentative superiority of evil. The gist of the matter is that the narrative plays exactly the same role in Plato as in the book of Job. This narrative cannot be traced either in *Gorgias* or in *The Republic*, yet we are aware of its existence. The narrative hidden behind the argumentation is that of the death of Socrates. Being aware of this narrative, we know that the man who argued for righteousness and who was unable to prove by arguments that it is better to suffer injustice than to commit it lived and died by his beliefs. The man of philosophy acted exactly the same way as the servant of God. Accused of crimes, he listened only to his daimon, his conscience. The daimon remained silent. The man of philosophy knew he was right; he knew that he was righteous and stuck to this conviction in the same way as Job. And it is this hidden narrative that makes the paradox complete. The act of righteousness, the *gesture*, lurks behind the arguments. The truth of righteousness is thus expressed in the gesture which no argument can justify; but this truth was the acting-out of the same argument that could not be proven. Socrates chose to suffer injustice rather than commit it; he justified it without justifying it; he observed philosophical reason beyond reason. And we should not forget the chronological factor. The dialogues of *Gorgias* and *The Republic* take place, unlike certain other dialogues of Plato, *before* the trial of Socrates. Socrates does not yet know his fate, but we do. We read the dialogues with hindsight, from the perspective of this gesture of the future. But this is not yet the entire paradox.

The wager between good and evil is made not in heaven but on earth; it is not only a wager about humans, but a wager between humans. The repositories of good and evil are humans. Socrates argues for righteousness; Callicles (in *Gorgias*) and Trasymachos (in *The Republic*), for evil and injustice. In this earthly setting it is the most righteous person who bets, and so the subjects of the wager are not the most righteous (as in the book of Job) but men of the middle ground, men with an inclination towards the good – Polus (in *Gorgias*), and Adeimantus and (in particular) Glaucon (in *The Republic*). Whether the argument for evil or the argument for good is the more convincing, or, rather, completely convincing for the average man, is what the wager is all about. And it is here that the paradox is fully elaborated. Rational argument alone does not justify righteousness. The truth of philosophy, the gesture of Socrates, is beyond argument. But this gesture is that of the philosopher who partakes of truth. How about those who do not? What about the non-philosophers? The finale of *Gorgias* and the finale of *The Republic* are variations of the same themes, though they are played in a more complex arrangement and on a higher note in the latter work. Two themes appear. One is the recapitulation of the fundamental statement that righteousness does indeed bring happiness, and this is demonstrated by recourse to subjective experience. The other is the theme of other-worldly justice, the myth of divine reward and retribution. The myth of Radamantus and the vision of Er are images the functions of which are to replace argumentation; images that tip the scale of balance to the right side, but only for those who believe in them, for the men of faith. Callicles and Trasymachos do not believe in 'silly tales', but the men of the middle ground still might. The myth is placed in the scales in an attempt to win the wager for the soul of these men of the middle ground. But the wager with reason cannot be won by invoking faith. Still, the gratifying subjective experience of goodness remains. But this experience only stands as proof for men who need no proof at all: for the righteous. Experience must be prior to argument. Socrates says, 'For myself, then, Callicles, I am persuaded by these accounts. . . . And so I dismiss the honours accorded by most men. . . . And I will try to be really the best that is in my power. . . . And I call other men, as far as it is in my power . . . to this life and this contest, which I say is worth more than all the contests here.'[9] Socrates pretends here to be convinced by the 'silly tale'. This can be read as a comedy, for the simple reason that Socrates cannot say he has been convinced by his own arguments, since his goodness existed prior to his arguments. Yet the most important issue here is not the source of conviction, but the invitation ('I call other men . . . to this life and this contest'), the waking and application of the charisma of goodness. The host invites the guests – those who do not possess the inner experience of gratifying goodness, and the experiences of the host must be accepted as a true account by faith. The paradox of reason ends in faith. Yet it still remains the paradox of reason. For it is philosophy and not religion that provides, in the last instance, the faith itself.

And what has Plato to say about evil?

Radical and tragic thinker that he was, fluctuating between comedy and pathos, destructive reasoning and moralizing preaching, Plato was still very parsimonious in making generalized statements about the 'human condition' *in time*.[10] He never said, 'This is an evil time.' He said that all states are badly governed, that Pericles corrupted the Athenian people, that the powerful are wicked, that wealth and poverty are hotbeds of injustice, and he made many statements in this vein. He also said, as did all Athenians before and after him, that bad constitutions breed unjust citizens, and that unjust people enact unjust laws. There is nothing new, much less astonishing, in these assertions. They are fairly commonsensical. Euripides expressed the life experiences of an 'evil time' far more dramatically and radically.

There is nothing astonishing or unique in Plato's conception of soul either. Wisdom is bound to keep both anger and desire under tight control. Anger and desire are destructive both in the soul and in the state. All the same, they do not constitute evil. That must be sought elsewhere.

What is both novel and grand in Plato's conception is the discovery that *evil is the misuse of reason*. The word 'misuse' should be noted here. The idea that evil is identical with the *use* of reason is a pre-Enlightenment statement or a statement stemming from the negation of Enlightenment. The idea that evil is the *misuse of reason* is the defence of Enlightenment against the conclusions drawn from the Enlightenment itself. In Plato, philosophy stands for the proper use of reason, whereas sophistry or rhetoric involves the misuse of reason.

Philosophy (the proper use of reason) is righteousness, wisdom, happiness. Rhetoric and sophistry, the improper use of reason, are evil, foolishness and misery. It is absolutely immaterial whether sophists or rhetors really held the views attributed to them by Plato. In Socrates' time this was obviously not so. In Plato's own time, some of them held views that were at least close to what Plato was talking about. But the full arguments of a Callicles or a Trasymachos were invented and construed by Plato himself. It was he who drew the final consequences from certain tenets: the game of argumentation was played and acted out in his innermost soul. Plato invoked his teacher, Socrates, to voice his arguments for the proper use of reason in order to prove righteousness to be the stronger than evil. Had Plato spoken in his own name, and not through the mouth of Socrates, the impact of the gesture would have been lost. Plato did not die for his righteousness. Moreover, he knew that he would not. Yet it is possible to distinguish between the proper use and the misuse of reason only if it can be proved that the former wins the wager. And, since Plato knew that argument alone does not settle the wager, he made Socrates, the clownish knight of righteousness, tip the balance in favour of the proper use of reason.

Evil makes its appearance as 'the argument for evil'; the *dramatis personae* (Callicles and Trasymachos) present a full argument. The difference between the lines of argument of Callicles and Trasymachos has often been pointed out. So has been the similarity between Calliclas and Nietzsche. And, if we want to find a modern counterpart to Trasymachos, it is Mandeville who comes most readily to mind.

Callicles makes his speech at the middle of the dialogue. He intervenes to remove Polus from the influence of Socrates, accusing Socrates of using the category 'justice' not 'according to nature' but 'according to convention' whilst pretending to speak of both.

For by nature everything is more shameful, which is also worse, suffering injustice, but by rule doing injustice is more shameful. For this isn't what happens to a man, to suffer injustice; it's what happens to some slave. . . . But in my view those who lay down the rules are the weak men, the many. And so they lay down the rules and assign their praise and blame with their eye on themselves and their own advantage. They terrorize the stronger men capable of having more; and to prevent these men from having more than themselves they say that taking more is shameful and unjust . . . they are satisfied, I take it, if they themselves have an equal share when they're inferior. . . . But I think nature itself shows this, that it is just for the better man to have more than the worse, and the more powerful than the less powerful . . . we mould the best and the strongest among us, taking them from youth up, like lions, and tame them by spells and incantations, until we enslave them, telling them they ought to have equal shares, and this is the true and the just. But I think that if a man is born with a strong enough nature, he will shake off and smash and escape all this. He will trample on all our writings, charms, incantations, all the rules contrary to nature. He rises up and shows himself master, this slave of ours, and there the justice of nature suddenly bursts into light.[11]

Whereas Callicles' argument against righteousness is based on the concept of 'nature', Trasymachos' point of departure is the character of law or convention. He argues that what is called 'just' is simply the expression of the 'interest of those who rule and of the stronger, and the loss of the subject and servant'. The truly righteous man (Trasymachos, in contrast to Callicles, assumes that there is such a man) will always lose. And those who rob their citizens, those who are the wicked ones, will be called happy and blessed. Hence the righteous man follows not his own interest, but the interest of the strong and mighty. Indeed, it is in his interest to be unjust: 'And thus, as I have shown, Socrates, injustice, when on a sufficient scale, has more strength and freedom and mastery than justice; and, as I said at first, justice is the interest of the stronger, whereas injustice is a man's own profit and interest.'[12]

The differences in position and argument do not obscure the common element here, which is not simply the making of a case for injustice, but something above and beyond this – the making of a case for *freedom* as against the *slavery of being subjected to norms*. This is an entirely new concept of freedom, a very far cry indeed from the 'freedom of free citizens'. It is a concept which changes the 'status' of happiness. In terms of this concept, the virtuous man cannot be happy, not only because he will not achieve either wealth or power, but because he is not free. In this respect it is of secondary importance whether freedom is defined as following nature or as following personal profit or interest. (It has to be mentioned, though, that following 'nature' as against 'convention' was not necessarily related to the praise of injustice in the ancient context either, for 'nature' could be interpreted in different ways.) For both Callicles and Trasymachos, freedom means the *absence* of any external authority whatsoever, be it collective, traditional, legal or divine, as well as the absence of any internal authority (conscience). Plato attributed an ethico-political concept of 'injustice' to evil. In this concept, external authority is slavery (the political aspect), while internal authority does not exist (the moral aspect).

Thus, for Plato, evil does not dwell in human nature, nor does it dwell in the city (or in the laws). Men can be wicked, the city can be badly governed, but evil is, to use Kant's expression, the *maxim* of acting in an evil way. But if the maxim of committing injustice is evil itself, then evil is nothing but *perverted reason*. The maxim of perverted reason is that no norm is valid. It is this maxim that *makes* men and times evil. It is wrong that laws are bad, that men do not observe them, that the just are poor whilst the unjust take pride in their wealth and power. But it is not evil that these things are so. To argue on behalf of all these things – herein lies evil. Plato is breathtakingly modern. That he is not completely modern is due to the lack of universalized values, and to the impossibility in his time of universalizing them. We must wait until the Enlightenment for this to occur.

But how does Socrates make a case for good reason against perverted reason? In both *Gorgias* and *The Republic*, Socrates–Plato applies the same method used many centuries later by Kant in *The Foundation of the Metaphysics of Morals*: he proceeds from common sense to philosophy. I shall restrict myself here to *The Republic*, where the speech of Evil does not sever the argument in two. The gist of the matter is that, although Socrates begins his argument with the thesis he will defend to the end, he is unable to make a case for it using common-sense arguments. When he ends the first round (first book) with the statement, 'For I know not what justice is, and therefore I am not likely to know whether it is or is not a virtue, nor can I say whether the just man is happy or unhappy',[13] this is surely a piece of comedy (for he knows quite well what justice is), but, again, it is *not* a comedy (for truth must be proved, and it has not yet been proved). So Glaucon's question (at the beginning of the second book) hits the nail on the head: 'Socrates, do you wish really to persuade us, or only to seem to have persuaded us, that to be just is always better than to be unjust?'[14] It is at this point that Socrates makes it clear that he is dealing not only with the ethical but with the ethico-political concept of justice: 'I propose therefore that we enquire into the nature of justice and injustice, first as they appear in the State, and secondly in the individual. . . .'[15] Thus the discussion of the state commences.

As is well known, the fourth book already includes the answer to the question raised above. We learn that, as far as the city is concerned, 'when the trader, the auxiliary, and the guardian each do their own business, that is justice, and will make the city just'.[16] And we learn that 'the just man does not permit the several elements within him to interfere with one another'.[17] But it is only after all this is said that we learn about philosophy.

The Republic, as depicted by Plato, is to be seen as a polysemic symbol. It offers three solutions to the question under scrutiny: that of justice as righteousness.

First, one can take the utopia of *The Republic* at its face value. It is the utopia of the city, where the virtue of justice pertains to the whole, and the three further virtues of wisdom, courage and temperance are distributed among the three classes or castes. This city is indeed the perfect embodiment of the formal concept of justice. It is a city where the formal concept of justice is the exclusive concept of justice. The norms that apply to the cluster of ruler–philosophers apply to every member of this cluster; the norms that apply to the cluster of guardians apply to every member of this cluster; the norms that apply to the cluster of traders apply to every member of this cluster. There are no transclusteral norms whatsoever because every cluster has its own distinct virtue. However, we know that righteousness entails the observance of certain transclusteral norms. Where there are no such norms, there is no righteousness. And this is exactly what Plato had in mind when he said that justice is the virtue of the city as the whole, and not of the individuals residing in different social clusters. The ethical aspect of the ethico-political concept of justice is lost for good, but the political aspect does not fare much better. Those living in an unjust city, like Socrates and all his interlocutors, can recognize justice as something to be realized in the image of a utopian republic. They can do this because they can choose to do it: they can choose the just over the unjust, can counterpose the former to the latter. But what about the people who might live in such a utopian city? Not being familiar with injustice, they could not juxtapose an unjust city to the just, and they would have no choice.

If we understand Plato's Republic as the idea or the model of a just city, we must conclude that Plato–Socrates, instead of solving the initial problem of righteousness, eliminated the problem itself. Socrates wanted to prove that it is better to suffer than to commit injustice. In the ideal city, where no one suffers and no one commits injustice, this question cannot even be raised. The initial thesis is not substantiated by the arguments, but, rather, circumvented.

But with this we have only touched upon the first and most superficial layer of *The Republic*. And, though this layer is superficial, it still exists. We know only too well that Plato genuinely believed that philosophers should rule the state, and that his conception of the state should be put into practice to a greater or lesser degree. However, the solution to the initial problem of righteousness begins to reveal itself if we proceed to the second layer.

Plato designed a city ruled by philosophers. In so doing *he founded the city called 'philosophy'*. For let us ask the question, 'Is there a city ruled by philosophers?' The answer is that such a city exists, and it is called 'philosophy'. In philosophy you can set up as many cities as you wish. Each and every philosopher establishes his city, the 'city in the sky'. The prophets said very little about the 'city of justice'; they only knew that it would be just, for God is just, and it would be His city. But philosophy is ruled by the philosophers; it is up to them to construct their city and to mould the 'city in the sky' according to the pattern of justice. Philosophy is the utopian reality. Whoever dwells in this city is righteous. Thus the political facet of the ethico-political concept of justice is shifted to the level of a utopian reality. The philosopher acts according to the norms of the 'city in the sky', and this is why he is righteous. The arguments of Trasymachos or Callicles do not prove anything for a philo-sopher, because his happiness springs from his own republic. Callicles and Trasymachos are ridiculous because of their blindness. They cannot hit their target (Socrates) with their argument, for they know nothing of the 'city in the sky'.

But it is only ironically that those living in this city can raise the question of whether it is 'better' to suffer or to commit injustice, not only because the inhabitant of this city is beyond choice, in that he cannot commit injustice, but also because he cannot suffer injustice either. As the Socrates of the *Apology* said, Anytos and Meletos can kill me, but they cannot do me harm. Where harm is not done, there is no suffering. The man who lives in the 'city in the sky' is happy irrespective of his circumstances.

The wager is about righteousness. The philosopher must argue on behalf of righteousness in order to capture the soul of the non-philosopher. Thus the argument on behalf of righteousness is to be the arrangement on behalf of philosophy, the 'city in the sky'. However, no one can *become* a philosopher simply by accepting a convincing argument. Discourse itself, as we know, ends in a stalemate between the repositories of perverted reason and the repositories of good reason. To catch sight of the idea is the revelation that opens the gate to the 'city in the sky'. The philosopher argues for something he already sees, *ergo* knows. Thus revelation precedes argument. Argument alone cannot lead to revelation.

The third meaning of the city is the city within us, the city called the 'soul'. The preliminary solution, that in a 'just soul' all parts must perform their own work, is now explained in full. We know not only that wisdom means keeping anger and desire under tight control, but also something beyond this: we know what wisdom is. Further, we know that, if there is true wisdom (that is to say, true philosophy) in the soul, then anger and desire should not be kept under tight control at all, for there is nothing bad left in this soul. Not only is the soul not destroyed by evil (as in the analogy of the cart), but it is indestructible, for nothing bad or evil remains within it. We cannot believe, so Plato says, the soul, 'in her truest nature, to be full of variety and difference and dissimilarity'.[18] The city in the soul, or rather, the city which is the soul, is no longer like the Republic. There are no castes, parts, differences in it, only homogeneity and the unity of the good. Man can be righteous if he becomes ruler of his own city, and, the more he rules it, the less it needs to be ruled. This soul, this true city, becomes indestructible, for, if something cannot be destroyed from the inside, it cannot be destroyed from the outside. Thus we arrive at the final stage; we meet the man of pure conscience. And here we also arrive at the myth of the immortality of the soul, a fairytale which reinforces the resolution in favour of the good in the soul of the common man. But, then again, this myth is not wholly a fairytale. It expresses the deep conviction of Plato that the completely good soul (which cannot be destroyed from inside) *deserves immortality.*

How, then, can we become the rulers of our own city: how can we transform our city into the homogeneous soul of pure conscience?

The answer is attempted in book VII, where Plato speaks about the disciples of philosophy. Socrates says,

> You know that there are certain principles about justice and honour, which were taught us in childhood, and under their parental authority we have been brought up, obeying and honouring them. . . . There are also opposite maxims and habits . . . which . . . do not influence those of us . . . who continue to obey and honour the maxims of their fathers. . . . Now, when a man is in this state, and the questioning spirit asks what is fair or honourable, and he answers as the legislator has taught him, and then arguments many and diverse refute his words, until he is driven into believing that nothing is honourable and more and dishonourable . . . do you think that he will still honour and obey them as before?[19]

This is a confession of defeat. Socrates makes a plea for good reason as against perverted reason, and comes to the conclusion that everyone who is not yet righteous would be defenceless against the maxims of evil. If you are already righteous, you can neither suffer injustice nor commit it. If you are not yet righteous, perverted reason will persuade you that it is better to commit injustice than to suffer it. The man of reason shrinks from reasoning and takes course to authority. Socrates makes a case for philosophical authority. The love of wisdom, the love of this authority, is the most reliable reader of the soul. But even traditional authority, that of the fathers, is better than none. Only through firmness in the acceptance of an external authority can internal authority (conscience) truly develop as pure conscience. The paradox of reason is thus formulated in the most extreme manner: reasoning leads to unreason. Faith surfaces three times and in three forms: faith in other-worldly justice, faith in authority, and faith in revelation (the sight of ideas). Enlightenment is thus revoked in the city on earth and wholly shifted to the 'city in the sky'. It can be never proven that it is better to suffer injustice than to commit it; but it is always proven, and it always remains true in philosophy, in this 'city in the sky'.

The paradox of faith and the paradox of reason were utterly radical positions in ancient times. Normally, both religion and philosophy stop short of radicalism when making a case for righteousness and justice. It is the deep crisis of the ethico-political concept of justice that gives birth to a radicalism of this kind. We have seen that the prophets of Israel, with the exception of

Habakkuk, did not arrive at the paradox, because they firmly believed in God as the just judge. Similarly, the paradox is eliminated in Greek philosophy after Plato. As mentioned, Aristotle discovered the polysemic character of the notion 'justice', and clearly distinguished the different uses of this term. However, amongst these distinctions he preserved intact the ethico-political concept of justice. Justice as 'the sum total of virtues' is the ethical concept of justice (righteousness), which has its political counterpart, the polity. It is in the polity, the just state, that the virtue of the good citizen and that of the good man coincide. Once again, the problem of happiness is soundly solved. Aristotle agrees with Plato that only the virtuous can be happy, but he does not add that the virtuous are always happy under all circumstances. I think one can understand Aristotle best by reformulating his statement: the non-virtuous cannot be happy, despite enjoying the 'goods of luck'. Virtue is the prerequisite of happiness, but is not happiness itself. After Aristotle, the decomposition of the ethico-political concept began.

The notion of righteousness in ancient stoicism and Epicureanism is a *purely ethical* concept. The city called the 'soul' is the only city left. But the city called the 'soul' is also the 'city in the sky'. The loss of the city as utopia and of the 'city in the sky' as the utopian reality marks the interpretation of righteousness itself. Practising righteousness is no longer practising the good, committing justice, but becoming indifferent to all injustices we might suffer. 'Unhappy consciousness' is the consciousness of pure conscience in its impotence. There is no longer any wager to be made.

THE DISSOLUTION OF THE ETHICO-POLITICAL CONCEPT
OF JUSTICE IN MODERNITY

The new ethico-political concept of justice ends rather than begins its historical vicissitudes with the modern wager as portrayed in Goethe's *Faust*. *Faust* is in every respect the antithesis of the book of Job. Whereas with Job it was God who acted, and finally argued, while Satan remained passive and waited for the outcome, here Mephistopheles is the stage-manager, the one who argues, while God is passive and waits for the outcome. The subject of the wager is not the righteous man but the man of knowledge. At stake is neither faith nor reason, but freedom. The paradox contained in *Faust* is the paradox of freedom. It is the modern paradox *par excellence*. In the book of Job the righteous man must experience all sufferings. In *Faust* the man of knowledge gains new life, and his wants are satisfied again and again. The first endures unlimited suffering, the second enjoys unlimited freedom. Faust is free even from the eclipse of his time and space. None the less, the outcomes of the two parables are amazingly similar, in a paradoxical vein as well as in other ways. In spite of winning the wager, both Satan and Mephistopheles end up losing. Job blasphemes God but sticks to his righteousness; he remains what he has been. Faust pleads for the moment to linger because it is beautiful, but God wins the wager and Faust is saved because his last vision of freedom was the freedom of all. What is so striking in comparing these two paradoxes is the more than perplexing fact that Job, who is restored to health and wealth, is a modern man, the man who believed himself righteous, whereas Faust is saved because he returns to the ethico-political concept of justice. The Faustian vision of 'free men on free soil' links, once again, the righteous life of the individual with the image of a just and free 'city on earth'. The dissatisfied modern man, who thirsts for knowledge, wealth and power while transgressing traditional norms, dreams of freedom within the limits of norm-regulated human co-operation.

But this particular wager was not about 'human nature'; it was not about 'righteousness as such'; it was not about the problem of whether it is better to suffer injustice than to commit it, a maxim in general, that is insoluble in its generality. It was a wager about modern man in particular. Since the wager is historicized, the dilemma at stake is no longer insoluble in principle. Yet still we are in the midst of the wager where righteousness is at stake. This wager is won neither by God nor by Mephistopheles.

The paradox of freedom is the paradox of modernity *par excellence*. Both the paradox of reason and the paradox of faith became facets, constituents, of this overarching paradox. This is why we are confronted with new problems and new puzzles, in the light of which even the ancient questions need to be reformulated. The greatest of puzzles is the problematization of 'good'. In ancient times everyone knew what was good and righteous, even Callicles and Trasymachos, who argued, in fact, that by being righteous we harm ourselves, and so it makes no sense to be good; but they never said that in being righteous we can harm others, that being righteous can have evil consequences. What is being righteous? How can we be righteous? What can we do if we are confronted with differing and even contradictory norms of righteousness? Righteousness is no longer 'prior to argument', which was the case with the prophets, for Job, even for Plato–Socrates and Aristotle. The kind of righteousness that is in fact righteous can only be found via reasoning, and reasoning is not restricted to self-reflection; it includes reflection on the norms themselves. Practical reason cannot make the right decision simply by applying valid norms to particular circumstances. It must test the norms themselves to determine whether they are valid. Conscience must legislate, instead of interpreting the laws (of convention). We have become free to reject norms by reason and to argue for the establishment of substitute norms, and there is no moral commitment without the use of reason. The paradox of reason, thus reformulated within the paradox of freedom in our search for good maxims, can cut both ways: it can lead to a post-conventional free morality, or to a stage where we can no longer tell good from evil. This problem becomes central in the modern ethical concept of justice. And, after the last great efforts to keep it intact, the concept of ethico-political justice is disintegrated. The *ethical* problem of justice loses its socio-political character, of which only remnants remain. These remnants are called *retributive justice, distributive justice* and *'just-war theory'*. These will be analysed in chapter 4.

The ethico-political concept of justice and the birth of modernity

A. MacIntyre asserts that in modern times we often use moral terms without being able to attribute meaning to them, because we have disconnected these very terms from the totality of moral beliefs that once gave meaning to moral concepts. In ancient times, MacIntyre reasons, there was a consensual knowledge of moral ends, of perfect virtues, and human nature was considered as the raw material to be shaped in order to achieve this end, this 'good'.[20] This consensual knowledge of the moral end, he continues, is now absent, and every discussion of 'human nature' and its moral potential is therefore meaningless.

Hegel was perfectly aware of this change; moreover, he knew more about it. He wrote as follows in the *Phenomenology of Spirit*:

Virtue in the ancient world had its own definite sure meaning, for it had in the *spiritual substance* of the nation a foundation full of meaning, and for its purpose an actual good already in existence. Consequently, too, it was not directed against the actual world as against something *generally perverted*, and against a 'way of the world'. But the virtue we are considering [the modern concept of virtue] has its being outside of the spiritual substance, it is an unreal virtue, a virtue in imagination and name only, which lacks that substantial content.[21]

The 'evil time' of the prophets was evil because men forgot the commandments of God and became wicked. It was a timeless time. Modern moralists of virtue are not confronted with the wickedness in this timeless time but with the times that bring about wickedness. But is virtue possible in a time that generates wickedness, a time where not God, but history, is the judge? Even though in Hegel the 'wickedness of times' is understood as the construct of mere subjectivity, and it is precisely this subjectivity that must be overcome, or rather abandoned, in his philosophy, the diagnosis of the modern notion of virtue is quite accurate. Modern practical reason and conscience become the ultimate arbiter in respect of good and evil.[22] Conscience nurtures an image of good and juxtaposes it to reality, so that reality becomes, via this juxtaposition, unreasonable and evil. Conscience, as the ultimate arbiter in moral decisions, can be bad conscience, sceptical conscience and legislative conscience. Since bad conscience has recourse to divine judgement, and sceptical conscience restricts itself to an ethical concept of justice, it is only legislative conscience that establishes new forms of the ethico-political concept of justice. Clearly, an image of human nature is by no means the real point of departure for legislative conscience. The procedure here is very similar to the ancient one described by MacIntyre. First there is the image of the end, the image of good itself. Human nature is constructed in a way that enables it to be the vehicle for the realization of the final end. Accordingly, human nature cannot be constructed in a way that is radically evil, for it could not then transform itself in line with the goal of the 'good end'. Yet human nature cannot be constructed as radically good either, for society would then be neither unreasonable nor wicked, and there would be no need for legislative conscience.

There is another similarity between the ancient and modern which is of the greatest importance for the problem under scrutiny. The end, 'good', is not only 'the moral man', but 'the moral man in a good society'. Legislative conscience legislates not only for men, but for society and the body politic too. The basic structure of the ethico-political concept of justice remains intact. Nevertheless, the differences are striking. First there is the difference between interpretative and legislative conscience itself. Interpretative conscience, as Hegel put it, can refer to an already existing good as its end, even if it reinterprets that good from the standpoint of true knowledge as contrasted with mere opinion. There is, however, no pre-existing good for the legislative conscience; it must construe this good. And one cannot construe good (in philosophy) by simply isolating or pointing out the voice of subjective conscience; one must prove the goodness of the particular good, must find 'evidence' on the basis of which good may be deduced. So we come back to 'human nature'. Good will be proved to be good by deducing it from human nature. The nature of the human race is to be the nature of all individual human beings, and all individuals must share the same nature. The best possible world is seen as the world of optimum (or maximum) freedom, optimum (or maximum) reason, and optimum (or maximum) morality. Human nature must therefore encompass freedom and reason, and goodness must be deduced from either one or the other or both. Freedom is not yet paradoxical, for it is not yet conceived of as absolute; it is optimum or maximum freedom (and even the maximum is an optimum) because it is freedom in a society (state) where the formal concept of justice still applies. But the paradox is avoided at a heavy price. The price paid by the modern ethico-political concept of justice was the construction of a substantive goal lacking 'a foundation full of meaning . . . and an actual good already in existence', to echo once again the words of Hegel. By constructing such a substantive goal, modern adherents of the ethico-political concept of justice solved a problem philosophically that cannot be solved philosophically at all. But Hegel, even if rejecting this problematic venture, did not fare much better. The modern ethico-political concept of justice was unproblematic only at the level of the poetic abstraction of the Faustian dream. The wager still stands.

Hobbes worked with a complete ethico-political concept of justice. Much has been written about the similarities and differences between Hobbes and Locke by comparing their respective views on human nature, on the relation between state and civil society, on the concept of contract, and on their respective options for a particular socio-political solution. Whether Hobbes defended the absolutist state or laid down the principles of liberalism is not our concern here. As far as the ethico-political concept of justice is involved, there is a clear split between the two men. It was definitely Locke who cleared the way for the dismantling of this concept of justice. It is in Locke that the *retributive* and *distributive* aspects of justice are (if not yet completely) severed from the general (ethico-political) context, and that the *formal* characteristics of the good state are to be substituted for substantive qualities (see tacit consent). Morality was to become a science (like mathematics), and was to be the same for all humankind.

Whatever the similarities between Hobbes and Locke in the 'scientific' conception of morals, Hobbes was none the less rooted in the Aristotelian tradition, both in discussing justice and in relating righteousness to the observance of socio-political norms. Whether political society was believed to come about as the 'natural goal' of men and of human associations, or was due to the famous 'covenant', makes no difference here. In *Leviathan* Hobbes says,

Justice is the constant Will of giving to every man his own . . . the Validity of Covenants begins not but with the Constitution of a Civil Power, sufficient to compell men to keep them: and then it is also that *Propriety* begins. . . . The names of Just, and Injust, when they are attributed to Men, signifie one thing; and when they are attributed to Actions, another. . . . A Just man therefore, is he that taketh all the care he can, that his Actions may be all Just; and an Unjust man, is he that neglecteth it. And such men are more often in our Language stiled by the names of Righteous, and Unrighteous; then Just, and Unjust; though *the meaning be the same.* Therefore a Righteous man, does not lose that Title, by one, or a few unjust Actions . . . nor does an Unrighteous man, lose his character . . . because his Will is not framed by the Justice, but by the apparent benefit of what he is to do. . . . This Justice of the Manners, is that which is meant, where *Justice* is called a *Vertue*; and Injustice a Vice.[23]

The law of justice, the third law of nature, is complemented by the eleventh, that of equity: 'if a man be trusted to judge between man and man, it is a precept of the Law of Nature, that he deale Equally between them'.[24] It is the sovereign who establishes the laws; that is, the rules of *meum* and *tuum*, of lawful and unlawful, of good and evil. The contempt of the legislator is referred to as a sin, as is the intention of transgressing. I shall not dwell on the illiberality of the above proposal; it suffices to say that in the final analysis Socrates was put to death for no other reason but 'the contempt of the legislator'. However, the Hegelian criticism, directed primarily against Rousseau, also found a target in Hobbes. For Hobbes had already created a political model that performed two tasks simultaneously. First, legal and moral norms should coincide, at least tendentially: the laws should promote righteousness. Secondly, the maximum liberty of the individual should be secured on the grounds of an absolute obedience to the laws and norms, including obedience in intentions (legality and morality). True enough, for Hobbes the state was rather the *means* to achieve just that degree of liberty that would ensure justice, righteousness and proper education – rather than the *end*, freedom accomplished. However, this *substantive model* was already highly speculative, being constituted by a subjective design, through a deductive procedure, and not being rooted at all in the pre-existing forms of *Sittlichkeit* (collective morality). The 'way of the world' took a different turn, and this turn was soon to be felt and expressed in Britain. There, the first great edifice of the ethico-political concept of justice was at the same time the last.

Much has also been written and said about the different images of human nature in Hobbes and in Rousseau. We learn that 'man' is evil by nature in Hobbes and good by nature in Rousseau. In fact, nothing could be more misleading than this interpretation. If we moved beyond the comparison of *single* statements, and compared the two philosophies as wholes, we could also come to the opposite conclusion. However, as I have already mentioned, human nature was neither radically evil nor radically good for either Hobbes or Rousseau, but rather malleable, adjustable to social requirements, or to the lack thereof. The difference between Hobbes and Rousseau lies in their philosophical frameworks and styles. Hobbes operates with the simple juxtaposition of the state of nature and the civil state, whereas Rousseau historicizes 'human nature' by distinguishing different steps in its unfolding. The style of Hobbes is objective, sceptical and even, whereas Rousseau constantly alternates between enthusiastic rapture and spiteful contempt. It is not true that Hobbes simply sees man as he is, and Rousseau as he ought to be: both see him in both these ways. Yet for Hobbes not a great deal is needed, only good use of reason and the desire to get rid of fear, to transform men into just and righteous persons (what they might become and ought to be), whereas Rousseau posits a gulf between utter degradation and perfect elevation. Hobbes is more pagan, Rousseau more Christian. Indeed, there is a striking difference between Hobbes's and Rousseau's images of human nature. But this is not because the former sees it as 'evil' and the latter as 'good', the former 'as it is' and the latter 'as it ought to be'. It is because reason is quite unproblematic for Hobbes, whereas it is deeply problematic for Rousseau. Since reason is the bearer of the 'laws of nature', good practical reason is, so to speak, 'natural' for Hobbes. The distinction between theoretical and practical reason is relative. Proper conscience is based on good understanding (Hobbes dwells on the etymology of the word 'conscience' in order to prove this point), although the 'voice' of conscience can be misleading, in that it might be the expression of unsoundly based promises and ignorance. Rousseau problematizes reason, and he is the first to contrast theoretical and practical reason: *will* and *understanding* are thus divided. This shift is responsible for the transformation of the notion 'virtue'. Virtue, which for Hobbes was still identical with justice and righteousness, and nothing else, has acquired a *double meaning*. On the one hand it is completely subjectivized in order to advance the Kantian notion of morality. On the other hand it is completely desubjectivized in the form of absolute republican virtue. Not only are the morality of the man and the morality of the citizen different in kind, but the first only exists where the second is absent, and *vice versa*. And yet Rousseau did not abandon the *full* concept of the ethico-political concept of justice, and never reduced it to a mere moral concept. There is no morality without some kind of ethico-social community. Lonely men (or men in loneliness) can be good, but they cannot be moral (virtuous). And goodness is merely negative, the absence of social perversions, for the positive aspect of natural goodness (benevolence or empathy) cannot be made use of in seclusion. Thus the interplay between righteousness and the just society remains in force. How can man be free and reason practical; how can society be such that man should be free, reason practical, and will good? – this is the question. And, as Rousseau developed two different notions of virtue, there are two distinct answers to the question.

Still, both solutions have one element in common: happiness, the central concept of the ancient ethico-political concept of justice, becomes marginal, and freedom moves to the centre of discourse. In modern, dissatisfied society, it simply could not be otherwise. The felicity of free speculation, or *amor dei intellectualis* (in Spinoza) is rather ecstatic in comparison with the happiness of the good life shared by all good men and citizens (in Aristotle), even in comparison with the Platonian happiness anchored in the good life, in harmony with the 'city in the soul'. And for Hobbes happiness simply means the constant satisfaction of desires; it is thus devalued rather than abandoned. True enough, unjust people cannot be happy in Hobbes's state because they are punished. But it is not made clear whether 'justice of manners' (righteousness) makes men happier than the mere avoidance of unjust acts. Rousseau goes even further when he sees happiness in the innocence of the noble savage. Happiness through a lack of reflection does not appear as a fascinating experience even if it was so regarded by certain readers of Rousseau. And the happiness of ignorance is a far cry from the reflected happiness of antiquity. Anatole France, in his story about the shirt of the 'happy man', understood more than the philosophical commentators about the Rousseauian notion of 'happiness'.

The subjective concept of virtue (as morality) is worked out in full in Rousseau's *La Nouvelle Héloïse*. The misfortune that this great and complex philosophical treatise was written in the form of a novel – and a bad one – makes it a tiresome reading. All the same, as far as the *ethical attitude* is concerned, nowhere is Rousseau so liberal and far-sighted.

The fact that Rousseau himself found decisive (and he was

disconsolate that his readers remained insensitive to it) was that there is no single negative ('bad') character in the whole novel, not even an unworthy or amoral deed. The story is about righteous, decent, good people, but all of them are righteous, virtuous and decent in entirely different ways. It is the *plurality* of righteous attitudes that the novel is all about. The romantic enthusiast, the mystic Christian, the rational disbeliever, the stoic, even the conventional person with a kind disposition – all of these characters are good, and equally good. Saint-Preux is undoubtedly the mouthpiece of Rousseau. He is the one who burns with moral fervour, has raptures over simplicity, nature and virtue, and nothing but bitter contempt for 'men of society'. He is the one who describes city life as the masquerade of empty selves – more than 200 years before Goffman invents the simile of the 'empty peg', where there is nothing 'inside'. But Rousseau relativizes his own enthusiasm here, as well as his conceit. He exposes himself, because he exposes Saint-Preux, his mouthpiece, to the friendly criticisms of other and equally righteous people.

The work is a credo against perfectionism. Righteousness has absolutely nothing to do with the 'perfectability' of human nature, only with its corrigibility. All the characters of the novel are righteous, but none is 'perfect'. All have faults and weaknesses. They are sometimes carried away by false ideas and unworthy passions. But, if this is so, why do they not commit wicked acts? The answer is straightforward: because they all belong to a 'network', the network of friendship, the network of an ideal, and, later, of a real community.

Since the novel is composed of letters, we have a direct insight into the operation of the 'network'. The intersubjective relations are based on a mutual recognition of all members. Recognition means the recognition of one another's needs, of one another's character, and – what is of the utmost importance – the recognition of one another's values. Only a few values are shared by all members of the circle. However, these shared values stem from and depend upon the plurality of values. It is a shared value that the friends respect each other's values. It is a shared value that everyone should be true and should live up to his or her own values. It is a shared value that members of the circle listen to each other's judgements, be they approving or disapproving. The friends are not sparing with their judgements: they praise and blame each other's intentions and feelings as disclosed in their letters. If they praise, they praise the personality; if they blame, they blame a particular intention, feeling or judgement while affirming the personality. Mutual recognition includes mutual confidence. But mutual confidence does not include complete self-disclosure. Although human relations are reciprocal and symmetrical, not all of them are equally intensive or intimate. Truthfulness is general, frankness is relative, to the intimacy of a particular personal relationship. Mutual help in critical situations is taken for granted; and the friends keep their eyes open to find out when such help is needed. But constant care for each other is not required, except the caring that occurs in the most intimate relationships, because the personal freedom of everyone is truly respected.

This model of personal relationships based on the plurality of righteousness and mutual recognition is apparently a *fuite en avant*. The word *fuite* ('escape') refers to the fact that all the friends experienced various disappointments in the 'wide society' before they found comfort and a home in the 'network' of friends. The term *en avant* ('into the future'), refers to the model itself, so far removed from the ancient image of righteousness, a model based on the pre-existence of commonly shared norms. Rousseau's model is utterly modern. It confronts us with the very question we must still raise: how is a world of *Sittlichkeit* possible if the 'good life' is pluralistic? How can we listen to each other's arguments if our ideas differ? How can we come to rational understanding and co-operation while preserving our uniqueness, freedom and disagreement? Had Rousseau only raised these questions, *La Nouvelle Héloïse* would indeed have been a *fuite en avant*. But to provide a solution, if only a relative one, was a temptation Rousseau could never resist. The contradictions had to be reconciled, first and foremost because Rousseau wanted to keep the ethico-political concept of justice intact.

The application of the Hegelian notions of 'subjective spirit' and 'objective spirit' to the composition of *La Nouvelle Héloïse* is not without foundation. In the first part of the novel all personal contacts are based on love, and love alone. The network is an 'ideal community' of friendly spirits, but it is not a real community because it is not yet institutionalized. The second part of the novel is where the real community (that of Clarence) comes into being. In contemporary jargon, Clarence can be referred to as a 'counter-institution'. There does not exist, nor can there exist, an ethico-political concept of justice that lacks 'objective spirit'. Indeed, the formal concept of justice does not apply to the 'network of friends', where people are recognized according to their uniqueness (singularity). This is why Rousseau wants to invent the very institution in the framework of which the model of the 'network' can become generalizable. As he undertakes this task he ends up designing a community of shabby paternalism. The paternalistic rule of a 'wise man' (or a wise king) was an idea of mainstream enlightenment. Should Sarastro sing the tunes of Mozart, then because of the power of the medium of music we accept the complete paternalistic message. Should Wolmar recite Rousseau's prose, we are thoroughly disappointed. Even if there are life qualities in Clarence which anticipate Fourier's phalanstery, the openly aristocratic tinge of the Rousseauean utopia, where virtuous enthusiasts and men of reason treat servants like naughty children, regulating their behaviour by rigorous norms far outstripping in fundamentalism the laws of the Hobbesian sovereign, and where all joy and pleasure is centrally organized and orchestrated, frightens us no less than does 'freedom by constraint' in the *Social Contract*. The relapse into mainstream Enlightenment is to be seen as an indirect confession. The questions of such foresight raised in the first part of the novel cannot be solved on the grounds of a full and complete ethico-political concept of justice. The 'networks' Rousseau alludes to can incidentally solve them, but in having recourse to such networks one can only prove the *possibility* of an ethico-political concept of justice appearing in times to come.

La Nouvelle Héloïse ends in tragedy. By not shrinking from this solution, Rousseau restores in the second part some of the philosophical merits of the first. Neither the best people, nor the best possible society, secure human happiness. Not even the liberalizing of attitudes can prevent conflicts of duties from occurring. The most that can be said of this best possible society is that its tragic events are deeply mourned, and that the tragedies themselves are built into the good life of all.

From what has been said, we can construct not two but three ethico-political concepts of justice in Rousseau – two of them complete, one of them incomplete. I termed the last *fuite en avant*. Since all three solutions follow from exactly the same philosophical premises, it is doubtful whether we can charge these philosophical premises, and these alone, with responsibility for the fundamentalist solutions of the paternalistic community depicted in Clarence and the republic designed in *Social Contract*. Let me briefly sum up the main premises.

1   The coalescence of virtue and freedom, and of wickedness and unfreedom (slavery). Where men are free, they are also virtuous, and *vice versa*. When in chains, they are also wicked, and *vice versa*. This is the basic statement of every ethico-political concept

of justice. However, the notions 'freedom' and 'virtue' had to be reinterpreted under the condition of modernity *in statu nascendi*.

2   Human passions in themselves are not to be made responsible for human wickedness. Rather, we are denaturalized in a competitive, divided and oppressive civilization. Even in respect of phenomena within the 'instinctive' domain, such as sexuality, it is vanity and not the desire itself that leads men astray.

3   Reason itself can be corrupted. And it is corrupted if it serves (rationalizes) the mere particularistic will. The progress of theoretical reason does not improve man; rather, the contrary is the case. In order to put reason right, certain norms (or laws) have to be established by the common reason of humankind or a human community. Right reason cannot be the expression of the particular will, just as it cannot be the expression of the sum total of particular wills ('the will of all'). It must be the expression of the 'general will'.

4   The 'general will' is (in its broadest interpretation) the collective internal authority, the collective conscience of humankind, the duty of which is to test the external authorities of norms, rules and public opinion. It is a legislative authority because it must establish new and rational norms that free and virtuous people are bound to obey.

5   There must be a procedure for distinguishing the general will from the 'will of all', the sum total of particularistic wills. Rousseau asserts at one point that it is very easy to be aware of the imperative of this general will: *'the general will is, in each individual, a pure act of the understanding which reasons, when the passions are silent, about what a man can ask of his fellows and what his fellows have the right to ask of him'.*[25] This formulation anticipates the outlines of the Kantian solution, but it has no socio-political relevance. Rousseau gives voice to the objection of the 'civilized man': 'I admit that I can clearly see there the rule that I must consult . . . but I still do not see *the reason why I should be subject to this rule*. It is not a question of teaching me what justice is; it is a question of showing me what interest I have in being just.'[26] As we know, this question has become, in certain modern philosophies like that of Strawson,[27] the central problem of ethics. Yet Strawson is wrong and Rousseau is right. The question is intrinsically modern and it is raised only by 'perverted' or, to apply a less demonic term, 'instrumental' reason. But Rousseau asserts that the question is indeed asked and that it must be answered. If we look back to the network of friends in the first volume of *La Nouvelle Héloïse*

(I have termed this model *fuite en avant*), we shall immediately notice that they never asked this particular question. They formulated their small number of norms from the reason of the 'general will'; and the latter coincided with 'the will of all' precisely because they did not ask this question. Every particular will expressed itself freely, and the plurality of values was respected because this question was never raised. The friends in this network were able to enter into rational discourse about the good and the bad, mutually reinforcing and correcting each other.

What I have tried to show here is the fact that the Rousseauian 'general will' does not necessarily contradict the 'will of all'. This is because the general will 'is in each individual'. In *La Nouvelle Héloïse* the particularistic wills (plural) express the 'general will' in different ways and in different forms. But in Rousseau's opinion readiness for a democratic–communicative procedure is a fairly rare event. And this is why the other model, which involves constraining people to freedom, was invented. No room remains for pluralism and discourse in the model of *Social Contract*: there are only uniform duties (obedience to the 'general will'). Here, the question, 'What interest do I have in being just?' is far from being superseded; it is rather reinforced. If one 'consults reason', one obeys; and it is indeed the interest of everyone to obey the sovereign dutifully. The 'general will' becomes an externalised and alienated 'categorical imperative', the embodiment of 'alienated conscience'. This is not only a retrospective view: Diderot, a contemporary of Rousseau's, summed up this solution in a similar way.

The grand dimensions of the enterprise cannot be denied. It is a radical – indeed, a radically modern – solution to the problem of the ethico-political concept of justice. All the traditional themes of the venture return in full orchestration: the just state, the virtuous man and citizen, freedom, happiness, reason and faith. All these qualities are to coincide, and they are to coincide under the aegis of popular sovereignty and equality, the totally new values of modernity. Yet there is a qualification to this, and an important one – namely, that the same paternalistic image lurks behind the façade of popular sovereignty and equality presented in the second volume of *La Nouvelle Héloïse*. We read in the *Social Contract* that the 'individuals see the good they reject; the public wills the good it does not see. All stand equally in need of guidance. The former must be compelled to bring their wills into conformity with their reason; the latter must be taught to know what he wills. . . . This makes a legislator necessary.'[28] Since every person is simultaneously an individual and part of the public, every person is in need of double guidance.

Rousseau's *Social Contract* shares the fate of the Platonian Republic. The attempt to solve the puzzles of the ethico-political concept of justice ends in the destruction of the very idea the project originally stood for: the idea of a free morality, a morality based upon the power of conscience. Is it better to commit injustice or to suffer it? – this is the question. Rousseau, like Plato, ends up with a double solution that is no solution at all. In the 'network' of *La Nouvelle Héloïse* people neither commit nor suffer injustice. It is better for them not to commit injustice (this and nothing else is the 'general will' which resides in their wills). They do suffer injustice from the outer 'social world', but they do not suffer injustice from one another because they do not commit injustice. (The tragic death of Julie is due to the original injustice committed by her father, representative of the 'social world', but Julie never believed her father's decision to be unjust.) Conscience as an internal authority, mirrored in the conscience of friends, the 'city of the soul', is the only guide. Justice becomes, once again, institutionalized in the republic of Rousseau. The formal concept of justice is the only justice left, and people who apply the norms to each and every person (on the grounds of the principle 'to each the same thing') are just. Either there is nothing but subjective morality, or there is no morality at all. The ethico-political concept of justice is once more proved to be self-contradictory. Yet, because of the shift in values, the paradox of reason is going to become the paradox of freedom. Plato did not endeavour to present a state in which the freedom of all would be guaranteed; nothing was so remote from the Greek mind. However, this was exactly what Rousseau opted for and was committed to; and that men must be forced to be free was the paradox in which the project resulted.

Hegel's *Philosophy of Right* is the swansong of the ethico-political concept of justice. This is not meant as a historical statement. Models based on a complete ethico-political concept of justice can be found throughout the nineteenth century, and even in the twentieth. However, they no longer embody the representative attitudes of their times, and mere 'school philosophy' is not our concern. But, putting aside the persistence of such hackneyed theories, a new ethico-political concept of justice (which I shall term 'incomplete') was to be born from the ashes of the old. I shall return to this particular concept of justice in chapter 5.

It was not Rousseau whom Hegel challenged. Yet the ethico-political concept of justice in Fichte was destined to repeat in full the structural patterns of Rousseau, if in a different philosophical context. The 'closed mercantile state', contrasted with the world of ultimate sinfulness, was designed in the vein of a fundamentalism which exceeds that of Rousseau's *Social Contract*. Romantic subjectivism, Hegel's other antagonist, had already renounced the ethico-political concept of justice or revitalized the familiar model of *La Nouvelle Héloïse*.

It is well known that Hegel overcame subjectivism by constructing a complete and self-contained philosophy of history. The term 'self-contained' means a philosophy of history in which the 'end of history' is posited in the present, and later I shall show that only a philosophy of history of this type can perform the task Hegel wanted to perform: the preservation and reinforcement of a complete ethico-political concept of justice that is both adequate to modernity and still anchored in reality. 'Adequate to modernity' means above all that freedom is the central value; 'anchored in reality' means that the conditions of individual righteousness are posited in the world of moral customs (*Sittlichkeit*) of a given socio-political order, and that Sittlichkeit is conceived as the idea of the existing world. A 'complete ethico-political concept of justice' contains three components and posits all three together: the real city (the 'city on earth'), the 'city in the soul', and the 'city in the sky'. Hegel keeps the coalescence of these three 'cities' intact by historicizing ethico-political justice. He posits the 'city on earth' as the 'end of history', alias the good: 'The good is the Idea ... freedom realized, the absolute end and aim of the world.'[29] The good is the idea of modern society and modern state in their difference and identity, the realization of the freedom of all as *optimum* freedom. The 'city in the soul' (of the ethical personality) represents the identity of the two kinds of righteousness (in their difference): obedience to the laws of the 'good city', and the moral motivation of the pure conscience as *maximum* freedom. The 'city in the sky' philosophy, as the vehicle of the recognition of this end of world history (the good), is *absolute* freedom. The three 'cities' (subjective, objective and absolute spirit) do not struggle against each other, are not tragically divided, because *ought* and *is* are reconciled. Hegel believed that he had fully accomplished what Plato could not possibly accomplish because world history was not then at the end of its march:

even Plato's *Republic*, which passes proverbially as an empty ideal, is in essence nothing but the interpretation of the nature of Greek ethical life.

Plato was conscious that there was breaking into that life in his own time a deeper principle which could appear in it directly only as a longing still unsatisfied, and so only as something corruptive. To combat it, he must have sought aid from that very longing itself. But this aid had to come from on high and all that Plato could do was to seek it in the first place in a particular external form of that same Greek ethical life. By that means he thought to master this corruptive invader and thereby he did fatal injury to the deeper impulse which underlay it, namely free infinite personality. Still his genius is proved by the fact that the principle on which the distinctive character of his idea of the state turns is precisely the pivot on which the impending world revolution turned at that time. '*What is rational is actual and what is actual is rational.*'[30]

Although Hegel rejects 'hyper-wisdom', both in Plato and in Fichte, he fully accepts the Platonian approach, and acquits the ancient philosopher of the charge of chasing 'empty ideals'. Plato's 'deep principles', the principles Hegel himself adopts, as illustrated in the final lines of the above quotation, could not stand the test of Plato's own time, but are completely relevant now. The task of philosophy is not to construct a state as it ought to be (and Plato did not attempt to do this), but to give instruction (*belehren*) as to 'how the moral universe should be known. *Hic rhodus, hic saltus.*' 'Reconciliation with reality' is an attitude, the only one to be taken by philosophy. The reason disclosed in present reality is the very idea that the reason of self-conscious spirit (philosophy) must grasp. The reason of reality is not to be understood as 'everything that is'; it is the *rose* on the *cross* of the present.

Hegel gathers up all the traditional categories of the ethico-political concept of justice in order to reinterpret them within the framework of his philosophy of history.

(1) Although Hegel rejects the concept of radical evil, he addresses the problem of evil in a far broader framework and with far more seriousness than Hobbes, Rousseau or even Kant. After briefly discussing the historicity of evil, he scrutinizes the modern form of evil. The question is raised in ★139 and its explanatory notes; it takes the form, 'How does the alien and the negative become the positive and the good?', and it is answered in the following way:

Once self-consciousness has reduced all otherwise valid duties to emptiness and itself to the sheer inwardness of the will, it has become the potentiality of either making the absolutely universal its principle, or equally well of elevating above the universal the self-will of private particularity, taking that as its principle and realizing it through its actions, i.e. it has become potentially evil.

The various forms in which evil of this kind appears is not our concern here. It should be noted, however, that Hegel did indeed discover the truly modern form of evil, which stems from our reliance on conscience as the *sole* arbiter in moral decisions, and which was still in its gestation in his time. His model for the study of the modern attitude is romanticism. This serves him well, for he can discover the 'ruse of reason' in the dialectics of conscience as the sole arbiter in moral decisions: the reversal of absolute subjectivism into absolute subjection (an attitude I have described in detail in my book *The Power of Shame*).

The particular content is not bound up with the general through itself ... as if we knew what good is when good [appears] as good for the sake of good. *In itself* it is ... (d) determined by the subject; (e) it is posited in it ... it is a mere matter of opinion – initially it should be equally suspended whether it is objectively good or not. Here *conviction* alone is objective. *No principles*. ... Groping for objectivity – in the other extreme – becoming catholic.[31]

What Hegel describes here as the modern form of evil is the spectre that has haunted us ever since, and the Hegelian ethico-political concept of justice was intended to overcome precisely this form of evil.

(2) Hegel distinguishes between virtue and righteousness in the following way:

Virtue is the ethical order reflected in the individual character so far as that character is determined by its natural endowment. When virtue displays itself solely as the individual's simple conformity with the duties of the station to which he belongs, it is rectitude. ... In an existing ethical order ... virtue in the strict sense of the word is in its place and actually appears in exceptional circumstances only or when one obligation clashes with another. ... It follows that if a 'doctrine of virtues' is not a mere 'doctrine of duties', and if therefore it embraces the particular facet of character, the facet grounded in natural endowment, it will be a natural history of mind [correctly, 'a spiritual natural history'].[32]

There are more connotations to this distinction than Hegel himself points out, all of them still relevant now. He describes virtue as 'ethical virtuosity', a notion which he realizes has become increasingly irrelevant in modern times – in particular, so he believed, for Germans. Modernity is for Hegel quite prosaic, without great conflicts, whereas only such conflicts call for intellectual sacrifice, and thus virtue. This distinction between virtue and righteousness suits well the restricted liberalism of the Hegelian ethico-political concept of justice, and it is taken up by all the brands of liberalism which were to abandon the ethico-political concept of justice altogether.

However, Hegel offered a second interpretation of the same distinction. Here virtue is relegated to the sphere of character, and the study of virtues becomes a character study. It can then be asked, 'Are virtuous characters still possible in societies with pluralistic social character types, and, if so, what makes them virtuous characters?' It is obvious that simply living up to our duties does not make us virtuous (this is still 'righteousness' in the Hegelian sense of the word). We are now familiar with the problem as it is presented in Rousseau's *La Nouvelle Héloïse*, but as yet we have no answers to it. At best we have some indications of where to look for the answers: for instance, towards German classicism, and in particular Goethe. The more that character patterns are individualized within the general framework of pluralistic social character types, the more our virtue dwells in the character which is 'made' by our individual selves. Character appears as if it were nature, but in fact it is 'second nature'. A character can be 'sublime' or 'low', 'elevated' or 'base', and from a moral standpoint this difference can be enormous, although it cannot be accounted for if we have in mind the 'performance of duties' alone.

(3) The political element of the ethico-political concept of justice becomes socio-political in Hegel. His distinction between state and civil society is well known; so is his differentiation between the 'internal' and the 'external' state. For us the latter is of interest because it is the secret of the unique venture. The unique features of the Hegelian venture is the grasping of the distinctness of civil society and of the state by on the one hand affirming their difference, and on the other keeping the complete ethico-political concept of justice intact. What generally happened in parallel philosophical attempts was to describe and affirm the first whilst abandoning the latter. The moment that civil society was conceptualized as the source of legitimation of the state, and the state was conceived as the trinity of constitution, the sum total of laws and the lawful government, the complete socio-political concept of justice had to fall to pieces, and it stands to reason why. In a complete ethico-political concept of justice, the political

aspect (the institution) must be the source of positive moral power: it must be the supreme good, not just an institution which exacts retribution for crime and guarantees negative freedoms. With the duplication of the state as an 'external' and an 'internal' state, Hegel conceived of the state as the legislative, administrative and judicial agent related to the 'common weal' of civil society, and simultaneously as the supreme good, the ultimate source of good and freedom. And yet the 'external' and the 'internal' state are the same state, and so the various and extremely heterogeneous institutions of collective morality (*Sittlichkeit*) must be brought together in a harmonious fashion, and Hegel had to show how this happens. In taking account of this final result, Hegel could not avoid enumerating certain substantive features characteristic of one or the other institution. Indeed, he avoided giving advice to wet-nurses or recommending the introduction of passport portraits, but he could not avoid the 'hyper-wisdom' he so firmly rejected in Plato or Fichte. It is because of this that he insists on the inferiority of women and on marriage as an 'ethical duty' (he even describes what a proper marriage looks like), and draws up a model of the intimate sphere and also of the estates, including bureaucracy as the 'general estate'. Even if he does not offer a complete picture, he still offers a complete X-ray of the good body politic when he depicts the idea of the existing order as 'good'. We need only recall here that Montesquieu had already insisted that this and similar questions should be left open to see that the intrinsic fundamentalism of all modern complete ethico-political concepts of justice was not overcome by Hegel. The swansong of the complete ethico-political concept of justice sounds a warning against mere formalism, and it is exemplary in this negativity. However, in its positiveness, it can offer very little; and even that small amount is deeply problematic.

Modernity threw itself back into antiquity to keep the ethico-political concept of justice intact for and against modernity. This was a rare historical moment. Time stands still while the owl of Minerva begins its flight. But, alas, time does not stand still. And we only need to cross the channel from the continent to see how far 'history' has already advanced.

The 'city of the soul' reconsidered

In England, the ethico-political concept of justice was broken into two distinct parts, the philosophy of morality and the socio-political concept of justice. The Continent followed suit with very little delay. However, a concept cannot be cut in two, each part being substantially altered in the process. The socio-political concept of justice became less and less concerned with the best possible moral world. It made recommendations for a legal-political order that might possible secure the *rights* (freedoms) of citizens, but not their goodness. It subjected morals to the inquiry of theoretical reason while being committed to a 'value-free' procedure. It criticized mores while explaining them (or interpreting them). The socio-political concept of justice addressed the issues of distribution and retribution. The question of the best possible *social* world was centred mainly on the problem of 'just distribution'. Just distribution, just punishment and – occasionally – *laissez faire* were substituted for the 'good life'. When Rawls analyses 'justice as fairness', he only pays tribute to the subsequent emaciation of the notion 'justice'. Justice, indeed, became fairness, and this result – wittingly or unwittingly – impinges on the moral issue of approval and disapproval. What is approved of is 'fairness', the shabby remnant of the 'sum total of virtues' that was once called 'justice'. (This reduction begins with Hume's notion of justice, and I shall discuss Hume – in conjunction with distributive justice – in chapter 4.) On the plane of socio-political justice, only *minima moralia* remain.

Social philosophy can stop raising questions about the supreme good and the good life, just as it can stop making inquiries into human motivations. But moral philosophy cannot do this, precisely because it *is* moral philosophy; because it raises these questions and makes these inquiries. But, if the idea of a 'city on earth' is not construed at the same time, the symmetry between macrocosmos and microcosmos cannot be posited. The 'city on earth', as Hegel remarked, has always been built on the foundation of a pre-existing moral order (*Sittlichkeit*). It is nothing but the idea of this collective morality. The norms and rules of this 'ideal' city were thought of both as the preconditions of the education (*paideia*) of virtuous (just) men and as the end result of virtuous activity. If there is no longer a pre-existing collective morality, the norms and values of the present cannot be idealized, and the ethics of the individual cannot be construed as the observance of these idealized norms and values. Morality thus loses its intersubjective foundation; it must be located in the *subject*. But, even so, morality cannot be subjective. If human action (or the maxim for action) does not carry a general validity, morality collapses and becomes a matter of taste. In modern times, generality is universality. I mention only as an aside that the breaking down of the ethico-political concept of justice, which operated with substantive criteria, contributed to the emergence of the idea of universal validity. The subject, as a moral being, should be the bearer of the ultimate universal: humankind. The reader may recall the statement about humankind in chapter 1, that it is not a social cluster. The formal concept of justice cannot be applied to humankind. That is why modern moral philosophy must leave behind the formal concept of justice. But, if subject and humankind have to coincide, one can leave behind the formal concept of justice not by underformalizing but by overformalizing morality. Moral philosophy becomes formalized and procedural in order to preserve and reinforce the idea of supreme good and the idea of the good life.

I agree completely with MacIntyre that intuitive and emotivist moral philosophies are no moral philosophies at all. In my view there are only two moral philosophies in modernity that can cope with all the problems briefly enumerated above: utilitarianism and Kantianism. However, even if both are able to cope with them, and cope with them equally (together with an equal number of insoluble problems, though different ones), the Kantian is far superior to the utilitarian solution, not only because it is better philosophically, but for two further reasons. First, Kant succeeded, through the (otherwise problematic) complete severing of theoretical and practical reason, in preserving the traditional meaning of practical reason as distinct from calculation. Secondly, he related righteous-ness to the postulate of the best possible moral world while keeping the idea of 'good' and of 'benefit' categorically apart. But, after openly stating my preference, I repeat that the question of 'What should I do?' or 'How should I act?' has been supported by complete philosophical argument only in utilitarianism and Kantianism in the last two hundred years. As yet, no convincing alternative attempts have been made in this direction.

The 'city of the soul' became the sole concern of the British moralists. Mandeville's comedy came as a salutary shock, even if it was merely experienced as a shock. Happiness and goodness, motivation and consequence, private (the individual) and public (the whole), so mockingly divided and juxtaposed, prompted the reconsideration of traditional moral notions and solutions. To restore the link between *summum bonum* and the good intention without returning to the ethico-political concept of justice was the task. I shall exemplify the concerns of the period via Hutcheson's moral philosophy, though I do not choose this philosopher randomly. Hutcheson's early utilitarianism (with pre-Kantian overtures) represents the basic tendency: the transformation of the 'city in the soul' into the modern city of London.

Hutcheson has very little to say about society, laws and state, and what he does say is not new. His basic question is this: morality exists; how is it possible? Three more questions follow from this: how can we distinguish between the supreme moral good and the supreme natural good; how are the two goods combined; and how can we distinguish between good and evil if social norms are relative and changing, and are thus unreliable as means of proper guidance? The answer to the first question is descriptive; the answer to the second is both descriptive and prescriptive; the answer to the third is prescriptive.

The assertion 'morality exists' is empirically proven. We always attempt to separate morally motivated actions from those based on self-love or self-interest, and we approve (respect, admire) the first, irrespective of whether the disinterested actions performed benefit us or others, or even whether they are performed in the present or were performed in the remote past. This empirical fact can be explained by the assumption that there is an inherent moral sense in every member of the human species and that this 'sense of virtue' is *antecedent* to ideas of advantage. The moral good is thus defined as acting out of benevolence. In our *de facto* actions we act both out of self-love and out of benevolence. In morally indifferent spheres of action, self-love cannot be censured. But, if we act towards other men as rational beings, we cannot be good if our motivations are mixed. In this we are good only if we are motivated by pure benevolence. We are at liberty to apply Kantian categories to this conception. Benevolence is humankind in us. In being benevolent we are members of the chain of rational beings. Thus benevolence is practical reason as the universal reason of humankind in us. Hutcheson calls benevolence the love towards rational agents. Humankind (rational humankind) is the source of good. If we are motivated by universal benevolence (and not by self-interest or self-love), we are morally good. Supreme moral good resides in this motivation.

In the second instance, humankind appears as the supreme natural good, and the happiness of humankind is the supreme natural good. The problem lies in the combination of the supreme moral good with the supreme natural good. And this is exactly the point where Hutcheson ceases to be pre-Kantian and becomes utilitarian.

It is obvious that, if moral norms and rules are particularistic, historical and changing, morality cannot be explained by the observance of norms and rules. Morality must be universal, the same for every human being (though humankind is not a social cluster). What Kant later calls 'heteronomy' is excluded by Hutcheson for two reasons: morality cannot be based on self-interest, but it cannot be based on the observance of any concrete norms either. At any rate, social norms carry sanctions that are invoked against those who infringe these norms, and motivation is only purely benevolent if the action is not motivated by fear of social sanction. There must be a formula to be applied to each and every choice and judgement; a formula applicable by all rational and benevolent human beings, a formula on the ground of which every benevolent man can choose the good. Indeed, benevolence is the moral motivation, but the moral motivation can lead us astray. If we do not apply a reliable and universal formula, we could choose evil out of moral motivation. There are many opinions, and many false opinions, in moral matters. Under the influence of false or 'partial Opinions of the natural Tendency of their Actions, this moral sense leads them to Evil'.[33] Evil can only be avoided if benevolent men can rely on a true opinion of the 'natural Tendency of their Action'. But here there is no such true opinion. It is up to the benevolent individual to determine in every single case how he or she should act in order that the action may be good. Only a formula which is empty (of which no content is given) and at the same time absolutely reliable can guide benevolent action.

Benevolence (disinterested moral motivation), the supreme moral good, includes the supreme natural good (*summum bonum*) as its intrinsic *end* (goal). This is why the result of the action to be undertaken (how far this action contributes to the *summum bonum*, the greatest happiness of humankind) determines whether benevolence is what it ought to be: the perfect good. Hutcheson's solution is the exact opposite of the Kantian, even though the problems he raised are exactly the same, and his conception meant formalizing morality to no less a degree. But it must be emphasized that Hutcheson's early utilitarianism includes rather than excludes *Gesinnungsethik*, an ethics of intentions. If two distinct actions of two persons lead to an equal amount of happiness, but one has acted out of pure benevolence, the other out of self-love, only the first actor is morally good. Natural good is not the criterion but the end of moral goodness. True enough, Hutcheson concedes that sometimes it is very difficult to tell whether a particular good act has been motived by pure benevolence, by self-love or by both. But it is equally difficult to know whether someone has acted out of duty, or 'only dutifully', if we think in terms of Kant. Hutcheson only states this much: if we act out of self-love, then we are motivated not by the natural good of humankind in principle, but by concern for our own well-being; the result can be the same, but not the end.

On the relative goodness of actions Hutcheson argues as follows:

in order to regulate our Election among various Actions propos'd, or to find which of them has the greatest moral Excellency, we are led by our moral Sense of Virtue to judge thus; that in equal Degrees of Happiness, expected to proceed from the Action, the Virtue is in proportion to the Number of Persons to whom the Happiness shall extend . . . so that, that Action is the best, which procures the greatest happiness for the greatest numbers. . . .[34]

But how can we know anything about the greatest happiness of the greatest numbers? Hutcheson argues that we can if we apply the proper axioms to our decisions. He invents six such axioms. These are formulated in order to prevent a mere quantitative application of the general formula (for instance, the happiness of morally good people weighs more than the happiness of people characterized by self-love, and the like) and are set forth in the form of mathematical equations. Good moral action thus depends on proper calculation, or 'computing', as Hutcheson calls it. If only you compute well, you make the right decision. However, Hutcheson is aware of the problem that we do not always compute well, even if we want to do so: 'Let us read the Preambles of any Laws we count unjust . . . and we shall find no doubt, that Men are often mistaken in computing the Excess of the Natural Good, or evil consequences of certain Actions. . . .'[35] But how do we know that it is they who are mistaken, and not us? Undoubtedly, it is the consequences that determine this. But how do we know that our actions will lead to the greatest happiness of the greatest number? And, even after the consequences are felt, how do we know that the happiness of the greatest number has been secured? Obviously, the 'greatest number' must declare itself happy. But, if it does, then its happiness depends on its opinion. If this were not so, computations would not be sufficient to achieve the greatest happiness of the greatest number; we should also have to know *what* this 'happiness of the greatest number' is. But there is no axiom available to help determine this. So we have to rely on our own opinion – this time, on our opinion of 'happiness'. But it was precisely 'opinion' that had been judged as relative, changing, and unreliable at the beginning of Hutcheson's argumentation. Such recommendations as 'they may not stupidly follow the first Appearance of public Good'[36] do not eliminate the fallacy. And Hutcheson is aware of this more than later utilitarians ever were. After having promoted the supreme natural good to the end of the supreme moral good, Hutcheson reverses his argument. It finally turns out that supreme natural good (happiness) is identical with supreme moral good. There are various notions of universal good, but the 'justest' notion of them all is 'That virtue is the chief Happiness in the Judgment of all Mankind'.[37]

In the end, then, 'the greatest happiness of the greatest number' is tantamount to the greatest virtue of the greatest number. But, if the latter is the *end*, the axioms become totally superfluous, and calculative 'computation' gets us nowhere. We can calculate with the natural good, but not with the moral good of others. It is up to others to be benevolent rather than selfish, and we cannot decide through any computation whether our act will make the greatest number more virtuous or not. The only thing we can do is to be virtuous, to act benevolently. By this act (or choice) we can increase goodness in the human universe, and we can hope that others will do the same.

It is obvious that the circularity of Hutcheson's argument (a circularity he is not fully aware of) stems directly from the breaking-down of the ethico-political concept of justice. If only he had said something like 'such and such are the socio-political preconditions for men becoming virtuous, such and such institutions should be established or discovered *as the supreme natural good*, and then supreme moral good will come about', his problem would have been solved, just as it had been from Aristotle to Hegel. But, if there is no 'city on earth', if there is not even the idea of such a city on the horizon, the difficulties of this theoretical problem become insurmountable. Hutcheson stands at the beginning of a long road; more precisely, at the junction of two long roads. He finds the utilitarian solution, but shrinks from it because of his insistence on morality as intention (*Gesinnung*). He leans towards the Kantian solution, but shrinks from this too, because he must maintain the view that the consequences of human actions comprise at least one criterion of moral approbation or disapprobation. He identifies moral man with rational man; but he also identifies reason with 'sense' as well as with 'computation'. He formalizes moral decision as computation but he fails to formalize the moral sense itself, to which he refers as an empirical fact. His man of good will is a man of good will by nature, or a man of good will by character. Put simply, his aim is to establish the following: human beings can be of good character under any circumstances; and, if they are, they will find pleasure in being good, and pain in doing something contrary to goodness.

And so, after all this, we return to Plato, to the idea that it is better to suffer injustice than to commit it – though with one proviso: this applies to the benevolent man. Yet the benevolent man is benevolent precisely because in his *opinion* this holds true of everyone. Philosophically, then, the solution is redundant. From the practical viewpoint, everything has been said that can be said. Hutcheson already evokes the idea of the *honest man* in our modern world. The honest man performs the amazing act of drawing strength from his own conscience when external norms and rules promote selfishness or intolerance; when dealing with a moral choice, he does not neglect his interest in morally indifferent matters, but relies on pure benevolence (or goodwill) in his relations with rational (human) beings. He is concerned with the natural good of others as well as with his own, but suffers injustice rather than commits it. The honest man does all this with a view to the idea of a humankind which does not exist. Hutcheson deduces this 'honest man' empirically; Kant constitutes him transcendentally. Kant writes,

to a humble plain man, in whom I perceive righteousness in a higher degree than I am conscious of in myself, *my mind bows*. . . . Why? His example holds a law before me which strikes down my self-conceit when I compare my own conduct with it. . . . I may even be conscious of a like degree of righteousness in myself, and yet respect remains. . . . Respect is a tribute we cannot refuse to pay to merit whether we will or not.[38]

The assertion shared by both Hutcheson and Kant is that we cannot help but approve of the benevolent. But only Kant provides a conclusive answer to the question of *how* righteousness can be achieved.[39]

Kant emphatically rejected the ethico-political concept of justice, which, as he noted, had in modern times disintegrated anyway:

The ancients openly revealed this error by devoting their ethical investigation entirely to the definition of the concept of the highest good and thus posited an object which they intended subsequently to make the determining ground of the will in the moral law. . . . The moderns, among whom the concept of the highest good has fallen into disuse or at least seems to have become secondary, hide the error (as they do many others) behind vague expressions.[40]

Kant's intention was to rescue the notion of the 'highest good' as the end of moral intention (*Gesinnung*) without relapsing into the fallacy of heteronomy implied by every ethico-political concept of justice. Instead of the interplay between righteousness and the supreme (socio-political) good, he designed a one-track solution:

supreme good is posited by the moral law, yet the reverse does not apply. The morality of any action depends on the maxim of this action; the will is to be determined by the moral law (freedon, reason) alone. There is no morally legislative instance but the moral law itself, for its task is to give moral law to nature. The subject alone posits the object (supreme good), yet not in his or her capacity as individual subject, but in that as a subject stripped of all individuality (feelings, desires, interests), as a pure intelligible being, as rational humankind.

This is, indeed, a perfect and flawless philosophical solution of the problem of how to unify supreme moral good and supreme natural good without taking recourse to the ethico-political concept of justice. And the solution is philosophically flawless not only as a whole but in all its details. The distinction between the general will and the will of all (which led Rousseau to the paradox of freedom within the framework of an ethico-political concept of justice) does not imply a paradox if the two wills are located in different worlds (in that of freedom and that of nature). The heterogeneity, contradiction and alteration of the empirically existing norms and duties does not pose any difficulty either, for any norm or duty can and should be tested as to whether it qualifies for universal legislation, and accepted or rejected accordingly. Only norms and obligations which qualify for universal legislation are duties, as all others are morally contradictory. The doctrine of virtues (*Tugendlehre*) is soundly based on this foundation because virtues and vices are to be deduced from the already tested duties and the neglect of duties. Thus, for Kant, the duty man has to himself is opposed to the 'vices of lying, avarice, and false humility (servility)'.[41] The virtue which he contrasted to these vices he called *Ehrenliebe (honestas interna)*.

The rigorous formalism of Kantian 'morality' has always been criticized, and rightly so, but the categorical imperative has never been replaced by an equally satisfactory philosophical solution to the problems to which Kant addressed himself. The limited fundamentalism of a resurrected ethico-political concept of justice in Hegel, or the limited neo-Platonism of Scheler, is not a viable alternative. Even worse is Weber's suggestion in his *Politics as a Vocation* of uniting the two conclusive moral philosophies of modernity (the Kantian and the utilitarian) within the empirical subject. We know from Kant's critics that the formal formulae of the categorical imperative can be applied as guidelines for our actions if no conflict of duties is involved, a problem eliminated by Kant because he was concerned only with intention (*Gesinnung*).

We know that the Kantian criterion of 'no contradiction' is redundant and empty. We also know that the dismissal of the 'empirical nature' of man from the realm of moral motivation is rigid and is not compatible with the pluralism of moral personalities that is so important in modernity. We know all this, and more. And yet, in my view, at least one formulation of the categorical imperative can never be surpassed by any moral philosophy: that man should never be used as a mere means, but should always be treated as an end-in-itself as well, because humanity must be respected in every human being.

Beyond justice, or the anthropological revolution

Both Kantianism and utilitarianism are philosophies beyond justice. We know that all kinds of justice must be of a nature that permits the application of the formal concept of justice. Kant himself did not dismiss the concept of justice, but kept it within the framework of the doctrine of law. In moral philosophy, rational humankind (intelligible humankind) is not a social cluster to which the formal concept of justice applies. 'To be just' does not figure among the norms which qualify for the maxim of the categorical imperative, and for good reason. Only absolutely concrete obligations qualify for 'duty as such'. If moral commandments stipulate, 'You should not murder', 'You should not lie', 'You should not embezzle', and the like, we all know what we should not do. If a commandment stipulates, 'You should not be unjust', we must first know what justice or injustice is. And indeed we do know: being just means applying the norm which constitutes a social cluster to each and every member of this cluster. However, according to the categorical imperative we must first test the very *norm* which applies. And, if the latter cannot be willed to be natural law, we obviously ought to be unjust, because we are not permitted to apply that norm. But to repeat: Kant goes beyond justice: we ought to act such that the maxim of our action could become the universal law; that is to say, the law for all intelligible beings. What Kant formulates thereby is the universal criterion for a non-existent justice. We ought to act as if this criterion existed, though it does not exist (empirically). We could even add that the formula according to which no man should be used as mere means by another man is the ultimate concretization of the criterion. You should use no man in this way, the commandment prescribes. In other words, each and every man belonging to the intelligible world of humankind should equally be treated also as an end-in-itself. On the other hand, utilitarianism remains 'below justice', as it does not suggest any universal criterion of justice either. The greatest happiness is to be achieved for the greatest number, not the same happiness for each and every member of any society or humankind, not even a happiness proportionate to something under the guidance of any idea of justice.

The great enigma of all moral philosophies, summed up in the celebrated statement that it is better to suffer injustice than to commit it, *seemingly* disappears for good. In utilitarianism the dilemma is easily (too easily) solved, whilst in Kant it is seriously faced and then dismissed. 'Phenomenal men', driven by the thirst for power, fame and possessions, obviously prefer to commit injustice than to suffer it, and their unjust acts may even benefit the public and accelerate material progress. 'Nuomenal men', on the other hand, cannot commit injustice, for this would be ethically self-contradictory. The moral law 'in us' hurts, it causes pain, in so far as it smashes the concept of self-love, desires and particularistic goals. Given the dual character of human beings, we cannot be simultaneously good and happy. But the righteous man, and the righteous man alone, is worthy of happiness. And Kant's argument does not stop here. If it did, the unification of supreme moral good and supreme natural good could not have been posited. Righteousness in Kant is not a mere subjective option: to apply a modern term, it is resoluteness (*Entschlossenheit*), resoluteness for autonomy, for freedom, for rational humankind; and, because of this, the universal, the end (supreme good) constituted by morality, cannot stop at the stage of a mere wish (as only phenomenal men wish). Since the possibility of supreme good cannot be deduced empirically, it must be deduced transcendentally, in the form of a postulate. Kant circumvented both the paradox of reason and the paradox of faith in an ingenious manner. The attempt to prove theoretically the unity of the supreme moral and the supreme natural good would have led to the paradox of reason. But it is Kant's point of departure that such an attempt cannot be undertaken. The paradox of faith is the result of belief in a hidden God (God is the fountainhead of justice but we do not know his ways). But, again, it is Kant's point of departure that we do not know and cannot know whether God exists at all. The transcendental deduction of the postulate of the existence of God avoids the traps of both paradoxes. 'Therefore, the highest good is possible in the world only on the supposition of a supreme cause of nature which *has a causality corresponding to the moral intention.*'[42] The postulate of the supreme original good backs the postulate of the supreme deduced good – of the best world. But we have no duties towards God (whose existence we only postulate): 'All that here belongs to duty is the endeavour to produce and to further the highest good in the world, *the existence of which may thus be postulated.* . . .'[43]

Thus Kant finally posits the possibility of the best possible moral world. But what is it like? The only theoretically possible way to conceive of this world, Kant conclusively argues, is to posit it as the unity of the realm of nature and the realm of morality. Thus the best possible moral world presupposes an anthropological revolution.

The solution, which only emerges on the horizon in the *Critique of Practical Reason*, is elaborated in full in *Religion within the Limits of Reason Alone*. The most serious problem of the categorical imperative becomes explicit here. Kant, who found the proper balance on the tightrope between the paradox of reason and that of faith, plunges headlong into the paradox of freedom.

The 'best possible moral world', and the possibility of it, must always be argued for anthropologically. One of the fundamental statements of any ethico-political concept of justice has always been that human nature does not resist reform. But no ethico-political concept of justice posits an anthropological revolution. Man, as he is, can change for the better, philosophers argue, and how better this 'better' might be depends on the end, the 'good society' posited by them as possible. Very little is required from people in Hobbes, or even in Hegel. No anthropological change was envisaged by Aristotle, and even Plato described a second-best possible state where recommended reforms in human nature were of a modest nature. We know that the members of the 'network' in Rousseau's *La Nouvelle Héloïse* often blundered, carried away by unruly passions, but they were able to correct each other's blunders with friendly criticism. Although some kind of anthropological revolution (the second denaturalization) was required in *The Social Contract*, the paradox of freedom (constraining people to accept their freedom) implied that this revolution cannot be fully achieved. We all know that Rousseau's model of freedom was not viable for Kant. However, when Kant rid himself of one paradox of freedom, he ended up grappling with a version of it of no lesser gravity. If righteousness is absolute morality, pure intelligibility, absolute freedom, then the supreme good posited by it, the best possible moral world, must be the world of absolute morality, pure intelligibility and absolute freedom. The whole of human nature must become intelligible, every necessity must become freedom, no particularity can remain in this best possible world. In short, the Kantian 'best possible world' presupposes the absolute perfectibility of human nature. This is indeed an extravaganza, but one that follows from the disintegration of the ethico-political concept of justice, given that (a) supreme natural good (happiness) is not abandoned, (b) the 'city on earth' is still posited, (c) freedom is absolutized, and (d) supreme moral good is unified with the notions of freedom and reason.

It is to the merit of Kant that, although the best possible world is conceived as the world of pure intelligibility, absolute freedom and absolute morality, he did not dwell at length on the realization of the 'city on earth', where establishment he sees as pertaining to a remote future.[44] But Kant's 'perfectibilism' does indeed rest on the *postulate* of the best possible world, and not on the image of its final realization. To paraphrase Marx, the Kantian 'first stage of communism', the establishment of the 'invisible Church', this precondition of his 'second stage of communism', the best possible moral 'city on earth' already presupposes an anthropological revolution, the revolution of intention (*Gesinnung*). As far as morals are concerned, the good civil state is still the 'state of nature':

But if a man is to become not merely *legally*, but *morally*, a good man (pleasing to God) ... *this* cannot be brought about through gradual *reformation* ... but must be effected through a *revolution* in the man's disposition (a going over to the maxim of holiness of the disposition). He can become a new man only by a kind of rebirth, as it were a new creation ... and a change of heart.[45]

In the 'first stage of communism' – that is to say, after the revolution in disposition – evil is still present in the senses. People still belong to two distinct states; the 'ethical-civil' (*ethisch-bürgerlich*) and the 'legal-civil' (*rechtbürgerlich*). All people must belong to both states, because the senses must undergo a reform after the revolution in disposition has taken place.

Accordingly, the result of the process is as follows. To the degree that we are imperfect, we belong to the 'legal-civil' society. To the degree that we are perfect, we belong to 'ethical-civil' society. In 'ethical-civil' society, or the ethical community, we are free, but above all we are virtuous, in so far as we have no choice between good and evil, not even between the good and the better. In short, we have no choice at all.

The 'ethical state on earth' envisaged by Kant is not a state at all, for obvious reasons. Angels do not need states. The member of Kant's 'invisible Church', who already live in the realm of freedom, resemble Kierkegaard's 'knights of faith'. Even the notion 'incognito' can be applied to them, for it is extremely difficult (if it is possible at all) to tell the members of this Church from people who only act dutifully. But, even if the end (supreme deduced good) casts its shadow on the categorical imperative itself, the post-Kierkegaardian existentialist solution and the Kantian solution of the moral problems are still worlds apart. As long as we live in both spheres (natural and intelligible), torn between the freedom of the moral law and the ethical arbitrariness of our natural inclinations, we are still moral human beings.[46] And we are human moral beings not because we are absolutely free, but because we are not so. And, even if we have no moral choice, we still have a choice between resoluteness (*Entschlossenheit*) and lack of resoluteness towards the moral law. It must not be forgotten that in Kant the concept of absolute freedom as absolute autonomy was meant to rescue morality after the fragmenting of the ethico-political concept of justice. But absolute freedom as absolute autonomy destroys human morals completely. This is the paradox of freedom, if freedom is interpreted as autonomy.

The idea of the anthropological revolution did not free Kantian philosophy from the paradox of freedom; just the contrary. It was Nietzsche who left behind this paradox by disclosing its hidden dimensions. Indeed, absolute harmony via the anthropological revolution destroys morality: so let it be destroyed. Once this step is taken, the paradox disappears. Although it is difficult to assess Nietzsche's aphoristic witticism in any coherent way, one does not err greatly if one views his philosophy as the most radical attempt at eliminating the paradox of autonomy, by pledging to smash the moral heritage of the biblical 'slab of stone'.

The Marxian project was even more ambitious. Marx did not simply piece together what had been torn asunder – namely, the socio-political and ethical components of the ethico-political concept of justice – but he did want to connect them in an indivisible whole. However, after separation, both these facets had already undergone substantial changes. The socio-political component had increasingly lost its ethical basis. Socio-political inquiry had become first and foremost the science of economy, where the 'invisible hand' reigned supreme. Social philosophy of justice concentrated on the problem of distributive justice under the alternative conditions of abundance or scarcity. The development of needs was seen as a self-perpetuating process (as it was also in Kant). Interest, as the motive force of socio-political action, was taken for granted. Liberated from the 'ought' and 'should' of supreme moral good (or supreme natural good), social inquiry had become 'positive' science. Simultaneously, the ethical component of the ethico-political concept of justice had also been 'liberated' from the obsolete task of assessing real possibilities, from the responsibility to search for 'ought' in 'is', to speculate about the substantive features of a good social order. Consequently, absolute autonomy and the extravaganza of the anthropological turn towards 'perfection' had been conceived, and the religious idea of the 'Kingdom of God' had been secularized. The task that presented itself was to combine the socio-political and the anthropological-ethical components of the ethico-political concept of justice, now worlds apart. And Marx succeeded, *almost* completely, in achieving this.

Marx's point of departure is the idea of absolute freedom, formulated as early as his dissertation on Epicur. Absolute freedom is equivalent to no authority and no constraint. All norms, rules and values external to individuals are authorities; all socio-political necessities and determinations are constraints. The Kantian distinction between phenomenal and nuomenal man is historicized. Nuomenal man is 'species essence' (*Gattungswesen*), alienated in history. Hitherto, history has progressed via alienation. But now the time has come for this trend to be reversed. The most alienated stage of history is also the last. Capitalism has already cleared the way for the historical change in so far as it has dismantled all traditional ethical authorities and institutions (norms, rules, values, duties). Economic constraint is now the only obstacle left. Should this obstacle be removed, the path to absolute freedom will lie clear. Capitalism also produces the social agent to remove the economic constraint, the proletariat, which cannot liberate itself without simultaneously liberating all humankind. With the removal of economic constraint, the real, the genuine history of humankind, begins. This history, communism, leads to an anthropological revolution, to de-alienation; that is to say, the unification of the individual and the species. Absolute freedom as the unification of individual and species, essence and existence, phenomenal and nuomenal man, reminds us of Kant (and Kantian Marxism did pay tribute to this resemblance). However, Kant's and Marx's methods of argumentation have nothing in common. In Marx, theoretical reason (critical science) performs a double task: the task of reconstructing history, and the task of deducing absolute freedom as a necessary future from a history already reconstructed. Practical reason is not a moral agency. It is identified with socio-political practice (class struggle). Revolution is not a revolution in intention (*Gesinnung*, maxims), but a socio-political revolution. True enough, *interest* cannot be the motivation for liberation in Marx either. But he distinguishes between needs and interests, and identifies *radical needs* as the true motive force. Radical needs exist but cannot be satisfied in the existing order, and this is why they motivate the bearer of social practice (the proletariat) to crush this order in the final act of liberation.

The traditional ethico-political concept of justice – good men create good society but only good society can make all men good – is thus transformed as follows: the liberation of humankind creates free society, and only in free society can all men be free. In societies of unfreedom all ethics are alienated because moral concepts are 'superstructures' of an alienated economic order. It is useless to 'preach morals' because there cannot be true morality where there is no freedom. Under the condition of de-alienation (or the end of alienation), where species essence and individual coalesce, everyone will be a moral being precisely for this reason. In the realm of absolute freedom, authority (species essence) is within and not above the individual. Marx thus eliminates 'ought' from both prehistory (where it is futile) and from real history (where it is redundant).[47] The ethical idea of justice (to each according to his merit), which draws its legitimation from the claim of righteousness to happiness, is completely absent from Marx.

But this is not the whole story. The absolute juxtaposition of unfreedom and freedom (realm of necessity – realm of freedom), together with the absolutization of freedom itself, makes all regulative ideas of justice irrelevant for Marx's project. For Marx, the only sensible concept of justice is the formal concept. In each society, the norms and rules of a social cluster are to be applied to each and every member of that cluster. In this sense, Marx reasons, all societies are just, capitalism included. In capitalism, the rules of the market are, indeed, applied consistently and continuously to all members of society. And, since all societies have been alienated and unfree, but at the same time just, justice is an empty value, and therefore irrelevant. In a de-alienated society, after the anthropological revolution, where no external rules and norms are left, and no constraint remains, all ideas and notions of justice will become irrelevant; but, then, abstract justice too will disappear for good. The society of 'associated producers' is a society beyond justice. We know that Marx later added certain qualifications to this concept, such as 'in the first phase of communism the form concept of justice still applies' (for we are not yet completely free), and 'the sphere of production will remain the realm of necessity even in communism', and this is why duty (and justice) cannot be eliminated here. But, whatever the specifications, the fundamental pattern remains intact. Freedom is absolute: where there is freedom, there are no duties or constraints; where there is freedom, individual and species coalesce; where there is freedom, there is no justice. Absolute freedom is beyond justice.

Without analysing the historical changes in the concept, it should be remarked here that the emphasis on the anthropological revolution, so forceful in the 'Paris Manuscripts', was later diminished, though it never completely disappeared. Marx later relied more and more on the liberal concept of freedom. This is why the notion of abundance became a central category in his work. To relate absolute freedom to the condition of absolute abundance is indeed an alternative to the theory of an 'anthropological revolution', although it is, philosophically at least, an inferior version. However, even this scenario excludes justice, because the idea 'to each according to his needs' is not an idea of justice. To be more precise, it might be an idea of justice in one interpretation (the needs of each and every person are recognized), but then it excludes absolute freedom. One cannot have absolute freedom and justice (of any kind) simultaneously.

Marx, like Nietzsche, succeeds in circumventing the paradox of freedom, though in an entirely different manner. Instead of positing the superman, he posits the supersociety, a society purely rational, intelligible (transparent) and absolutely free. Absolute freedom is a state without moral norms and moral choice (between good and evil, or even between good and better). Men are unique and different, yet their difference resides not in their morals (as all individuals share 'species essence') but in their abilities and capacities, which they fully develop. Thus individual uniqueness and singularity is aesthetic and not ethical in character. (When Marx considers what people will do in a communist society, he always mentions artistic activities.) Righteous persons are not considered to be the repositories of the supreme good; no moral claim is realized in the realm of freedom. The all-embracing category of alienation stands for the alienation of the process of individual objectification into a cumulated social wealth the individual cannot appropriate. Those who cannot develop their own selves, whose abilities are crippled, whose desires are trampled underfoot, are the ones who raise the claim to absolute freedom. In short, it is not righteousness but suffering that raises this claim. Absolute freedom is the end of human suffering (though not the end of human pain), and not the promised land of the righteous. This is a grand idea and it is rooted in a religious tradition to the same extent as the Kantian image of the 'ethical state'. The conception is very close to a 'theodicy of suffering' in that the promise pertains not to those who do not commit injustice but to those who suffer the greatest injustice. The proletariat suffers most, and consequently it is the bearer of the promise. The people of Redemption are chosen not on the grounds of their righteousness but on the grounds of their suffering. It is in this way that the paradox of freedom is circumvented.

However, the reconstruction of the complete ethico-political concept of justice fails. The end of suffering is not to be the dawn of justice, but the end of justice. The idea of absolute freedom hinges either on the extravaganza of the anthropological revolution (the coalescence of all individuals and the species essence) or on the self-contradictory concept of absolute abundance.[48] Putting aside the theoretical fallacies incumbent upon the Marxian philosophy of history (which I analysed in *A Theory of History*) – namely, the obvious *transcensus* of theoretical reason of which Marx is guilty, and the neglect or misrepresentation of the political domain, cultural value patterns, and the like – the Marxian solution does not hold water for other reasons. Hegel was right: the edifice of the ethico-political concept of justice can only be built upon the idea of an already existing moral order (*Sittlichkeit*). In so far as it is built on this idea, the theory presupposes a *change* in society to match the idea, and a change in human nature to live up to it. If the concept is built upon morality, the posited 'macrocosmos' must be already present in the 'microcosmos' of the 'city in the soul'. Human nature, being what it is, must have all the propensities of the 'good', and by virtue of a certain 'original' goodness or the 'laws of reason'. The assertion, 'It is better to suffer injustice than to commit it', must be argued for. Marx designs his 'city on earth' without reference to the 'city in the soul'; there is no place for the latter in his theory. Consequently, it is not only the extravaganza of the anthropological revolution that is built on sand; in terms of this theory, not even the betterment of an existing human nature can be envisaged. One could, in principle, make a case for 'radical needs' as the main constituents of, or at least the motivations for, the 'city in the soul', but Marx does not consider this option. Had he done so, he should have substituted a democratic concept of freedom for the liberal notion of absolute (and empty) freedom. But he subsequently substituted the development of forces of production for the 'city in the soul'. The ethico-political concept of justice in Marx does not separate into its ethical and socio-political components, because the latter absorbs the former. However, it does separate into a reconstructive (critical) component and a prophetic component, in a manner whereby the two can never meet on a rational plane. Marx's failure to combine necessity and absolute freedom, critical science and an anthropological revolution, can be viewed as an indicator of the demise of the complete ethico-political concept of justice, and as a warning against any attempt to revive it.

Towards an incomplete ethico-political concept of justice

In a work of Diderot's unpublished in his lifetime, *A Refutation Following the Work of Helvetius Titled 'On Man'*, we find the following important passage:

We all are born with a just spirit! But what is a just spirit? . . . A commonly well-organized man is capable of everything. Believe this, Helvetius, if it suits you. . . . I have not found justice, and I have looked for it with more effort than you demand. . . . For example, I am convinced that even in such a badly organized society as ours, where successful vice is often applauded and failed virtue is almost always ridiculed, I am convinced, I say, that all in all one cannot do better here for one's own happiness but by being a good man. . . . This is a question upon which I have meditated a hundred times and with all the spiritual intensity I am capable of; I had, I think, the necessary gifts: shall I confess to you? I would not even have dared to seize the pen to write the first line otherwise. I said to myself, if I do not emerge victorious from this attempt, I will become the apologist of malevolence; I would have betrayed the cause of virtue, I would have encouraged man to commit vice. No, I do not feel myself sufficient for this task; I would dedicate in vain my life to it. . . . Do you want a most simple question? Here it is. Is or is not a philosopher who is summoned to a court of law obliged to confess his feelings and put his life thereby at peril? . . . What is the best government for a great empire, and by what solid precautions would we succeed in limiting sovereign authority? . . . What are the circumstances in which a simple individual might believe himself to be the interpreter of all wills? Is eloquence a good or a bad thing? Do we have to sacrifice to the hazards of a revolution the happiness of a present generation for the happiness of a coming generation? Is a savage state preferable to a police state? These are not childish questions, and you believe that every man received from nature the ability to solve them? Without false modesty, please give me dispensation.[49]

This passionate statement carries a triple message:

1 The problems worthy of philosophical reflection are the ones that were raised, and eventually solved, by various ethico-political concepts of justice.
2 The solutions presented by the ethico-political concepts of justice are wrong. (And here Diderot has Rousseau in mind as well.) They are wrong because philosophers do not delve into the depths of the problems they address. Even if the courage to do so

is there, one inevitably runs into contradictions. To solve these on a philosophical level is not tantamount to solving the problems themselves. Ethico-political concepts of justice fail to make this distinction. This is why philosophy can become a dangerous and even a demonic enterprise, and can make a case for evil in its quest for truth. Modern philosophy carries the burden of an *enormous responsibility*. It is preferable, for it is more responsible, simply to raise the questions, without making a hasty attempt to solve them. It is preferable, for it is more responsible, to live together, along with those same contradictions we cannot overcome in our actions and decisions, in our capacities as human beings and citizens. Yes, it is better to suffer injustice than to commit it. We can live according to this principle, but we cannot prove it. And we should not pretend that we can. The philosopher must forgo construing a complete ethico-political concept of justice.

3   The solution of the supreme philosophical problems is possible. Resignation should not, therefore, be final. To raise the questions, to face the contradictions, to penetrate the depths of the issues, presupposes the regulative idea that such issues can be solved. But it is indeed a regulative and not a constitutive idea. Philosophy must remain unfinished, incomplete, if life does not provide the solid basis of its completion.

If we cast only a cursory glance at the works of Diderot, we see how many paths he embarked upon. He experimented with several solutions. We can recognize Rousseau, Goethe, Kant and Hegel, and sometimes even Burke and Kierkegaard, in his invariably brilliant ideas. He anticipated or influenced many of these figures, but is identical with none of them. The multifaceted character of Diderot's inquiry does not stem from an inability to systematize. Diderot searched for answers in many directions. He did not restrict himself to any particular avenue of enquiry. He was the first to formulate the programme of a deliberately incomplete philosophy, which remains incomplete not because it turns away from the supreme (and traditional) issues of philosophy but precisely because it addresses them, and only them.

The advocate of activity in the public sphere never published his most original manuscript. Diderot's contributions to the *Encyclopaedia* were written in the spirit of the mainstream Enlightenment, which he believed in and represented with such a pure conscience. The fear of retribution cannot explain his reluctance to publish (he outdid all his contemporaries in his displays of civic courage). The fear of harming his allies is not a sufficient explanation either. (*Rameau's Nephew* did not hit any of them.) We simply must accept that the reasons he gives in the above passage were the decisive ones.

Moreover, we must bear in mind that the most novel and pioneering works of Diderot (except for the criticism of Helvetius) are written in the form of dialogue (*entretien*). At the time when philosophy made the last adequate attempts to systematize its sublime issue in a complete ethico-political concept of justice, as well as its first attempts to go beyond this concept, literature could make headway in the presentation of problems as problems. After all, Rousseau's *fuite en avant* (the first part of *La Nouvelle Héloïse*) is also a literary work. So is the satyr play of Enlightenment, Sade's *Justine*. German literature perfected this tendency. Of course, both Lessing and Goethe were greatly indebted to Diderot. Lessing followed in the footsteps of Diderot in working out his incomplete ethico-political concept of justice,[50] and *Rameau's Nephew* first appeared in Goethe's translation. *The Wise Nathan*, on the one hand, and *Wilhelm Meister* and even *Faust*, on the other, raise the problems of Diderot's spirit. The distinction between a regulative and a constitutive idea, so strict in philosophy, can be overcome in fiction, as it was overcome in Faust's last daydream, where the wager was won by God.

In Diderot's *Rameau's Nephew*, a philosophical work *par excellence*, there is neither winner nor loser. The dialogue differs substantially from the Platonian, and even more from the Renaissance dialogues (for instance, those of Giordano Bruno). Plato's dialogues were timeless, for truth was believed to be timeless. Renaissance dialogues were time-bound: the clash depicted in them took place between the new and the real, and the old and outdated truth. Whether it was in the complex and sophisticated manner of Plato, or the simple and one-sided manner of Bruno, true knowledge always won, and won by argumentation. Diderot's dialogue has an affinity with the Renaissance dialogues in that it is time-bound. However, here it is not the old truth that clashes with the new, but two interpretations of the new and the modern that clash with each other. Diderot's dialogue has an affinity with Plato in a decisive way: the protagonists do not simply mouth ideas; they also stand for ideas, they lead a life in harmony with their ideas. They not only *have* characters, they *are* characters. The representative of 'good' is in both cases the philosopher who is committed to the principle that it is better to suffer injustice than to commit it, the incorruptible ethical principle of all moral philosophies. However, the representatives of 'evil' in Plato and Diderot have nothing in common but the propositional element of their arguments. In Plato, every character is a rational agent. The tyrant, the sophist, the rhetor are successful, wealthy and powerful, and they defend their way of life. However, Rameau's nephew makes a plea for evil in a non-rational way, for living up to his theory makes him utterly unhappy and despondent. It is Socrates who plays the comic in Plato, whereas his adversaries are serious and pompous. The cast is reversed in Diderot: Rameau is the clown, stating, 'I don't know anything', whilst the philosopher remains serious, like B in Kierkegaard's *Either/Or*. To avoid any misunderstanding, the 'I' of the dialogue is not a solemn preacher who censures laughter, gaiety or human weaknesses. But the ironic attitude is only ethical if it clears the way for the new 'city in the sky', so he cannot be ironical and still keep his human dignity intact. Rameau becomes a master of irony and self-irony, and he uses irony not as a means of clearing the way for the insight into truth, but as a form of life, and, as such, a mode of self-abasement and frivolity. Diderot divided the personality of Socrates into two parts, the moralist and the jester, and made both problematic, even if not to the same extent.

In all probability, the discussion between Rameau's nephew and Diderot did take place. Diderot was known as a great *causeur*. He loved discussing matters of life with everyone, as well as translating seemingly banal issues into philosophical problems. The fact that Diderot committed to paper exactly this conversation indicates his deep concern not only for the topic of the dialogue but also for the way the discussion was conducted. Diderot's visionary eyes transform the real character of Rameau into a 'prophetic character', to use Lukács' term. Indeed, Rameau is a figure befitting Dostoevsky's pen a century before Dostoevsky. Diderot puts himself (the 'I' of the dialogue) into an unusually weak position (unusual in philosophical dialogues). He improves this weak position not via the argumentative reaffirmation of his own propositions but by arguing in line with Rameau's fundamental proposition against Rameau. This is what I had in mind when I mentioned Diderot's concern for the way the argument was conducted.

Had Rameau only repeated the ideas of Trasymachos or Mandeville (which he did), Diderot could have proceeded on a well-worn path and proved the superiority of virtue. But Rameau's trump card was the assertion that he had 'chosen himself', to which Diderot could only answer that he too had chosen himself ('I am an honest man and your principles are not mine');[51] the result is thus a stalemate. Yet the problem goes even deeper. Although Diderot despises Rameau, the two men have one thing in common: they put

the genius at the pinnacle of the human race. The Achilles heel of
the moralist is laid bare by Rameau at the very beginning of the
discussion when he states that the moral man and the genius rarely
coincide. Rameau resents men of genius because he is not a genius.
Had he (Rameau) only Diderot's talents, he would have been like
Diderot. But Rameau wants to be a genius at all costs, and so he
chooses himself as the genius of evil: 'If it is important to be sublime
in anything, it is specially so in evil. . . . What you value in
everything is consistency of character.'[52] It is here that Diderot
makes a new move. One cannot choose oneself as the genius of evil,
because being a genius is not a matter of choice. Rameau's claim to
have chosen to be a genius is therefore self-contradictory. What he
had in fact chosen was mimicry; he is everyone else but himself.
'And yet there is one person free to do without pantomime, and that
is the philosopher who has nothing and asks for nothing'[53] – and
Diderot refers to Diogenes. But this switching of the trump card is
not particularly convincing. If the philosopher is the only person
who can choose himself, and can do so without pantomime, and if
we cannot choose to be a genius, then choosing ourselves without
pantomime is also a gift of nature, and not a choice open to all.
Once again, the result is a stalemate. And the finale of the dialogue
registers this stalemate. 'Goodbye, Mr Philosopher. Isn't it true that
I am always the same? – Alas, yes, unfortunately. – So long as I have
that misfortune for another forty years! He laughs best who laughs
last.'[54] And, indeed, who laughs last?

The problem is raised, but not solved. Yet there is no doubt to
which position the author is committed. The interpretation that
Diderot divided himself into two parts is untenable. The relation of
'I' to 'He' is not only explicitly accompanied by negative accents; it
is also detached: Diderot despises Rameau but finds him amusing.
(The lack of hatred, which might be problematic in respect of this
point, is due to this detachment.) The roles are not only cast
between virtue and vice, but also between the sublime and the base,
between human dignity and the lack of it. Yet the arguments are not
convincing, though I must repeat that it is Diderot who made them
unconvincing, and he did so not because good became problematic
in his philosophical universe, but because truth did.

Diderot went to the extreme in scrutinizing the paradox of reason
('Is eloquence a good or a bad thing?'). Argument serves evil as well
as good. Good will be no less good because evil can equally be
proved by reason. However, we have not yet found the philosophical means to ascertain the superiority of good, and we should
not pretend that we have. We have seen how close Plato came to the

same conclusion. But Plato had his protagonist, Socrates, who died for the true and the good. His martyrdom was put on the scales as the final proof. Diderot does not fail to refer to this proof either. 'I: Who is disgraced today, Socrates or the judge who made him drink the hemlock? – He: And a fat lot of good it has done him! ... Because he despised a bad law, did that do anything to prevent his encouraging fools to despise a good one?'[55] This argument is not pushed further, because Diderot himself did not believe that the gesture of dying for a cause can prove the truth of it. And, indeed, almost every position, faith or knowledge would prove true if we accepted voluntary death on its behalf as the single proof of truth. What speaks for the morality of a person does not necessarily speak for the truth of the cause the person advocates. That is why Diderot listed among the unsettled questions the one of whether or not a modern philosopher should act as Socrates did.

Diderot arrived at the historical distinction of theoretical and practical reason. We cannot and we should not accept the separation of the two attitudes, but we must live with this separation. We must act as moral agents, despite the ambiguity of theoretical reason. But we cannot give up the claim for the reunification of theoretical and practical reason. Had Diderot known Kant, he would have rejected him. Had he known Hegel, he would have rejected him as well. Keep raising and discussing the problems. Keep living an honest life, and exclude solutions which might conceivably play into the hands of the devil. Philosophy as a perpetual 'dialogue' (*entretien*) conducted from the standpoint of practical reason – this was Diderot's legacy. It is this legacy that I termed the 'incomplete ethico-political concept of justice'.

3

The Concept of
Dynamic Justice

In this chapter I shall return to the method of the first chapter. The presentation will therefore be analytical (in the Aristotelian sense) rather than historical. Since it is dynamic justice that is to be discussed, I can concentrate on modernity in the course of explication.

If we assert that X norm(s) or rule(s) is (are) unjust, we pass a judgement. This is a value judgement and, simultaneously, a statement of fact. In its *form*, this judgement does not differ from judgements passed within the framework of static–formal justice, such as 'Act X is unjust', which is a shorthand formulation of an evaluative sentence deduced from a statement of fact (e.g. 'A is innocent; B nevertheless sentenced him, which is act X; therefore act X is unjust'). However, the identical form covers a quite different procedure. If norms and rules are taken for granted, it is also taken for granted that, if A acts in such and such a way, B will (for she or he should) act in this way as well, and, if B acts otherwise, injustice has, by definition, taken place. This is why evaluation follows from the statement of facts, even if the process is obscured by the shorthand formulation ('Act X, the act of B, is unjust'). Should we, however, assert that the norms and rules themselves are unjust, the procedure follows 'in reverse'. I have certain values, norms, virtues, principles or maxims in mind from the perspective of which I evaluate (or interpret) facts as unjust. The facts are *de facto* existing (valid, observed, legitimized, customary) norms and rules themselves. In respect of the application of 'taken for granted' norms and rules (static justice) matters can end up at an empirical consensus about the truth or falsity of the evaluative statement, and, if rules are applied, this is never in doubt. (In case of a foul, the referee of a soccer match *should* grant a free kick to the offended party.[1]) However, if we state that X or Y norms and rules are unjust (dynamic justice), there will always be others who state that they are just. If there were no one to make such statements, *the norms and rules in question would no longer be existent*, and so there would be nothing to test and reject.[2]

At this point I accept Baier's proposal that we distinguish between verification–falsification on the one hand, and validation–devalidation on the other.[3] If norms and rules are taken for granted (static justice), the truth of the evaluative statement ('This is just or unjust') can be verified or falsified. However, in the dynamic procedure when norms and rules are rejected as unjust and the proposal has been made to substitute alternative norms and rules for the existing ones, the truth of the evaluative statement can neither be verified nor falsified, only validated or devalidated. And, as I have briefly pointed out, such statements are *simultaneously* validated by some, devalidated by others. Norms and rules can be devalidated as unjust if the critics of the norms and rules have recourse to normative criteria the observance of which contradicts the norms and rules which are to be devalidated; if the statement 'These norms and rules are *unjust*' *follows* from the observance of those criteria.[4] Finally, critics of norms and rules can make claims to alternative norms and rules they believe would be just because they would be in harmony with the observed criteria.[5]

If we undertake a hypothetical survey of different instances where critics of certain norms and rules denounce them as *unjust*, we can divide those criticisms into two *ideal types*. Either it is claimed that *another idea of justice* should constitute the norms and rules in one or another form of social relations (and, in an exceptional case, in all of them), or it is claimed that the standards of the idea of justice should be *redefined*. Obviously, both can be claimed. The questions raised here are thus the following.

To whom should the same thing be due (while it is not)?
What is the same thing that should be due (while it is not)?
What should be due according to merit and excellence (while it is not)?
How should merit or excellence be interpreted for which those things are due (while they are not)?
What should be due to someone who belongs to X, Y and other essential categories (while it is not)?

What should be the ranks to which something should be due (a new
  kind of ranking)?
What should be due to a certain rank (while it is not)?

Let me repeat: critics of norms and rules devalidate existing (still
observed) norms and rules by invoking normative criteria whose
observance contradicts those norms and rules.

Such criteria can be different in kind. They can be (1) particular
principles (or ideas), (2) moral norms and practical maxims (in the
Kantian understanding of the concept), (3) pragmatic maxims or (4)
substantive values. I wish to set forth the following hypothesis: the
first three kinds of criteria are either directly or in the last instance,
rooted in substantive values (in one or in several). Ultimate criteria
are always substantive values. In modernity, to which for the time
being I restrict my analysis, the ultimate substantive values are
universal values. Universal values themselves can be interpreted
either as *universal principles* or as universal goals (ends). One
substantive value is, however, excluded from the criteria of justice,
the value 'justice', and it stands to reason why. If someone
devalidates existing norms and rules as unjust and raises a claim for
any alternative system of norms and rules considered by that person
as just, it must be *argued* why this is so, and justice, as value, cannot
be part of this argument because it would be *petitio principii*, which
is not a rational answer to a problem. Recourse must be had to
another value, and it should be proved that the accepted value (or
the one recommended for acceptance) is completely observed in the
alternative set of norms (and this is why they will prove just).

Particular principles (ideas) can perform the devalidation of
norms and rules in cases I may describe as instances of a 'cultural
gap', to paraphrase Ogburn's expression. It is relevant to speak of a
'cultural gap' if there is inconsistency among the different sets of
norms and rules in a given society. A particular principle of this kind
is the principle 'equal wages for equal work for men and women' in
a society where the equality of the sexes has already been recognized
in certain important social relations (members of both sexes are
equally regarded as legal persons, have equal civil rights, and the
like).

In a democratic society, devalidation of norms and rules by
particular principles is a normal and, in a manner of speaking, an
everyday occurrence. Moreover, it is a constant and continuous
procedure. There are always certain norms and rules (even many)
that we consider unjust. A great proportion of public debate centres
on such issues.

Not everyone who devalidates norms and rules by particular principles has recourse to ultimate and substantive values. On occasion, reference to other norms and rules and to the inconsistency between these and the devalidated one may suffice for that purpose. But, even so, one can at least have recourse to such ultimate values if one chooses to argue in full.

It is not always possible to reject norms and rules as unjust from the vantage point of a moral virtue or value or maxim, even if they can be rejected on the grounds of being bad, wicked or inhumane. Both *moral norms* (virtues, values) and *moral maxims* serve as frames of reference for such a procedure if they satisfy the third requirement set forth above (to propose an alternative set of norms or rules). Devalidation based on moral maxims is a sub-case of devalidation based on moral norms. If one devalidates norms and rules from the vantage point of a moral maxim, one does not devalidate one or another set of norms and rules, but *all* norms and rules the observance of which contradicts the moral maxim. If one subscribes to the famous Kantian maxim that no person should serve as mere means for another person, one can thereby devalidate as *unjust* all norms and rules the observance of which implies the use of others as mere means, provided that one is ready and able to argue for the acceptance of alternative norms and rules the observance of which is in harmony with the moral maxim in question.

The rejection of norms and rules as unjust from the vantage point of a moral maxim is as rare as the rejection of norms and rules on the basis of particular principles is frequent. People who devalidate one or another norm or rule by resorting to a moral value do not normally simultaneously test and query *all* of them. But revalidation or devalidation by moral maxims is tantamount to the simultaneous devalidation (or eventual revalidation) of all norms and rules. The procedure requires *complete* consistency and conscious consistency. However, that which is rare is not unheard-of. There are people who reject all kinds of violence and all norms and rules which enjoin or even permit the use of violence (for example, they are pacifists, and reject even the concept of the 'just' war).

If a *pragmatic maxim* posits one or another concrete substantive end (goal) as just, everyone who raises the claim for the realization of this (just) goal rejects norms and rules the observance of which prevents the realization (achievement) of that goal. In a particular field, norms and rules are regarded as so many means of preventing, or eventually achieving, the realization of the goal in question. In the course of establishing a welfare state, several former norms and rules in particular fields are devalidated as 'unjust', and replaced by others regarded as consistent with one or another substantive (particular) aim, such as a national health scheme, or blanket access to higher education. Naturally, there still exist substantial numbers of people who consider the new norms and rules unjust from the perspective of another substantive goal, a particular principle, and the like. This has been mentioned as an aside because the reader should not forget that we are dealing here with the concept of dynamic justice.

As mentioned, whether one devalidates norms and rules as unjust through the use of a particular principles, moral values or maxims (imperatives), or pragmatic maxims, the rejection of each and every system of norms and rules is, in the last instance, rooted in a substantive *value*. In modernity, there are two universal values in which all principles or maxims are rooted: freedom and life.

This statement can be verified with *all* modern versions of the ethico-political concept of justice, complete or incomplete. It can also be verified by reference to the various declarations of human rights. When philosophers pondered the 'just society', they always designed the constitution, laws, norms and rules of this society to ensure either the life of all (Hobbes) or the freedom of all. Life and freedom (or both), as universal values, are *presupposed*, and in this sense they are *axiomatic*. Unlike in Rawls's model, life and liberty are not *deduced* from justice, but the reverse: a society (or constitution) is stipulated as just in so far as it ensures the life and/or liberty of the citizens. In the idea of justice, recourse has been had to the substantive values of freedom and life; in the American *Declaration of Independence*, or in the French *Declaration of the Rights of Man and Citizen*, to both.

The assertions that there are only two universal values in modernity, and that all principles and maxims which devalidate norms and rules as unjust have, in the last instance, recourse to these two values, do not yet seem convincing. If we cast even a cursory glance at the discussion of principles and maxims and at the cases which exemplify their application, we rather see *equality* as the guiding common value in all of them. Theories of natural law stress not only that we are born free and that we all have a right to life, but also that we are all born *equally* endowed with reason and conscience. Furthermore, if we define 'conscience' as 'involvement in practical reason', as I have done elsewhere,[6] this would in itself suffice to posit *reason* (rationality) as yet another ultimate value. Thus we would end up with not two but four universal values: life, freedom, equality and reason.

In chapter 1 I argued for the assertion that equality and inequality are not natural propensities. People are unique. Equality and inequality are created by norms and rules. People who belong to the same social cluster are socially equal because the same norms and rules apply to them. I have also pointed out that we can (and should) claim that humankind should be the overarching social cluster, but only under the condition, suggested by our sense of justice, that the common norms and rules should be such as to diminish, or eventually abolish, domination, force and violence. Put simply, the common norms and rules which constitute the overarching essential social cluster should ensure *freedom*. If we do not posit the common norms and rules constituting humankind, the overarching social cluster, as rooted in *freedom*, our sense of justice will raise a powerful protest against the recommendation that humankind should be the overarching social cluster at all. I have also argued that we *cannot* will that humankind should be the *only* social cluster, because rejecting the plurality of normative systems (ways of life) is tantamount to rejecting freedom. The claim to equality is *subject* to the claim to freedom. In other words, equality cannot be considered an ultimate universal value.

Moreover, whenever people claim equality, they claim equality in *something*. 'Something' can stand for many things, but all of them can be reduced to two forms of equality: equality in freedom(s), and equality in life chances (termed by the popular political philosophy of the Jacobin period *égalité de fait*). Anatole France's famous *aperçu* about that equality of bourgeois society, which equally forbids rich and poor to sleep under the bridge, points out the injustice created by the blatant inequality of life chances, even if equality in a kind of freedom (equality before the law) is indeed guaranteed.

The claim to equality of freedom can encompass, first, two claims, where both claims can be related, and secondly, two interpretations of freedom. The first *interpretation* of freedom is the *democratic*, the second is the *liberal*. (Isaiah Berlin termed these 'positive' freedom and 'negative' freedom, respectively.) One can claim that each person should have equal *rights* to participate in all decision-making processes concerning his or her community or body politic, and also that each person should have the equal right to do so *and* the possibility of doing so. Thus two different claims pertain to one interpretation of freedom, the democratic. Next, one can claim that each person should have the right to decide his or her own fate, to choose his or her own way of life, to do anything that does not prevent others from doing what *they* like doing, and one can also claim that each person should also have the *possibility* (life chances) of practising this right. Thus two different claims pertain to one interpretation of freedom, the liberal. Both claims and both interpretations can be brought together under the following formula: 'The norms and rules of society should be such as to ensure to every person the right (and eventually the ability) to participate in all decision-making processes concerning his or her community or body politic (which is the pursuit of public happiness), and, in consequence, *all* norms and rules, whatever social cluster they may relate to, should ensure the same.' And further: 'The norms and rules of society should be such as to ensure to every person the right (and eventually the ability) to decide upon his or her own fate, to choose his or her own form of life (which is the pursuit of private happiness); thus each and every person should have the right (and the equal ability) to leave one social cluster and join another.'

It is obvious that in the above formulation equality in freedom and equality in life chances are conceived of as being actualized simultaneously. It is equally obvious that equality is regarded not as an independent universal value, but rather as a *condition* of the complete and unfailing actualization of the values of life and freedom. Furthermore, the idea 'to each the same thing' is being applied here without making the persons involved each other's equals. In so far as norms guarantee freedom, they guarantee equal rights. However, people can still choose to be unfree, or else freedom would not be guaranteed. In so far as norms guarantee equal life chances, they do not exclude unequal life chances, for some will make better use of these equal chances than will others. This is the case with all *norms*, though not with all rules. One person will live up to moral norms completely, another to a substantial degree, a third not at all, even if their respective life chances are entirely the same. Moreover, there are primary values in the 'good life' which cannot be either guaranteed or 'distributed' by any norms and rules, for the simple reason that they are beyond justice. Love is one of these values, though it is no less sublime a value than freedom or life. No idea of justice applies to love. Not even Christianity, which preaches love, the love of your enemy included, commands you to love each and every person equally, or according to merit and excellence and the like (in fact, it demands inequality in love, for the believer ought to love God above anyone else).

Although logically there is no conflict between equality in freedom and equality in life chances, since we can lay claim to norms and rules which encompass both, in reality there are such conflicts. It was precisely this fact that prompted the attempt to raise equality to the level of universal values; moreover, the claim that it should be the supreme (ultimate) value. In this attempt, *égalité de fait* is indeed intepreted as the factual equality of all, and not as the equality of life chances. Since all people are (ontologically) unique, and as wholes incommensurable, such a project includes the acceptance of a dictatorship over needs, values and opinions.[7] To cut a long argument short, *égalité de fait* is, in this extreme interpretation, a *self-contradictory* project, for it excludes equality in freedom, both positive and negative (some practise the dictatorship; others are subjected to it). Accordingly, those who recommend the acceptance of 'equality' as a human universal, and the supreme one, do not choose equality as a human universal at all. To repeat, equality cannot be conceived as a human universal, because it is conditional and not unconditional.[8]

I have argued that equality does not qualify as an ultimate universal value: that it is, in fact, not such a value because the use of equality as a universal is self-contradictory. I shall follow a similar path in my discussion of *reason*. By way of introduction, we must probe further into the problem of equality.

All of us, all human beings, are equally born with reason. Should this statement have the formulation, 'All human beings are born with the endowments to appropriate the use of ordinary language, the use of man-made objects, and the observance of the norms and rules of their human community, and all human beings are *equally* born with such endowments', the statement is undeniably true. However, to be born *equally* with these things does not mean that our endowments are equal (or that we are equals in our endowments). Even less does it mean that every human being makes equal use of his or her endowments. Thus, here as well, 'equality' refers to the condition(s).

To act according to reason (speech acts included) means to act rationally. One is a rational being if one is competent in observing norms and rules the observance of which is the prerequisite of self-preservation as an adult member of the relevant societal environment. The application of the norms and rules to everyone to whom they indeed apply is, by definition, included in the 'observance of norms and rules'. Thus *static justice* is a rational procedure. Static justice is, in the form analysed in chapter 1 (on the formal concept of justice), practised by the kind of rational procedure I have termed 'rationality of reason'.[9] It is obvious that, if reason is understood as the practice of 'rationality of reason', 'reason' cannot be the value the observance of which devalidates as unjust those existing norms and rules which are, for their part, observed rationally. However, I have distinguished between two attitudes of reason, and I have termed the second 'intellect'. 'Rationality of intellect' (acting according to reason as intellect) encompasses all acts, speech acts included, which have recourse to at least one norm the observance of which is juxtaposed to the observance of at least one norm or rule 'taken for granted'. Consequently, dynamic justice presupposes the attitude of 'rationality of intellect'. Obviously, *reason* cannot serve as the universal value in which the principles and maxims of dynamic justice are ultimately rooted, because only *one* attitude of reason, not reason as such, may qualify for this position.

It seems obvious at first glance that rationality of intellect indeed qualifies for such a position. Rationality of intellect devalidates norms and rules taken for granted in a *rational procedure*. Or, in a more cautious formulation, at least the highest (the most adequate) kind of rationality of intellect is tantamount to the performance of such a rational procedure. If rationality of intellect devalidates certain norms and rules taken for granted by observing at least one (alternative) norm, devalidation happens in the *form* of rational argumentation. The repositories of rationality of intellect *argue* for the observance of the norm they already observe; they simultaneously argue against the observance of norms and rules taken for granted, and, in so doing, against the validity of those norms and rules. Thus the process of devalidation is always an argumentative process.

All this considered, rationality of intellect only *formally qualifies to occupy the position of an ultimate universal value in modernity; it does not*, however, qualify *substantively*.

Since *any* norm can be juxtaposed to *any* norm and rule taken for granted, and since one can argue for the rejection of any norm and rule from the standpoint of an alternative norm, the question, 'Of which kind should the alternative norms be?' has been left wide open. Among others, one can subscribe to the value 'elite'. One can also formulate the norm 'Society should be such as to engender a new ruling elite, a new superman', thus devalidating all democratic norms and rules. This position can be argued for rationally. As a result, the full argument on behalf of rationality of intellect can also *devalidate universality*. An obvious objection to this is that an argument is only rational (in the sense of communicative rationality) if a (domination-)free *consensus omnium* is virtually hypostasized. However, if we formulate such, as Habermas normally does, then we have already accepted *freedom* (equality in freedom) as the ultimate value. Should we take recourse to the 'ideal speech situation' as the idea of a situation in which rational communication can indeed hypostasize a *consensus omnium*, we have already posited *life* as a supreme value (in the form of equality in life chances for the free use of reason). The concept of rationality of intellect, formal as it is, does not encompass the value of freedom or life *unless we so define it*, unless we make these substantive qualifications. Thus rationality of intellect does not qualify as the ultimate (or as one of the ultimate) universal values, because the *norm* of rational argumentation must be such as to encompass the values of freedom and life (or at least one of them).

Thus, there are only two ultimate universal values in modernity: freedom and life. *Equality* is the *condition* (in the forms of equality in freedom and equality in life chances) under which any *universal* goal or any *universal* principle based on universal values can be posited or formulated. If this condition is not met, neither goals nor principles can be thought of as universal. *Rationality of intellect* (argumentative rationality) is the *procedure* by which we revalidate or devalidate any norms and rules with universal principles constituted by the ultimate values of life and freedom. To put it succinctly, the procedure of rationality of intellect is *the* universalistic procedure if universal principles *regulate* this procedure. This can also be formulated the other way round: the values of freedom and/or life can only be observed as ultimate–universal values if norms and rules are devalidated by arguments and if all norms and goals rooted in the values of life and freedom are *argued for rationally*.

Irrespective of whether or not norms and rules are taken for granted, there are times when a moral decision has to be taken in the situation of a conflict of duties. Conflicts of duties occur if at least two moral norms or values can guide our moral choice and both or all, if observed, enjoin us to take *different* courses of action. If a conflict of duties is the case, the actor must give priority to one of the norms, observing this norm and infringing the other(s). Which norm should be given priority in a concrete situation is to be decided by *good judgement* (practical wisdom, *phronesis*).

If we recall all that has been said about the two (supreme and universal) values of modernity, and about the procedure of devalidating (or revalidating) norms and rules taken for granted as unjust (or just) under the guidance of those universal values, we shall immediately become aware of an analogous problem, or rather an analogous conflict situation. Although the universal principles of freedom and life do not *logically* contradict each other, for their simultaneous observance can be conceived without logical contradiction, there are innumerable concrete situations where our actions cannot be guided by *both* principles, or at least *not* by both *equally*, cases where we must decide for one against the other by giving one priority over the other in our concrete choice. If we assume that the actor accepts the validity of both ultimate values and both universal principles unconditionally (and the analogy with the conflict of norms would break down if we did not do so), the same actors *cannot observe* both these values and principles unconditionally, if they must give priority to one over the other in any concrete situation.

I wish to set forth the hypothesis that all value discussions which remain *unsettled* in modernity can, finally, be reduced to two types: first, those where freedom and life are interpreted in eventually conflicting ways; and, secondly, those where there is a conflict between the values of freedom and life. The first type of conflict, although it remains sometimes unsettled, can in principle be settled here and now.[10] However, the second kind of conflict cannot be settled − at least, not in certain cases, even the most important ones.

The two value conflicts discussed by MacIntyre (abortion and taxation) are undoubtedly conflicts between life and freedom (one interpretation of freedom as against life, one interpretation of life as against freedom). We can add the current value discussion about pacifism to this list, or the current value discussions between movements which opt to defy freedom if life chances can be improved, and those which reclaim freedom even at the cost of worsening life chances. Although I believe that freedom and life chances for all can simultaneously be improved, such an option is not open in *all* concrete situations of decision.

We must live with the awareness that conflicts between life and freedom may occur, with the awareness that, even if we uphold both universal principles, we cannot observe both of them unconditionally in many highly sensitive situations. If we ask questions such as the following − Is there a 'just war'?, 'Can violence be just?', 'Can depriving a person of his or her liberty (eventually life) be legitimately called 'justice'?' 'Are we authorized to alter the life chances of one social cluster in order to improve the life chances of another, and, if so, in what cases, how, and under what conditions?', 'Are we entitled to save the life of a person against his or her will (for example, with life-support machines)?', 'Can people be freed against their own will?', 'Can we opt for genetic engineering in order to increase life expectancy?' − then we are living with precisely this awareness.

I have discussed briefly universal values/principles as the ultimate criteria of dynamic justice in modernity. However, it should always be borne in mind that the history of dynamic justice (and of the concept of dynamic justice) reaches back long before the emergence of modernity, before the universalization of the values of freedom and life and the principles related to them, although neither dynamic justice nor its concept can be regarded as human universals. The procedure of dynamic justice – devalidation or revalidation of norms and rules taken for granted – can be performed at any time when people have recourse to any value, norm, virtue, rule, principle or maxim which has already been accepted (validated), at least somewhere and somehow, and from the vantage point of which the statement 'X norm or rule is unjust', or, conversely, 'X norm is just even if it is rejected or infringed', can rationally be supported as a true statement. Values cannot be 'invented' by any subject, but subjects can offer new interpretations of pre-existing values, or can formulate principles to clarify them. In pre-modern times, contradictions between the validity and the actualization of a value, contradictions between the abstract and concrete facets of the same norm, did serve as points of departure for dynamic justice. Clearly, this point of departure offers itself in modern times as well. Values and principles can be obtained or extracted from the set of norms and rules of our society or of a society other than ours (and this still happens today), and they can be obtained and extracted from objectivations-for-itself[11] created in earlier periods (works of art, philosophies, religions, and so on). All this happens today as well, only the empirical variety of such procedures in contemporary dynamic justice has been neglected here for the sake of analytical clarity.

THE SENSE OF JUSTICE

In chapter 1 I referred to the 'sense of justice'. I suggested that it is the 'sense of justice' that denounces the use of different standards as *double standards* if we come to judge acts of domination, force and violence. Thus the 'sense of justice' makes the claim that humankind should be the overarching human (social) cluster. I have therefore set forth the hypothesis of the existence of a 'sense of justice' without supporting it with any evidence other than the denunciation of the use of 'double standards'. Nor has anything been stated at all about the sources, propensities and functions of that sense (if such exists).

I now make the following theoretical proposal: *the 'sense of justice' is moral sense concerning the matters of justice and injustice.*

There is nothing novel in this idea. Roberto Mangabeira Unger writes of Confucianism that

It held that the moral sense exists in man either as a general disposition toward humanity (*jen*) and righteousness (*i*), from which standards might be drawn, or as a tacit code of conduct. Under proper conditions of upbringing and of government, this moral sense could develop so as to ensure harmony in the individual, in society. . . . The aim was to elicit latent, pre-existing notions of propriety.[12]

In order to clarify the narrower category, 'sense of justice', I shall first briefly discuss the broader one, 'moral sense'.

The notion 'sense' carries two connotations: that of mental ability (in such expressions as 'common sense', which can be understood also as *recta ratio*), and that of 'feeling'. None the less, irrespective of whether the first or the second connotation is the stronger in the use of the notion 'sense', it always refers to an ability to *discriminate* between good and bad, good and evil, beautiful and ugly, true and false, useful and harmful, right and wrong, correct and incorrect, and to discriminate between these qualities in action and in judgement. Having a 'good sense' of something means being able to tell, almost without fail, true from untrue, useful from harmful, beautiful from ugly, correct from incorrect, in the particular field under consideration, be it music, business, mathematics or politics. Obviously, it is possible to have a 'good sense' of something only if one is cognizant of the norms and rules of the specific field. If I suggest, 'All men are born with reason', I suggest thereby that all men are born with the ability to discriminate according to all categories of value orientation as presented (and embodied) in the *primary set of norms and rules* of the world they have been born into.[13] But the statement 'All men are born with reason' *does not necessarily suggest* that everyone is born with the ability to discriminate in *other* spheres of objectivation, for not everyone comes in fact to know and practise the norms and rules of these 'other' objectivations. Even less does this statement suggest that everyone is born with a *good* sense of discrimination in relation to these objectivations.

If one accepts this course of interpretation so far, *moral sense* must be tantamount to the ability to discriminate between good and evil as well as between right and wrong, provided that at least one facet of the latter distinction includes discrimination between good and evil. (If 'right and wrong' stands for 'correct and incorrect', this is indeed not the case.) Everyone is born with moral sense, because the imperative that everyone should discriminate properly between good and evil (and, with the above-mentioned proviso, right and wrong), implies that everyone can do it.[14] (Kant was right: if you *should* do something you *can* do it.) However, as with the comparable proposition (discussed earlier) that every human being is equally born with certain endowments, the statement 'Everyone is equally born with moral sense' is *not* tantamount to the statement 'Everyone is born with *equally* good moral sense', only to the assertion 'Everyone is equally born with good moral sense.'

The statement 'Every human being is born with moral sense' implies that every healthy specimen of our species has the ability *to discriminate between good and evil* (or right and wrong). If this ability is absent, the person is morally insane ('moral *insanity*' is an extremely accurate expression). The statement 'Everyone is equally born with a good moral sense' implies that *everyone can do what is good* (that which one should do), even if one does not do it because of contrary motivations or goals the pursuit of which might include the use of good sense, but in terms of *another* value orientation (for example, useful–harmful 'for me'). The assertion 'Everyone is born with equally good moral sense' implies, though, that it is *equally easy* (or difficult) for everyone to do what they should do (and can do), or at least that this is so under similar or identical conditions. Apart from the fact that we have ample empirical evidence proving that this assertion is not true, there is a perfect analogy here with all possible cases of 'good sense': we are equally born with 'good sense' (of something), but we are not born with equally good sense (of the same thing). In the case of good moral sense, the empirical evidence of this is represented by the type I have termed 'the transculturally good person',[15] a *virtuoso* of morality. Yet to practise 'good moral sense' does not require virtuosity.

I began this section with the assumption that the notion 'sense' has two connotations: mental ability (as *recta ratio*) and feeling. Philosophy has invented the idea 'reason' as an evaluative abstraction in reference to 'good sense' and 'good practical sense'. The same is obviously true of 'moral sense'. It has two aspects: discrimination, and involvement in the *positive* side of what has been discriminated (good or right). As suggested, the attitude of reason can be called 'rationality of reason', if 'taken for granted' norms and rules are being observed. The observance of such norms and rules presupposes positive involvement in both the norms and their observance. I have elsewhere defined 'to feel' as 'being involved in something'.[16] The feeling of shame is our involvement in the 'taken-for-granted' norms and rules and their observance. Norms and rules are the external authorities of the judgement of conduct. If certain norms and rules are rejected from the standpoint of observing alternative values, norms, rules, virtues and the like, then rationality of intellect (practical reason proper) becomes the authority of judgement in human conduct. I have defined *conscience* as the involvement in this (internal) authority as the secondary moral feeling (secondary *historically*, not as far as its sublimity is concerned, both philogenetically and ontogenetically).[17]

The reader must further remember that norms and rules can be devalidated from the standpoint of a value, virtue or moral norm as bad, wicked, evil, even if not as unjust (under certain conditions, this term would not make sense). Equally, we can *reject actions* by denouncing them as evil or wicked, but not as unjust. This may happen the other way round as well: we may appraise an *unjust* act as meritorious or supererogatory. All this only indicates (and this has been presupposed in the first place) that 'moral sense' is a *broader category* than the 'sense of justice'. But no moral sense can approve of *norms* and rules as good or sacred if they are considered *unjust*. Likewise, and this is only another formulation of the same assertion, if a set of norms and rules is considered unjust, it cannot simultaneously be judged as 'good'. This again suggests (something presupposed in the first place) that the 'sense of justice' is a specific manifestation of the 'moral sense'.

It stands to reason that, if we take the position of the ethical concept of justice, and understand justice exclusively as righteousness (the sum total of virtues), the distinction between 'moral sense' and the 'sense of justice' is an empty one. But, if we include sociopolitical justice in the concept of justice, the distinction will be of the utmost importance.

Let us consider static justice. If norms and rules apply to a social cluster, the 'matter of justice' is applying the same norms and rules to each and every member of that cluster consistently and continuously. In other words, the 'matter pertaining to justice' is the *right* application of these norms and rules. 'Right' also means *correct*. In respect of 'following rules', 'right' is identical with 'correct', although this is not so if norms are to be observed. A 'correct person' is a just person in the following of rules. I stated in chapter 1 that the norms and rules which constitute a social cluster are by no means mainly of moral provenance. But I also stated that the consistent and continuous application of any norms, moral or not, is a moral matter. Thus the concept of 'right' (right judgement, right decision) implies the concept of 'good', and, as a consequence, the distinction between 'right' and 'wrong' (as well as between 'correct' and 'incorrect') includes discriminating between good and evil, even if the norm or rule to be applied 'rightly' has nothing whatever to do with morals.

Let us now consider dynamic justice. If we reject norms and rules as unjust, we normally do not call them unjust *because* they are not (or cannot be) followed or observed (even if sometimes we seem to argue in this manner): we rather assert, first, that because they are unjust their observance is unjust; secondly, that because they are unjust they cannot be (or are not) observed or followed; thirdly, that because they are unjust they should not be observed or followed; and, fourthly, that in spite of their being unjust they are and should be observed and followed until they are replaced by an alternative set of norms and rules considered just. In all these cases the distinction is made according to whether the norms and rules themselves are right or wrong *and/or* whether their observance is right or wrong.

One can, theoretically, reject any sets of norms and rules. However, as mentioned, one cannot reject all of them as *unjust*. We reject norms and rules as unjust if we can prove (or substantiate) that the rejected norms are *wrong*. Unlike in the sphere of static justice, 'wrong', in this case, cannot stand for 'incorrect', and for obvious reasons. 'Right' only stands for 'correct' if we are speaking of rules that are being followed, and not norms that are being observed. Rationality of intellect always has recourse to norms, values, principles, maxims and the like, but it *cannot* have recourse to rules. It can make a claim, as it indeed does, for an alternative, and right, set of rules to be substituted for the existing ones, but these are *not yet* rules. Of course, one can reject existing rules as 'incorrect', but only if the value on the basis of which this judgement is passed is *technical* in character. In this case, though, the rejected rules are not devalidated as *unjust*.

Purely moral (interclusteral) norms can also be devalidated by moral maxims or by interclusteral norms *in statu nascendi*. But they can only be devalidated as *unjust* if they have served as *legitimizing* moral norms for a socio-political system rejected as unjust. If this is not the case, the devalidated moral norms can be rejected not as unjust but as *inhumane* or *wicked*, or simply as *irrational*.

Thus neither merely technical rules nor merely interclusteral moral norms are normally devalidated as *unjust* (or revalidated as just). None the less, socio-political norms and rules are devalidated and revalidated as unjust/just. Interclusteral moral norms can perform the process of devalidating and revalidating socio-political norms as unjust/just, even if *they* cannot be devalidated or revalidated as unjust/just. But merely technical rules (or goals) cannot even perform the process of devalidation (revalidation), let alone be judged just/unjust.

We devalidate socio-political (social and/or political) norms and rules as *wrong*, or revalidate them as *right*. The distinction between 'right' and 'wrong' *includes* the discrimination between good and evil, though the former is not identical with the latter. I shall argue for this thesis in chapter 4, where the three great problems of the socio-political concepts of justice – retributive justice, distributive justice and the problem of the 'just war' – will be discussed. If we assume that the hypothesis has already been substantiated, we can come to the following conclusion: *the sense of justice is moral sense in its capacity to discriminate between 'right and wrong', if at least one aspect of the latter distinction includes the discrimination between good and evil.* If all aspects include this discrimination, we are speaking of justice as *righteousness*. If not all facets of the distinction include the discrimination between good and evil, we are speaking of *socio-political justice*. A judgement can be just, in both cases, if the mental process of reflective *and* determining judgement is *conclusively* and *consistently* performed.

The discrimination between right and wrong is performed by judgement (both determining and reflective). Sense of justice is *actualized* by judgement. This is where I must make a clear distinction between 'sense of justice' and 'good sense of justice', which so far has not been done.

'Sense of justice' is the ability to discriminate between right and wrong (if at least one aspect of this distinction includes the discrimination between good and evil), both in determining and in reflective judgement. Everyone is born with the 'sense of justice', for everyone can make judgements by means of this discrimination. Everyone is endowed with *both* the cognitive and the emotive aspects of the sense of justice.

Everyone is *equally endowed with the good sense of justice* as it is actualized in static justice because everyone can do what she or he ought to do – namely, pass just judgements. It is perhaps superfluous to add that this does not mean that everyone actually passes good judgements concerning right or wrong.

Yet *not everyone is equally endowed with the good sense of justice* as it is actualized in *dynamic* justice. This statement means the following. Everyone learns how to be just and how to pass good judgements according to the existing norms and rules (static justice). What you should do, you can do. However, construing alternative (imaginary) norms and rules and devalidating existing ones as unjust is not an 'ought' for all human beings. Not all human beings *can* perform this procedure. One cannot assume that the *heightened* intensity of both the *mental* and the *emotive* aspects of judgement is present in every human being. There are always a few supersensitive but not necessarily superintelligent people who make the first steps in this direction. The more numerous these people are, the more they create a 'social climate' wherein *the procedure of dynamic justice itself becomes taken for granted*. Of course, the statement 'The procedure of dynamic justice itself becomes taken for granted' is not tantamount to a statement that the norms and rules newly recommended become taken for granted. This would be contradictory. It is only in modern times that the procedure of dynamic justice has become more and more, if not completely, taken for granted. This being so, now, but only now, can it be said that every human being is endowed with a good sense of justice as it is actualized in dynamic justice. Now, and only now, everyone can, from early childhood onwards, view existing (concrete) norms and rules from the vantage point of ideas, principles and values. Now, and only now, can judgement be 'well-informed', where the qualification 'well-informed' includes factual and judgemental information about social, cultural and political patterns, procedures, options and perspectives on an incommensurably wider scale than our immediate life world. Despite this, the statement 'Everyone is endowed with an *equally good* sense of justice' remains no less false than the statement 'Everyone is endowed with an equally good moral sense.' We can even say that the first statement, as well as the second, is *generally* false, and not only in our times.

The distinction between moral sense in general and the sense of justice in particular has still further ramifications. It is of the utmost importance that the sense of justice discriminates between right and wrong, and not between good and evil (even if the latter distinction is included in at least one of the aspects of right and wrong, respectively), whenever we ask the question 'How far are *right* norms binding?' This question cannot be raised about *moral norms* (the norms of good) *for they are by definition binding.* In the case of a moral *conflict* (if two or more equally binding norms cannot be simultaneously observed, and I must give priority to one), I am obliged to *justify* my decision. And I can only justify it in the clear awareness of the morally painful fact that I have infringed one moral norm by giving priority to another. Universal principles as moral maxims operate in exactly the same way as has been argued in relation to the problem of value discussion (the conflict of life and freedom). However, if we say, 'These norms and rules are unjust', and if we recommend an alternative set of norms and rules as substitutes – to put it simply, if we state, 'These norms and rules are wrong' – such a statement is binding as far as *judgements* are concerned, but not necessarily in respect of direct *actions*. If we state that the ensemble of rules called 'the market' is unjust (wrong), and still go to the supermarket to shop, we do not need to justify our actions: we can hardly be expected to act otherwise. We can state that a particular set of norms and rules is wrong and still be justified in acting according to that same set of norms and rules (unless the moral aspect of the 'wrong' norms and rules – bad, evil – enjoins us to act otherwise). Kant's distinction between the private and public use of our reason is relevant here. If we state, 'These norms and rules are wrong', the very statement is *binding* in public debate because we ought to argue for the claim for devalidation in full, and are obliged to present alternative and right (*alias* just) norms and rules as substitutes for the existing ones. However, the same statement is *not binding* in the so-called 'private sphere', in actions performed in accordance with the existing norms and rules, unless such actions also infringe *moral maxims* (norms). In the latter case, we can still continue to act according to norms and rules denounced as unjust if, and only if, we can *justify* this practice with the observance of a moral norm (maxim) other than the infringed one. We cannot be justly called 'unjust' simply because we observe norms and rules we reject as unjust (for 'right' is not binding in the same way and in the comprehensive manner that 'good' is). But we can justly be called rascals, hypocrites or insincere if we conform, in speech or action, to the very element of the wrong norms and rules that involves the morally bad (evil). Also, we can justly be called biased (and thus unjust) if we publicly argue for the devalidation of one norm or rule and yet refrain from arguing for the devalidation of another norm or rule which contradicts our professed values or norms just as much as the former. Finally, we can be justly called hypocrites and unjust if we observe certain norms and rules but censure the same behaviour in others.

I have assumed that the sense of justice devalidates norms and rules as *wrong*, and not as evil, even allowing that at least one element of the devalidated norms and rules includes the morally evil. I have concluded from this that the devalidation of norms and rules is binding in *judgement* (one cannot argue that one norm or rule is unjust but another norm or rule of the same kind is just), but is not necessarily binding in *action* (one can still observe norms and rules one has rejected as wrong and unjust, with the provisos discussed above). Now, how can this distinction be made in the case of the sense of justice which transforms different standards into double standards?

To judge in accordance with the sense of justice is unconditionally binding. If someone denounces the application of double standards but makes an exception of his or her own country, or of a personally revered or highly valued country, culture or political system, that person can *justly* be called unjust or a hypocrite.

Accepting this, what can be said about action? Let us assume that everyone behaves and acts exclusively in his or her socio-political environment and culture. This is clearly a simplification, but it is a worthwhile point of departure. If I state that, in comparison with other cultures, my own culture (system) includes more (or more serious) acts of domination, violence, force and coercion (that in this respect it is worse – less just – than others), then my speech act is tantamount to direct action. More precisely, the speech act increasingly constitutes direct action the more that my statement approaches the pure truth. (This is not the case if I pass just judgements about cultures or socio-political systems other than mine.) It is binding upon me to stick to my judgement and to argue for it rationally, but, the more my statement is true, *the more I shall myself be subjected to the acts of domination, force, violence and coercion that I denounce.* When I say, 'It is binding to stick to my judgement', I mean that it is a *moral act.* However, the statement that *my own* socio-political system or culture is wrong and unjust (in that its norms and rules include a high degree of domination, force, violence and coercion) is made from the standpoint of the values of freedom and life. If professing such a judgement publicly endangers *my* freedom and life (or eventually the freedom and life of my relatives and friends and of those who have simply listened to my judgement without denouncing me), then my judgement is absolutely true (and not even arguable), but it is *not morally binding* for me to profess this judgement publicly. This would be a *supererogatory* act. If my ultimate values are life and freedom, the observance of these values cannot compel me to sacrifice my freedom and life. The same applies to direct action. If I judge that the norms and rules of my socio-political system or culture are wrong and unjust, in that they entail a great amount of violence, force, coercion and domination, I am bound to act according to my belief that they should be changed, so long as I do not endanger my life or freedom or those of others. If acting so does not endanger my life or freedom, the statement 'The norms and rules of my socio-political system or culture are wrong and unjust' can still be true, though open to argument, but an assertion such as 'The norms and rules of my socio-political system or culture entail a far greater amount of violence, force, coercion and domination than those of others' is undoubtedly untrue (and therefore my sense of justice will definitely *not* prove to be a *good* sense of justice). Thus we come to the seemingly paradoxical conclusion that the judgement 'The norms and rules of my socio-political system or culture are worse than those of others' is not unconditionally binding in action if the statement is true, but is definitely unconditionally binding in action if the statement is untrue. But the paradox only appears in the two extreme cases, and even here it is only an *apparent* paradox. For the *good* sense of justice performs the comparison (ranking) well, and passes true judgements. Thus, if I make the comparative statement that the norms and rules of my culture or socio-political system are *worse* than those of others, I am bound to judge and act according to my belief that they should be changed for the better, but to do so *conditionally* if doing so *unconditionally* implies a *moral conflict proper*. For, if the proviso is not made use of, is not relevant to the case in question, the comparative statement is by definition false, and we are thus entitled to *generalize* the theoretical claim that, if the above comparison is made with the help of the good sense of justice, the validity claim is only conditionally binding for actions. This theoretical proposal can be the guideline in all sorts of comparisons and rankings. Thus, if I acclaim the norms and rules of my culture or socio-political system as superior (as being amongst the most right of all), I am obliged to undertake the following *mental experiment*: what would happen to me (and others) if the exact opposite was my judgement, and would I be exposed to a moral conflict in this situation? If my judgement was to the contrary and I would not be subjected to acts of force, violence and coercion, nor would I be instrumental in subjecting others to such acts, then my *first* comparative statement would be true.[18]

However, the notion 'binding' has so far been used only in the interpretation of judging and acting *according to* our judgement passed on norms and rules. But what if we interpreted the notion 'binding' as 'not to act, not to judge in a manner contrary to our judgement passed on norms and rules'? In the case of judgement, such an interpretation would imply the following imperative: if your sense of justice judges that such and such a norm or rule is *unjust*, you should not pass a judgement to the contrary, either privately or publicly. I suggest that, if we interpret the notion 'binding' in this sense, every judgement concerning right or wrong is equally binding, regardless of conditions and consequences. You should not state, 'These rules are right', if you judge them wrong, even if the price of being consistent in this way is your freedom and your life. This is so because in this case the *supreme* interpretation of life and freedom is at stake: personal autonomy as human dignity. The eventual loss of this supreme expression of life and freedom overrules the value of physical freedom and mere life. Thus, even if no one is morally obliged to profess publicly, 'The norms and rules are all wrong', if one's life (and that of others) is at stake one is always morally obliged *not* to profess that the wrong norms are right. The refusal to renounce one's own convictions cannot be called a supererogatory gesture, because every human being *should do it* and *can do it*. The same holds true of actions. No one is obliged to act such that the norms and rules should be changed if his or her life and freedom (and that of others) is at stake. But no one who rejects norms and rules as wrong and unjust *should be instrumental* in practising those same acts of violence, coercion, force and domination as are being rejected. Everyone familiar with the inner workings of totalitarian societies is aware of the enormity of the distinction between the two kinds of 'binding' in relation to our statements. People who reject all the social norms and rules of such societies are not thereby unconditionally obliged to participate in open acts of dissent. For example, in Stalin's Russia such acts were tantamount to suicide, to the sacrifice of the life and freedom of family, relatives, friends and neighbours, and a loss of freedom is still the price generally paid for such acts. Clearly no one can be obliged to commit suicide, to sacrifice others, or even to condemn him- or herself to a loss of freedom. Yet crying along with the wolves, volunteering to do the dirty work, climbing up the ladder of power to become a fountainhead of force, violence, coercion and domination, is absolutely impermissible, even if the price of reluctance to do so is one's freedom or life (as is sometimes the case).

As a result of this, the judgement 'These norms and rules are utterly unjust in comparison with those of other socio-political systems or cultures because they include the greatest amount of force, violence, coercion and the like', or 'These norms and rules entail as great an amount of force and violence as systems or cultures having the most unjust norms and rules', is not unconditionally binding, if the notion 'binding' is interpreted in a positive sense. None the less, the same judgement is unconditionally binding if 'binding' is interpreted as forbearance.

Only in exceptional cases are systems of norms and rules comprised entirely of domination, violence, force and coercion, even if they include acts of the latter kind to a greater or lesser degree. We know that the sense of justice does not require a comparison among the *actual* systems of norms and rules unless they include such acts, and then only as far as they do include them. Since only those aspects of norms and rules which directly relate to the universal values (principles) are affected by the comparison, the Kantian distinction between private and public use of reason, in respect of this particular situation, has to be modified, for all the examples of observance or infringement of that *norm* of *comparison* are also moral matters. Of course, all aspects of the norms and rules we do *not* compare can still be subjected to judgement by the sense of justice. Everything that has been said about the 'private' use of reason applies here. It can be argued that the rule of obligatory education includes coercion (it is enforced), but it cannot be said that the acts performed in educational institutions are acts of force, though they can be. Even in the most violent and coercive societies innumerable acts are performed according to norms and rules which do not involve violence, force or coercion (or involves them only if one chooses this course of action). The ultimate argumentative rejection of those norms and rules can thus be considered simultaneously with the due observance of those norms and rules that do not involve moral contradiction.

SOCIAL AND POLITICAL CONFLICTS VIEWED FROM THE PERSPECTIVE
OF DYNAMIC JUSTICE

In chapter 1 I gave a brief overview of the possible social (and political) conflicts viewed from the perspective of the formal concept of justice as static justice. I shall now address the problem in full, including the social and political conflicts which arise from, or conclude in, the process of testing and querying norms and rules as to their justness or unjustness. A firm division between 'non-testing' and 'testing' cannot be made. Obviously, if I claim that certain norms and rules should constitute a broader social category than they do now, I pass the judgement that the present sphere (extension) of validity of those norms and rules is unjust. Social conflicts over such issues can also be categorized as dynamic justice *in statu nascendi*. However, if social conflicts spring from the inconsistent application of norms and rules pertaining to a social position (for example, a peasants' revolt against tax-collectors), they must be solely examined from the standpoint of static justice.

In the preceding section I stated that, whenever we reject norms and rules as unjust, our judgement is guided by the sense of justice. Wrong norms can be called unjust (and not only incorrect) because they have a moral aspect we reject as bad (evil). But the norms and rules we reject as unjust are not moral, but social and political. Thus the statement 'These norms and rules are unjust' expresses a *social* and *political* conviction. Those claiming, 'These norms and rules are unjust', and those saying of the same norms and rules, 'These norms and rules are just', stand in a social (or political) *conflict* with one another. The former want the norms and rules changed or abolished (replaced by others); the latter will defend them because they either take them for granted, or have revalidated them, or both. Social (political) conflicts can be worked through by speech acts alone *only* if this procedure is a *norm* of the community (rank, estate, institution, the entire society) recognized as valid by both parties. If not, the conflict is worked through via direct actions (practices), in the course of which the following alternative solutions emerge. First, one party may *force* the other to listen to its *arguments*. Secondly, one party may *force* the other *to obey* norms and rules the latter believes unjust. Thirdly, a *compromise* may occur where norms and rules are more or less changed but the suggested alternative rules are not substituted. Social conflicts can be settled in the first and third of these solutions if in time both parties agree that the new norms and rules are *fair* (as just as possible), but they are never settled in the second case, only temporarily suppressed.

I make the theoretical proposal that *all* social and political conflicts arise around the matter of justice/injustice (of the application, the area of validity, of norms and rules, or of the norms and the rules respectively); further, that all social and political oppression is the suppression of a particular claim to justice, and that all social and political compromises are compromises concerning the justice or injustice of certain norms and rules.

Of course, this is a matter of definition, and every definition also means exclusion. Accordingly, I exclude from the category of 'social–political conflicts':

1 those clashes of interest where none of the conflicting parties challenges either the norms and rules or their application as 'unjust' (competition among individuals or organizations, conflicts arising from personal ambition, thirst for power, following the 'rules of the game');
2 all wars where neither of the contestants has *any* restrictive norms and rules concerning this particular war or wars in general (this can legitimately be called a relapse into the 'state of nature');
3 those conflicts where the dispute concerns the correctness or

incorrectness of a *merely technical rule*;
4 *purely moral* conflicts – that is to say, conflicts between interclusteral moral norms (or maxims), irrespective of whether such a conflict occurs in the soul of an individual or in discourse, even if such conflicts occur in conjunction with, or on the occasion of social conflicts;[19]
5 disputes about the truth/claim of any statement of fact if, first, the acceptance or rejection of the statement is not evaluated either as good or as evil, and secondly, if no evaluation follows directly from the statement, or if the evaluative conclusion is accepted by all parties, provided the statement is true;
6 all conflicts of emotion and passion, unless it can be rationally proved, most preferably by a third party, that the *trigger* of the passion was a matter of justice or injustice – clearly, if emotions or passions are manifest in any particular matter of justice, we are dealing with socio-political conflicts.

The statement that *all* social and political conflicts arise around the issue of justice/injustice thus leaves wide open the problem of the *motivating forces* of social and political conflicts, for it by no means amounts to the statement that groups or individuals in social conflicts are *motivated* by an idea of justice, even less that they are exclusively motivated by such an idea. I would instead say that being exclusively motivated by an idea of justice is a rare phenomenon, in respect not only of groups but also of individuals. People who defend norms taken for granted as just are *normally* motivated by vested interest (or, along with other things, by vested interest), and those who challenge the same norms and rules as unjust are often motivated by dynamic interest. (An interest can be called 'dynamic' if its pursuit concludes, or might conclude, in the alteration of a norm or rule.) Particular social conflicts often emerge, or eventually gain momentum, through the private or public display of passions (for example, the outburst of rage or irrational disobedience that I have termed 'rebellion'). Such passions, which cannot be understood in terms of 'interest', may continuously fuel such conflicts. World views, immanent or transcendent, in a legitimizing or critical role, are of tremendous motivating force. This is an obvious and almost redundant statement, for all norms and rules are legitimized by dominant world views, and all alternative world views, including the dominant one in its critical use, challenge at least the application of the prevailing norms and rules, and eventually also their justness. But, whatever the motivations are, whether one or the other has more influence, whether all three are of equal influence, or perhaps one is more or less absent, the fundamental motivation formulated, or only displayed, in and through them is a *social need*,[20] or a structure of needs, claiming satisfaction.

Whether the idea to defend or to achieve social justice (or political justice) is also a powerful motive in a social conflict is an important question, but it has no crucial relevance for the problem being examined here.[21] I have only stated that all social and political conflicts arise around the *matter* of justice and injustice.

A conflict arises around the matter of justice/injustice if an observer (participant observers included) can describe or reconstruct the conflicts in terms of justice/injustice; if the observer can identify the norms and rules challenged, or the norms and rules devalidated or revalidated by the actors in that conflict. If this cannot be done, the conflict under scrutiny is neither social nor political in character.

Despite its apparent meagreness, the proposition that all social and political conflicts can be understood as arising around the matter of justice/injustice allows several important conclusions to be drawn.

In the discussion of the criteria of justice we saw that in the modern age we have recourse, directly or indirectly, to two ultimate values, freedom and. life, every time we devalidate or revalidate norms and rules as just or unjust. Further, we saw that equality is a conditional value (equality *in* freedom, equality *in* life chances), while 'reason' (as rationality of intellect) is the supreme *procedural* value. I shall now develop this further.

Life and freedom as such – that is, as universals – are the ultimate values only in modern times. Yet in any past instance when conflicts centred upon justice or injustice – in other words, in every political or social conflict – the very values, principles or hypothetical imperatives which performed the task of devalidation or revalidation were embedded in, and related to, *one specific interpretation of freedom or of life* (or both). Two kinds of claim could define the conflict. The contesting parties could state, 'The norms and rules are wrong and must be replaced, because freedom means this and not that, life chances are indeed these and not those' (the interpretations are different but the social clusters to which freedom and life are allocated remain constant); or they could claim, 'Freedom should be "more or less" for everyone; it should be more for some, less for others. Life chances should be increased or decreased for everyone; they should be increased for some, decreased for others' (the interpretation of freedom and life chances is constant). Normally, the two kinds of claim merge.

Some additional remarks are necessary. The claim that freedom should be decreased for everyone is the only contestation of justice by freedom that can be made in a typically *social* (*not* political) conflict. All other contestations of justice due to any particular interpretations of, or claim to, or invective against, freedom, are *political* conflicts *par excellence*. Similarly, the claim that life chances should be decreased for everyone is the only contestation of justice by the idea of 'life' which can be made only in a typically *political* (*not* social) conflict. In a generalized form, the following conclusion can be drawn: conflicts are political if justice is contested on the grounds of freedom(s); conflicts are social if justice is contested on the grounds of life (chances). Although I have discussed the problem here from the perspective of dynamic justice, the conclusion would be the same if we turned to static justice. If norms concerning life chances are inconsistently applied, social conflicts may occur. If norms concerning freedom(s) are inconsistently applied, political conflicts may occur. Of course, one can devalidate or revalidate the same norms and rules by having recourse to both ideas (those of life and of freedom). If this happens, social and political conflicts merge or overdetermine one another.

It has been argued that political conflicts arise around matters of freedom and social conflicts around matters of life chances. Are the conditional value of equality and the procedural value of rationality also constitutive in all social and political conflicts?

As we know, social equality is constituted by norms and rules. Norms and rules 'equalize' people of the same social cluster and 'unequalize' people of different clusters. It then stands to reason that every time social and political conflicts emerge around the widening or restricting of a social cluster (the application of the same norms and rules), or every time that such conflicts involve the claim for introducing and founding alternative norms and rules to constitute new, broader or narrower, clusters, the matter on the agenda is equality or inequality in freedom or in life chances or in both. This assertion simply follows from the definition of 'social equality'. Socio-political conflicts attempting to change social clusters contest, by definition, the very kind of equality and inequality constituted by the established norms and rules. A claim such as this is far from being equivalent to the specific claim that people should *generally* be less unequal in their freedoms and life chances, just as it is not equivalent to the claim that *some* people should be less unequal in one or both respects than some other people, though this latter claim is quite frequent. The *reversal of roles* can be claimed as well (for instance, that the present hierarchical 'upper' cluster should become the 'lower' cluster, and the like). The claim to equal freedom and equal life chances for everyone appears in pre-modern histories only as the exception, and even then as a dream and a wish rather than a real claim, for it is not, and cannot be, made by actors in social-political conflicts. The universalization of the values of freedom and life in modernity is both the precondition and the consequence of the emergence of this claim as a *real* one. A claim is real if it is regulative and can also be constitutive in political and social conflicts.

All the same, not *all* political and social conflicts aim at increasing or decreasing equality or reversing the hierarchy of social and political clusters (which can be called the restitutive or retributive application of the concept 'equality'). If neither the substance of the norms and rules nor their width is queried, and social and political conflicts still arise around the matter of the *inconsistent* application of norms and rules, the claim for greater or lesser social equality is absent (the contestants claim greater *justice* in terms of static justice). This is equally true if social conflicts appear in the form of disobedience or rebellion.[22] It is *not the form* of a social or political conflict that decides whether a greater or lesser degree of equality is at stake, but the overt or implicit *claims* made by the social (eventually individual) actors. (The claim is implicit if the observer can rationally interpret or reconstruct the social or political conflict as the contestation of equality and inequality, even if the participants do not overtly make such a claim.)

What is the rational procedure for carrying out our political or social conflicts? I have defined 'rationality of reason' as 'observing norms and rules', whereas I have defined 'rationality of intellect' as 'observing at least one norm or value while querying, testing and rejecting others'. Rationality of intellect is in the final instance communicative reason, because the value (or norm) observed devalidates or revalidates existing norms and rules, and this can only happen by way of rational argumentation as justification. Consequently, *a procedure is rational in so far as the norms and rules of a society or a social cluster include such a procedure*, or, alternatively, if the value or norm observed does so.

Normally, the system of norms and rules of any society does include procedures for handling social or political conflicts. There are usually *different* procedures for handling intraclusteral conflicts and interclusteral ones, and sometimes other procedures for dealing with both kinds of conflicts depending on whether they occur within or among higher, or lower, clusters. In other words, there are different procedures for social and political conflicts among equals and among unequals, for conflicts among the more free (or free) and those with optimal life chances, and among the least free (or unfree) and those with the least life chances. If norms and rules are taken for granted – at least, for those people who take them for granted – all such procedures *are rational*, where 'rationality' stands for 'rationality of reason'.

There are *three kinds of procedure* for settling social and political conflicts: *discourse, negotiation* and *force*. All three are rational if, and only if, the preference given to one or the other procedure in a particular type of conflict is normatively imperative or at least optative (according to the norms and rules). The procedure is just if the norms and rules prescribing it are applied consistently and continuously. The ideas of justice applying here are 'to each the same', 'to each according to rank' and 'to each according to merit', where 'merit' stands for social and political merit and not for purely moral merit. The other ideas of justice do not apply here.[23]

The use of force as a procedure for settling social and political conflicts is *unjust* if, and only if, the norms and rules enjoin us to settle this kind of conflict by discourse or negotiation. Except under tyranny (the state of absolute injustice), there are always norms enjoining us to settle at least a few types of conflict by discourse, just as there are established institutions to conduct such discourse. But only intraclusteral social–political conflicts can be settled by discourse. Interclusteral social–political conflicts cannot be, and have never been, settled by discourse alone. However, there are usually *optative* norms recommending the settling of certain conflicts by negotiation rather than force, or by force only if negotiation is totally exhausted. Finally, in all societies where political freedom is allocated to a rank, there are certain inter-clusteral social conflicts which *should* be settled by force (or, at least, where it is optative to do so). Where there exists a system of laws, procedural imperatives and options are prescribed or circum-scribed by those laws. By 'imperative' I mean the following formula: 'Each and every time such and such a conflict occurs, an attempt must be made to settle it by either discourse, negotiation, or force, and in that order.' By 'option' I mean the following formula: 'If social or political actions are conducted in one or another way by one party (or by any party), an attempt must be made to settle the conflict by this or that procedure, and in that order.'

The justness of a procedure for settling social and political conflicts can also be examined within the framework of static justice. Here the following statement is possible: 'This procedure *should have been* chosen to settle the conflict, but another has been chosen.' (For example, negotiation was still possible, so the use of force was unjust.) We come across such statements as this in all history books. The authorities which use force legitimately are generally inclined to do so even if the norms stipulate a different procedure. It appears rational to try to settle social and political conflicts quickly and for good, and force seems the best means to this end. But this option of purposive rationality is not as rational as it seems. If purposive rationality overrules the norms and rules of procedure, the person or persons opting for it may pay dearly: with their lives, with a change in the institution of authority, eventually even with the loss of sovereignty.

The justness of the procedure for settling social and political conflicts can be queried too by the sense of justice as the sense of dynamic justice. (See the preceding section of this chapter.) X can say, 'Such and such social or political conflicts should be settled not by force but by discourse or negotiation.' By saying this much X claims that the procedure of using force (in these particular situations) is unjust, and cannot have just results. And Y can say, 'Such and such social and political conflicts *cannot* be settled by discourse or negotiation; thus they should be settled by force.' Since the formula here involves the phrase 'cannot be settled' instead of 'should not be settled', it does not query the justness of the procedure *per se*, but only asserts that this procedure cannot have just results. This is why force should be used, because then a just result will eventuate.

Let us now suppose that both X and Y observe a norm or have recourse to a value from the standpoint of which they devalidate the current procedures. Both must produce arguments to justify their claim and both must be consistent in the argumentation. Let us first examine the claim of X.

The moment X claims that such and such a conflict should not be settled by force but by discourse and negotiation, X *commits* himself *not to use* force, but rather to use negotiation and discourse. Thus X is committed to devalidating the existing norms and rules and validating alternative (still imaginary) ones by discourse, or to the actualization of alternative ones via successful negotiation. Thus X is only ready to participate in movements committed to the procedure suggested by him. X also recommends to all parties in the relevant political and social conflicts that they proceed via negotiation and discourse, and may add that, given the asymmetrical conditions between the challengers and the challenged in the imaginary social and political conflicts, the challenging party may use force up to the point where it ensures that negotiation and discourse become the methods of settling the conflict. It would indeed be totally inconsistent to devalidate a current procedure by the use of the same procedure.

Let us take now the case of Y. The moment Y claims that certain social and political conflicts cannot be justly settled except by force, he is in no position to devalidate the use of force by the challenged party. Y cannot claim at all that the use of force is an unjust procedure. Y can only argue as follows: 'They should not have done what they did.' Yet what is the standard here? This can obviously be the standard of the *challenging* party alone. Thus Y devalidates the norms and rules of the challenged party (those of the existing social system) from the standpoint of alternative ones. But the alternative procedural norm is, by definition, supposed to be *force*. To blame the challenged party for the use of force on the grounds that they 'should have acted otherwise' implies the *devalidation* of the same norms as have been revalidated. We come across this almost ridiculous inconsistency daily. Sorel is the only completely consistent modern advocate of the procedure of force (as violence): he argued that it is *equally just* for *both* challenged and challengers to settle the social conflict by violence.[24]

Of course, we can devalidate (query, test, criticize) concrete norms and rules in many respects without rejecting the norms concerning procedures embedded in them. Further, we can give conditional support to social actors who query the justice of certain norms and rules we query ourselves but who settle the conflicts with a procedure we believe inappropriate. We can eventually agree with the measures taken against such actors and still state that their claim is just.[25]

All claims to justice raised by any challenging party in social and political conflicts include a retributive or restitutive element or both. It is in static justice that both elements are always present, even if the challenging party does not take justice (as retribution) into its own hands, which it sometimes does. This is obvious, for in static justice the norms and rules of the existing social order have been infringed. 'Social justice' is restored if the same norms and rules are continuously observed, the challenged party is compensated, and persons and institutions infringing the norms (laws) are punished. In dynamic justice the matter is far more complex. But in societies where the social order is legitimized by *tradition*, dynamic justice follows, more often than not, the logic of static justice. Norms and rules are devalidated and challenged from the vantage point of norms and rules (eventually laws) that have already at some time existed. It is of secondary importance whether the 'original state of affairs' really existed, and, even if it did, it appears embellished and idealized in the imagination of the challenging party (witness the perpetual references to the laws of Lycurgus in Sparta). The challenging party claims that the contemporary norms and rules are distortions of the 'original' ones, that their very existence is an *infringement* of the original normative and legal system. Thus the proposal to substitute other norms and rules for the existing ones is tantamount to, or rather, appears in the disguise of, the proposal to *restore* the factual validity of those *still valid*. The claim to restoration includes the claim to restitution (returning land, annulling debts, and the like), and usually to some kind of retribution. The more the challenged party forcibly defends the existing order, the more it is guilty of offence against the 'original' laws and norms. And, unless clemency is granted, this guilt must be treated retributively.

Although theories of 'social contract' introduce new elements into dynamic justice, as do political actors relying on or supported by such theories, there are striking similarities between their argumentation and the traditional one. The supposition that there exist certain 'laws of nature' continuously infringed by the existing legal and normative system, and particularly by the supreme authority of this system, and, consequently, the belief that *right* is with the offended and not the offender, is not far removed from the supposition that the laws of Lycurgus have been infringed and the belief that right is with those wishing to restore them. In both cases, justice should be done by *restoring* the 'original laws'. Restitution is part of the act of restoration, but even additional compensation can be claimed. Although legal thinking cannot be reconciled with the idea that retribution is justly exacted against those observing a law and acting according to the authority in force at the time of their actions, it is still the case that political actors have very often taken the theory of 'natural law' at its face value. The verdict against, and subsequent execution of, Charles I and Louis XVI rested precisely on this embracing of the theory of 'natural law'. Whether the actors were right or wrong is another matter; what is relevant here is their conviction of being right.

All secularized Western theories of natural law are based on the assumption that we 'have' certain rights 'by nature'. Rights are ours 'by nature' even if the Creator has endowed us with them. There are two basic rights of this kind: life and liberty (freedom). Being natural rights, no one can appropriate or alienate them. What is ours can only be relinquished by us. We may eventually decide to alienate and delegate our freedom (or certain elements of our freedom) for the sake of life. (For the theory of contract this is irrelevant, but in principle we can proceed in the reverse fashion as well.) All social systems, norms and rules, legal systems and authorities which deny these rights in any way (deny them to any social cluster or individual) are illegitimate and thus unjust, unless the person or group concerned has decided to relinquish (delegate or alienate) them. Thus the devalidation of norms and rules, legal systems and authorities (the latter embody the legitimized norms and rules of a particular kind) is effected by having recourse to the values of 'life' and 'freedom'. But this always happens when any norms and rules are devalidated. Norms and rules cannot be, and never have been, devalidated except by claiming the reinterpretation of freedom and/or life chances respectively. Theories of 'natural law' only *codify* the usual procedure; and, by codifying it, universalize, generalize and delimit it.

They universalize the usual procedure because the statement 'Every human being is born with the right to life and liberty, and equally so' is here substituted for the traditional statement that 'We (our social cluster) have the right to life chances and freedom(s) equal with yours (those of another social cluster).'

They also generalize the usual procedure because 'freedom' and 'life' do not stand for a *particular interpretation* of the notions 'freedom' and 'life'. The claim to freedom is not specific (for example, 'We should be eligible for this office as well as you'), and the claim to life chances is not specific either (for example, 'We should get a share of the spoils of war as well as you'). In traditional societies specific claims normally relate to a specific interpretation of freedom and life chances ('We, too, should have the right to own land', or 'We should also be exempt from corporal punishment'). Life and freedom in their totality, to which all humans have a right, are, however, *unspecific*. Both values are usually specified, although not in one interpretation but in many, and different social and political actors can define, interpret and specify them in various ways. The interpretation of these values can thus become a matter of contestation, and modern social conflicts mostly arise around diverging socially and politically relevant interpretations.

Theories of natural law also delimit the usual procedure. Since the right to freedom and life is universal and general, we cannot propose (as a just claim) a *general decrease* in respect of either one or the other compared to the existing normative system. (Only with respect to an alleged 'state of nature' can this claim be just.) Thus we cannot claim that everybody should be less free or should have fewer life chances than the current norms and rules allow. Claims of this kind are raised even now, but cannot be based on any secular theory of natural law.[26] A limitation such as this upon the usual procedure is but one expression of the universalization and generalization of both values.

If we accept the theoretical proposal that in a specific interpretation norms and rules are always devalidated and revalidated as just and unjust from the perspective of the values of freedom and life, or both, and if we are also aware that in modern times the values of freedom and life have been universalized and generalized, we can easily relinquish the makeshift theory of 'natural law' without weakening the ground under the argumentative justification of claims for greater (or more equal) freedom and greater (or more equal) life chances. In fact, we can gain even more ground, because theories of natural law have never seriously assumed the existence of a 'once upon a time', a 'state of nature', or that 'natural rights' were the 'original rights' of man. 'Original' means 'timeless', but the conclusions drawn from the construct of the 'original' rights are 'in time', and this time is the present and the future of the present. Since the 'original state' does not stand for the past, and the devalidating power of the 'original' rights is being asserted in the present, the justification of the process of devalidation is put forward within a fallacious argument. To repeat, the argumentation is analgous with the Spartan argument. However, the laws of Lycurge had indeed existed, or at least it was common belief in Sparta that they had existed at such and such a time in the real past of that city. However, to speak again with Croce, the problem with natural law and natural rights is that they do not exist and have never existed, yet we employ them as if they do and they have.

We can relinquish this makeshift construct if we anchor ourselves both in the *real past* of humankind – that is, of all human histories – and in the real present, and future of the present, of our own (Western and modern) history. If we accept that norms and rules have always been devalidated from the perspective of the values of freedom and life, in all human histories, then *our right* to do likewise needs no further justification. The manner of proceeding itself entails a restricted empirical universality. It is restricted in the sense that, where social and political conflicts are absent, this procedure is also absent. It is *empirically* universal in the sense that all social and political conflicts are carried out via such a procedure. Thus working through *our* social conflicts via such a procedure is only the manifestation of universality, and, as such, needs no further justification.

Let us consider at this point a possible objection to my argument: even if we accept that norms and rules have always been devalidated (or revalidated) by the process of resorting to one or another interpretation of the values of freedom or life (or both), we have not yet ascertained that those acting in this way have the right to do so. Consequently, the *right* to devalidate or revalidate any system of norms and rules by having recourse to the universal and general values of life and freedom is not a right either, or, if it is, this has not yet been proved.

What does it mean that I 'have a right'? It means that I am entitled to do something. And who or what entitles me to something? Norms and rules do. If I do something I am entitled to, my action must *not* allow for social sanctions. If it does, I suffer injustice. If I do something I am not entitled to do, my action does allow for social sanctions (irrespective of whether or not they are applied). Can I claim that I have a right to do something if this action carries social sanctions? Is there such a right? Do we know about such a right? In chapter 2 I argued that *moral norms* are interclusteral norms, and that we observe them *irrespective of social sa·ctions*. Everyone is entitled to act according to interclusteral (**moral**) norms, because they are accepted as valid. So the right exists to act according to moral (interclusteral) norms, even if this action allows for social sanction for having infringed *social* norms. In this sense we are aware of a right different from those secured and guaranteed by intraclusteral social norms and rules. I term this *moral right*. Hence we can consider the following possibility: the people of group X are not empowered by concrete norms and rules to contest and eventually devalidate any of these norms and rules, but they still have a *moral* right to do so. They have this moral right any time they observe interclusteral (moral) norms in the process of challenging taken-for-granted norms. It is too far-fetched to insist that any time people devalidate norms and rules as unjust they have a moral right to do so; sometimes they have, sometimes they haven't. However, I need not prove that every contestation of justice is based on rights (which I do not believe to be true at all). I only have to argue for the following (weak) statement: the contestation of justice *can* be based on a right even if the contestants have no social right to contest.

By saying this I have not annulled the previous distinction between social–political conflicts and moral conflicts. In moral conflicts it is the observance of moral (interclusteral) norms itself that triggers the conflict. In social–political conflicts it is the non-observance of the moral norms by the challenged party, or the contradiction between the moral norms and the social norms in a challenged institution or order, that *legitimizes* the challenge in moral terms. Of course, the contradiction between interclusteral (moral) norms and concrete institutionalized norms is itself constituted by the *regard* of the *challengers*, because the challenged party does not detect any contradictions. This *can* be the case in moral conflicts as well, though not always. If it is, the moral conflict has socio-political relevance (it can be the point of departure for socio-political conflicts). In moral conflicts the motivation of the actor in conflict is also moral. In social–political conflicts the motives are rather mixed. Moral motive can also be absent. In this case the moral right (or eventual lack of it) can be imputed by the observer. The observer can assert that this or that social or political action accords with moral (interclusteral) norms, although the actors are unaware of it and/or their motivations are different in kind (such as sympathy or despair). If the observance of moral (interclusteral) norms is inherent in the ideas and the motives of the challenging party, such moral norms are normally included in the 'package' of a world view. This is exemplified by heretical movements, which normally rejected the norms and rules of the Church by claiming that it had abandoned the original teachings of Jesus Christ, teachings of eternal validity. But, even if moral ideas and motives are present, they merge with different ones (passion triggered by miserable living-conditions, selfish interests, and the like). There is always a difference between moral and social–political conflicts, even if they arise around the *same* matter.[27]

Moral conflicts, as mentioned, can trigger social ones, or can make the individual in the conflict susceptible to joining actors in social–political conflicts (if such conflicts exist), but neither the former nor the latter process is perforce the case.

The idea that the claim to justice draws its authority from moral right, even if the claimants are *not empowered* to raise this claim by the current norms and rules, has been tacitly presupposed throughout this analysis. If, in the assertion 'these norms and rules are wrong', 'wrong' means *unjust*, and not merely 'incorrect', there must be something in these norms and rules that we judge as morally bad (evil): this is how I have argued. This morally bad (evil) element is precisely that which contradicts moral (interclusteral) norms, and this is so by definition. This is exactly why the delegitimizing claim can be based on authority, *alias* moral right.

But what happens when such moral right does not exist? And there must be instances of this, because it was presumed that the challenging party in a social or political conflict *may or may not have* the moral right to challenge. The answer is simple. If there is no moral right to challenge, then either the devalidating claim or the validating claim of the challengers is false, or both are false. The devalidating claim is false if the statement 'These norms and rules are unjust' is false. The statement is false if those norms and rules do not contradict valid interclusteral (moral) norms and rules in the very interpretation claimed by the challengers. This happens if the challenged party can revalidate through full arguments (of a rationality of intellect) the existing norm under challenge, or at least a third party (an observer) can do so, and the devalidating claim cannot be supported by such arguments (even by a third party). The validating claim is false if the claim '... and the recommended alternative norms and rules will be just or even more just' is false. The validating claim is false if the recommended (alternative) norms and rules contradict interclusteral moral norms, irrespective of whether the actors are aware of this. This happens if the challenging party cannot justify the acceptance of alternative norms and rules with a full argument, and no third party (observer) can do so.

4

The Socio-Political Concept
of Justice

The term 'socio-political concept of justice' does not stand for
'concept of social and political justice', because the latter is included
in, and is therefore addressed by, all versions of the ethico-political
concept of justice, complete or incomplete. In chapter 2 I spoke of
how the moral and political aspects of the traditional ethico-political
concept of justice were torn apart during the eighteenth and
nineteenth centuries, and how both have been integrated into
separate areas of theoretical inquiry. The 'socio-political concept of
justice' is a product of this development. The question of justice and
injustice is addressed within the framework of the scientific (or
quasi-scientific) understanding of society. Moral considerations are
not completely neglected, but no motivational force is attributed to
morals in the sense of 'righteousness', to perseverance in acting
according to moral principles.

The socio-political concept of justice has brought into focus
certain fundamental themes of justice. The dissection of the socio-
political body has offered a deeper and clearer insight into the
functioning of its organs. Being a modern theory, the socio-political
concept of justice has illuminated traditional problems of justice
from a new viewpoint and has raised new problems concerning the
functioning of modern societies. However, during the twentieth
century, in particular after the Second World War, it has shown
signs of decay, and manifested its incapacity for coping with the
postulates of our times. The crisis of modern consciousness cries for
a new ethico-political concept of justice. All the innovative discoveries
of the socio-political concept of justice can be incorporated, if
with certain – and sometimes considerable – modifications, within
this concept. The works of Rawls, Nozick and Dworkin are
important precisely because of this. Still anchored in the tradition of
the socio-political concept of justice, these writers have widened its

scope in the direction of an ethico-political concept of justice.

Therefore, despite my radical criticism of the socio-political concept of justice, and in particular of two of its main elements (retributive and distributive justice), I do not dismiss the problems raised by these writers as irrelevant for understanding *justice*. I do not agree with Kaufmann's proposition that neither the problem of retribution nor that of distribution can be legitimately discussed under the heading of justice. Even if I subscribe to Kaufmann's thesis that '*preoccupation* with retributive justice is inhumane', if this is meant as *pure moral* judgement, and if the word 'preoccupation' is heavily emphasized, I strongly disagree with his concluding thesis that 'punishments can never be just', or his thesis that 'distributions can never be just'.[1] Even if I agreed that the former statements were true, I should not thereby be accepting the proposal that retribution or distribution cannot be rationally discussed under the heading of justice. Neither do I share the position of Menninger, who comes to exactly the same conclusions by hopelessly confusing the two distinct understandings of the notions 'right' and 'wrong' (as correct/incorrect and just/unjust), dismissing thereby the whole concept of retributive justice.[2] My criticism has an entirely different source and direction.

In modern Western societies dynamic justice is taken for granted. Since dynamic justice emerges when existing norms and rules are no longer taken for granted, if dynamic justice is taken for granted then *it is taken for granted that norms and rules are not taken for granted*. Those who challenge the existing norms and rules devalidate them as unjust; those who defend them revalidate them as just. Nozick distinguishes historic from patterned models of justice. Generally speaking, historic models serve better the purpose of revalidation, whereas patterned models serve better the purpose of devalidation (although even patterned models normally operate with one or the other streamlined version of natural right and natural law). All models, patterned or historic, have recourse in the last instance to one interpretation of 'freedom' or of 'life'. They are different (and competing) because they have recourse to either one or the other, and because they interpret the ultimate values in different ways. I must mention as an aside here that some of the challengers strongly believe that they have recourse to *equality* as the ultimate value. I am positive that they are mistaken in this. If Dworkin believes that 'equal respect' is a category of *equality*, he is completely mistaken. Equal respect is equality of *respect*, where the supreme value is *respect* and not equality (and 'respect due to all' is one interpretation of equality of freedom).

Obviously, both challengers and challenged have an affinity with the interests, desires, projects, dreams and world views of different social groups or strata, for this is so whenever the justice or injustice of a normative or rule system comes into question. Mannheim's conception of 'ideology' and 'utopia' is clearly relevant here. Even the most esoteric analytical model takes issue with one or the other social or political actor, challenger or challenged. One need not be familiar with any branch of the sociology of knowledge to understand that taking issue with a social or political group, their interests and needs, is not tantamount to being simply a mouthpiece of particularistic interests. It takes the professional arrogance of Anthony Flew to 'unmask' Rawls's theory – in the spirit of the most dogmatic Marxism – as a straightforward expression of the interests of the 'new class' (although Flew despises all kinds of Marxism, the least dogmatic versions included).[3]

The very fact that the dynamic concept of justice is now taken for granted has transformed dynamic justice into static justice from one very important aspect: the framework of contemporary Western society is dealt with ahistorically. On the one hand we live in an hermeneutical age; the relativity of our cultural values is hammered into us. On the other hand, various models of '*the* just distribution' or '*the* just retribution' in '*the* just society' are made available to us. Justice is treated as a substance, like sugar or iron, either contained or not contained in norms and rules. Most of the new theories of justice depart from the analysis of the modern welfare state. Both the challengers and the challenged treat the need structure and the personality structure of 'men' as identical with the need structure and personality structure of modern Western man. The things *we* want are believed to be the things 'men' want. The things *we* feel entitled to are the things 'men' are entitled to. Of course, Rawls hid the rabbit under the top hat (this time called the 'veil of ignorance') in order to conjure it out again, but all his critics do likewise. For example, the Lockean theory of 'mixing' nature with labour as the source of entitlement is neither less nor more ingenious than just another rabbit under the hat. Nothing is wrong with this magic, for it is the magic of philosophy. However, if we reflect on the historicity of our consciousness, we must be aware that *we* in fact *have put* the rabbit under the hat, because we consider it a valuable rabbit. And then the questions arise. What kind of rabbit should go under the hat? Why is one rabbit more valuable than another? Do we have a yardstick to compare the relative values of these rabbits? But there is no answer to these questions within the framework of the socio-political concept of justice.

In the preceding chapters I simply followed the logic of my arguments. This time the subject matter itself puts constraints on the procedure. So this chapter will simply comprise three sections dealing with the three major themes of the socio-political concept of justice: (1) retributive justice, (2) distributive justice, (3) the 'just' or 'unjust' war and peace.

RETRIBUTIVE JUSTICE

When social norms and rules are infringed, retribution is social sanction effected according to these norms and rules. The sanctions inflict suffering so that the offender pays his 'debt', and this in turn reinforces the validity of the norms and rules. Social justice is thus restored.

The modern concept of retribution excludes *revenge*. Yet if the norms and rules of a society include revenge, the form of revenge carried out in terms of the norms and rules is retribution proper.

The modern concept of retribution excludes *collective retribution* for the simple reason that we ascribe the act solely and excusively to the individual (its actor). The notion of 'moral personality', so strongly developed through, and emphasized by, the Enlightenment, can be listed among the few indicators of ethical progress. To exact retribution for the sin or offence of an actor through the suffering of his children may sound absurd, but many different gods of the ancient world indeed substituted for the father's suffering the suffering of the offspring. However, though the modern concept of retribution excludes collective retribution, the *idea* of collective retribution has not completely withered.[4] Balzac's question, 'Who is responsible for collective crimes?' has been repeatedly raised in our century.

Even this much makes us wonder why the problem of retributive justice is usually tackled only in relation to criminal law. Retribution as *social sanction* and retribution as *legal sanction* do not now coincide. Though in bygone days these two forms of sanction were not easily distinguishable, in modern times they are, but there still exists a great variety of social retributive sanctions apart from the legal ones. If, owing to mischief, parents punish children, or teachers punish pupils, this is retribution proper. If two or three children refuse to play with another child because the latter has infringed the rules of the game, this is retribution proper. If members of a party are obliged to vote in parliament according to the decision of their executive, and one of them acts otherwise and is expelled from the party, this also is retribution proper. A person can be expelled from a social club because of heavy drinking, and this again is retribution proper. Even today, criminal law presides over only minor territory in the world of retributive sanctions.[5]

Retribution has been defined as social sanction, but 'social sanction' is far from being identical with retribution. It was Austin who spoke strongly for the identification of sanction with retribution.[6] Yet there are a great number of negative sanctions which are *not retributive*, since they are *not punishments* exacted because norms and rules have been infringed. Dismissal from a job for being a 'security risk' is undeniably a sanction, but not a retributive one. Likewise, a person may be quarantined as a health risk. *Preventive* sanctions are by definition not retributive, irrespective of whether their aim is to prevent crime or to safeguard against some other harm. They rest on the principle of utility, and have absolutely nothing to do with justice, even when applied justly (to every person who belongs to the same cluster – for instance, the cluster constituting a 'security risk'). Social sanctions instigated because of lack in excellence (a particular kind of excellence) are in most cases neither preventive nor retributive. They are not preventive, because the sanction is a *response* to a failure to properly follow particular rules. They are not retributive, because no wrong requiring 'restoration' has been committed. To repeat a point from a previous discussion, failing someone on an examination is a sanction, though not a retributive one.

The ethico-political concept of justice has always dealt with sanctions, negative sanctions included, and with the specific problem of retribution. However, there is no trace in it of any 'preoccupation' with retribution. Very little can be learnt about this matter from Aristotle's *Politics* or his three ethics. In modern ethico-political concepts of justice (in Hobbes, Rousseau and Hegel), the problem of retribution appears in conjunction with other problems, and is not of central importance. Even taking Hegel, one could not support the thesis that the division between state and civil society and the affirmation of this division necessarily concludes in a preoccupation with retributive justice, let alone a preoccupation with criminal law. But, if today someone mentions 'retributive justice', we associate this kind of justice with 'meting out punishment' according to the authority of criminal law. No wonder then that the preoccupation with retribution and the identification of retribution with the administration of criminal justice made the notion 'retribution' itself problematic. The moment that retribution became the exclusive concern of criminal justice, it became questionable whether criminal justice could or should involve retribution at all. The principle of 'deterrence' has been increasingly substituted for the principle of retribution, first and foremost in utilitarian legal theories. The principle of *reform* followed suit.

Upon comparing the 'state of nature' in Hobbes and in Locke, one becomes aware of the absence of the notion of deterrence in the former, and of its presence in the latter. It is not too far-fetched an interpretation of Locke's contract theory to say that the contract became indispensable *because* the deterrence of *single criminal acts* had become too troublesome a matter. Locke writes,

> In transgressing the Law of Nature, the Offender declares himself to live by another Rule, than that of *Reason* and common Equity . . . every man upon this score . . . may restrain, or where it is necessary, destroy things noxious to them, and so may bring such evil on any one, who hath transgressed that Law, as may him repent the doing of it, and thereby deter him, and by his Example others, from doing the like mischief.

Further, 'Each Transgression may be *punished* to that *degree*, and with so much *Severity*, as will suffice to make it an *ill bargain to the Offender*'; and again: 'I easily grant, that *Civil Government* is the Proper Remedy for the Inconveniences of the State of Nature, which must certainly be Great, where Men may be Judges in their own Case.'[7] As is well known, Locke asserts that not all kinds of civil government propose proper remedies, for some of them (such as the absolutist state) are greatly inferior to the 'state of nature'. Locke still applies the concept of 'deterrent justice' in both of its understandings. Even so, the emphasis on deterrence is so strong that it anticipates Beccaria's formulation.

Beccaria's short masterpiece opens several new chapters in the story of retributive justice. He is unusually outspoken, lucid and utterly modern. A disbeliever, he is not concerned with sin and divine justice. He cannot use – as Austin later still could – 'divine justice' as the criterion for gauging the justice or injustice of laws. Beccaria completely deprives the notion 'punishment' of the vestiges of the notion 'retribution'. Speaking of the *purpose* of punishment, he writes, 'the purpose of punishment is neither to torment and afflict a sensitive being, nor to undo a crime already committed. . . . The purpose can only be to prevent the criminal from inflicting new injuries on . . . citizens and to deter others from similar acts.' And further: 'For a punishment to attain this end, the evil which it inflicts has only to exceed the advantage derivable from the crime. . . .'[8]

The complete rejection of the principle of retribution, on the one hand, and the subdivision of society into 'law-abiding citizens' and 'delinquents', on the other,[9] follow from the same premise – that virtues belong to despotic societies and not to free ones. In a despotic society one 'needs' domestic virtues, needs the virtues of friendship or even of patriotic self-sacrifice. But in a free society virtues are superfluous, all the more so because they inspire submission. Public 'morality' 'teaches the pursuit of personal advantage without the violation of the law'.[10] Beccaria denounced the principle of retribution in criminal law, since he renounced the principle of retribution altogether, from the position of *purposive rationality*. The authority of (clusteral) norms is oppressive, and since morality is the observance of norms, morality is oppressive. The logic seems to be fallacious (in positing the identity of clusteral and transclusteral norms), but it is only so if one presumes that transclusteral norms exist at all. If one asserts that transclusteral norms are but fancies 'enveloped in obscurities',[11] the conclusion that morality is oppressive is quite straightforward. In the main, the belief that transclusteral norms are but fancies is Beccaria's position, though it is held with some inconsistency.

Beccaria's book lends itself perfectly to the study of the 'dialectics of Enlightenment', a task I cannot undertake here. The utilitarian position, the division of society into 'law-abiding' (normal) and 'criminal' (abnormal) clusters, was accompanied by great humanitarian concern for the criminals. The conviction that moral norms do not exist, that retribution is a false principle, fostered rather than hindered the full development of that humanitarian concern, unless such concern contradicted the utilitarian principle itself. It is well known that Beccaria made a strong case against torture and the death penalty (even if he supported his claim with manifestly incorrect arguments) and presented these issues to the public eye. It is perhaps less well known that he suggested *refraining from legislating* against infanticide, for this act is not easily detectable, and so such a law can be more harmful than useful. Since there is no other authority than that of the law, and we may pursue every personal interest unless we break the law, infanticide, if it is not legislated against, belongs to the domain of 'pursuit of personal interest'. Of course, even on this subject Beccaria had a humanitarian frame of reference: he referred to the misery of fallen women.

Beccaria's proposals produced one of those rare occasions when Kant and Hegel reacted in concert. Both viewed his proposals with abhorrence; both rejected the principle of deterrence as *a*moral, as unworthy of free human beings. Kant mentions Beccaria's 'sentimentality' and 'affection of humanitarianism', and denounces his argument against capital punishment as 'sophistry' and a distortion of law.[12] Kant is full of bathos when he presents his defence of the death penalty: 'I say that a man of honour would choose death and the knave would choose [penal] servitude ... because the first recognizes something he prizes more highly than life itself, namely, honour, whereas the second thinks that a life covered with disgrace is still better than not being alive at all.'[13] Utilizing the categorical imperative, Kant argues for the principle of retribution. Since humankind dwells in all of us, since we can all do what we should do, evidently we can all do what is *permitted*. It is humankind in us that punishes us, should we fail to act in this way. If we do not crave for retribution, this only indicates our lack of humanity.[14]

Hegel's argument is different, more 'down to earth', more embedded in the traditional view of retribution:

The deed of offence is not primary, a positive to which punishment would come as something negative, but is rather negative in itself, so that punishment is a negation of a negation. The real right is the sublation of this offence, which displays its validity precisely in it and is preserved as a necessary mediated being.[15]

In terms of his philosophy, Hegel reaffirms that crime is a 'debt' which must be paid back to restore social justice. However, his conclusions are exactly the same as those drawn by Kant. Against the principle of deterrence he argues,

However, right and justice must hold their seats in freedom and volition, and not in unfreedom which is addressed by threat. In this way punishment is established as if we raised a stick at a dog, and man will not be treated according to his honour and freedom but like a dog. But a threat which so insults a man that he proves his freedom against it, sweeps aside justice completely.[16]

Arguing against Beccaria's rejection of the death penalty, Hegel adds,

what is involved in the action of the criminal is not only the concept of crime, the rational aspect present in crime as such whether the individual wills it or not, the aspect which the state has to vindicate, but also the abstract rationality of the individual's *volition*. Since that is so, punishment is regarded as containing the criminal's right and hence by being punished he is honoured as a rational being.[17]

I have dealt with the controversy of 'deterrence versus retribution' at some length because I wish to make a case for the principle of retribution as the sole principle of punishment which can legitimately be called a principle of *justice*; moreover, as the sole principle of punishment which can be *implemented concomitantly* with full respect for the person who is to be punished. Neither the principle of deterrence nor that of reform has this potential. However, the assumption that the principle of retribution can be *thought* together with full respect for the person and his or her moral freedom does not mean that punishment administered via the principle of retribution does *in fact* go together with the latter. It is at this point that the problem of 'retributive justice' must be inserted into a framework of an 'incomplete' ethico-political concept of justice. I shall return to this problem later.

I have described Beccaria's book as a typical case of the 'dialectics of Enlightenment'. Although I have set forth my rejection of 'deterrence' and 'reform' as principles of (just) punishment, I have not touched upon the problem of the type and the 'quantity' of punishment. Subscribing to the principle of retribution also means subscribing to the idea of *proportionality* between crime and punishment, but not to any particular kind of punishment. Beccaria made a strong case for the *inviolability of the human body*, and thus a case against corporal punishment, the death sentence included. The body was regarded by him as the inalienable *property* of every human being. The formula was more consonant with the imagery of capitalist society in the making than with the traditional Christian view of the body as the 'house' of the immortal soul. In Beccaria's view, all other properties are accidental, and so can be alienated as well. The property of the body is, however, essential, and this is why even the law must not cause it injury.

What is regarded as corporal punishment and what is not is always a matter of judgement. As Bonner and Smith note, 'Demosthenes speaks of imprisonment as a corporal penalty: "In the first place, men of the jury, it would not have been lawful for you to determine what penalties corporal or pecuniary a man should suffer ... for in the expression 'corporal penalty' is included imprisonment." '[18] Thus for Demosthenes there are only two kinds of punishment: pecuniary and corporal. Among our contemporaries, Foucault subscribes strongly to Demosthenes' views. Yet for Beccaria and his followers imprisonment is not to be regarded as a facet or instance of corporal punishment. By providing this option, for it is indeed an option, Beccaria did put one universal value of modernity, the value of *life*, at the pinnacle of the value hierarchy. Although he recommended punishment in a *free* state, he valued life above freedom. This is why freedom can be 'alienated' but life (and the body as the symbol of life) must remain inviolable. Kant and Hegel opted for freedom as the supreme universal value. They valued freedom above life. In their view, not the body but the person as a *free person* was inviolable. The conflict between the two universal values made its appearance right at the beginning of the controversy about punishment.

Indeed, the principle of retribution gives priority to the value of freedom as against that of life. All the same, does such a priority necessarily entail the acceptance (and defence) of the death penalty, as Kant and Hegel believed? As mentioned, the principle of retribution implies the idea of *proportionality* between crime and punishment. But proportionality itself does not call for the *lex talionis* in general, or make the demand of 'a life for a life' in particular. Or does it?

The answer is not as simple as it seems. Accepting the principle of retribution, it is easy to reject capital punishment in all cases bar one, that of murder. If someone commits premeditated murder, it is just that the person should die. Whether or not capital punishment deters this extreme act is irrelevant here. This is the very juncture where the two universal principles (of life and freedom) are in harmony. Taking a human life on purpose is a simultaneous violation of the value of life and of freedom. If a person guilty of this crime respected humankind in him- or herself, then this person, acting as a free being, would experience the *will* to die. Taking his or her life, then, would amount to the administration of justice.

I do not think this argument wrong, nor do I believe that Kant and Hegel were 'cruel' or 'inhumane' or even simply misled when thus arguing. However, there are two strong arguments against capital punishment which do not *invalidate* but which do *overrule* the above argument.

If we state, 'X is guilty', we mean, 'X is guilty beyond reasonable doubt', for absolute, incontestable guilt is only rarely established. This is particularly so in a case of suspected murder, where circumstantial evidence, motives and confessions are usually the only material one can draw upon to reach a verdict. *Should an innocent person be sentenced to death, even once in a million cases* (something unavoidable, given the relative unreliability of available evidence), *every member of society commits an injustice.* Thus, in terms of a Kantian–Hegelian logic, *everyone should make retribution.* Clearly, we cannot will this to happen. Thus the abolition of the death penalty does not contradict the logic of retribution, but rather follows from it.

Secondly, the retributive principle is *past-oriented.* A crime committed (in the past) is completely ascribed to the free person as the author of the deed. However, to attribute freedom to the person is tantamount also to attributing the faculty of human reason as a possible source of self-punishment. Taking a life for a life means excluding even the possibility of self-punishment. True, the *objective* of retribution is *not* 'reform'. None the less, irrespective of the quality and quantity of punishment, giving every human being the *chance* of self-reform, slim as this chance often is, does not contradict the principle of retribution; rather, the opposite holds.

Granted this, there is one highly relevant area where the Kantian–Hegelian principle of retribution must not be overruled: the matter of crimes committed against humankind. Here the guilt is not simply 'beyond reasonable doubt', but is absolute and incontestable, for the guilty party *publicly* occupies the institutional position which orders the mass murder of the innocent, executes the order, or is party to it. 'Excommunication from the human race' implies that no *human chance* should be given the guilty person. This 'excommunication' accompanies the death penalty. If crimes are committed against humankind, the arguments of Kant and Hegel retain full force.

I have advanced the hypothesis that deterrence as the principle of punishment has nothing to do with justice. But why is this so? Only an act already committed can involve punishment, and the punishment should be proportionate to the offence (once again, a past-oriented relation). However, if in meting out punishment one considers whether the person is likely to commit the same (or a similar) crime again, or whether the degree of punishment will affect the likelihood of others committing the same crime – in other words, if one considers if consequences other than the consequences of the very deed under judgement have an influence upon the sentence – then punishment simply *cannot* be proportionate to the crime. In past ages, slaying one's next of kin, and in particular parricide, was believed to be the greatest crime and sin, sometimes even the only type of killing regarded as murder. And our moral sense has not moved all that far from this position. Still, if the principle of deterrence is taken seriously, parricide ought to be punished only very lightly, or even not at all, for it is simply impossible to murder one's father or mother twice, whereas one can steal any number of cars. If punishment is governed by the principle of deterrence, no genocidal criminal could be punished after the collapse of the regime under which his crimes had been committed, because in all probability this person would become a 'law-abiding citizen' under different circumstances.[19] To conclude, the principle of deterrence, even if it can be applied justly, cannot be the principle of justice. The quality and quantity of punishments can only be consistent as well as proportionate if they are compared with one another. Yet, when the deterrence principle is applied, *punishment cannot be proportionate to the offence*, and this is exactly what justice in punishment is all about.[20]

Moreover, the principle of deterrence permits us unrestrictedly to administer *negative sanctions* as *preventive sanctions*. I have already mentioned negative sanctions which are not punishments (dismissal from a job through being a 'security risk'; being quarantined as a 'health hazard'). Preventive sanctions prevent an evil from occurring to others (as in the examples just given), or to the persons themselves (for example, forced evacuation from a disaster area). But preventive sanctions are not usually implemented with the intent to deter (quarantine regulations are not aimed at deterring people from travelling through Africa). The moment they are, individual and group *rights* have been violated. And, indeed, should we go all the way in applying the principle of deterrence, all claims for human rights, individual and collective, are overruled.

Deterrence is proposed as an alternative principle of *punishment*. Preventive sanctions carrying the intent to deter are *forms of punishment in situations where there is nothing to punish*. Not crimes committed, but crimes expected, are the focus of this principle. Totalitarian societies operate with the deterrence principle. Internment and concentration camps deter political enemies, potential enemies and members of 'hostile' classes and ethnic groups from 'doing mischief', and thus the whole populace is 'deterred' from obstructing measures taken on behalf of the 'common weal'. One could object that partisans of the deterrence principle in 'open societies' do not go this far. But, even if this is correct in respect of intentions, it is wrong in respect of the principle: the latter goes precisely that far. Hegel put it correctly in stating that, when the deterrence principle is used, the situation is one not of a free man being punished, but of a dog being kept at bay with a stick; and who the dogs are, and how big the stick is, are decided by the self-appointed guardians of this 'commonweal'.

The principle of 'deterrence' also lends itself to quite a different interpretation. One can say that deterrence is not an alternative principle of punishment to retribution, but that it is *the function of the law to deter*, irrespective of the principles of punishment. Yet the less a *criminal offence* is considered a *moral offence*, the stronger is the deterrent function (or value) of the law. If no moral norm or rule forbids an act which is otherwise pleasant or accords with our collective interests, but the same action is legally forbidden – and, even further, if an action is morally commendable but is punishable by law – then the criminal law does act to deter, and deters more successfully, than in all other possible situations. Consequently, the less democratic a state, the greater the deterrent function (or value) of its laws.

The statement that those who do not kill their spouses (even if they intensely dislike them) are not as a rule restrained by the deterrent value of the death penalty (or a life sentence) does not stem from a particularly optimistic view of the human race. It may be no more than guesswork, but I strongly suspect that the few who do indeed reach the brink of committing an act of murder can no longer be deterred by prospective punishment, or *perhaps* only a minority of them can be. In this case, then, the deterrent value of the law is almost negligible. If, however, incitement to strike, or participation in strike action, a 'normal' act that is encouraged rather than discouraged by our moral sense, becomes punishable by the death penalty (as it was in Hungary in 1957, in the wake of the revolutionary general strike of the Hungarian working class against the Soviet invasion), one can be pretty sure that almost no one will strike. Under such circumstances the deterrent value (function) of the law is very strong.

There are indeed instances where the 'common weal' demands that certain actions (or acts of forbearance) should be legislated against, though in themselves they may be morally neutral. If drunken drivers pay a heavy fine or lose their licence, this is a penalty imposed on an act not in itself considered morally 'wrong' (for example, if no accident has occurred). And so it is with those who defy customs regulations, evade tax-paying, and the like. If these acts were not punishable by law, people would not care much about such regulations. In these matters the law does function as a strong deterrent, but only because something is amiss with civic morals. It is not too far-fetched to imagine the emergence of a civic morality rational enough to induce every person endowed with civil rights, upon embarking on an action similar to those just mentioned, to ask the question, 'What would happen if everyone did the same?'[21] Of course, if only so many people raised this question as people who do not murder their spouses (although they might no longer want to live with them), the laws would penalize only moral offenders and their deterrent value would be negligible.

Reform, as a guideline of punishment, is just as future-oriented as the principle of deterrence. In terms of this principle, punishment occurs *in order* to reform the wrongdoer or criminal. The simile of the stick and the dog is relevant here in modified form: one does not just show the dog the stick; one uses it in the belief that a beaten dog will be a good dog. However, the obvious link between the principle of 'reform' and that of 'deterrence' already casts a shadow on the former. If the dog has already been beaten, it will suffice merely to show the stick again: 'reform' may mean increasing a person's apprehension about potential future punishment (deterrence).

The principle of reform cannot be a principle of justice. It does not even allow for the same degree of just application of a standard as the principle of deterrence does. Given that no one can know what kind or amount of punishment will actually reform a particular person, punishment becomes guesswork, and can be entirely out of proportion, as well as arbitrary. This fact alone would not make the principle irrelevant. It can be argued that the principle of reform is beyond justice because it resembles *charity* rather than justice, and charity is above and not below justice. But then it must be proved that the principle of reform is indeed related to the gesture of charity, or that the principle is indeed humanitarian.

The principle of 'reform' is as old, and has been as generally accepted and applied, as the principle of deterrence; it has played a constant role in bringing up children, determining behaviour towards wives and servants, and also, though far from always, in treating offenders, sinners and malefactors. A person was considered to be reformed upon leaning to observe the norms and follow the rules, irrespective of motivation. Fear and pain were regarded as apt devices for bringing people back to the right course. It would be ridiculous to deny that the traditional practice of 'reform' has normally been successful in the manner depicted in *The Taming of the Shrew*. And it would be superfluous to cast a glance at the other side of the coin, so well known and so generally discussed today. But there is one fundamental contradiction in punishment administered for the sake of reform. 'Reformed people' act and behave according to the norms and rules of their environment. Thus they learn to act and behave *rationally* – in the sense of the rationality of reason. If fear and pain, if punishment *alone*, or even primarily, compels them to act and behave rationally, then impulses, desires and also 'rationality of intellect *in nuce*' will be repressed, and these people socialized by punishment will seek and find outlets in irrational acts. Consequently, the very reform attained solely or primarily by punishment promotes a certain kind of rationality and simultaneously unleashes irrationality.

Authentic reform is always self-reform, or, to express myself more cautiously, reform of *character* is always self-reform. It begins with insight. Punishment can be the *occasion*, but not the *cause* of such insight. If punishment is administered to reform, it is seen as the cause of reform. If punishment is administered by those sharing the principle of retribution, such a belief is absent. It is left to the offender to change character, if the punishment serves to elicit insight.

The principle of retribution gives the offender freedom of choice. Even disregarding practical reason (and conscience) as the authority of moral insight, if someone is put to shame by the 'eye of others', this shame alone can cause a change in character. However, 'being put to shame' cannot bring reform, only 'being ashamed' can. If pangs of conscience do not accompany punishment, if someone put to shame does not feel ashamed, no authentic reform follows. Real reform depends not upon *the punishment but upon the deep internalization of norms*. Fear and pain can be, and mostly are, the *affects* which motivate and activate reform. But the fear must be the fear of evil (the fear of norms, the fear of God) and the pain must be the pain of being ashamed or the pain of conscience. The fear of punishment (even of divine punishment), and the pain accompanying punishment, will never suffice. This ancient truth was brought out in the Aristotelian notion of 'catharsis', the Christian metaphor of the black sheep.

If it is true that the principle of 'reform' has always had self-contradictory results and has never achieved reform of character, this is immeasurably more so in *modern* society. In times when social (and moral) norms and rules were generally taken for granted, when rationality of reason guided rational behaviour proper, when norms and rules were not queried and tested, 'insight' simply meant insight into the validity and propriety of these taken-for-granted norms. This is no longer so. If nowadays parents or teachers punish children and pupils in order to reform them, these children will probably have quite different moral values to begin with. Punishment will not only be resented, but also be ridiculed. Since the attitude of rationality of intellect has become widespread, we need a *reason* for doing one thing, instead of another, and the traditional command, 'Just do it, because you should do it', is no longer accepted as rational (for the 'ought' is not obviously valid). Punishment as an incentive to reform seems to us utterly irrational, and, if we are punished with the intention that this should reform us, our moral sense is hurt to the extent where we would rather not do the thing we are expected to do, even if it is quite a rational action. It is a mystery why the principle of reform as a guideline for legal sanctions has become widely accepted at a time when the idea itself has undergone an unprecedented crisis and is regarded as irrelevant in relation to all kinds of non-legal sanctions. Moreover, the principle unmasked as *inhumane* as the principle of social sanctions, shines in the light of supreme humaneness as the principle of legal sanctions. It comforts law-abiding citizens to believe that 'criminals' are punished for their own sake – that is, for the sake of their reformation – and not 'for us' (which would accord with the deterrence principle), or because they have 'simply done something' that demands punishment. This is so even though the same citizens would be utterly shocked to hear that they are to be sacked 'for their own sake', or that their former friends avoid their company 'only in order to reform them'.

Still, fraudulent as it is, the principle of reform is undoubtedly more humane than the principle of deterrence. If punishment is a deterrent, human beings affected by it serve as mere means to a goal (the 'common weal'). If punishment aims at reform, one can at least think that people are treated as ends as well. However, one can only imagine this, because it is not in fact the case – at least, not if one interprets 'end-in-itself' in the way Kant did. Man as an end-in-itself is man as a rational being, the man of free volition. Punishment, as the means to reform, does not treat man as a rational being or a being of free volition. For Kant, the insight into duty makes volition free. And, as we have seen, this insight cannot be *caused* by punishment, so in the end the principle of reform treats men also as means, though more subtly than does the principle of deterrence.

To repeat, legal sanctions as well as moral sanctions can be *occasions* for reform if, and only if, the punished person is ashamed or tormented by pangs of conscience. With punishments other than legal ones, this is so if the punished person accepts the norms and rules as valid, and thus accepts punishment as right and just. Similarly, punishment by law can be the occasion for reform if the offender regards the law as just and the punishment as just punishment, and even these two conditions do not necessarily coincide. However, the people who do feel shame and pangs of conscience, who do recognize the law as just and who want to be punished, usually receive milder punishment, whereas those who do not recognize the justness of the law, or have any guilt feelings, are usually more severely punished. Notwithstanding the exceptions, the milder the punishment, the more it can become the occasion for reform, whereas, the more severe the punishment, the less it can be the occasion for reform. Reform, as the principle of punishment, is obviously false.

Nevertheless, and this is a very strong proviso, why are there so few 'criminals' who recognize the law, and so few who recognize their own punishment as just? Can we really throw all these 'rejectionists' into the wastebasket of the 'wicked mind' (where the term is used as in ordinary language and not as a legal expression)? Again, we arrive at a question unanswerable unless we break out of the circle drawn by the topic of 'retributive justice'. If we depart from society as it is, from the legal system as it is, it is natural to divide society into 'law-abiding citizens' and 'criminals', and to divide criminals into those with wicked and those without wicked minds. And we must conclude that the three principles (retribution, deterrence and reform) must be mixed, as crimes must entail retribution, but in a way that 'protects' 'healthy' society from offenders, and punishment should reform, if this is possible, although people with 'wicked minds' should be locked away. This is straightforward legal thinking, and matches the interests of the citizen, who wants to be protected from murderers, thieves, drug-pushers, rapists, corrupt officials, embezzlers, extortionists and child-molesters. This is my interest as well as yours. However, moral sense and the sense of justice do not find peace in the pursuit of this interest. The widespread acceptance of the fraudulent principle of reform evidences our ambivalence when confronted with the ambiguity of criminal justice.

I shall now sum up my basic statements about retributive justice.

(1) The only principle of punishment worthy of human beings is that of retribution. From the viewpoint of this principle man is always treated as an 'end-in-itself', and the individual is regarded as responsible for the deed, is seen as a free and rational agent. A person who offends norms (and violates the law) should expiate this offence by paying the debt due and thus restore justice. Once the debt is paid, the offence expiated, the person is no longer guilty. Retribution can also be self-punishment.

If punishment is administered via the principle of retribution, people are treated as free and rational beings, as the sole authors of their deeds. But are they?

(2) The deterrence principle views people as mere means, and I find this morally impermissible. This principle allows for punishment without offence (preventative action). The more moral an offence (i.e. the graver the moral transgression involved), the lower the deterrent value of the law. None the less, the practice of employing the law as a deterrent cannot be discarded today, because of the lack of civic morality in cases concerning the public weal.

(3) The principle of reform is morally ambiguous. Punishment is not and should not be the *cause* of reform. The more an individual internalizes norms and laws, the more that punishment can be an occasion for reform. But, the more that punishment can be the occasion for reform, the milder this punishment should be. And, usually, the harsher, the more severe the punishment, the less it is an occasion for reform. The principle of reform leaves us with the 'wastebasket' of the 'wicked mind'.

The 'wicked mind' can be neither reformed nor deterred, so deeds stemming from this mind must entail retribution. If we subscribe to the principles of deterrence and reform, we come to the *absurd* conclusion that only the 'wicked mind' is the mind of a free and rational agent. This is obviously a conclusion that no one would accept. Thus we have reason enough to accept the principle of retribution as the *only* rational and moral principle of punishment.

But we must now return to the initial question: are we indeed free and rational actors, are we really the sole authors of our deeds? For, if this is not so, retribution is *unjust*, and *there is absolutely no just method or principle of punishment*. If we are not free and rational authors of our deeds, 'retributive justice' is a chimera, and punishment a convenience to keep our bodies unharmed and our house clean.

In discussing the constitution designed by Phaleas, Aristotle, with his usual brevity, gave an account of the *causes* of theft, immediately widening the topic to explain the causes of crime in general. However, contrary to Durkheim, he immediately suggested remedies, for he believed that remedies existed. Crimes against property are committed in the first instance because of *poverty* (cold and hunger being the motives). The same crimes can be committed out of *greed*, or because some people simply *enjoy* pleasures which bring no pain.

Thus there are three different sets of persons to be considered and three different cures: for the first set (those who steal in order to live) a modest competence and employment; for the second, self-control (they must learn to curb their desires). As for the third, if they wish to find enjoyment not in coveting anything but in themselves, philosophy alone . . . will provide the answer; unlike the other two sets of people, they stand in no need of a third party.

And Aristotle adds that *major crimes* are not committed through lack of necessities: 'Who ever heard of a man making himself a tyrant in order to keep warm?'[22]

If we broaden the first and second cluster of causes and the motivations of moral offence, we can say, with Aristotle, that there are but three such causes: (1) strong and primary *social constraints*, such as dire poverty, ignorance (about what is good or bad), education in crime, social discrimination, and frustration through being an 'outcast'; (2) strong interests and passions of a morally negative bent, notably greed, lust for power, jealousy, and the like; and (3) the pleasure of committing a crime (the 'kick'). One may object to this that Aristotle unduly neglected the so-called 'psychological' causes. Obviously, he was not familiar with modern psychology. Indeed, even the third Aristotelian cluster does not stand simply for 'psychological constraints', for it also encompasses intellectual crime. Moreover, if only psychological constraints were to be blamed for the 'kick' in crime, philosophy could not have been suggested as the only effective remedy against such crime. However, even after a century-long tradition of the dissection of soul, I still give credit to Aristotle for his blessed neglect. If a crime can be explained solely by psychological constraints, it can no longer be attributed to a free and rational actor. If it is not explicable *solely* via such constraints, the crime can be *understood*, though never completely *explained*, by placing it in one of these three clusters.

The distinction here between understanding and explanation is of great importance, because we are dealing with justice. I have emphasized several times that all persons are *unique*, and cannot be ranked or compared as wholes. If we desire to know why X committed crime Y, why X, as a unique person, has committed exactly this crime, (under circumstances A, at time B, against person C, and the like), we shall always end up with an infinite number of interpretations, most of them constituting a complete explanation. Obviously, the psychological constitution of X, and his or her unique biography, will form the point of departure in all interpretations. To grasp the single case is a great theoretical challenge, and the need to meet this challenge is perfectly legitimate. Still, there are two very good reasons for not dwelling upon the explanation of uniqueness in the just assessment of the criminal act. First, both in making judgements and in meting out punishment we rank and compare. Yet we can only rank and compare those patterns of action open to ranking and comparing. Since uniqueness cannot be either ranked or compared, we forgo justice if we get stuck on the (potentially endless) matter of explaining uniqueness. The second reason is just as weighty. Explaining the unique actions of a unique character via psychological motivations means robbing the person being judged of the most precious quality possible: freedom.

Let us return to the three clusters. We can attribute *limited* responsibility to an actor only if the act can be understood in terms of the first cluster. But we should attribute full responsibility to the actor if the act is explicable in terms of the second and third cluster. If we attribute limited responsibility to the actors of the first cluster, we do not rob them of the most precious quality of freedom. We only apply a different *yardstick* for comparison and ranking. But are we entitled to do this? Can we do it without being unjust?

Before answering this question we need briefly to examine the second cluster. One could object to the restriction of the category 'social constraints' to the first cluster. Is greed not a social phenomenon? If wealth and extensive property did not offer access to luxury and power, who would commit crimes out of greed? So, if someone commits crimes for this reason, does not this person act under social constraints? The answer is in the negative. That everyone acts under given social conditions is a truism, and an irrelevant one when it comes to explaining a criminal act. The temptation to crime (and offence), and the norms, rules and laws in their capacity as obligations and safeguards against temptation all belong equally to the realm of 'social conditions'.

We judge as members of our community. Because we judge, we are also responsible for, our community. If certain social strata in our community live in dire poverty, if others are discriminated against or are social outcasts, if children have cruel parents and are abused before our eyes, then, if we let all or any of this pass, we are *jointly responsible* for the offences committed by people socialized under such constraints. For *we are the social constraints*, or, at least, we are *part of* those constraints. We have the right to judge because we assume that everyone is the free author of his or her deeds. However, we ourselves are the free authors of the *circumstances* which at another level are nothing but social constraints for those whom we judge. Consequently, we must judge ourselves as well. But, given that our condemnation is dual (condemnation of others and ourselves), we must lower the standard of judgement. Of course, this does not mean that we stop treating others as free authors of their actions. It means that we hold ourselves jointly responsible for those actions. In such cases, as private persons, we can withhold our right to judge.

However, if people belonging to the second cluster are to be judged, then we are to judge people like ourselves, people who act under exactly the same circumstances as we do, and who have committed an offence, a crime, that we have not committed at all. We are thus in no way responsible or jointly responsible for their actions. There are no mitigating circumstances to be attributed to 'social causes'. The offence is moral and the full responsibility lies with the offender. To have been a child of criminals and brought up in an atmosphere where crime is taken for granted; to be unemployed without the slightest hope of earning a living; to be born an outcast or a member of an outcast race – all these are real social constraints. But to be a child of divorced parents is *not* a social constraint; failing a high-school examination is *not* a social constraint; the discrepancy between high aspirations and limited opportunities is *not* a social constraint; bad luck in relationships with others is *not* a social constraint. Everyone has had a childhood, everyone has been subjected to frustration, everyone is constrained, in varying degrees, in their aspirations, everyone has bad luck: if all these circumstances were reckoned as 'social constraints' which would legitimize moral (and legal) offences, who could avoid being a scoundrel or a criminal?

Let me recapitulate the problem under discussion. Retribution is the only just principle of punishment. Retribution can be just if all deeds can be imputed to their authors as fully free human beings. If people are affected by social constraints, we still can, and should, attribute their actions to them. If we treat them as puppets moved by the strings of circumstances, we rob them of their most precious possession: moral freedom. And yet we should not impute their deeds to them *in full*. This is why we must lower the standards of judgement. If the social constraints are immense, we should even withhold judgement. Yet it is always X (a member of the community as a whole) who sits in judgement on Y (another member of the group, though affected by social constraints), whereas X, in the capacity of member of the community, is jointly responsible for the social constraints themselves, and so is also jointly responsible for the deeds of Y. It is exactly the difference between the standard applied to members of the second cluster and the lowered standard applied to members of the first cluster that indicates the *degree* of responsibility of the person sitting in judgement. But it almost never happens that a person sits in judgement to condemn those who are jointly responsible for the actions of the person under constraint – the 'accused', the 'defendant' – in proportion to *their* responsibility.[23]

But, if this is so, the principle of retribution is not a just principle of punishment, though it is the only *possible* just principle of punishment. And this is why the problem of 'retributive justice' cannot be solved within the sphere of justice called 'retributive justice'. As long as the first cluster exists, as long as people commit crimes (or moral offences) under social constraints, retribution cannot be just — at least, not fully. And only full justice is justice. Only in designing socio-political models that exclude social constraints can we recommend for the future the principle of retribution as the only fully just principle of punishment.

Let us turn now to the second cluster. The people constituting this group are fully responsible for their crimes and wrongdoings. Of course, their acts are limited, as well as induced by 'social and personal conditions'. But acts committed under particular conditions and acts committed under duress cannot be treated alike. Clearly, people are unique. One person has a stronger desire, another a weaker desire, to commit a prohibited act. It may be easier for X not to commit the prohibited act A than it is for Y. Good luck for X can be bad luck for Y, but this is irrelevant in respect of justice. If X strongly desires money, while Y does not, X may have the greater temptation to embezzle. But embezzlement is prohibited, and equally prohibited for everyone. In this respect moral norms are just like laws. If aggressiveness or lying is disapproved of, in our moral judgement we equalize those who would not harm a fly and those strongly inclined to be aggressive. *No one should* behave aggressively. So far as the validity (the binding character) of a norm is concerned, personal inclinations and the uniqueness of psychological disposition are left out of consideration. But moral norms, unlike the criminal code, also put a premium on merit. If an aggressive person develops the will to control this trait, credit will be given for it.

People living under the same law also live under the guidance of different moral norms. Ours is a pluralistic moral universe. This in itself is a good thing, and I shall discuss later why it is. Some moral life worlds have stricter norms, others more lax ones. This is not an issue in respect of the problem presently under scrutiny. But it is a problem that in certain social milieux all moral norms have disappeared, or moral worth is attached to the pursuit of personal interest. Social success by itself is considered the greatest of merits: those who achieve it are the good guys, those who don't are the bad guys. People raised by the norm of success will never be able to curb their desires, to restrain their impulses, to resign certain interests, and to do so for *moral reasons*. So now the problem can be stated in the following terms. If we judge two people for the same criminal act, for example embezzlement, and one has been socialized by moral norms which credit honesty and decency above all else, whereas the other was brought up in the belief that gaining wealth is the only path to merit, we still condemn both equally. This is a just judgement because no 'social constraints' appear which would pressure us to lower our standards of judgement in the latter case. But is this an *equitable* judgement? Is a person responsible for his or her upbringing? The principle of retribution demands the same degree of punishment for crimes of the same nature, as long as the criminal has not acted under duress. Accordingly, condemnation will be just but not *equitable*, and what is not equitable is not fully just. And, to repeat, only the fully just is just.

If this is so, the problem of 'retributive justice' cannot be satisfactorily solved within the branch of the theory of justice called 'retributive justice'. As long as such a 'moral vacuum' exists, as long as people are raised in social milieux where success is identified with merit, where human relations, acts and decisions are seen as means to achieve success, and where success is the final goal, retribution cannot be equitable, and thus cannot be just. Only if we design social models where in all these different social milieux a *righteous* way of life is advocated, where every person is given a particular idea of righteousness (all such ideas having at least one element in common) can we recommend the principle of retribution as the only fully just principle of punishment.

I have not addressed the third cluster identified by Aristotle: that where people sometimes commit crimes simply for pleasure. Here, crime (or any moral offence) is a 'goal-in-itself'. Dealing with this cluster requires caution. Sometimes the original (first) action of wrongdoing of a person belonging to this cluster is performed under social duress or because of greed, the thirst for power, or various passions, and the pleasure taken in crime is, strictly speaking, the outcome of the original act (like an appetite which grows with eating). A typical situation in war is where a soldier, initially reluctant to kill, becomes intoxicated with killing, and comes to find pleasure in doing so. The purely intellectual pleasure taken in crime is often nothing but the consequence of the degeneration of moral norms within a particular context. Crimes can then be regarded as a matter of virtuosity, as pure problem-solving, as an intellectual game. If the third cluster exists at all, and is not simply a derivative of the first two, it must be minute and socially insignificant. Yet, if we do assume the existence of this cluster, the principle of retributive justice can and must be applied as the principle of punishment in every matter pertaining to it. The application of this principle is always just, and fully just, irrespective of any and all social and psychological factors.

It is a reasonable guess that most criminal offences are now committed under social constraints. It is also a reasonable guess that the gravest crimes are either committed, or at least planned by, people motivated by greed, the thirst for power, or strong and unruly passions, and by those, few in number, who commit crime for pleasure.

To avoid any misunderstanding, I repeat that so far I have discussed only an *abstract* model. I have presumed that the laws (and first of all the criminal law) enjoy legitimacy and are regarded by the majority as just. It is obvious that in a period of dynamic justice the situation is complex. Certain laws are constantly criticized and rejected as unjust, even if the legal system is considered just. None the less, this abstract model makes sense, for, as long as a law remains in force, to breach it is prohibited, even if we regard it as unjust.

Everywhere there are unjust laws; that is to say, everywhere there are laws *regarded as unjust*. If people have the right to query and test the justness of a law in public, and if a change in the sense of justice can make this law change, then laws should normally be obeyed for as long as they exist. They should be obeyed, first and foremost, by the judiciary, by state officials, administrators, and everyone in a position of power. I completely agree with Dworkin[24] (as against legal positivism) that the administration of legal justice is not tantamount to applying rules, and that, at least in the 'hard cases', the judge must have recourse to general or universal *principles* to arrive at a correct decision, even if the relevant laws are considered just. But what if the entire legal system is unjust? Should the judiciary then apply the rules at all? Or should they resort to *principles*, and in the first instance to moral principles, in every case involving judgement? This is the matter Hart addresses in his discussion of the Radbruch case. Radbruch, once a legal positivist, in drawing the lessons of Nazism and its 'legal system', concluded that 'every lawyer and judge should denounce statutes that transgressed the fundamental principles not as merely immoral or wrong but as having no legal character'.[25] In a brilliant paper on the Jewish question in Hungary, touching upon the last chapter 'The Holocaust', Istvan Bibo, the Hungarian political theorist, concluded precisely the same thing. Bibo argued that the laws of a genocidal regime are null and void, and outrightly blamed Hungarian officials for their reluctance to forge papers for the persecuted because of an ill-conceived sense of legality.[26] Our sense of justice suggests that both Radbruch and Bibo were right. But why is this so?

To answer this, the following questions must be answered:

1   Can *single unjust* laws make the *whole* legal system *unjust*, irrespective of the justice or injustice of all other laws?

2 Can *single evil* laws make the *whole* legal system *evil*, irrespective of the justice or injustice of all other laws?
3 Can the administration of justice be a criminal act?
4 Can obedience to the law be morally evil? (Can disobedience to the law be morally good?)

My statement above, 'Everywhere there are unjust laws', must thus be complemented by the statement, 'Everywhere there are certain just laws.' Even an unjust or evil legal system contains just laws. A further qualification is that, since I am dealing with the *present*, I am working in terms of dynamic justice.

As to question (1), the statement 'This law is unjust' is a statement of devalidation. We claim that the law is *wrong*, where 'wrong' does not mean 'incorrect', for one aspect of the law is believed to include evil. If people have the *right* to state *publicly* that such and such a law is unjust, and to argue for devalidation, and if it is so that, if this devalidating statement were generally accepted, or accepted by most of the population, the outcome would be that the law in question would be replaced, then, if the law in question really is unjust, its injustice will not make the entire legal system unjust. And this is so for the following reason. If people believed that the entire legal system was unjust, they would *publicly declare* it unjust, seeing they have the right to do so. If, however, they stated that law A was unjust, but did not simultaneously devalidate law B and law C, then clearly they would consider B and C just.

But what happens if people devalidate a law as unjust but *do not have the right* to claim this in public? Here the devalidating statement itself is *outlawed*. And this means the outlawing of *dynamic justice*. It then follows that to outlaw dynamic justice means to outlaw the claim to justice, to outlaw just procedure, thus to outlaw justice itself. Where justice is outlawed, the legal system cannot be just. Laws do indeed include an evil element, illustrated by the fact that people (a minority or majority) believe that a certain law involves evil (in part or wholly), and, if they suffer via the same law if they speak their minds, the law indeed includes an element of evil. Consequently, the very law that makes the criticism of any law punishable makes the entire legal system unjust, but not necessarily *evil* or *criminal* (where the exact meaning of 'criminal' will be defined in what follows). If the entire legal system is unjust but not criminal, all the laws are still valid with the exception of the one outlawing the criticism of laws, and the administrators of justice are not criminals simply because they follow the stipulations of the existing laws. To suggest to officials and legal administrators that they should forge papers and documents because the criticism of the law is outlawed would be ridiculous. However, the judges who try to sentence those criticizing the laws, who mete out (sometimes heavy) punishments to these people, are *morally and personally responsible for the injustice of the legal system*, even though it is obvious that they do not take the brunt of the blame. Political rulers, the genuine fountainheads of an unjust legal system, are fully responsible for the injustice of the law.

If criticism of the law is outlawed, there exists no just procedure for changing the laws considered unjust. Normally, people resort to violence to change such a system. Though violence is always illegal, it can be based on moral right, if, for example, the original violence is incumbent in a law authorized by a dictator. To outlaw just procedure is an act of pure violence. Retribution against free speech is retribution against a rational and moral claim.

Most of the presently existing legal systems are unjust. In an unjust legal system all laws are considered arbitrary. No wonder then that in such a system 'legal thinking' is not well developed, either in the minds of the legal authorities or in the populace. Where free speech and criticism are outlawed, political considerations always overrule legalistic ones. Where there is moral merit in defying the law in one particular matter, moral indifference develops in other matters. In East European societies, 'stealing from the state' (for example, from state-owned factories) is usually seen as a good joke, though the average person still regards stealing from another person as downright theft.

Concerning question (2), legal systems are *evil* if they contain even one evil law or statute. A law or statute is evil if it *declares war on a group of citizens* of the state without *real* provocation. Declaring such a war means attempting to *exterminate* the members of this group. This extermination can range from 'extermination as citizens' to 'extermination as living beings'; from enslavement to deportation to genocide. The last was the logical outcome of evil laws as they appeared in Nazi Germany, in Russia under Stalin, in Cambodia under Pol Pot, these embodiments of states with a criminal legal system.

Since we live under modernity, since life and freedom have become universal values, since we can judge as repositories of humankind, we can prove our case by having recourse to the supreme values – we can juxtapose the 'inalienable' laws of nature as moral laws to the legal system of the regimes under scrutiny. We can do this, though we *need not* do this, in order to prove our case.

It is not necessary to resort to natural law to regard the

unprovoked enslavement of the *citizens* of a state by *their own* state as a criminal act. *This has always been regarded as a criminal act.* The qualification 'without provocation' means that no connection whatsoever exists between the act (or forbearance) of a person and the legal sanction. The sanction is levelled at the person as a member of a group independently of any act committed. This is the 'absolute tyranny' I referred to in chapter 1. And the contention that absolute tyranny is *evil par excellence* within the state is as ancient as social philosophy itself. In absolute tyranny the law is nothing but the expression of the tyrant's will, and, even if this will dons the guise or adopts the shape of the law, *it is not law.*[27] In fact it contradicts the spirit of all laws. In the passage partly quoted above, Aristotle remarked that the tyrant is the greatest criminal. If this is so then the law expressing the will of the tyrant is also criminal. And it has always been regarded so.

But if the law is criminal, the administrators of justice are the administrators of injustice – moreover, the administrators of evil. The sense of justice demands that the legal system of the absolute tyrant *should be disobeyed.* Morality and legality are not in contradiction here (as sometimes happens when the legal system is unjust but not evil), for in the criminal legal system there is no law, only the semblance of law.

It is now possible to answer questions (3) and (4). Can the administration of justice be a criminal act? Can obedience to the law be morally evil? If the legal system is a system of evil, a state of absolute tyranny, the administration of justice is a criminal act. Obedience to the law *can* be morally evil, but is *definitely* evil if obedience encompasses actions where evil is administered in the name of justice. If the legal system is completely unjust, but not criminal, the judging of political dissidents is an act of injustice (it *can* be a criminal act, but is not necessarily so). Obedience to the laws is not in itself morally evil. But any authorization of unjust laws, any participation in legislating injustice, is morally evil.

Happy are those who can take legal positivists seriously; who have confidence in the justice of their judges; who believe that laws are important; who can publicly state that some of the laws they live under are unjust. There are very few such people.

I have briefly discussed my design for a utopia. But even the *reality* to which this utopia has been contrasted is a utopia for most of the denizens of our world. The state of arbitrariness, the state of lawlessness, the state of injustice, the state of evil – these are the overwhelming realities all theories of justice must cope with.

DISTRIBUTIVE JUSTICE

Doing justice or injustice involves distribution. In judging others and ourselves we distribute blame and praise, approval and disapproval. Retribution, in proportion to the offence, is also distribution of punishment. Certain honours should be distributed equally among members of the same social cluster, and unequally between people of differing clusters. Yet 'distributive justice', as a separate branch of the socio-political concept of justice, does not address the distributive aspects of all types of justice. Rather, just (or unjust) distribution refers to the just (or unjust) distribution of *material resources and goods*. At first, 'distributive justice' was concerned with distributing *property*. Since the emergence of the welfare state, the distribution of general income (salaries and wages included) has been the focus of attention.

The distribution of material goods had always been of concern in images and theories of justice, but, even when the issue was given the highest importance, it was subjected to and understood within a general theory of justice, and addressed within the framework of a complete socio-political concept of justice. As we have seen, in the prophetic concept of justice the misery of the poor called for divine retribution, since alleviating misery was believed to be a matter not of optional charity but of *moral duty*. To neglect this duty was to sin, to breach the divine laws. Plato proposed the abolition of private property for the caste of guardians in order to make the Republic *as a whole* just. Aristotle, who coined the term 'distributive justice', recommended a *relative* equality of wealth – neither too much nor too little, but 'medium wealth' – as a condition of the *good life* of the good citizen and the good city. Even Rousseau, the most egalitarian philosopher in respect of distribution, subjected the solution of this problem to the general patterns of an ethico-political concept of justice.

Locke did not completely break with this longstanding tradition either. As we have seen, he contributed to the emergence of the concept 'retributive justice' rather than 'distributive justice'. However, he had already presented a sophisticated theory legitimizing inequality in property ownership, a theory deriving property from work. I have mentioned that Locke did not support the idea 'to each according to his entitlement', for he put 'entitlement' into the 'to each' category, whereas the 'according to' category was defined by 'work' (mixing work and nature). But Locke never claimed that entitlement was the *main* issue, let alone the only issue of justice.

Hume is undoubtedly the founding father of that branch of socio-political justice now called 'distributive'. He even claimed that property and *property alone* is the subject matter of justice. He asserted too that *retribution* (negative sanctions) is the *suspension* of justice for the sake of social utility: 'When any man, even in political society, renders himself by his crimes, obnoxious to the public, he is punished by the laws in his goods and person; that is, the ordinary rules of justice are, with regard to him, suspended for a moment. . . .'[28]

Hume also deduced justice from 'public utility'. Inequality in property ownership is just because it is useful. We can imagine two cases – and extreme cases – where property (inequality in property ownership) *qua* justice loses its social usefulness: the situation of *absolute abundance* and the situation of *absolute scarcity*. In the former, property is useless, redundant because, if all needs can be satisfied, we are beyond justice. In the latter situation property rules are violable, thus justice must be suspended. Yet we live in a situation of limited abundance (or limited scarcity). This is why property *qua* justice is useful. Thus in Hume the concept 'justice' reduces to the idea 'to each according to his property entitlement'; all other uses of the notion 'justice' are seen as relating to the 'suspension of justice' (although the term 'equity' can remain relevant in these other contexts).

Hume, an extremely sincere man, did not shirk from facing proposals alien to his own. He stated,

nature is so liberal to mankind, that, were all her presents equally divided among the species, and improved by art and industry, every individual would enjoy all the necessaries, and even most of the comforts of life. . . . It must also be confessed, that, wherever we depart from this equality, we rob the poor of more satisfaction than we add to the rich. . . .[29]

None the less, he then continues,

Render possessions ever so equal, men's different degrees of art, care and industry will immediately break that equality. . . . The most rigorous inquisition too is requisite to watch every inequality on its first appearance; and the most severe jurisdiction, to punish and redress it. But besides, that so much authority must soon degenerate into tyranny, and be exerted with great partialities; who can possibly be possessed of it, in such a situation as is here supposed?[30]

The same problem still haunts contemporary theorists of distributive justice, though answers have become diversified. Attempts are made to reconcile the value 'equality in freedom' with the value 'equality of life chances', especially by leading theorists of American liberalism, whereas an orthodox Humean view, though with certain modifications, persists amongst British liberals and American conservatives. In what follows I shall not focus my criticisms on any particular theory of 'distributive justice', but rather on certain crucial issues addressed by most of them.[31] Further, I do not offer either a historical or a patterned model of just distribution. Indeed, this is far from my intention, for I wish to make it clear that the questions raised under the heading 'distributive justice' should be handled within models of an ethico-political concept of justice.

The liberal models rest on the following assumptions. Persons are *atoms*. They all pursue their interests. They are endowed with a greater or lesser degree of talent. Some of these talents are won in the 'natural lottery'; others *could* be considered as meritorious. The more talent one has, the greater the chances of high income, success and the like. This is unfair. The state must perform the task of redistribution, preferably with the consent of all. The state must 'confiscate' income (as progressive taxation) from the most talented and redistribute it to the least talented. The theories differ in their arguments for redistribution. They also differ on whether they still consider property relations, or only inequality of incomes (goods and services included), as the problem. Furthermore, they differ as to whether certain *moral* norms are considered decisive in achieving the consent in question. Finally, they differ in whether they aim at equality in satisfaction or equality in resources. But, whatever the differences, and regardless of how important they might be for the theoretical argument, in practice we are always confronted with a *triad*. This consists of (1) the individual (the atom) endowed with interests and a certain degree of talent as the *competitor* and the *receiver*; (2) the state as the *redistributor*; and (3) money (in the form of income, welfare spending and the like) that is *redistributed* by the state and *received* by the less fortunate individual atoms.

Justice means that the norms and rules constituting a social cluster are applied to every member of the cluster consistently and continuously. If the *idea* of distribution is 'to each the same thing(s)', then equal distribution applies. Equal distribution within an entire social body is the case if the cluster to which the norms and rules of 'to each the same thing(s)' apply includes the entire populace of the society in question. Justice will then mean the distribution of exactly the same things, and the same amount of things, to each and every member of society consistently and continuously.

This is a model no liberal would accept, and with good reason.

First, it is impossible to attain the consent of all concerned regarding the implementation of this model. Not only would the wealthy reject it, but, I suspect, even the poorest would do so, or at least a majority of them would. Secondly, complete distributive equality is strikingly *unequal*. It is based on the assumption that the needs and need structures of all persons are alike. This assumption is false (a matter to which I shall return). Thus, if the model of complete equality were implemented, the needs of some people would be satisfied in full, those of others only in part, those of yet others not at all. The outcome of rigorous egalitarianism is inequality.

And, indeed, when liberal theorists formulate the claim to *equal* distribution they are in fact supporting a specific type of *unequal* distribution. Upon what criteria inequality should be based, *what kind of inequality* should be achieved, *how far inequality can go, what is the just limit to inequality* – these are the questions they address. (An example from Rawls's theory is that the most disadvantaged groups should benefit from the inequality of incomes.) They argue not for equality of income but equality of *life chances*. With this I agree. However, they believe that equality in life chances depends first, or even solely, on income. Here I disagree. Of course, if the triad (the individual atom as competitor and recipient; the government as redistributor; the money to be redistributed) is the *sole* model of distributive justice, then, as far as the power of social regulation goes, life chances do indeed depend on the amount of money (in the form of cash income and services provided by the state), because the satisfaction of non-monetarized and non-monetarizable needs cannot be catered for by *any* social regulation. Since the way of life (a single way of life as a generalized model) is taken for granted, theories of distributive justice must address the problem of just distribution adequate to this form of life. They can only differ in their recommendation of different kinds and forms of, and different limits to, inequality, and they see recommendations as the only road to *the* just distribution. Nozick has detected the fallacy implicit in such proposals. This is why I agree with his *criticism*, if not with his proposals.

Once the triad model is accepted and equality of life chances is taken as the major value, or one of the two major values, on which distributive justice rests, we can still choose between two (secondary) principles in our argument. As Dworkin stated, we can depart from the principle of 'equality in satisfaction' or from the principle of 'equality in resources'.

Equal satisfaction means one of two things. We can either say that the *same* needs should be equally satisfied for all, or say that the needs of all (whatever they are) should be *equally* (to the same extent) satisfied. Equality in satisfaction is not tantamount to the Marxian idea of 'to each according to his needs', for the latter means satisfying *all* needs, whereas the former does not (although it *can* raise this claim).

By the first interpretation (the same needs should be equally satisfied for all), we can mean the same *concrete* (single) needs or the same *cluster* of needs.

We can define the *sameness* of needs on the ground of objective criteria or of social value preferences. We can also accept a person's claim that his or her needs are 'the same' as someone else's.

The same needs can be held to be satisfied with the same amount of satisfiers, and also with a different amount of satisfiers: with one particular or another particular satisfier.

Finally, we can attribute the *same* needs to social clusters as well as to individuals.

It is impossible to conceive of any model of distribution covering all these interpretations, as well as all aspects of the programme stipulating that the *same* needs should be equally satisfied for all.

I shall take the simplest of cases. In a concentration camp a group of ten people (men, women and children) have two loaves of bread and one packet of cigarettes. Among them are three smokers. All ten are hungry. We can assume that all have the *same* need for bread, but not for cigarettes. What can they do? They can distribute the bread equally among all ten, and the cigarettes equally among the smokers. This means presupposing that their needs are not the same; that the smokers have an additional need compared with the others. Consequently, this form of distribution is unequal, for the smokers obtain a disproportionate share of the common store. There is also another method of distribution. One could distribute the cigarettes equally amongst all ten people in the awareness that either the cigarettes will not satisfy any need at all, or that the smokers will exchange some of their bread for cigarettes. In the latter case the *same* need for bread will *not* be equally satisfied. And what would happen in the former case? The non-smokers will suggest offering the cigarettes to the smokers, and so will opt for unequal distribution. Granted this, there could be yet greater complications with this simple model. There may be sick people present. These people have the same need for bread as the healthy, but also require the opportunity (in the form of goods such as medicaments) to restore their health. There may be people present who perform particularly exhausting work. They too have the same need for bread as the others, but in addition they need something extra to maintain their strength. There may exist *fixed values* shared by all the group, that the survival of children must take precedence over the survival of adults, for example. All these possibilities affect, and in fact make outright impossible, the equal satisfaction of the same needs, even in this relatively uncomplicated situation.

For these reasons, even if so-called basic needs are taken for granted and assumed to be the same for everyone (that is to say, the quality of the need is not socially evaluated), even if the quantity of the need is initially equalized (the assumption that everyone is equally hungry), the postulate that the *same* needs should be satisfied for each can trigger *entirely different*, and equally *unequal*, patterns of distribution. This is so because needs normally appear in *clusters* (people never have single and isolated needs), and because social value preferences are attached to need satisfactions even if one abstracts from the evaluative character of the needs themselves.

The more complex the model, the deeper we are in trouble.

The satisfaction of higher education is denied people if they fail their exams. They may claim to have exactly the *same* need for higher learning as those who pass. We can contest this, referring to lack of diligence or ability, but it is better to recognize this need whilst admitting that we cannot now satisfy it. We have of course the option of satisfying the same need for all by abolishing exams. However, providing everyone with the opportunity *for* higher education does not guarantee satisfaction *in* higher education. Means to satisfaction do not guarantee actual satisfaction. There are ineliminable idiosyncratic elements in need satisfaction. If two people claim to have the *same* need, the same object might satisfy the need of one but not of the other.

The proposal 'The same needs should be satisfied for all' only makes sense if (a) we impute certain kinds of needs at all, (b) we define the quantity and quality of satisfiers to meet those needs.

Both the imputing of needs and the definition of the quantity and quality of satisfiers have a lower and an upper limit. The closer we approach the lower limit, the more the same needs imputed to all are truly the needs of every individual belonging to the 'all'. The closer we approach the upper limit, the less the same needs imputed to this 'all' will truly be the needs of every individual belonging to the 'all'. If we refer to a minimum calorie intake necessary for biological survival, we can assert without further ado that this need is a need of each and everyone within the 'all'. We can also define the quantity and quality of nourishment (the satisfiers) which meet this need. If, however, we refer to strongly evaluated, socially and culturally determined needs (cleanliness, education, housing or entertainment), we can be pretty sure that these needs are not the same for every person in the 'all'; that different quantities and qualities of satisfiers are required to meet the needs of every member of this 'all'. What then are the social options here?

The state (the ruling elite) can apply the method of *need imputation*, which is only relevant if we are close to the 'lower limit', to *all needs*. In so doing, the state (elite) will *define* arbitrarily the quality and quantity of the needs of all, *and* for every person within that 'all'. The state will also define the quality and quantity of satisfiers which meet the needs already arbitrarily determined. Whereupon the state can claim the satisfaction of the *same* needs for all. This model can be termed the 'dictatorship over needs'.[32] The 'ideal type' of dictatorship over needs is a centralized and complete determination of all needs, biological and sexual needs included (for example, propagation is centrally organized, the need for population growth – and in a related vein the need for offspring – quantified). Here the concentration camp serves as a model, where free decision and arbitration are relegated to the niches of life, the uncontrollable or not totally controlled loci of society. Societies of 'dictatorship over needs' can and do diverge from the ideal type, but can also completely personify it (for instance, Cambodia).

The second option is to impute the *same need* to all where at least a *large number* raise the *claim* to the *same* satisfiers. It can then be justly assumed that, if the same need-satisfier meets the need of many, it will meet the need of everyone, even if it is not assumed that the same satisfier will satisfy the needs of every person equally. The *same* needs are thus *not equally* satisfied. This is the case with all *services* provided. Hence, even if it is the *claim of many* (for the satisfaction of certain needs) that engenders methods and modes of satisfaction in the form of services, the provision of services in itself homogenizes different concrete needs and is thereby a *limited paternalistic need imputation*. It is limited because there is always a *limited amount* of national wealth invested in services. It is paternalistic because the *government* (or the expert) decides the matter. It is need imputation because the authorities that *determine* the 'real' *average* needs cater also for their satisfaction. The same needs cannot be *equally* satisfied (if needs are socially and culturally determined) unless *the needs themselves are defined* as the *same* from the perspective of the available satisfiers.

The third option is that of *complete monetarization*. Everyone *buys* the satisfiers. Whoever has more of the 'same' need will spend more on its satisfaction; whoever has lesser or less urgent needs will spend less on their satisfaction. Taxes can be distributed in cash form among lower income-earners to make the model work. This cannot be done in all cases, especially if the theory aims at just distribution.

These three options have been discussed in terms of the famous 'triad'. The first accompanies political dictatorship; the second and third accompany political democracy. Even if we now disregard the first and remain with the other two, we must face the disquieting fact that the same needs cannot be satisfied equally, and that the 'sameness' of needs is always imputed. In the democratic model, imputation is the outcome of a double-edged procedure. First, claims are accepted as needs; secondly, they are interpreted and 'averaged' from the standpoint of the available satisfiers. This is a paternalistic system of need imputation which cannot be eliminated (within the triad model).

Turning now to the other interpretation of 'equal satisfaction', we can claim that all human needs should be *equally satisfied*. Here it is no longer important whether they are the same needs or different ones, or whether or not their satisfaction is costly.

How can we *know* that all needs are equally satisfied? If everyone is equally free to voice dissatisfaction, and yet everyone claims to be completely satisfied, then all are indeed equally satisfied. All the same, the theory of 'equal satisfaction' does not stipulate that everyone must be *completely* satisfied, only that they must be equally (to the same extent) satisfied. And with good reason. *Complete* satisfaction is relative to the system of needs. Should everyone need only water and bread, everybody in the 'first world' would be completely satisfied. If we are completely satisfied, we need nothing else. Whether complete satisfaction is desirable or undesirable is a matter addressed in the next chapter. Yet one thing is beyond question. If all needs are completely satisfied, we have a situation of complete abundance, a world where, as Hume correctly observed, the notion of 'justice' makes no sense. If we insist on 'distributive justice', then 'equal' satisfaction cannot be 'complete satisfaction'. However, if equal satisfaction is not tantamount to complete satisfaction, how do we know that people are equally satisfied? We may try to answer this by reversing the question: people are equally satisfied if they are equally dissatisfied. But, again, how can we measure the *amount* of dissatisfaction? Moreover, how can *any* social regulation achieve an equal amount of satisfaction or dissatisfaction? There is an ineliminable individual (subjective) aspect to the matter of satisfaction and dissatisfaction, even if we restrict ourselves to socially produced and scarce satisfiers. An obvious objection to this is that 'equal satisfaction' means equal satisfaction as far as *income* and *share in services* are concerned. But, even if we were all satisfied with our income and services (a question to which I shall return), we should still not be equally satisfied. For satisfaction with our income and services means equal satisfaction only if we are *completely* satisfied in all our needs.

Dworkin is probably right in rejecting the 'satisfaction' paradigm. His own paradigm, 'equality of resources', circumvents most of the problems we have encountered in discussing the theory of 'equal satisfaction', in both of its interpretations. The rendering of this paradigm is as follows. We all get (symbolically) the same bundle of resources. Because we are all aware of the risks involved in the gamble of life (including the risks of taking and not taking risks), because, moreover, we can be handicapped, and experience other misfortunes, we take out a life-insurance policy. If we are among the fortunates, we simply pay the premium to those who have failed; they on their part collect this premium. Dworkin does not assume, as some of his critics believe he does, that people *in fact* start their lives with an equal share of resources; in other words, the term 'initial' in the expression 'initial equal share of resources' represents not an empirical fact, but a *constitutive idea*. Since equal concern and respect are *due* to every community member (for everyone's life matters and matters equally), the authority of redistribution must establish and re-establish continuously such an equality of resources. Put simply, perhaps even simplistically, the equal 'start' upon the gamble of life is given everyone, throughout the entire life of every member of the community, by the authority of redistribution.

The theory has its highlights. It conceives of welfare not as a goal, but as a principle. Also, equal respect and concern are *due* to everyone irrespective of merit. Being a member of a social community means having the *right* to such equal respect and concern. Next, as already mentioned, the insoluble problems of the paradigm of equal satisfaction are circumvented. However, the theory has great blemishes too. Although the 'initial' equality of resources does not represent the *de facto* equality of life's commencement, the *de facto inequality* of this beginning casts a deep shadow on the theory. There are real inequalities in the start to life which no redistribution can overcome. Since Dworkin's recommendation is endowment-insensitive but ambition-sensitive, I do not mention endowments. However, the opportunity for gambling and taking risks is also unequally divided from the outset. There is a significant difference between starting to gamble by leaving the parental hearth or by reinvesting your parents' legacy as capital. Besides, an important group of satisfiers cannot be redistributed. This is the group encompassing such things as prestige, honour and power, results of the gamble on which no insurance policy can be taken out.

I shall not present any alternative 'patterned' model of distributive justice because I believe that the justice or injustice of distribution cannot be defined *in abstracto*, but can be defined only as an element of a particular way of life. In addition, I see no reason why the way of life illustrated in the 'triad' model must be taken for granted. Nevertheless, I still want to discuss certain problems addressed by liberal welfare theories by having recourse to the supreme values of freedom and life. As I have forgone the presentation of any alternative 'just' model, I cannot claim that the models of justice based on the 'triad' pattern are unjust.[33] Moreover, I assume this statement to be untrue. If the 'triad' pattern is taken for granted, and if distribution is regarded as the sole *variable* factor within this pattern, there must be models of more just (or almost perfectly just) distribution fitting this pattern. Rawls, Dworkin and others have produced just such models. They have undoubtedly made a case for a more just (or almost just) distribution in terms of the 'triad' pattern. In what follows I address *problems* which have emerged in discussions about just distribution without being critical of any current opinion in particular.

For the moment I am not concerned about the *sources* of inequality or equality (property, income, welfare spending, and so on). By distributive equality I mean that every member of a society (nation, community) receives an equal *share* of the disposable wealth created by this society. By distributive inequality I mean that, according to certain (as yet unspecified) yardsticks, some people get a larger share than others. My aim is to determine whether the realization of the universal value of 'equality in life chances' presupposes distributive equality or some form of distributive inequality.

Unequal distribution can be proposed on the grounds that certain types of work are more important than others, more useful than others. This argument fails. Given any particular form of social division of labour, all kinds of work contribute *equally* to the reproduction of society. From this point of view, the doctor's work is not 'more important' than the plumber's, the prime minister's work is not 'more important' than the farmer's, for all are equally necessary to social reproduction. Within leftist discourse, the converse should rather be argued: that the doctor's (or lawyer's) work is as important as the farmer's. The fact that certain types of work bring far better remuneration than others has absolutely nothing to do with the intrinsic 'usefulness' of different kinds of work. The evaluative basis of income differentiation is intrinsic to the actual structure of domination, and the distinction between less useful and more useful is enhanced by the latter.

Even if this conclusion is accepted, it could still be added that not everyone performs the *same* work equally well. Those performing the same task better (in respect of either quality or quantity) deserve higher remuneration (a larger share of the created wealth). They contribute more to that wealth, and so should receive more. But there is no common yardstick for measuring the greater or lesser importance (or usefulness) of similar accomplishments. Yardsticks vary according to ways of life, and, even within the same way of life, different yardsticks are applicable to different kinds of accomplishment as well as to similar kinds of accomplishment. Finally, even if a certain person's contribution to the social wealth might be greater than that of others, it is far from being self-evident why the recognition of this greater contribution should take the form of remuneration through a greater amount of wealth (material goods, income, and the like). Praise, approval and moral reward can be substituted for monetary or material remuneration. Even today, certain achievements are recognized in this way (citations, awards unaccompanied by prize money, and so forth). This is how adolescent peer groups normally recognize a special achievement. Justice is not curtailed if the reward for a 'greater contribution' to social wealth is confined to respect.

Still, there are arguments to the contrary, and arguments neither more or less convincing than those above. The main one goes as follows. In contemporary (Western) society, the more talented you are the greater will be your income. This is unjust. Our talents are not merits (they are not 'deserved'), but are gained in the 'natural lottery'. We are simply born with greater and lesser, with more subtle and less subtle talents. If something is not to our moral merit it should not be rewarded by greater income. A modified version of this suggestion is that talents themselves consist of two facets: one facet covers the genetic lottery (endowments), and should not involve remuneration; the other facet deals with merit. Different people use similar endowments in different ways. Ambition (a shorthand formulation of 'doing something with our endowments') must then be rewarded with higher income.

To my mind the initial thesis of this argument is utterly false. It is by no means true that in contemporary societies, even in the best of them, income depends on the quality and quantity of talents in general, be they 'endowments' or 'ambitions'. But, since Rawls and his followers do not comment on the empirical state of affairs in the modern democratic welfare state, but rather comment on its idealized and perfected mirror image, I shall not support my arguments with empirical facts either. Therefore I assume, as an initial thesis of my argument, a *real* (and not just imaginary) equal opportunity for all. I thus assume that everyone has an equal opportunity to develop certain endowments won in the 'natural lottery', to become a highly paid movie star, politician, fashion-designer, manager, businessman or businesswoman, academic, pilot, tennis-player, writer or general – whatever the person concerned deems fit. Can we seriously believe that people, even in such imaginary circumstances, are paid according to their general *talents*?

It is a commonplace wisdom that every person is born with innumerable endowments. Which of these become 'talents' depends as much on the 'social lottery' as on the 'genetic' one. We are thrown into a particular world by accident, and we become what we are in coping with both the 'social' and the 'genetic' *a prioris* of our existence. Hannah Arendt drew well enough in the 'genetic lottery', but had she lived 500 years earlier the same draw would not have been enough for a Jewess, regardless of her level of endowment. Many of us realize that we were born with a number of endowments which might have developed into 'talents' but did not, either because of our bad luck in the 'social lottery' or because we transformed one particular endowment into talent while leaving the others dormant. There is no *single* way of life, and there never can be, providing a social *a priori* favourable to the development of *all endowments* into talents. The greater the variety of social *a prioris* (ways of life) in the world we are thrown into by accident, the greater the possibility of developing all endowments into talents. Even so, not everyone will develop all his or her endowments into talents – for the development of one may still impede the development of others; at best, each person will have the *chance* to develop any particular endowment. '*Equal opportunity*', even if real, does not provide us with *equality in life chances* if we must find our way in a single particular social *a priori*.

It is true that people can now convert a greater variety of endowments into talents than ever before (if equal opportunity is indeed the case). The pursuit of no excellence is beneath human dignity. Yet it is equally true that, since certain talents are better paid, or bring more power or fame, people will develop exactly those endowments which, upon becoming talents, will elevate them to a position of greater wealth, power and fame. It is not written in the stars that, had they developed other endowments, they would not have had different (or greater) talents. If we have the 'triad' model in mind, we may rest assured that, whatever *particular* talents people unfold, they must *simultaneously* unfold either the talent to *make money* or the talent to *manoeuvre* well within the framework of rationalized institutions, or eventually even both. Those not born with endowments convertible into these two talents will on average score far lower than those who are, irrespective of the quality and quantity of talents they develop in their profession. Exceptional individual achievements could, if they met social needs, result in great income, fame and perhaps eventually power. However, on the average it is not excellence in the particular profession but the two talents I have referred to (the talent to make money and the talent to manoeuvre well under institutional constraints) that will bring the higher yield. Those who write books on talents must not forget that income, power and fame within the academic institutions, for example, hardly depends on professional excellence. To be a good power-broker, to understand how to flatter whom and when, to quote copiously from the works of people in positions of power, to be good, first and foremost, at 'powerspeak', as well as at playing the *social* role of the 'efficient academic', is what really matters. I would not deny that proficiency at 'powerspeak' is a *talent*, but it is not the *same* talent as required in philosophy, physics, literary criticism or biology. Regardless of however talented somebody is in other respects, the talents for money-making and 'manoeuvring' are important in achieving success. Thus some people develop these two 'endowments' *malgré eux-mêmes*. To improve their life chances of income and power, they limit their life chances in the development of endowments closer to their heart. 'Ambition' cuts two ways. One can draw a losing number in this particular lottery not because one has too little ambition, but because one has too much.

Rawls's suggestion (the 'difference principle') does not envisage change in this respect. Let us assume that the income differentiation betters the lot of the 'worst-off'. I shall momentarily disregard the fact that the term 'worst-off' is itself subject to evaluation (for example, one could say that the worst off are those not loved by anyone) and will continue to make my analysis via the 'triad' model. In this model the 'worst off' are those with the lowest incomes, people also assumed (though to my mind without foundation) to have the fewest (or weakest) endowments. Mandeville was cynical enough to state that every public vice, every inequality, the pursuit of all forms of luxury, power and fame improve *de facto* the lot of the worst-off. If he was right (and if we take a long-term perspective on capitalist development in the West, he did prove right), the Rawlsian viewpoint may accept things as they are. Yet Rawls not only had the interests of the worst-off in mind, but also a highly evaluative conception of what 'improvement' should mean in the context of a radical welfare state. But it is very difficult, if possible at all, to decide which *activities* contribute to helping the worst-off in a qualified sense. (For example, do successful novelists help these people or not? If perhaps they do, do they deserve a higher income?) And who *decides* this is yet a different matter. However, if the differentiation of *incomes* is the differentiation of rewards, and if higher incomes are due to those who improve the lot of the worst-off, then people will seek to develop into talents those endowments which will help the worst-off because they wish to earn more money. What is wrong with such a brand-new utilitarianism? Obviously, the decrease in the equality of life chances. And this decrease will occur not because the practising of certain talents will incur lower payment (if they do not improve the lot of the worst-off), but for another reason. If monetary reward is *the* reward proper, if 'better-off' and 'worst-off' are gauged by income, and by that alone, most endowments will not be developed into talents at all, or at least such developments will not be encouraged by the social *a priori*. However one modifies the 'triad' model, a state of equal life chances for all is unattainable. We should not even get closer to the realization of this ideal.

I shall now address the problem of 'talents' from another angle. If endowments are won in the 'genetic lottery', there is no moral merit in possessing talent. *Therefore* payment should not increase for excelling in something. This is an odd argument to say the least, for it implies the following: *if* talents were morally meritorious, *then* it would be just and fair to be paid more for the possession of such talents; thus we should be paid better for our *moral* merits, and for them alone. The point is that, if we were paid better according to our moral merits, we should have no *moral* merits at all. We ought to observe moral norms irrespective of social sanctions (rewards or punishment). We can say that respect should be given to moral merit even if one does not act morally *in order* to receive such respect, or *not solely* for this reason. The substitution of pecuniary rewards for due respect is very telling. It suggests that the supreme material good is money (happiness is money), and thus, if the moral person deserves happiness, by definition he deserves more money. This is definitely *not* the conclusion drawn by Rawls. Yet, if we suggest that talents are not morally meritorious and *therefore* should not be rewarded by higher income, the conclusion is implicit in the initial statement. I see no reason why any society should block the allocation of a greater amount of social wealth for the development of *undeserved* human abilities. People would probably say 'this practice is unjust!' But why? What is just or unjust depends on the social norms and rules recognized as just or unjust. If we accepted as a social rule the idea that, if the development of certain endowments requires greater social spending (in any form), society should consistently and continuously dispense 'surplus goods' in every relevant case, then it would be just to do so, without even considering whether the endowments are also merits. Moreover, if any community deems by consensus that it is just to spend more on developing the endowments of one single individual than on developing the endowments of many people, this is again a just act, irrespective of 'merits'. In fact this is beyond mere conjecture: both in 'primitive' tribes, where for example, chiefs are 'remunerated' according to their social functions and not merits, and in kibbutzim, where people are often 'unequally' treated in that certain people, because of their endowments, are sent to receive higher education at a greater expense than others, and *this* practice is regarded as justice, the procedure suggested above is clearly accepted.

Certain critics of Rawls have pointed out that the practice of developing endowments into talents is indeed morally commendable, or involves such merit. As I have already rejected the theoretical proposal that non-meritorious endowments have no just claim to greater social spending, this counter-argument is not of primary importance for me in the present discussion. But it must be said that developing endowments into talents can involve both *moral merit* and *moral demerit*. Whether one or the other of these is predominant depends on many factors (which talent is developed, in what way, at what cost, and the like). Will-power, diligence, sacrifice, courage, enthusiasm are qualities and acts of merit. But turning endowment into talent can also imply the use of people as mere means; cruelty, insensitivity to suffering, selfishness – these are acts of demerit. Rarely, if at all, does it happen that the development of talent is exclusively invested with moral merit. Even the most talented of those who have achieved success have acted sometimes for the sake of this talent as against their moral conscience. And too many have trampled others underfoot in order that their talents should flourish. The story of Faust and Gretchen is a profound and typical metaphor. The point of balance can shift now towards credit, now towards demerit. In any event, the person in question is at least jointly responsible for the unfolding of his or her talent, though this is *not* tantamount to saying that excellence is a result of deserved moral merit. The former can be true even if the latter is false.

On the other hand, not only are our initial endowments concerning skills and talents undeserved; so are our initial moral endowments. If we assert that skills and excellence cannot be rewarded because their original source does not involve merit, we can equally say that virtues cannot be rewarded unless they 'repress' our natural endowments. If our virtues also facilitate the development of the endowments we have won in the 'genetic lottery', we cannot claim recognition for these virtues, because there is a gratuitous aspect to them. Moral virtuosity is also a kind of talent, though our respect for saints is not diminished by knowing this. I also mentioned earlier that not everyone is born with an equally good moral sense, even if everyone is born with good moral sense. However, whatever talents people either promote or leave barren, it is essential for everyone to promote his or her moral talents, even though not everyone can do it equally well or in the same way, even though it is easier for some and difficult for others. Aristotle knew clearly that not the *genesis* but the *norm or rule* makes all the difference between endowments in skill and moral endowments. The rule for developing skills is the rule of differentiation; everyone should do what she or he can do best; the norm for developing moral endowments is the norm of fusion via generalization; all types of endowments are absorbed in the resolution to observe general norms; all men should observe norms but come to do so in different ways, according to their own nature. Here we arrive at the final but crucial issue of 'distributive justice' as presented in contemporary discourse: at the distribution of *respect*. Is respect due to endowments won in the 'genetic lottery' or only to moral merit? Is respect due 'according to something' or is it due to everyone, and to everyone equally?

I recommend that here we distinguish between recognition and respect. Recognition is due to the person *qua* person – it is due to specific being, to ipseity. Respect is due to humankind (to humaneness) and thus to every person as a member of the human race. Recognition must be *equally* distributed both in our judgements and in our action. Recognition of all endowments means that we confer the right to cultivate endowments upon every person, and every person *equally*. Our recognition is not proportionate to merits. To what extent a certain endowment has been won in the 'genetic lottery', and to what extent it is the result of meritorious efforts, is irrelevant in relation to recognition. It is not only the government or any agency responsible for distribution or redistribution of goods and services that should grant equal recognition to each and every person; so should each and every individual. Dworkin is right: we cannot enjoin that every person should care equally for every other person. Yet we can enjoin that every person should recognize every other person. Respect is due to every person equally as a member and as a repository of the human race. Kant would say that it is to human practical reason that equal respect is due. However, equal respect is not due to the specific being (ipseity) of every individual person. People should be respected equally as members of the human race, and *in proportion* to their moral merit, although not in proportion to their excellence. If someone develops his or her talents in a wicked way, recognition is due to these talents, but disrespect to the ways in which they have been developed. We can simultaneously recognize needs in full and condemn the mode of their satisfaction, if people are used as mere means in need satisfaction. This follows from the injunction that humankind should be respected by every person. Whoever satisfies individual needs by withdrawing recognition from others as fellow human beings forgoes the right to be respected in his or her specific being, ipseity, although this person still deserves respect as a member of the human race. What is true about recognition and respect should be the guideline of self-recognition and self-respect. Every person has the right to self-recognition. It would contradict the norm of 'equal recognition of ipseity' if we required that people should recognize others *to a greater extent* than themselves. 'Altruism' cannot be postulated as a general attitude. The right to self-recognition is the right to develop one's endowments, to satisfy one's needs, to develop one's personality, and to claim legitimacy for this venture from all one's fellows. There simultaneously exists the legitimate claim to be respected by all others by virtue of being a member of the human race. Thus I should respect myself ('humankind in me') as much as I respect others. None the less, personal self-respect of ipseity should be proportionate to moral merit and demerit. Kant expressed this view with bathos: I must compare myself, he said, not to my fellow creatures but to the moral law, and respect myself according to the results of this comparison.

Obviously, the distinction between these two forms of respect is irrelevant at the governmental level or that of any central distributive or redistributive agency. At any rate, if we have only the 'triad' model in mind, not even recognition, which must be equally distributed, is distributed among individuals; rather, it is distributed among *typical* 'bundles' of endowments appearing as needs. The

Rawlsian 'worst-off' constitute a social cluster (the lowest income group), and every member of this cluster is equally recognized, not in his or her ipseity, but as a member of such a group. If any central agency undertakes to distribute proportional respect, the result is usually completely *contingent*, and the distinction between endowments and moral merits is rarely made (except for the saving of lives or self-sacrifice in war). In certain other models pertaining to the distribution of recognition and respect, for example in a community, equal recognition can indeed be due to individual persons, and the distinction between the two modes of distributing respect can be completely implemented. This is one proof amongst several that distribution is embedded in a particular way of life, and that a certain kind of distribution can therefore be perfectly just in one particular way of life and unjust in another. In the 'triad' model, doing justice to moral merit is simply a personal matter. And herein lies one of the gravest shortcomings of that model: the gulf between social recognition and personal respect.

Endowments and talents should be equally recognized. Endowments are won in the 'genetic lottery'. However, as argued, the transforming of endowments into talents and the practice of talents can be due to moral demerit as well as merit. Society puts a premium on certain kinds of talents as against others (in respect of monetary rewards, they are *not equally* recognized). Moreover, 'getting to the top' (in income, power, fame, or all of these) requires specific talents – among others, those of making money and of manoeuvring successfully. Being good at making money and 'manoeuvring' under various institutional constraints means being *more likely* (at least on average) to use other people as mere means. For this sort of competition is not like that between two poets writing on the same topic or two athletes competing at the Olympic Games. I am not concerned here with whether or not competition in general is a good or bad thing. An athlete who wins the race does not use others as mere means for this goal. Yet, should competition occur in the making of money or in 'manoeuvring' within institutional constraints (for example, factory management, a political party, an academy), it is very likely that in order to 'win' people will use others as mere means. It is equally likely that people who abstain from using others as mere means will never reach the top, however good their endowments or their talents in other fields. Only good luck or extraordinary achievement can outweigh this tendency.

The problem is not simply that moral merits are debited instead of credited as far as pecuniary reward, power and fame are concerned, but that large salaries, great power and widespread fame are social rewards, whereas no social rewards exist for human goodness. Social rewards do not mean to me *awards*, but proportional distribution of *respect* due to moral goodness. Indeed, morally good actions are performed irrespective of social sanctions, but respect is *due* in proportion to goodness, and where such respect is not granted there can still be goodness, but no justice. Proportionate respect can still be distributed on the private plane, but, if thinkers such as Dworkin can refer to 'ambition' as 'merit', it is no wonder that non-philosophers do likewise. If 'ambition' means 'merit', and not also potential demerit, the proportionate respect due to persons according to their moral goodness will be misplaced. Success will indicate moral merit. Social distribution of recognition will be unequal, despite all promises to the contrary, and the distribution of personal respect will, in the main, follow the patterns of unequal distribution in recognition.

All human endowments must be equally recognized. The development of certain endowments is a need. One must recognize all human needs, and all equally. Under the condition of relative scarcity, not all these needs can be satisfied – at least, not simultaneously.[34] However, not all needs awaiting satisfaction are concomitant with the development of our endowments. In connection with this I wish to make the following theoretical proposal: realizing the universal idea of 'equal life chances for all' does not presuppose either the satisfaction of all human needs or the distribution of an equal share of the available material resources to everyone. What it does presuppose is the satisfaction of all needs for the cultivation of our endowments, whatever these endowments may be, unless the satisfaction of an endowment as a need implies the use of others as mere means.

The postulate 'satisfaction of all needs for the cultivation of our endowments, whatever these endowments are' (with the above proviso) sounds familiar. The suspicion may arise that I have only suggested another formula for an old demand, that of fair and equal opportunity for all, which is only one possible interpretation of the 'triad' model. The formula can mean that everyone gets the same amount of 'manna' at the outset (Ackermann's simile) and subsequently makes the best or worst of it, or that each individual atom departs from the same point, some finishing well, others not. It can even imply that the poor runners or the unlucky investors of the manna may be compensated later with some 'welfare sugar'. Yet, irrespective of whether we like or dislike the 'triad' model, it is obvious that what is called fair and equal opportunity facilitates the development of certain endowments into talents and impedes the development of others. Endowments must be known in order to be developed, and, where there is only one way of life, certain endowments which may have been fully developed remain infertile, while less promising or even inferior endowments are developed. Only if different ways of life and different social patterns coexist, only if a person is free to change a way of life to find more adequate values and means of unfolding his or her endowments into talents, can the idea of 'equal life chances for all' be actualized. I subscribe emphatically to the conception of Nozick in this respect: the utopia worth pursuit is the realization of *all* utopias, not just of one.

Still, though one may dwell in such a utopia, it may not be true that an equal 'start' will lead to the satisfaction of all needs for the cultivation of one's endowments, or that an equal distribution of 'manna' will ensure this. I return to the problem discussed earlier: the promotion of certain endowments requires greater social spending than does that of others, and society must spend precisely the amount necessary for promoting a person's talents. In other words, this expenditure must be *unequal*.

Having in mind the actualization of the ultimate value of 'equal life chances for all', I *reverse* the qualification signs between 'start' (or 'opportunity') and 'end state'. In the usual 'triad' model we have *initial equality* (equal start, equal distribution of manna, equality in resources, and the like), after which competition begins; and the end state involves achieving the proper (or permitted) level of inequality of *incomes* and wealth.

My model would involve *initial inequality* in that everyone receives what is necessary for the development of his or her abilities into talents and the practising of these talents. As endowments are unique, this is a principle of inequality. But I see no reason for anyone to get a higher income as a *result* of this. This is especially so considering that I believe all talents to be equally precious, and that no particular one of them contributes more to the good life of all than the others. However, while stating these preferences I do not exclude the idea of the 'triad' model from the Utopia (the realization of all utopias) – whoever likes this model best may embrace it.

An ironical rejoinder is almost inevitable here. If the 'triad' model is open to choice, no one will be foolish enough not to run the race that has the highest stake: a bigger salary. This is the prime article of faith with all liberal theories of distributive justice. The idealized image of the 'triad' model is presented as the form of life every human being would subscribe to, if rational choice were not inhibited by vested interest or prejudice. The 'original position' under the 'veil of ignorance' is only an elegant and witty presentation of a common view. Distributive equality is tantamount to equality of incomes, whereas distributive inequality is tantamount to differentiation of incomes (restricted by welfare) and nothing else. The 'triad' model is taken for granted because certain structures of needs are taken for granted. And, if the structure of needs enhanced by the way of life of the 'triad' is taken for granted, then, of course, a streamlined version of the original model seems to be the only and ultimate choice of all. If, however, one posits different need structures, among them structures which are enhanced by, while being constitutive of, social models other than that of the 'triad', then we must assume that at least some people will opt out of the 'triad' model, streamlined as it may be, and will choose other ways of life; and that, the more different ways of life develop their own need structures, the more people may freely opt for the new ones. On these grounds I allow myself to believe that the distributive patterns which reverse the qualification signs between 'start' or 'beginning' and 'result' or 'end' in matters of equality or inequality could, and perhaps would, be chosen by many.

Let me again summarize what this alternative distributive model is all about.

1 Everyone receives from the social wealth what is necessary for developing his or her endowments into talents. This means *unequal distribution at the start.*
2 Everyone receives from the social wealth what is required for the use of his or her endowments (inequality remains in force).
3 When someone decides to develop any other endowment, this person receives what is required to achieve this (inequality remains in force at the second 'start', third 'start', etc.).
4 To meet needs other than those necessary for developing endowments, every person gets an *equal* share (be it in the form of distributed goods and services, income, dividends or whatever).

Distribution along these lines is by any measure either irrelevant or downright unjust in terms of the 'triad' model. It can only be just and fair in *communities*, in a particular form of communal life. There can be several different ways of life wherein such a distributive model works, but there must be one common denominator among all of them: the collective ownership of what was called by Marx 'the means of production'. In other words, every member of the community must be a co-proprietor of the sources of social wealth of that community. Co-proprietorship entails an equal and genuine right of every community member to dispose of the social wealth created by all. The kibbutz lifestyle, or the way of life in commonly owned and managed factories encourages, or at least permits, the theoretical possibility of the implementation of the 'reversed' form of distribution, equal or unequal. True enough, there are few kibbutzim, and few employee-owned and managed factories, or other forms of the business co-operative. Their paucity may be taken as an indication of a lack of social need for them. But this objection is very questionable, for two reasons. The need structure of today is not indicative of 'need structures' as such; the current needs will change, as they have always changed. Further, the distributive pattern I have described and the need structure adequate to it exists even today, and more generally than one is inclined to suppose – namely, in every democratically structured family. If the *ideal image* of the current democratic family structure is drawn, this will match exactly the pattern of my distributive model with 'reversed qualification signs'. And we can be assured that there must exist some powerful needs which make this structure survive in the macrocosm of the 'triad' model, to which it bears very little resemblance.[35]

To avoid misunderstandings, I am not arguing that there is no need for the distributive model of the 'triad', or that this need is 'false'. I am contesting the stance that the streamlined version of the 'triad' model presents the *only* model people would rationally choose if they were presented with a variety of ways of life, and the accompanying view that the suggested pattern of distribution in terms of the 'triad' model is the only just distribution possible or imaginable. I also contest the view that the idea of 'equal life chances for all' can be realized if a single way of life is posited within the model. Only if all endowments have a chance to be developed into talents, and equally so, can we get closer to the realization of this universal idea.

Those taking it for granted that everyone would choose initial equality in the race for the biggest stake may be puzzled to realize how easy it is to accept the 'reversed' model of distribution in respect of collective ownership. Rosner comments, 'Interesting enough, the kibbutz has succeeded in the realm of economic equality and common ownership far more successfully and homogeneously than in other areas, and fewer threats exist to its economic structure than to other conditions of participatory democracy.'[36] Since I am only dealing with the problem of 'distributive justice' here, I cannot formulate the political and other kinds of constraints that may arise within purely communal models. At this point it appears sufficient to stress that a plurality of ways of life, and the inalienable right of everyone at any time to quit one way of life and join another, can counterbalance such constraints.

It may seem that, in suggesting an alternative model of 'reversed' distribution, I have left far behind all mental experiments with 'equal resources', 'initial equal distribution of the manna', and the like. This is not so. I have instead shifted the problem to another level.

Ackermann writes,

According to Nozick, so long as the first generation began from a just starting point at Time One, individual seniors may pick out particular juniors for special favour – by gift, inheritance, or otherwise. The fact that a rich junior can trace his title through a series of voluntary actions to an initially just Time One discharges him – so far as Nozick is concerned – from any claim of injustice made by his second-generation contemporaries. In principle, all eternity could be barred from all claims of injustice so long as a single generation had attained a just starting point for a single moment. . . . For it should be very obvious by now that the human race has *never* in its long history approached a single moment at which a single generation's starting point was arranged in a way that approximated the liberal ideal of undominated equality. We are, in short, at generation zero . . . the problem of inheritance is of such great theoretical importance that we must confront it head-on if we hope to grasp the shape of liberal ideals.[37]

Ackermann is undoubtedly correct. Nozick's position of excluding all forms of redistribution as acts of injustice is indeed untenable from the position of our dominant sense of justice, but not for historical reasons. Of course, historically speaking there has never been 'Time One'. However, if we were to establish Time One here and now, and if we also remain with the idea of *nil redistribution*, 'tomorrow' would not differ from 'yesterday' as far as distributive inequality is concerned. This problem was mentioned by Hume, and was well-known to socialists of the nineteenth century. To abolish the right of inheritance was always on their agenda. Whether right or wrong, it can still be stated in good faith that X acquired greater wealth than Y because X was more talented or more frugal than Y, but if X's son inherits this wealth it is hard to deny that the son possesses something that has not resulted from *his own* talents or merits. Therefore the son should not have this wealth. And what is true about individuals is equally true about communities and nations. The generation of fathers and mothers of community X (at

Time One) has accumulated greater wealth than the generation of the fathers and mothers of community Y at the same Time One. Consequently, the juniors of community X inherit far more than the juniors of community Y. They can thus capitalize collectively on a wealth they have no merit in owning. Of course, we inherit far more than just wealth, but I shall return to this matter very shortly.

I think that here we arrive at a point where theoretical suggestions might indeed clash with what I believe to be 'human nature'. Humans are mortal and know they are, but they do not acquiesce in this awareness. We all feel the need to leave behind some trace of ourselves and we generally accomplish this by offering the fruits of our lives to the future generation. Only a very strong belief in the hereafter can outweigh this desire. In fact, some have the tremendous consciousness – and justifiably so – of bequeathing *humankind* the fruit of their efforts. But these people are few. Most of us wish to bequeath our legacy to people bound to us by direct ties, to people we know, to people whose future joy may fill us with anticipatory pleasure. The children who spring from our bodies, the youth of our community, our friends, carriers of ideas we have stood for – all are *visible and perceivable* continuations of ourselves, and as such they are our heirs by right, choice, and desire. Whether we make our bequests to others during our lifetime or leave our legacy behind us is of secondary importance.[38] It is also of secondary importance whether we draw up a will or whether we witness (as in a collectivity) how the future generation capitalizes on the fruits of our labour. No *absolute* Time One is possible (now or at any time) for any member of any society, only a very *relative* Time One for each and every *concrete* community at the moment of its establishment.

But, even if there is never an absolute Time One, and even if the inheritance of wealth cannot be completely eliminated – since, if it were, a basic human need would be doomed to eternal dissatisfaction – the *continuous redistribution of wealth* can still be attained. Moreover, this goal should be attained, because it is not contrary to but rather *accords completely with* our desire to bequeath the fruits of our lives to the future generation. Why this is so becomes clear if we look at forms of inheritance other than the strictly material.

We cannot favour the actualization of all utopias (all utopian ways of life), as Nozick did, *and* reject the principles of redistribution, as he did, without self-contradiction. Certain ways of life may be more able to cope with material exigencies, others less able. Certain communities may flourish, whereas others, owing to the efforts or shortcomings of previous generations or because of factors beyond human control (for instance, natural disasters), may perish. So what, one might ask? If people are free to quit one particular way of life and join another, those who prefer wealth will choose ways of life which ensure such wealth, and those preferring different ways of life will freely choose a reduced standard of living. These solutions may be viable, but only up to a certain point. Ways of life which do not ensure the development of the members' endowments into talents because they cannot secure the reproduction of communal life, *at least at the same level as was established at the outset*, will stagnate, or even become extinct, but, regardless of the degree of this degeneration, the universal value of 'equal life chances for all' will not be actualized. The very fact that a way of life has been established and supported indicates the presence of men and women who seek to develop their endowments into talents within this way of life. If this way of life becomes extinct, the life chances of its adherents (or of those who might have chosen it) will diminish. If the ways of life in question stagnate, and cannot ensure their own reproduction on the level they had experienced at the beginning, the life chances of the members also decrease. Furthermore, the extinction of a particular way of life does not happen at Time One, but at Time Two, Time Three, and so on. However, from Time One onwards, generations who have lived a particular way of life have already passed on the fruits of their lives to future generations; not only material yields, but also values, behavioural patterns, emotional idiosyncrasies, forms of intercourse, modes of discourse, plays and dreams – everything we mean when we speak of 'culture'. If a way of life becomes extinct, a culture is doomed, and all the dreams and labours of former generations pass into oblivion. This is why *redistribution* is not the opposite of inheritance, but in fact is necessary for the preservation of inheritance.

These days, people are ready to make sacrifices to save animal species from extinction, even going so far as to endanger the livelihood of the Eskimo to save the baby seal. If we unhesitatingly sacrifice part of our well-being to save an animal species from extinction, why do we experiment with patterns of distribution which, once accepted, would doom entire human ways of life to extinction? If all utopias should flourish, we must do our best to make them flourish. Of course, not everything should be redistributed. Redistribution should only go so far as to ensure that no way of life falls below the level of wealth and well-being at which it was originally established. A *greater amount* can be redistributed, and just how much more this should be always depends on the sense of justice of those doing the redistributing. But the situation where *less* is distributed should never occur.

To sum up: as far as redistribution among various forms of life is concerned, the arguments of modern liberal theory for 'initial equality in resources' or 'equal amounts of manna (at Time One)' remain in force. As far as just distribution *within* each form of life is concerned, however, no general 'pattern' of justice can be invented or established. To each way of life must go its own distributive justice. What form of distribution is just or unjust is something that only members of each community – each way of life – are qualified to decide.[39] I am not qualified to do so. And neither are those who take the 'triad' model of a way of life for granted, and believe they have found the golden formula of just distribution.

Liberal theorists offer their goods with the certification 'envy-tested'. One can doubtless suggest and invent models of distribution which do not actively *promote* envy. Still, no model can be 'envy-tested'. Envy is an irrational feeling. Patterns of distribution are rational constructs. People do not usually envy others because they have *reasons* to be envious. Men with superior talents in a particular field can envy others with inferior talents in the same field. People can envy others for things (goods, propensities, and the like) they do not even want. 'Envy-testing' patterns of distribution is a process tantamount to 'jealousy-testing' patterns of sexual relations or 'vanity-testing' reviews written on scholarly books. To restrain envy or to check our impulses of envy is a *moral* matter and a *moral* task, and no quantity of sophisticated patterns of distribution can substitute for the ethical 'atmosphere' indispensable to the 'good life'. Distributive justice is but an aspect of the ethico-political concept of justice.

'JUST' AND 'UNJUST' WAR

To begin with I shall put this matter in the form of simplified Hegelian terminology. It is war that accomplishes the *synthesis* of retributive and distributive justice and injustice. In all wars both power and wealth are redistributed. If warring is a way of life, and in that sense a goal-in-itself, winning battles and campaigns is all that the warring parties aim at. Acquisition of bounty, women, slaves, herds, precious metals, new regions and lands the inhabitants of which augment the ranks of the taxpayers, and sources of raw materials – these are the objective results and the evidence of triumph. Wealth can be redistributed by looting, by destroying the enemy's livelihood, by exploiting the labour of the inhabitants of enemy territory, and by various other means. In this sense wars promote an ongoing redistribution. Yet it is also true that, aside from instances where the warring parties do not speak a common cultural language at all, and thus violence is not regulated to any degree by custom, ceremony or norms, or where constraining norms that would normally operate are dismissed and rendered ineffectual by overwhelming justificatory considerations[40] – in other words, except for situations of the 'state of nature' – the element of *retribution* is present in both motivation and end result. The attacker presents the war (justifies it) as *punishment* for crimes allegedly committed by the attacked, while the latter regards the attack as a crime requiring punishment when the wheel of fortune turns. The factor of 'deterrence', this particular principle of retributive justice, makes headway in a situation of war. *Si vis pacem, para bellum*: preparation for war deters the aggressor, and to instigate a war is to act so as to deter the other party from launching future attacks, employing blackmail, and the like. Even the principle of *reform* is at work in war. 'Holy' wars are allegedly waged to also save the souls of the vanquished, seen as pagans and heretics. If the war is won, the survivors among the enemy will 'reform', 'mend their ways', leave their devilish customs behind. Though it does not happen in every instance, it is usually the case that one or another principle of retributive justice (retribution, deterrent, reform) always serves as a legitimating principle in war, in conjunction with the goal of redistribution. These two facets can of course overlap. The wealth of a neighbouring people or their ownership of a particular territory could be regarded as an insult.

The intention to regulate the conduct of war has a very long history. If people at war share a cultural language, at least in some respect, they normally distinguish between 'right' and 'wrong' methods of warfare. True enough, the ultimate goal of winning more often than not overrides the norms concerning just conduct. The Trojan War, one of the first campaigns of which we have a detailed report, displays a combination of all the elements discussed here. This was a war of retribution in that the abduction (or seduction) of Helen demanded punishment and her return to the marital bed. The result of the siege was redistribution: Troy was looted and destroyed, and women and children were taken as slaves. For many years, both armies held to the rules concerning behaviour in war, and on the battlefield these rules reigned supreme. Granted this, the ploy involving the wooden horse was outside the just conduct of war. Putting it simply, as the war could not be won by just conduct, the rules determining this conduct were waived. It was supposedly the just nature of the war (retribution) that legitimized for the Greeks this final suspension of the rules regulating just conduct. And this first war to be recorded in full displays patterns that have characterized most wars ever since.

Theory about the 'just war' does not simply summarize the results of behaviour throughout thousands of years of warfare whilst applying political theories of war and peace. Such theory is a branch of the modern socio-political concept of justice. 'Just-war' theories are roughly based on the assumption that wars are waged between sovereign nation states. All other wars are regarded as exceptions, or at least as 'irregular cases' ('private wars'). Also, 'just-war' theories value peace above war. This is why their adherents advocate that all wars (breaches of peace) must have a strong justification. In fact these people list the various situations where the waging of war is justified. Actions aimed solely at redistributing land, wealth or population are generally excluded from this list of justifying circumstances. So is proselytism. Neither the possession of rich lands, nor the worship of different gods, is considered a situation or act of injustice. Thus the *principles* by which it is thought that the justice or injustice of a particular war can be decided are modern and rational ones.

Although the notion 'just war' was first coined by Augustine, 'just-war theory' is as much a challenge to the Augustinian interpretation of the concept as it is a rehashed version of it. For Augustine a war was absolutely just if waged under the direction of God with the aim of fulfilling the commands of God. It is exactly this kind of interpretation that is excluded by modern theorists of 'just war'. Wars have come to be considered as completely secular undertakings. That is why people must invent (or discover) principles which are (or should be) binding to all states as far as they enter a situation of war and as far as they fight a particular war. What is new is not the distinction between *jus ad bellum* and *jus in bello*, but the principles on which these two rights rest and the metaprinciple that the *same* principles apply (or should apply) to *all* warring parties. Thus the principles of just war are considered *universals*, which for earlier theorists in the modern tradition were restricted to the then 'civilized' world. No particular traditional justification is valid if it contradicts these universal principles of justice and injustice.

Just-war theories are rational in terms of *rationality of intellect*. When listing universal principles of justice in war they reject all other principles as unjust. ('Not this is just, but that is just; what *is* just is just for *all*, hence *should* be accepted as just for all.') Rational argumentation is the only way to justify a war. The warring party must have recourse to the universal principles of war and *prove* that the other party has infringed the norms of international justice, and that for this reason the waging of this particular war is justified, it being in accordance with the universal principles of just war. The chief values maintained and reinforced by all these principles are freedom and life. Injustice occurs if the freedom or survival of a nation state is endangered, when the freedom of the subjects (citizens) of this state is threatened or their life chances are purposely decreased. Consequently, an act such as the abduction of Helen could not justify a war in terms of modern theories of just war. Also, even if both universal values (freedom and life) underlie the principles of just war, freedom is the guiding value in all these theories. This stands to reason if one addresses matters of war, for war goes anyhow with loss of life. Yet it must once more be emphasized that in just-war theories peace is more highly valued than war. These theories are aware that most wars are unjust, at least with respect to appraising the justification offered by the aggressor. Just-war theories do not legitimize wars. Rather, they restrict legitimation to particular wars – namely, those which are just.

The modern character of theories of just war makes any historical application of them to pre-modern wars highly problematic. This is one of the main objections Turner Johnson raised against the outstanding work by Walzer. But Johnson goes too far in rebuking Walzer for making 'universal claims on the basis of less than universally recognized values' in and for the present.[41] This is not an accurate description of Walzer's procedure. What Walzer really did was to neglect and phase out certain values not universally recognized today but which none the less serve to justify wars. In my view this 'neglect' is the expression of a resolution to think and judge according to our 'sense of justice', in that the latter does not apply different standards to different cultures, but rather rejects different standards as if they were double standards.

However, Johnson is right when he traces back the modern theory of just war to Franciscus de Victoria's work (*De Indis*, *De jure in bello*), and when he considers the seminal work of Grotius (*De jure belli ac pacis*) as the paragon of all subsequent theories. In discussing the problem of 'just' and 'unjust' wars within the framework of the socio-political concept of justice, we can still heavily rely upon Grotius, even if some of his arguments and concrete analyses are historically outdated.

Although 'retributive justice', 'distributive justice' and 'just-war theory' as separate branches of justice have emerged simultaneously, and can be regarded as three answers to the same historico-social challenge, the vicissitudes of the theory of just war are unique compared to the story of these other two branches of the socio-political concept of justice. The evolution of the theories of retributive and distributive justice has been *continuous*. Since first formulated, they have always been appraised, upheld and modified. The case with just-war theory is different. There have been important periods in modern history when theories of just war were relegated to the background, even rejected outright. It has never been questioned in modern times whether the categories of justice or injustice can be applied to retribution and distribution. The only concern has been whether principles of retribution and distribution are just or unjust. Yet there have always been times when it has been questionable whether wars can be categorized as 'just' or 'unjust' at all. It is possible to insist (with Hegel) that all wars are just, or else state (with Kant) that none are. Leading theorists of the Napoleonic period made no use of the theory of just war whatsoever, irrespective of whether they supported the Emperor (as Hegel did) or fought him (as Clausewitz did, both on the battlefield and with pen).[42] Indeed, if peace is not valued more highly than war, a theory of 'just war' makes little sense. By contrast, if a person such as Kant holds firmly to the view that the achievement of eternal peace is within our reach, a theory of 'just war' again makes little sense. However, at the times when just-war theory was accepted, the *principles* themselves which underlay this theory did not undergo substantial change.

Principles of 'just war' have been more firmly established since Grotius' time than the principles of retribution since Locke's time, or those of distribution since Hume's. Sometimes the principles of just war have been supplemented by certain procedural and/or substantive criteria. By procedural criteria I mean conditions such as *who* decides to launch a war or to defend a country by means of war, and *who* wages the war (the armed citizenry, conscripts, professional armies, or other forces).[43] By substantive criteria I mean conditions such as *what kind* of ideas the war is waged for, *what kind* of institutions the warring parties defend or fight against. These additional criteria can *relativize* the consistent and continuous application of the principles themselves. Although the formal concept of justice (the maxim of justice) demands that the principles, and they alone, should determine the justice or injustice of wars, it is not easy, and sometimes even problematic, to abstract completely from the additional criteria of *jus ad bellum*, and for obvious reasons. In theories of 'just war' justice involves inter-state relationships. Even so, one cannot, and sometimes should not, abstract from the socio-political structures and institutions of particular states at war with one another. If the institutions of a particular state are considered *unjust* by a substantial part of the populace, and the war, if it ends in victory, will strengthen and stabilize internal injustice, the shadow of injustice might fall on the war as well, even if it is waged in accordance with the universal principles of 'just war'. The same holds true if the war is agreed upon and initiated by agencies unauthorized by the constitution of the warring country to initiate that particular war. Put simply, internal consensus or the lack of it can partly determine the justice or injustice of war, and, the less limited a war is, the more this is so. Whether fredom or unfreedom is defended can also partly determine the justice or injustice of a war, and, again, the less limited the war is, the more this is so. But there is an inherent danger in bending the principles via procedural or substantive criteria so long as matters are considered and judged in terms of 'just-war theory'.[44]

It is well known that the tradition of 'just war' distinguishes between two kinds of justice and injustice in war: between *jus ad bellum* and *jus in bello*. *Jus ad bellum* establishes principles for entering into à state of war; *jus in bello* establishes principles for the conduct of war. Countries entering into a particular war in accordance with the principles so established *have a right* to wage this war, whereas countries entering into a war in a manner in conflict with these principles have no right to wage that particular war. No country has the right to conduct a war while breaking the principles of just conduct. For centuries the tradition of just war advocated these ideas only on a theoretical level. The concept of 'right' had no legal backing; it stood for *moral right*. Theories of just war raised the claim to an international law that would codify moral right in legal terms. 'Laws of war' started to become *lex lata* at the close of the nineteenth century. Henceforth international conventions have codified certain traditional claims of theories of just war, to begin with those of *jus in bello*, and later even some pertaining to *jus ad bellum*. All the same, this consensual and transcultural acceptance of certain principles of just war has had little or no impact on warring parties since this time. Value-rational limitations are of almost no avail if the action itself is by definition purposively rational. War is about winning. The view of Trasymachos that the right is always the right of the strongest is unfortunately true in war. Principles of just war can have a *limiting* effect on the conduct of war in *utilitarian* terms only (as calculated by Sidwick). Warring parties might forgo the use of means contrary to the principles of just conduct of war, if the use of such means is *superfluous* for achieving the goal of victory. Principles of just war can also have an ideological function: warring parties always find it necessary to engage in distorted communication by 'justifying' their wars with these principles. And if this is impossible they simply lie, and generally get away with it, at least as long as they have the resources to back these lies up.

In a civil state laws generally carry sanctions; in the international arena they do not. International organizations, if they exist at all, cannot implement sanctions in a manner that penalizes every country, and every country equally, for breaching the 'laws of war'. Put simply, international law has neither the force to carry out retribution nor the power to deter. Only arms can achieve these aims. And, unfortunately, as the world stands now, it is better that this is so. Our world is divided into spheres of influence between two superpowers (and other local powers) in mutual hostility. It suffices to glance at the resolutions of the United Nations in instances of war to realize that these judgements passed on warring countries are not genuinely based on the principles of 'just war' but are based on vested interest, power affiliations, dogmatic beliefs, and the like. Had the United Nations the effective power to implement real sanctions (and not only nominal ones), our world would be even more unjust than it is.

Not only the idea of 'eternal peace' is utopian today (in the sense of 'unrealistic'); so is the consistent and continuous application of the principles of 'just war' to every state. True enough, the two universal values (freedom and life) and the two universal principles ('equal freedom to all', 'equal life chances to all') can only be fully realized in a world of peace. Kant once called peace the supreme political good. I would say that peace is the supreme *inferred* political good. Peace is the supreme political good in so far as it is inferred from the equal freedom and equal life chances of all, where 'all' stands both for 'every sovereign state' and 'every citizen'. Taking the world as it stands, the idea of just war must have *temporal* priority over the idea of 'eternal peace', even if the idea of 'eternal peace', on the level of values, must have *absolute* priority over the idea of 'just war'. Thus the principles of just war must be constitutive ideas but ideas considered to be *temporal*. Fighting only just wars is the first and necessary step towards a world peace based on equality of freedom and equality of life chances.

For all of this, the postulate that only just wars should be fought still takes the form of an *ideal* obligation, since this norm is nowhere observed. There is no parallel to the infringement of civil laws. In relation to the principles of just war, the situation is rather that people break the law (the principles) whenever it is in their interest to do so, and are outraged when another party acts likewise, and this is *not identical* with the attitude that the majority of the population have towards the law, even in countries with non-democratic constitutions.

At this juncture I must hark back to the last section of chapter 1. I there addressed the problem of whether cultural patterns can be compared, and the answer was that they should be compared (and ranked) as far as they involve domination, the use of force, and violence. War is the typical manifestation of force and violence. Warring countries, as well as those preparing for war, must be compared and ranked, and this can only be done by applying the 'principles of just war'. The civilian population of countries (irrespective of whether they are at war) should pass judgement on wars by applying the principles of 'just war'. All wars failing to observe these principles should be *condemned*, and condemned according to the amount of injustice they involve, irrespective of our affiliations, sympathies and ideological or cultural preconceptions.

In what follows I shall attempt to enumerate the principles of just war. Since these principles have not significantly changed since Grotius' formulated them, I need only adjust them to the circumstances of modern international relations and to the technological exigencies of modern warfare. Apart from reshaping the principles of *jus ad bellum* and *jus in bello*, I shall add a third cluster of principles to the list: the principles of just peace. Every war ends in peace, and the just or unjust character of that peace codetermines retrospectively the just or unjust character of the war in question. This is not a completely novel idea, although not all theories of just war have taken it into consideration. Kant, however, although himself not an adherent of the 'just-war tradition' made a very strong case for this appendage. In the opening lines of his study on perpetual peace, he wrote, 'No treaty of peace shall be considered valid in which there is tacitly reserved matter for a future war.'[45] Kant refers here to a very specific example of an unjust peace, but it deserves mention that he could picture a peace treaty that is by definition invalid.

The right to war holds if there is an *initial just cause for waging war*. There are four situations where such a right to war exists and makes the war *absolutely just* (in terms of *jus ad bellum*), and there are two additional situations where an existing right to war makes it *conditionally* just (just subject to certain qualifications).

1   If a state is attacked in breach of a *valid* pact or treaty which was
    not signed by the attacking nation in a situation of duress, the
    war is absolutely just from the side of the attacked.
2   If a state is attacked without provocation, or if provocation
    could have been dealt with by peaceful means but such initiatives
    were rejected or left unexplored by the attacking nation, the war
    is absolutely just from the side of the attacked.
3   If the sovereignty of a nation state is not recognized by its
    enemies and so the sheer survival of this state – and the life and
    freedom of its citizens – is under constant threat, or if the life
    and freedom of a state's citizens is threatened by a potential or
    actual genocidal enemy, even though the sovereignty of this state
    is recognized, the nation state under threat has the right to wage
    war. Waging war against such an enemy is wholly just even if the
    threatened country is the attacker.
4   If a once sovereign state is dispossessed of its sovereignty *under
    duress* and begins a war against the dispossessor so as to regain
    its sovereignty, the war is absolutely just from the side of the
    dispossessed.

In all these four cases, the *allies* of the country waging a just war are
also waging a just war, provided they do not seek any other benefit
than the successful defence of the just cause.

The principles of the absolute *jus ad bellum* enumerated above are
completely *formal*. As far as *relatively* just wars are concerned,
procedural and substantive qualifications cannot be entirely left out
of consideration. More precisely, if the mere formal criteria of just
war are modified by the addition of certain procedural and
substantive criteria, wars can be called only relatively just; that is,
they can be just to a lesser or greater extent. Two types of war
belong to this category: (i) those waged with the purpose of
regaining a territory lost in a previous war, and (ii) so-called 'wars
of liberation'.

If the purpose of a war is to regain lost territory (and if the formal
criteria of absolutely just war do not apply), the war can be
relatively just if (a) the former peace treaty was signed under duress,
and (b) there are certain procedural and substantive criteria present
for waging this particular war. By *substantive* criteria I mean the
following: that the populace of the territory in question is exposed
to harsher forms of domination, to more violence, than the
indigenous populace of the country to which they now belong; that
they are exposed, moreover, to harsher forms of domination and to
more violence than they would be had they remained citizens of

their 'original' country. If *both* these criteria apply, then the war waged to regain this territory is *also* a war of liberation. If *neither* of these criteria apply, the war cannot be *justified* by having recourse to the value of *freedom*; and, since all wars cause loss of life, the war waged in order to regain territory will be unjust (to a lesser or greater extent). By *procedural* criteria I mean the methods for deciding upon the matter of war and peace. If it is only a small ruling elite of a country that makes the decision to wage war to regain territory, the war cannot be even relatively just. With a completely just war, where the life and freedom of the state as such, as well as the life and freedom of all its citizens, are at stake, consensus about waging the war can be taken for granted. This is not so if the war is waged to regain lost territory. This is why such wars can be relatively just only if the decision to wage a particular war is made by the entire population.

Wars of liberation aim at liberating the people of another country. Since nowadays the cause of 'liberation' serves to justify wars waged solely with the intent of gain, the formal principles of *jus ad bellum* must be firmly adhered to and not allowed to be distorted by or become subservient to the substantive criterion inherent in the term 'liberation'. Put bluntly, the tyrannical, despotic and dictatorial character of a regime does not suffice to justify any external armed action against it. Only the rescuing of a whole mass of people threatened with genocide can be accepted as a just cause of war in such a case. However, *jus ad bellum* will be heavily relativized if the warring party simultaneously pursues goals other than the goal of rescue, be they territorial or ideological in nature. (Of course, this only applies if the conditions of an absolutely just war do not apply.)

The allies of a country waging a relatively just war have the right to enter this war if, without their participation, the relatively just cause would be lost (and this is the only condition under which they may do so). By contrast, if a country fighting a relatively just war (in order to regain lost territory) make an alliance with countries that engage in unjust (aggressive) wars, this country forgoes the right to war.

Jus in bello, the just conduct of war, has never ceased to be a source of recommendation and speculation. The harassment of civilian populations, the wilful victimization of non-combatants, the violation of neutrality, looting of cities, raping of women, killing of the defenceless (including soldiers upon their submission), abandonment of the crews of disabled or destroyed ships, the use of inhumane weapons, attack without preliminary warning, and several other conditions, have been added to breaches of the unwritten code of law by the 300-year old 'just-war' tradition. These days, the just conduct of war has become *lex lata*, covered by different conventions, ratified by almost all states. The conduct of war is considered unjust if any of the conventions are infringed.[46] But the more codified *jus in bello* has become, the greater the number of conflicts and contradictions that occur in applying the principles it entails.

If the initial cause of war is absolutely just, occasional breaches of *jus in bello* do not annul this initial justice. If through no fault of its own the life and freedom of an entire nation is under mortal threat by an aggressor, this nation cannot be held fully responsible if illicit means are used to prevent this ultimate catastrophe. No one can reasonably blame Yugoslav partisans for failing to adhere to the Geneva Convention concerning the treatment of prisoners of war. These partisans were acting under extraordinary circumstances, perhaps the most relevant being their lack of territory unaffected by war, one resource all belligerent state possess which allow them to provide for prisoners of war, aliens, and so on. Conversely, just conduct of war does not cancel the initial injustice of an aggressive war. It is easy for the powerful to victimize the weak without offending the code of just conduct; it is difficult for the weak to secure even mere survival. Moreover, in the case of victory the powerful normally break the code of just conduct with impunity. The just conduct of war establishes principles equally valid, and valid to the same extent, for both mighty and weak, for both aggressor and victim of aggression, for both just and unjust. It would be unthinkable to suggest that the norms of just conduct be valid only for the aggressor and not for the victim of aggression, only for the unjust and not for the just. Such a stipulation would annul the principles of just conduct as principles. But we simply cannot suggest to parties fighting an entirely just war that they *should* lose this war if they cannot win it by just conduct, for in so doing we are siding with the aggressor. And we should hope that the aggressor loses the war, irrespective of the way in which that party conducts it. The unjust conduct of war is really an 'aggravating circumstance' added to the initial breach of *jus ad bellum*.

Furthermore, since the just conduct of war has become *lex lata*, it is increasingly difficult, once war has begun, to observe the principles of *jus in bello* in full. Most modern wars, and not only the 'world wars', are not limited but total in nature. There is no strict separation between combatants and non-combatants. It is more or less the entire populace that caters for the military machine. And so munitions factories automatically become targets. Similarly, the strategy of destroying internal support for unjust wars by indiscriminately bombing the civilian population is always to some degree employed. Valid arguments against such measures rely upon utilitarian considerations rather than on the code of just conduct of war in general. It is obvious that the napalm bombing of Dresden did not contribute to the Allied victory, but was an unnecessary cruelty. We recall with justified outcry the nuclear attack on Hiroshima and the indiscriminate bombing of Tokyo. However, if use of the nuclear bomb had been the only way of preventing a final victory by Hitler, we should assess the use of it in different value terms.

We must conclude that, because of the purposive rational character of war, the value-laden principles of the just conduct of war can aggravate or eventually attenuate the infringement of *jus ad bellum*, and can blemish otherwise just wars; but they are not the decisive factors. Accordingly, if we adhere to value rationality and to judging wars according to their just or unjust character, we must instead focus on *jus ad bellum* and on *just peace*. It can rightly be said that no country *should* start a war or be party to a war without *jus ad bellum*. Before the state of war sets in, everything is still *open* to value-rational considerations and decisions. No Machiavellianism, no utilitarian principles are allowed to guide decisions at this stage. No party has the *right* to start a war for ideological reasons or territorial goals.

Peace can only be just if the victorious parties have waged a just war. Wars won by aggressors cannot in principle end in just peace. (The same is true if both parties wage an unjust war, though even then *restraint* in negotiations for peace can retrospectively lessen the unjust character of the war.) As just war is not distributive but retributive (restitutive), the parties which have fought a just war should not pursue any distributive objectives on the eve of triumph. The winner imposes a particular peace on the loser (this is unavoidable), but the imposed peace should not contain any conditions beyond the just cause of war. The recognition of the sovereignty of a nation state; the security, freedom and life of the state; the freedom and the well-being of its citizens: these should be the aims of the peace treaty, nothing else. If something more than this is gained the peace will be unjust, and it will surely serve to legitimize further (just or unjust) wars. If the peace is just, the wounds of the defeated may in time heal, though not necessarily. If the peace is unjust, this is highly unlikely. The Second World War did not come out of the blue. Hitler himself was an unintended and far from necessary product, yet a product of an unjust peace. The genocidal regime which drew the world into the most total war ever known would not have gained control over the German nation if there had not been an unjust peace at Versailles. All this does not mean that just wars simply forfeit their initial justice if they end in unjust peace. The assessment of this varies from case to case. The Second World War, in one of the areas where it ended in peace at all, Europe, produced an unjust peace. It even ended in an unjust peace in countries themselves nominally belonging to the victors (for example, Poland), yet the victors did not forfeit the initial justice of this war, so monstrous was the enemy. However, an utterly unjust peace can retrospectively cast a gloomy shadow over the initial justice of the war it concludes – as the Holy Alliance did over the patriotic war of Russia in 1812.

Just-war theories cover the social cluster of 'all sovereign states'. It is taken for granted that serious conflicts of interest might, and do, arise among sovereign states, and that such conflicts are normally solved by the use of arms. At the same time, a standard is provided for comparing and ranking wars: wars fought 'according to standards' are initially just; wars fought by infringing these standards are initially unjust. The standards provided by theories of just war are not only standards for judgement (comparing and ranking) but also norms of action: sovereign states *should not* solve conflicts by aggression, though they may settle conflicts by the use of arms if, and only if, they are in the right. Two conclusions follow from all this. First, conflicts among sovereign states which should not be settled by aggression should be settled by means other than force. This is obvious. But what kind of means? Is a choice of means available? How can such conflicts be settled? Secondly, even if states have the right to settle conflicts by force, this is a right and not an obligation. But are there means other than force available to settle such conflicts? Or is force the only possible answer to the challenge, if the cause is just?

All states are equal in the sense that they are all sovereign states. They are equal in so far as they are equally sovereign. They are also equal because each can equally decide in matters of war and peace. If their life and freedom is at stake, they *equally* have the right to war. If they are not provoked, then all of them, in an equal manner, have no right to wage war. The equality conferred by membership of the group 'all sovereign states' is, however, completely formal. The only common denominator among all the members is their sovereignty. There are big states and small states. There are states of great military strength and states with no such strength at all. There are states with inexhaustible natural resources and states with almost no resources. There are wealthy states and poor states. There are democracies, military dictatorships, traditional monarchies, and despotic and totalitarian states. Nowhere does there exist such a gap between 'equal rights' and 'equal opportunities' as in the case of military conflicts; nowhere does there exist such a gap between initial justice and just result as here. Theories of just war can give moral support to those choosing to die standing rather than live on their knees; these theories can condemn the aggressor, denounce the unjust peace, but this is all. Since inter-state conflicts (or conflicts between people) are no longer settled by the duel, where the initial justice of the cause could provide the knight of justice with additional force, David rarely, if ever, beats Goliath. So, if we care about a just result, it is best to solve all conflicts between states by means other than force.

Further, even if the claim to redistribution cannot provide a *just cause for war*, such claims can still, to varying degrees, be just. So what if such claims have a large element of justice but do not satisfy the criteria of *jus ad bellum*? Should the needs behind the claim never be met? If such claims can never be met by means other than war, unjust wars will always be fought, and people will still believe in the justice of these wars because the initial claim was relatively just.

Further, even if the claim to 'liberation' does not constitute a *just cause for war* (except in the case of a genocidal regime), claims to 'liberation' can still, to varying degrees, be just. They are more just if a populace suffering from despotic rule joins the liberator in the struggle. If people cannot be liberated by means other than war, unjust wars will always be fought, and people will still believe in the justice of these wars because the initial claim was relatively just.

Gandhi made a strong case against this second argument. Self-liberation from despotism and tyranny does not require resort to arms; nor does the restoration of national sovereignty. General, absolute and active civil disobedience suffices. Such disobedience is the only means leading with certainty to the collapse of tyrannies and of imposed colonial control. Gandhi was unquestionably right. *If* the populace as a whole resists the violence of an oppressive power, no violent means are needed to make that power collapse. However, what Lessing had already known, and Gandhi did not take into consideration, is that tyrannical power is not just naked violence but also a source of temptation. Lessing's Emilia Galotti exclaimed, 'Violence: who *cannot* resist violence?' But resisting temptation is difficult. Even if the entire populace is ready to resist violence, not everyone would resist temptation. As long as tyrannical power exists there is temptation, and usually the majority cannot resist temptation. But, if this is so, tyranny does not collapse without the use of violence of a kind.

I repeat that the claim to 'liberation' cannot provide a just cause for war (except where a genocidal regime exists). However, this claim will not lose its relative justice as long as there are nations subjected to political powers they have neither elected nor authorized to rule, or where nations are subjected to socio-economic structures they have no right to query or to change.

How can conflicts among sovereign nations be settled by just procedure if neither the political rule nor the socio-economic structure of the states in question result from just procedure? How can international affairs be settled by negotiation or discourse if matters concerning political rule and socio-economic structures are settled by force *within* states? How can retributive justice be carried out by any international agency if retributive injustice is experienced within states? How can just distribution be negotiated between states if all kinds of distributive injustices are experienced by people within states? How can standards of justice in war be accepted and simultaneously observed by all sovereign states if there are no common standards concerning *procedures* of just retribution, if the preconditions of just retribution do not exist, if one claim for distribution marks another type of claim not merely as false but also as criminal, in the great majority of states?

Only if the ultimate and universal values of freedom and life are *realized* in all states (cultures) or, to formulate this more modestly, only if these universal values are observed as regulative ideas in all actions and judgements, would we enter a period where conflicts between sovereign nations could be settled by negotiation and, in the optimal case, by discourse, without resorting to force. Just peace, as the final objective of just war, is beyond the scope of competence of theories of just war. This problem, like the problems of retributive and distributive justice, can only be addressed within the framework of an (incomplete) ethico-political concept of justice. Theories of just war can only provide us with standards to judge justice and injustice in war. Their unquestionable merit is their capacity to lend moral support to states fighting just wars, irrespective of results.[47]

5

Towards an Incomplete Ethico-Political Concept of Justice

The incomplete ethico-political concept of justice seeks to establish a *common normative foundation for different ways of life*. It does not intend to mould ways of life in a single 'ideal' pattern. It does not recommend a single ethics (*Sittlichkeit*) intrinsic to such an ideal pattern. It posits the simultaneous existence of ways of life all bound to one another by ties of symmetric reciprocity. Ways of life can be bound together in this way if (a) they have certain norms in common, and (b) if they are 'equalized' by common norms. The question raised by the incomplete ethico-political concept of justice thus runs as follows: how is a pluralistic universe possible in which each culture is bound to every other culture by ties of symmetric reciprocity?

No incomplete ethico-political concept of justice can purport to be able to design the best possible way of life. If we assume that there are many ways of life, each of which is the 'best possible' for those living it, we must renounce, and in fact we have renounced, the ambitious project of the complete ethico-political concept of justice. Nevertheless, all adherents of the incomplete ethico-political concept of justice stand in a particular historico-cultural tradition; they all have a particular life experience (a biography); they all elaborate ideas in affinity with certain social needs. All of them will therefore recommend utopias, ways of life in harmony with their traditions, life experiences and particular ideas. It is possible to reject and criticize existing norms and rules as unjust only if one can recommend alternative norms and rules as just. We cannot design such alternative norms and rules except by departing from the life experiences we share with at least some members of a particular culture. If we renounce the intention to design the way of life we stand for, we cease to stand for this way of life, and we also relinquish the goal of actualizing the particular utopia we believe to be the best for us. Our ethico-political concept of justice is incomplete not because we forgo the designing of a way of life best for us (where 'us' stands for people sharing a particular historico-cultural tradition), but because we are aware that what is best for 'us' may not be best for everyone, that a particular utopia may be best for a particular group of people, even though it is not the best for 'us'. As far as the design of concrete utopias is concerned, theories conceived in the spirit of an incomplete ethico-political concept of justice complement one another.

In addressing the question 'How is a pluralistic cultural universe possible in which each culture is bound to every other culture by ties of symmetric reciprocity?', we cannot stretch our imagination beyond what is possible. This is why the common normative foundation of various ways of life cannot be based on, or conjectured on the basis of, two assumptions: abundance, and the perfection of human nature. Of course, concrete utopias (arising out of a single way of life) which do assume abundance or perfectibility cannot be simply dismissed. Since abundance and scarcity are relative to needs, particular ways of life with complete abundance are not beyond imagination. Nor is a community in itself inconceivable in which all participants excel in complete human goodness (for example there is the eventual actualization of the Kantian 'invisible Church'). However, neither abundance nor perfectibility can be regarded as a precondition of the good life, even less as pertaining to the normative foundation of all forms of life.

I first spoke of 'symmetric reciprocity' in the first chapter of this book, which dealt with the formal concept of justice (the maxim of justice). 'Symmetric reciprocity' was said to be the condition of the application of the 'golden rule' of justice. If we ask, 'How is a pluralistic universe possible in which each culture is bound to every other culture by ties of symmetric reciprocity?' we project the possibility of the universalization of the 'golden rule'. The normative foundation of the incomplete ethico-political concept of justice is not the normative foundation of *morals*, but the *normative foundation of justice*. Just norms are *socio-political* norms (as are unjust ones). As mentioned, we can denote socio-political norms and rules as just (or unjust) only if they have a *moral aspect*. This moral aspect of just norms is the *good*. It has been mentioned too that to apply just norms to every person to whom these norms relate is always a moral matter, and to be just is a moral virtue. Thus the normative foundation I have in mind is that of *just socio-political norms* which include this element of moral goodness.

Symmetric reciprocity (the precondition of the universal actualiza-

tion of the golden rule of justice) excludes relations of superordination and subordination, hierarchy and domination. It includes social
intercourse, communication, mutual understanding, co-operation,
and the like. Common normative foundations must be theoretically
proposed for the actual normative foundation of social intercourse,
communication, mutual understanding, co-operation, and the like.
The kind of procedures that secure the full universal actualization of
the golden rule of justice, the question of whether procedures alone
can secure this end, or whether certain substantive qualifications
must be accepted as guiding ideas of such procedures – these are the
main issues I shall address.

IS A COMPLETELY JUST SOCIETY POSSIBLE? IS IT DESIRABLE?

Moralists, dreamers and religious enthusiasts have rejected the
norms and rules of their times as wicked. They have cried out that
virtue is trampled underfoot and evil flourishes and that no justice
exists on earth. The actualization of the idea 'to each according to
his or her moral goodness' is justice, and nothing short of this is
just. But such justice will never be.

Social contestants of injustice have very rarely, if ever, had this
kind of justice in mind. When contrasting their imaginary norms
and rules to the existing (institutionalized) ones, they have not had
as their objective a world of perfect moral goodness. Rather, their
objective has been to secure a greater amount of, or a different kind
of, freedom: an increase in life chances (of everyone or a particular
social cluster); new, alternative political and social institutions; or
admittance (of everyone or of their particular cluster) to the old,
existing institutions. Such objectives have shone in the light of
perfect justice. If only society would accept the new norms and
rules, the world (our world) would be what it is not: it would be
just.

The more justice becomes dynamic and the more dynamic justice
is taken for granted, the more rapidly justice transmutes into
injustice. Yesterday's justice is today's injustice; today's justice is
tomorrow's injustice. Justice becomes a chameleon in reverse: it
always assumes colours *other* than those of its environment. The
moment the environment assimilates to its colour, justice itself
changes colour. We chase justice without embracing it. We correct
particular injustices, we achieve particular justices, but we never
achieve full justice. Justice is a phantom of different shapes. Can this
phantom be caught at all? Is a just society possible?

There are a number of different answers to this question. I shall enumerate only four, and shall leave aside their variations and combinations.

1 All societies have been just, at least as long as a particular form of domination has enjoyed legitimacy. Just society is possible, but 'justice' is not an indicator of the desirability of a society.
2 All hitherto existing societies have been unjust, because, owing to exploitation, domination and the division of labour, they have not experienced factual equality (*égalité de fait*). The future society will abolish the social division of labour, and all exploitation and inequality, thus the future society (socialism) will be the perfectly just society. This society has not so far been possible, but it is possible now. Indeed, a completely just society is desirable.
3 We must accept 'chasing the phantom' as part of our human condition, and live with it. We are always able to correct some injustices. New injustices will undoubtedly occur, and in time be corrected. Progress is piecemeal. The just society is indeed a phantom, because it is neither possible nor desirable.
4 A society beyond justice is impossible and undesirable. A completely just society is possible but undesirable.

Since this last statement coincides with my own standpoint, I shall elaborate on it in some detail.

A society 'beyond justice' is one where no concept of justice applies. A completely just society is a society where *only the static concept of justice* applies. I shall begin with a discussion of the former statement and proceed to the latter.

Only where there is justice is there injustice. If there were no injustice, there would be no justice either. If we opt for a society where there is no injustice at all, and where there cannot be, we opt for a society without justice, for the notion 'justice' would no longer make sense. Thus we would opt for a society *beyond justice*. Since the formal concept of justice is the *maxim* of justice, a society beyond justice must be one where the formal concept of justice does not apply. The formal concept of justice, as the maxim of justice, enjoins that, if certain norms and rules constitute a social cluster, these very norms and rules must be applied to every member of the cluster consistently and continuously (both in action and in judgement). The formal concept (the maxim) of justice can only be eliminated if *all norms and rules are eliminated*, for, if even one norm or rule remains valid, this norm should be applied consistently and continuously to all members of the cluster it in part constitutes.

A society without any norm or rule is only conceivable if we subscribe to the chimera of an 'anthropological revolution' – that is, if we project a humankind in which every single human being is the *embodiment* of morality (rational humankind) or of the 'human essence'. However, should normative authority only dwell 'within' individuals, should it become completely 'internal', it could still provide us with a yardstick to measure action and judgement, and this yardstick should then be applied consistently and continuously in our interaction with all other people. When the young Marx insisted that in a future (non-alienated) society punishment would become self-punishment, and our fellow creatures would provide our absolution, he was still operating with the notion of formal justice, even if he considered that he had moved beyond justice. This self-punishing individual of the future has reason for self-punishment upon failure to act according to a norm, and has committed an injustice in failing so to act. Self-punishment will follow in proportion to the injustice committed. The transgressor's fellow creatures will be able to grant absolution because they will know as well that an injustice has been committed (otherwise they would view the self-punishment as stupidity), and they will confer absolution only because (and in so far as) self-punishment has already occurred. In other words, not even the notion of an 'anthropological revolution' leads us *per se* beyond justice. It only does so if we imagine that every person is *equally* and *completely* identical with rational humankind (or human essence), a situation where no one can commit injustice. And, if no one can commit injustice, there is neither justice nor injustice; thus 'justice' as a concept makes no sense at all, and we are indeed 'beyond justice'.

The 'anthropological revolution' is an absurdity, and not simply something 'not yet feasible'. That which is not yet feasible (not within reach in the foreseeable future) can still capture our imagination as a *rational utopia*. And such a rational utopia can still provide regulative ideas for our actions and judgements. Yet the situation projected by the notion of an 'anthropological revolution' is a *non-rational utopia*, because it includes a self-contradiction. What is more, it is self-contradictory not only as a socio-political utopia but also as a moral utopia, as I argued in the first section of chapter 2. Briefly, this argument was as follows. A person who prefers suffering injustice to committing injustice is a righteous person. If no injustice *can* be either committed or suffered, it is not the case that *everybody* will be righteous; rather *nobody* will be. That is why the 'best possible moral world' must be one wherein wrong can still be committed, as well as suffered.

The arguments used to show that the 'anthropological revolution' is neither viable nor desirable as the basis of a moral utopia can equally be used to show its insufficiency as the basis of a socio-political utopia – all the more so in that the moral utopia serves as the foundation of the socio-political utopia. However, such a socio-political utopia can never even be imagined, for the simple reason that it is beyond imagination. Anarchists are, as a rule, caught red-handed if they try to answer the question 'How are social institutions possible without any social norms and rules?' They usually reply that these and other norms will be abolished (made redundant), and, while such propositions are always arguable, they cannot present us with even the most abstract and abstruse image of a society where no norms and rules exist. Where there are no norms and rules, there are no institutions, no communities, no human bonds, no human existence.

It is unnecessary to touch upon the problem of 'human nature' in order to reject the utopia of a society beyond justice projected on the basis of an 'anthropological revolution'. One could ponder the questions (of no small relevance) of whether our psychological make-up, our fragility, the limits to the use of our reason are so many insurmountable obstacles to any such revolution. These and similar considerations could provide new arguments for the unfeasibility of the idea, but they would add nothing to the fundamental view that a society beyond justice, and the 'anthropological revolution', are undesirable. The latter is the stronger argument.

Of course, making a case against the 'anthropological revolution' is not tantamount to making a case against changing our social nature. Up to a point, human nature is very elastic, in ways that are for the better as well as for the worse. Even individuals can undergo quite substantial changes in the direction either of moral elevation or degradation. Considered commitment to positive norms and values can bring out the best in us; unconsidered attachment to untested norms, or, alternatively, the dissolution of normative structures and commitments, the worst. The limits to our nature are set by the 'human condition', by the substitution of norm regulation for instinct regulation. Instead of pondering a world 'beyond justice', a world without any kind of norm and rule regulation, if we address the following questions we should be considering something not only more 'feasible', but also more humane.

a   What type of norms and rules are desirable?

b   What are the desirable procedures for constructing such valid norms?
c   (On an even more utopian level.) What could be the normative foundation of the best possible moral world?

Thus I have reached the conclusion that to go 'beyond justice' is neither possible nor desirable. I shall now take up my statement 'A completely just society is a society where *only the static concept of justice* applies.'

Whether and to what extent a particular society is just or unjust depends first and foremost on the attitude of the members of that society. If all norms and rules of a society are taken for granted, if no one utters the devalidating sentence 'This norm/rule is unjust', then the society can legitimately be called 'just'. Yet members of other societies or cultures (either as contestants or as observers) can still utter the devalidating sentence 'Such and such norms and rules of the (first) society are unjust.' Since the devalidating sentence is not simultaneously delegitimizing, the society contested or observed from without will remain just, but its justice will be relativized. It will not be completely just.

A society can be completely just if in one of following two alternative situations holds.

1   There is a single set of norms and rules in *all* societies and every norm or rule is taken for granted (it is not queried or contested by any member of any society).
2   There are different sets of norms and rules in different societies and cultures, but, none the less, every one of these different norms and rules is taken for granted by all members of all cultures. No member of any culture makes a devalidating statement about any of the norms and rules of any other culture (society).

In the history of humankind there have existed several societies unfamiliar with dynamic justice. However, their justice was subsequently relativized by other cultures, marking the departure from the attitude of 'natural' ethnocentrism, and increasingly also from the position of rationality of intellect. The emergence of dynamic justice has transformed our regard in such a way that no society can ever again be completely just, only just 'to a greater or lesser extent', and similarly, unjust 'to a greater or lesser extent'.

Even in these terms, a completely just society is clearly *not impossible*. It is only impossible under the condition that justice will always remain dynamic. But we cannot make true statements about the future. The statement 'Justice will always be dynamic' is neither true nor false.

Should justice cease to be dynamic, a completely just society would become possible both in a prospective and in a retrospective sense. More precisely, it would become possible in case (1) only prospectively, in case (2) both prospectively and retrospectively.

In terms of model (1), the social norms and rules are to be established for the whole of humankind. From the perspective being taken here it is quite irrelevant *what kind* of norms and rules they are, and how they would be established. What is relevant is that all of them will be taken for granted. They could be norms and rules initially established by consent; they could be norms and rules initially established by a central agency of domination. In addition, they could be either egalitarian or strictly hierarchical rules. In any case, though, this society would be completely just, because no one could say (or would say) that any of the norms and rules in question were unjust. The norms and rules, whatever form they took, would be consistently and continuously applied to every member of any given cluster constituted by them. Static justice would remain in full force. If Huxley's imaginary institutions in *Brave New World* were to be established on our planet, society would be completely just. The norms and rules constituting the alpha cluster would apply, consistently and continuously, to all members of the alpha cluster, and the norms and rules constituting the beta cluster would apply in the same way to all members of the beta cluster. And so it would also be in the lower clusters. A society like this would develop the self-identity of the only true, complete and absolutely just world order, and this is why no other society could be regarded by its members as completely just, not even as just in retrospect.

Model 2 is the negative utopia of *total cultural relativism*.

I have hinted in chapter 1 at the self-contradiction inherent in theories of total cultural relativism. If the statement 'Each and every culture is unique and cannot be either compared or ranked' is true, and if the evaluative conclusion drawn from this statement ('Cultures should neither be ranked nor compared') is right, then the ranking and comparing of different cultures has already taken place, in that the cultures which permit the above statement to be made and the above evaluative conclusion to be drawn are seen as superior to others: they contain one more true sentence and one more right injunction than any other culture. This self-contradiction could only be eliminated if both the statement and the evaluative conclusion were accepted by all cultures. If the members of all cultures agreed that neither their truth claims nor their validity claims could possibly be compared to the truth claims or validity claims of any other culture, then no member of any culture could devalidate any norm or rule of any other culture. It would then become impossible to make the statement 'This norm is unjust.' One could only go so far as to say, 'This norm is different.' To renounce devalidation procedures altogether is a commitment with retrospective force. If the justice of no contemporary culture could be 'relativized', the justice of no previous culture could be 'relativized' either. The relativizing tendency of dynamic justice would disappear for ever.

And in this way too dynamic justice would disappear in every single culture. If any given norms and rules are just as good as others, how could we make the devalidating claim 'These norms are unjust' in our own culture? Once again, we could only go so far as to say, 'Our norms are different from yours.' And, indeed, the model of total cultural relativism does not allow the image of a culture in which norms and rules are genuinely contested: no reason could possibly exist for such a contestation.

Although sophisticated theories could still invent an (imaginary) process of new culture formation within a universe of hermetically closed cultures, strong arguments would support the prediction that in such a universe all norms and rules within all cultural units *should be taken for granted.* If all norms and rules are considered only as *different* in kind, and no norms and rules can be devalidated as unjust by the members of any other culture, and *if* the norms and rules are taken for granted within each and every culture, *then* all societies are *completely just.*

A completely just society of this kind is unlikely to come about, but it is not impossible.

Thus a completely just society is possible, but a completely just society is a *nightmare.*

The negative utopia of a completely just society contradicts the supreme universal principles. It contradicts the conditional value (equality) and the procedural value (communicative rationality). If one is committed to realizing the universal values, one *cannot want* a society where no one can make the devalidating statement 'This norm/rule/law is unjust.' However, a society in which people can and do make this devalidating statement is *not* a 'just society'; certainly, it is not a completely just society. Members of a free society, a free humankind, are, by definition, free to test and query norms, rules and laws again and again, for these are not taken for granted. They are not taken for granted because dynamic justice is taken for granted.

Are people, then, simply 'mistaken' in cherishing dreams of a 'just society'? Is their dream nothing but a kind of 'false consciousness'? Are not those theorists right who describe such dreams in terms of 'chasing phantoms'? Is it not true that all recommendations concerning justice as such are futile, seeing that, in correcting certain injustices, we inevitably create new ones: the process of piecemeal progression?

Such a conclusion would reaffirm dynamic justice as a taken-for-granted procedure, but it would simultaneously delimit the scope and force of dynamic justice. Those cherishing the dream of a 'just society' do not delimit, however, the scope and force of dynamic justice, but, rather, live up to it fully. 'Just society', in the everyday use of the term, is only a shorthand formulation for the image of a society where alternative norms and rules are substituted for existing ones considered unjust.

The statement that a just society is not desirable is not tantamount to saying that seeking alternative norms and rules, not merely in respect of replacing one particular norm or rule with another, is 'chasing phantoms', and is thus either futile or undesirable.

The incomplete socio-political concept of justice does not aim at constructing the image of a just, or completely just, society. Rather, it addresses two related problems. The first concerns the initial establishment of socio-political norms and rules (and laws). The second concerns the procedures through which socio-political norms and rules (and laws) should be contested as unjust.

The firt problem can be briefly formulated in the following way: how can socio-political norms and rules (and laws) be established by equally free people rationally, so that, at the time of being established, these norms and rules (and laws) provide equal life chances and equal freedom for all?

The second problem can be briefly formulated thus: if any of the socio-political norms, rules, and laws are seen as unjust by members of the generation which initially established them, or by members of a future generation, how should this contestation be carried out rationally, by equally free people, so that the result ensures anew the equal life chances and equal freedom of all?

The normative foundation of justice is not the normative foundation of a 'just society', but the normative foundation of all possible societies where the 'golden rule' is actualized in any form of socio-political intercourse. I turn now to this question.

THE NORMATIVE FOUNDATION OF AN INCOMPLETE ETHICO-POLITICAL
CONCEPT OF JUSTICE: THE SOCIO-POLITICAL ASPECT

The normative foundation of an ethico-political justice is tantamount to the normative foundation of an idealized model of the best possible socio-political world. The theory is constituted by certain value premises as grounding norms already selected, interpreted and formulated in view of the ideal model allegedly conjectured from those premises and norms. However, even if the selection, interpretation and formulation of value premises and grounding norms happens to be performed under the guidance of the 'model idea', neither the value premises nor the grounding norms are 'irrationally chosen', nor are they arbitrary. As Hegel's dictum correctly stated, the *Sittlichkeit* of the age serves as a real starting-point. The grounding norms and the value premises of both the philosophical theory and the ideal model of the best possible socio-political world cannot be termed 'empirical', but they must have, and indeed do have, an empirical 'backing'. There must be at least some people committed to the very values, and guided by the very norms, which constitute the 'normative foundation' of the theory and the ideal model of the best possible socio-political world. Of course, it is by no means necessary that the social actors committed to those value premises and norms should philosophically reflect upon what they are doing and why they are doing it.[1] The 'empirical backing' of the ethico-political concept of justice can be understood in terms of a *bet*, to touch upon Lucien Goldmann's interpretation of Pascal's theory. The philosopher bets on both the present and the future simultaneously. This bet is on actors of the present committed to the same value premises and norms in their actions, interactions, forms of communication and lifestyles here and now (in the present), in which the future society, the ideal society, the 'model' of a good society, must be grounded. To bet on this model, idea or utopia is to bet on the actors who advance, represent and embody this model, idea or utopia in their lives. Such a bet is not arbitrary. Good reasons can be given, and first and foremost good moral reasons, why one does in reality bet on this actor and not that actor. Nor is such a bet irrational. A philosopher does not enter into philosophical speculation with a mind free of all normative commitments. This person bets on particular people (particular forms of life) in value-rational terms; the bet itself is a considered act resulting from previous value commitments. Although the bet is neither irrational nor arbitrary, a bet it remains. The model, the idea, the utopia cannot be conjectured from the socio-political structure of the present, although modern philosophers often venture into sham deductions. Only the bearers of alternative and utopian ways of life could actualize models, ideas and utopias of this kind, but whether they would do so or not is unknown at the time of the bet (that is why it is a bet). If we design an ethico-political concept of justice, if we ponder justice and injustice in our everyday life, neither our value commitments nor our norms remains hidden behind the veil of ignorance. But what does remain hidden under this veil is the relevance or irrelevance of the idea, and the future of the values and norms we stand for.

The incomplete ethico-political concept of justice I am going to recommend is committed to answering the question 'How is a pluralistic universe possible in which each culture is bound to every other culture by ties of symmetric reciprocity?' Thus the normative foundation of the philosophical theory must be simultaneously the normative foundation of such a pluralistic universe. The question to be answered runs as follows: 'What kind of norm(s), if obeyed, would make possible a pluralistic universe where each culture is bound to every other culture by ties of symmetric reciprocity?' The actualization of that which is possible is hidden under the 'veil of ignorance', and this is why it is of no *cognitive* relevance for the theory. The theory I am going to recommend is not empirically founded. It has, none the less, an empirical 'backing'. One can always point to the *fact* that there are indeed people here and now who observe the 'golden rule' in all their social and political actions (speech acts included). Those who, if it comes to judging acts of domination, force and violence, in whichever culture they may appear, denounce the application of different standards as if they were double standards, belong to this group of people.

The generalization and universalization of the 'golden rule' is the generalization and universalization of the 'just procedure'. Generalization means that the golden rule, traditionally viewed as a rule of *static justice*, becomes the rule of *dynamic justice* as well. In other words, the golden rule not only informs the proper application of pre-existing norms and rules, but also informs the establishment and contestation of all possible norms. Universalization means that the procedure enjoined by the golden rule (in both static and dynamic justice) is conceived of as the *common* norm of the overarching cluster 'humankind'. It follows not only that each culture of a pluralistic universe is tied to all others by the bonds of symmetric reciprocity, but also that the denizens of any particular culture within the pluralistic universe are tied to each other by these bonds.

I term the generalizing and universalizing of the 'golden rule' the *supreme political good*. I term the plurality of cultures and ways of life which meet the standards of the supreme political good the *supreme social good*. The supreme political good actualizes the universal norm 'equal freedom for all'. The supreme social good actualizes the universal norm 'equal life chances for all'.

The actualization of the supreme social–political good is the 'best possible social–political world'. The best possible social–political world is, however, not identical with the *best possible moral world*. And this is so not only because the very idea of the supreme social good (plurality of ways of life) carries the claim that there may exist several different 'best possible moral worlds' (plural), but also because the best possible social–political world is only the *precondition* of best possible moral worlds; it is not yet such a world. The 'best possible moral world' is the *telos* inherent in the life and actions of righteous persons.

All the same, if we believe that actualizing the supreme social–political good is the precondition for actualizing the supreme moral good, we cannot impute the supreme moral good (the best possible moral world) as the inherent *telos* to the actions and ways of life of *all righteous persons*. We must then assume that righteousness must be somehow informed by the idea of the supreme social–political good. Only thus can a form of righteousness come about which indeed posits the *telos* of the best possible moral world – in other words, the supreme moral good.

An incomplete ethico-political concept of justice includes two elements, as do all ethico-political concepts of justice: the political (socio-political) element, and the ethical element. The socio-political aspect is the normative foundation of the possibility of a pluralistic universe in which every culture is tied to every other by bonds of symmetric reciprocity. The ethical aspect addresses the problem of the *moral–ethical propensities* required for the *readiness* to actualize such a universe – in other words, to live up to its normative requirements. It must be repeated once again that the normative foundation of the best possible social–political world must not presuppose the state of 'abundance', and that the discussion of moral propensities required for the readiness to actualize such a world and to keep it running must not presuppose any 'anthropological revolution'.

The formulation of an incomplete ethico-political concept of justice poses several serious difficulties. This is so because the concept is simultaneously universalizing and deuniversalizing. That which is to be universalized (and generalized) is the 'golden rule' of just procedure. However, if the simultaneous existence of several different cultures and ways of life is posited, everything else should be deuniversalized. No particular patterns of political institutions, retribution, distribution, ethics or particular cultural values can be designed as befitting the idea, because it is assumed that all patterns are to be in accordance with particular forms of life, and thus different. The only institution to be addressed in concrete terms is the procedure inherent in symmetric reciprocity, for this alone is posited as universal. Similarly, only that aspect of ethics is to be addressed in universal terms which keeps the universal institutions running. Complete ethico-political concepts of justice have the advantage of concreteness. Since they reflect upon one single way of life, since they idealize one particular kind of *Sittlichkeit*, they experience no restraint in universalizing it. Authors of complete ethico-political concepts of justice can rationally *intuit*, for we can all intuit within the tradition of our own culture. An intuition of this kind can be good and fruitful and garbed neatly in the mantle of conjectures and refutations. Rawls's *Theory of Justice* is a good example of a complete ethico-political concept of justice of this kind. Rawls operates with the idealized model of the 'triad' pattern, and conceals his own intuition behind the ingenious construct of the 'original position'. The model of 'just distribution' becomes *concrete* because it is the idealized distributive model of a particular way of life. The price to be paid for such concreteness is a kind of fundamentalism. A particular model of distribution is presented in such a way that it appears *the* model of just distribution. The concrete, if idealized, *modus operandi* of a particular way of life is universalized as such, and no other types of distributive patterns can claim 'justice'.

How can this pitfall be avoided? How can anyone design a model without relying upon his or her own intuition? Also, how can anyone then resist the temptation to set the imagination free and commit to paper the very ideal arrived at? The incompleteness of ethico-political justice is apparently fraught with a dilemma. Either we restrict ourselves to the discussion of a few norms, substantive or procedural, that we conceive as the sole universals, and thus completely forgo any discussion of political institutions, social structures, property relations, technologies and moral norms proper, or we fall prey to the 'universalizing fallacy'. Yet I believe that this dilemma can be circumvented. In this chapter I discuss only the norms I recommend as universals, and I do so in highly abstract terms, without making any attempt at concretization. I willingly admit that my cultural background, my intuition, my tradition, are the sources of my concrete ideal.[2] But I do not intend to universalize my ideal. Instead, I invite all those committed to generalizing and universalizing the 'golden rule', regardless of philosophical persuasion, to present their own social ideals, and to do so whilst relying upon their own traditions, their own cultural background, their own intuitions. If no one is trapped by the universalizing fallacy, the plurality of such social ideals can be nothing but the happy anticipation of a pluralistic universe, where each culture is tied to every other by the bonds of symmetric reciprocity.

In his study 'Diskursethik' ('Discourse Ethics'), Habermas proposes the theoretical acceptance of the 'fundamental principle of universalization' (*Universalisierungsgrundsatz*) as the *sole moral principle*. 'Discourse ethics' is described there as the procedure by which human beings can completely live up to the imperative of the moral principle. The conclusion is self-evident (within the philosophy of Habermas), for the 'fundamental principle of universalization' itself has been founded via a quasi-transcendental deduction from the conditions of argumentation (*Argumentationsvoraussetzungen*). For our purposes it is not necessary to follow the logical (and critical) steps which have resulted in Habermas's theoretical proposal. It suffices to discuss the proposal itself.

I can sum up my view of the 'discourse ethics' advocated in Habermas's paper in the following steps.

1   Both the 'fundamental principle of universalization' and the procedure by which men and women can live up to 'discourse ethics' can be viewed as *alternatives to a social-contract theory*. Habermas proposes a principle under the guidance of which, and a procedure via which, *socio-political* norms can be tested and established in a world of general and universal symmetric reciprocity. To put this the other way round, only if socio-political norms are tested and established under the guidance of the fundamental principle of universalization and via the procedure of discourse ethics are socio-political relationships established as relationships of symmetric reciprocity. This is why I accept both the fundamental principle of universalization and the discourse ethics as the *basic normative foundation* of an incomplete ethico-political concept of justice, and simultaneously as the normative foundation of a (possible) world in which all cultures (ways of life) are tied to one another by the bonds of symmetric reciprocity. However, I add that the basic normative foundation is not yet the complete normative foundation, and I

shall adduce suggestions as to how to complement it.

2 I shall show that Habermas's 'sole moral principle' is not a substitute for the categorical imperative (as he believes it is). Habermas's 'sole moral principle' is the *principle of justice*. Of course, justice includes a moral aspect, and for this reason the principle of justice is *also a moral principle*. But the principle of justice is not a pure moral principle *par excellence* (as the categorical imperative truly is), because it has to have recourse to interests and consequences, which a pure moral principle must not do. From this respect the Habermasian proposal is utterly un-Kantian. Yet in another respect it is Kantian in an orthodox sense. Habermas wants to reduce all moral principles to one 'sole' principle, and he does so more conclusively than Kant ever did. In my view (and I shall return to this point in chapter 6), morality cannot be grounded on one single principle, not even on one *kind* of principle.

I turn now to Habermas's proposal in detail.

The 'fundamental principle of universalization' is formulated twice. I quote the first formulation: 'Thus every valid norm must satisfy the condition that the consequences and side effects which would (predictably) result from its general observance in the course of satisfying the interests of each and every individual, could be accepted (and preferred to all known alternative regulations) by all those concerned.'[3] Habermas also defines 'discourse ethics' twice. Again, I quote the first formulation: 'In a discourse ethics, a norm may only claim validity when all those potentially concerned with it, as participants in a practical discourse, achieve (or could achieve) a consensus that this norm is valid.'[4] The second formulation is more laconic, but it is also stronger: 'Only those norms which find (or can find) the consent of all those concerned as participants in a practical discourse may claim validity.'[5]

Habermas assumes that the choice of norms can be rationally grounded. Further, he imposes a restriction on the factual universality of the fundamental principle of universalization: 'I have introduced the fundamental principle of universalization as a rule of argumentation which makes consensus possible in practical discourses when matters can be settled in the general interest of everyone concerned.'[6]

In formulating the fundamental principle of universalization, Habermas has taken a decisive, if not yet the final, step away from his own orthodox consensus theory of truth (rightness) in practical discourse. Within the framework of the orthodox consensus theory, discourse is not guided by any principle at all. The rules of speech themselves engender the true (and right) consensus. The participants in discourse live up to the rules of speech, and to these rules alone. Living up to the rules of speech is not dependent on the empirical will; it is not a matter of choice. Prior to writing his paper on discourse ethics, Habermas was in complete agreement with Apel, who insisted that the moral 'founding norm' is *implicit* in the *will to argumentation*, and that this is why this will can be termed 'unconditional' and 'categorical'.[7] True enough, Apel restricted this proposal to *philosophical argumentation alone*, whereas Habermas applied it to *every discourse*. As many critics of Habermas, myself among them, have pointed out, no discourse can result in a 'true consensus' unless the participants share at least one value, norm or principle before entering discourse ('higher-order consensus'). It is obvious that Habermas, in his paper on discourse ethics, has modified his theory along the lines suggested by certain of these critics. The 'founding norm' is no longer implicit in the argumentation, but prior to it. Discourse does not engender true consensus unless it is conducted under the guidance of the fundamental principle of universalization. One could even apply the Kantian–Hegelian distinction of *morality* and *Sittlichkeit* to this theoretical recommendation. The *Sittlichkeit* of discourse is informed by morality – namely, by the fundamental principle of universalization.

Despite this departure from his former theory, Habermas, in my view, has not as yet gone far enough. The fundamental principle of universalization has been kept completely formal. Habermas wants to avoid the traps of a complete ethico-political concept of justice, and to my mind rightly so. He is fully aware of the dangers implicit in the attempt to suggest *any substantive norm* as the norm of 'higher-order consensus'. Succumbing to such temptation would be for him tantamount to *superimposing* a norm (value) native to our culture, tradition, biography or intuition on the participants in the discourse, and thus tantamount to *anticipating* the result of the discourse itself. (This is exactly what Rawls has done.) However, if no substantive value is provided, anticipated or suggested in the 'higher-order consensus', the principle itself cannot possibly provide the guidance it is supposed to provide for the discourse.

Since in my view Habermas's fundamental principle of univer-salization is a sensible alternative to the 'social contract', but not to the categorical imperative, in what follows I shall refer (with certain modifications) only to social and political norms, not to moral norms proper.

The fundamental principle of universalization is about testing any given social or political norm or rule. Social–political norms and rules must stand the test of whether the foreseeable consequences and side effects they would exert, if accepted, on the satisfaction of the interests of every single person would be accepted by every person.

At first sight this formula seems to meet all the requirements of the normative foundation of a society based on symmetric reciprocity. If the consequences and side effects experienced by every single person are considered, 'equal life chances for all' are secured. If these consequences and side effects are not only considered but also accepted by every person, 'equal freedom for all' is secured as well. Consequently, under the guidance of the fundamental principle of universalization, and via rational discourse which lives up to this principle, social–political norms that *actualize* the universal principles ('equal freedom for all', 'equal life chances for all') can be established, designed and followed. Moreover, the formula leaves the door open for any further contestation of justice ('not this is just but that is just'). Indeed, only the *foreseeable* side effects and consequences can be considered. Should unforeseen consequences and side effects occur, an alternative norm must be suggested and accepted under the guidance of the same principle.

What then, is the problem?

For some time now Habermas has been a principal exponent of the view that the validity of all norms should be tested in a cognitive procedure. His paper on discourse ethics contains a lengthy discussion of Tugendhat's proposal, one which is the very opposite of his own. For Tugendhat, Habermas argues, discourse aims at 'will formation'. Consensus is free and true if it results from the will of all – that is, from each and every will. Once a common will has been achieved, it is irrelevant to ask whether or not it issued from a rational argumentation procedure. Against Tugendhat, Habermas contends that such a proposal does not permit us to distinguish between a true and a false consensus. In this I agree completely with Habermas. Tugendhat succeeds in merging the 'will of all' with the 'general will', but is the will of all as the general will also, by definition, the *good will*?

Despite having provided sound reasons for rejecting Tugendhat's consensus theory, Habermas, in my view, actually ends up proposing something very similar. If we accept the fundamental principle of universalization as the guiding principle of discourse, the discourse itself will aim solely at 'will formation'. The *sole criterion* of the rightness (justness) of norms will be whether every person accepts the side effects and consequences ensuing from the acceptance of any given norm. The discourse will centre on the free acceptance of consequences and side effects, and not on determining via a cognitive process whether the norm is *right or just*. The following is suggested to us: the *sole* criterion of the rightness and justice of a socio-political norm is the free acceptance of all side effects and consequences which the norm, if accepted, would impose on every individual by each and everyone. Here again the 'will of all' becomes tantamount to the 'general will', but whether it is the 'good will' we do not know, nor can we know, for there is no substantive criterion provided for gauging the goodness of the will.

In Habermas's formula very little room has been left for cognitive procedures proper. It is the 'satisfaction of interests' which informs the will, and does so *directly*. However, interests (or needs, as I should prefer to call them, 'interest' being fully 'booked' by the 'triad' model in the context of a specific understanding) are not 'natural entities': they are themselves informed by values and norms. Moreover, interests (needs) themselves cannot be subjected to discussion at all. More precisely, they cannot be thus subjected if we are to achieve consensus at all, and they should not be. As to the first point, Hume already knew, and he was right, that the discussion of needs is never conclusive. One justifies needs with other needs, and so it goes *ad infinitum*. As to the second point, if we take the notion 'equality of life chances' seriously, then *all* needs must be recognized, and recognized equally (recognition of needs is included in the full recognition of the personality). Habermas's formula suggests this too. But how can we escape this vicious circle where needs themselves are informed by values and norms, but where the will to the acceptance of a norm is informed by needs (interests)? There is no way other than by suggesting that the discourse should be conducted *among values*, provided that each value has an affinity to one or another need of individual actors. And this is indeed the only viable way because the concrete need structure (if you wish, the structure of different kinds of interests) is strictly individual. Habermas's formula covered this problem, for he did not suggest that the side effects and consequences resulting from the validation of a norm should promote in full the interest satisfaction of every individual; he only suggested that every individual should accept those consequences and side effects *on the grounds* of his or her interest. However, this proposal *implies* (if we do not assume that interests or needs are given as 'nature', and Habermas does not) that the discourse conducted should be a *value discourse*. (One can say, 'I vote for Labour and not for the Conservatives, although progressive taxation is not in my interest.

But I do this for reasons of principle. I support the value of social equality.') It should be added that one can enter into rational discourse by having recourse to interests and needs only, and we do so all the time, but such a discussion cannot result in consensus; it can only result in rational compromise.

Thus the discourse (in both a real and a hypothetical situation) concerns *values*, and this is why the will cannot be directly informed by interest. Still, if discourse takes place among values, the *cognitive process* proper sets in. What is to be tested in this cognitive process is the truth (or falsity), the rightness (or wrongness) of values. Only if consensus is reached about the *goodness* of a value (or certain values) can the 'general will' (tantamount to the 'will of all') be in fact the good will of everyone.

Granted this, a value discourse cannot be settled in the particular way Habermas insisted it should (by the *free* consent of *all*) without a 'higher-order consensus' about the *unconditional and absolute* validity of at least one single value (prior to the discourse). Contestants enter the discourse with different values, and they all try to justify their values (as right and true). They do so by resorting to values higher than those which they want to justify, by proving that the latter are but an interpretation of the higher values, or that they can be related to these higher values without logical contradiction. If the participants do not share any supreme value, they will resort to different kinds of supreme values, and the discourse must then remain unsettled. However, if they share one supreme value, the discourse can be settled in one of two ways (or by a combination of these ways). The positive outcome of the discourse can either be that all contesting values can be related to the supreme shared value without self-contradiction, or that they are only different interpretations of the same value. In both these cases it has been proved that all contesting values are *true values*, and the socio-political norm to be established should be such as to facilitate the actualization of all of them. The result can also be that certain values cannot be related without logical contradiction to the supreme (shared) value, and that they are not interpretations of that value either. But, since *all contestants* have already accepted this supreme value as absolute and unconditional, those unable to relate their values (without logical contradiction) to the supreme value will concede, by their free will, that their values are wrong (untrue). For consensus is always free if the person who resigns a particular value does so out of rational insight.

The value of the 'higher-order consensus' must be taken for granted as self-evident, for it has a *normative power beyond reasoning*. What I termed the attitude of 'rationality of reason' is the foundation of all kinds of rationalities. Even the attitude of 'rationality of intellect' cannot completely circumvent it. We can reach agreement about something we disagree upon if we already agree on something else. If we do not accept *any substantive value* as taken for granted, as *not open* to testing, consensus can be based on will formation alone, thus it will not be rational. Total rationalism is self-contradictory.

It is thus seen that Habermas's fundamental principle of universalization does not provide us with the guidance intended by Habermas himself (aiming at the cognitive testing of the justice or injustice of norms and the rational establishment of just ones) unless at least one substantive value is 'given', a substantive value which informs the fundamental principle of universalization itself.

If we have only the *formal* fundamental principle of universaliza-tion in mind, and if we abstract from all substantive values which may inform this principle, we must reach the disquieting conclusion that *any* norm or rule can be proved just and right. Everyone concerned can agree to accept the norm that every man and woman over sixty years of age should be abandoned in the desert to die of starvation.[8] All that is required is that every member of the community in question should freely consent to the consequences (and the side effects) of this action, and that they submit to the same fate when reaching the age of sixty. This follows strictly from the fundamental principle of universalization, and it only sounds absurd because we have already accepted freedom and life as universal values, and because we cannot imagine that people might freely renounce those values. Habermas's fundamental principle of uni-versalization sounds correct because Habermas himself accepted those values unconditionally (something which shines throughout his text), and because he surmises that everyone else has done so. But there is a major difference between accepting a norm freely and accepting a norm which actualizes freedom.

Let me now reformulate Habermas's fundamental principle of universalization and the definition of 'discourse ethics' as *the normative foundation of an incomplete ethico-political concept of justice* and, simultaneously, *the normative foundation of a pluralistic cultural universe*, where each culture is bound to every other culture by the bonds of symmetric reciprocity.

My reformulation of the fundamental principle of universalization runs as follows: 'Every valid social and political norm and rule (every law) must meet the condition that the foreseeable conse-quences and side effects the general observance of that law (norm) exacts on the satisfaction of the needs of each and every individual would be accepted by everyone concerned, and that the claim of the norm to actualize the universal values of freedom and/or life could be accepted by each and every individual regardless of the values to which they are committed. The consequences and side effects of these norms must be preferred to those ensuing from all alternative regulations, and the norm must actualize the universal values of freedom and/or life to a greater extent (more fully) than other alternative regulations would do.'

Thus, in my conception, the fundamental principle of universalization is the principle of *socio-political legislation*.

No single individual, no 'authoritative body', can live up to the fundamental principle of legislation. Not even the wisest legislator endowed with best of will can substitute his insight for the insight of everyone concerned. In ancient communities, given their roughly homogeneous system of values and needs, a substitution like this might have been possible, but not today. In a modern society *real discourse* must be conducted with the participation of everyone concerned. *Discourse* is the *only possible*, and not just the best or most preferable, *procedure of legislation*, if the requirements of the fundamental principle of legislation are to be met. Consequently, I subscribe to Habermas's definition of 'discourse ethics', with one modification: I do not speak of norms in general, only of social and political norms (laws) in particular. My formula reads as follows: 'According to the ethics of discourse, a social–political norm (law) can claim validity only if all those concerned, as *participants in a practical discourse*, aim at (or would aim at) agreement about the validity of that norm.' Discourse ethics is doubtless an ethics because it includes, as well as excludes, certain attitudes towards values (norms), and at the same time provides a *yardstick* for the recognition and/or non-recognition of practical claims. To my mind, discourse ethics is the central moral institution of the *ethics of citizenship*, although it does not encompass all of its aspects.

I have restricted the applicability of both the fundamental principle of universalization and discourse ethics to the process of legislation. I subscribe to them (in a modified form) only in so far as the validation of socio-political norms and rules (just norms and rules, just laws) is concerned. I have advanced my view that the fundamental principle of universalization is not a viable alternative, and in fact is no alternative at all, to the categorical imperative. Although the basic problems of moral philosophy will be raised only in my final chapter, I shall give some reasons at this point for rejecting Habermas's formulas as irrelevant in any moral philo-

sophy. However, certain qualifications must be made. The fundamental principle of universalization has absolutely nothing to do
with moral philosophy, whereas ethical discourse does. Yet the kind
of ethical discourse of utmost importance in morals simply does not
fit the straitjacket of discourse ethics, for the former is *not* informed
by the fundamental principle of universalization. Consequently, it
does not and must not live up to that principle.

To judge by his paper, Habermas himself is more than aware of
this fact. He raises almost all the genuine moral issues, only to brush
them aside as so many obstacles to the full observance of the
'fundamental principle'. At one stage he even poses a restriction on
the applicability of that principle. Let me quote the relevant passage
for the second time: 'I have introduced the fundamental principle of
universalization as a rule of argumentation which makes consensus
possible in practical discourses when matters can be regulated in the
general interest of everyone concerned.' If this is true, we are left
with the following alternative. Either the opening sentence of
Habermas's first formulation of the principle ('Thus *every valid
norm* must satisfy the condition . . .') is untrue, or all norms (moral
norms included) *must* meet the requirement that 'matters can be
regulated in the general interest of everyone concerned'. The latter
restriction is not untrue if applied to moral norms proper, but it is
completely irrelevant.

Take for example the value 'human dignity', and the norm related
to that value, 'keep your human dignity' (preserve your human
dignity, live up to your human dignity, and so on). In my view this
norm qualifies for a universal maxim, but we need not dwell upon
this problem now. Yet is this norm valid, or should it be recognized
as valid, only because all those 'concerned' accept the consequences
and side effects (what an awkward formulation!) that the validation
of this norm would exert on the 'satisfaction of their interests', and
because they have preferred this norm to an 'alternative regulation'?
To be more specific, if A keeps his/her moral dignity, he/she observes
 this norm irrespective of side effects and consequences (normally
painful ones), and at the same time wishes that everyone else would
do the same. But, if everyone did in fact do the same, 'keeping our
dignity' would *not* result in painful side effects and consequences. If
the norm were to be validated by the rule of the 'fundamental
principles', side effects and consequences would be completely
different from what they are *now*, and the norm is valid now.
Moreover, if I recognize and observe the norm 'keep your human
dignity' in retaining my dignity, and I wish that everyone would do
the same, I do *not* assume that 'keeping human dignity' in fact meets

the interests of 'everyone concerned' (every human being). Rather, I insist that everyone *should be* concerned with keeping his/her human dignity, and that the moral interest invested in keeping one's dignity should be preferred to other interests. Finally, I keep my human dignity even if *no one else* is actually concerned with keeping their human dignity.

What if we now take a norm which does not qualify for a universal maxim, such as 'solidarity with my brethren'. In this case, who are those 'concerned'? My brethren alone, or everyone who has 'brethren' (and how about those who have none)? Let us assume that only my brethren are concerned, and that the side effects and consequences following from the observance of this norm are accepted by all my brethren. But why should this norm be 'generally observed'? If half my brethren did not recognize this norm as binding for them, and would not agree to observe it, the norm would not *cease to be a norm*, and would remain firmly valid for those recognizing and observing it. If those observing the norm 'solidarity with my brethren' were not intent on imposing this norm on those brethren who did not recognize it as binding for them, and if the latter recognized the validity of this norm for those observing it, then the norm would be 'freely accepted' by everyone concerned, even though it would not be generally valid.

The proposal that the only moral norms that should be generally valid are those that can be generally validated is tautological. The proposal that the only moral norms that can be recognized as valid are those that can or could be generally validated is false. Let us quote the stronger definition of 'discourse ethics' again: 'Only those norms which find (or can find) the consent of all those concerned as participants in a practical discourse may claim validity.'

The qualification 'consent of all those concerned' could imply consent to the validity of that norm (recognition of the norm as valid). It could also mean that the norm is recognized as valid and *as binding* for everyone concerned. As I have argued above, the two suggestions are different in kind. But, since the discourse ethics is to be informed by the fundamental principle of universalization, the recognition of a norm must imply that this norm is binding for everyone concerned (that it is generally binding). Now, moral norms which are not simultaneously moral maxims are not necessarily generally binding. Moral maxims which, on their part, should be generally binding, are usually not tested in a real discourse, but intellectually intuited (occasionally with a view to an 'imaginary' discourse), and validated in terms of 'ought', irrespective of consequences and side effects. From whatever angle one approaches the fundamental principle of universalization and the definition of 'discourse ethics', the result is the same: they do not qualify as formulas of morality and moral philosophy. The questions 'How should I act?' and 'What should I do?' are not answered at all by these two formulas.

None the less, as I have already suggested, they do qualify as the formulas of just legislation.

The preconditions of the relevance of the formulas (in their modified version) are as follows.

1   A group of people has a *problem* to solve or an *objective* to achieve which concerns all members of that group.
2   The problem to solve or the objective to be achieved requires a standing *regulation*. This regulation can be substantive as well as procedural.

If this is the case, all members of the group must conduct a real discourse concerning the problem and the objective at hand, and concerning the standing regulation (law, convention, norm, rule) relating to the solution of the problem and the realization of the objective. The discourse is to be informed by the fundamental principle of universalization. The rules, regulations and laws which are to be validated can be seen as *means* to achieve the end, to solve the problem under discussion.

Moral norms are related to values and not to problems or objectives. They cannot be established (or seen) as *means* to achieve something. Even if morality were completely rational, moral norms would (and could) still not be constituted with a view to problems to be solved or objectives to be achieved. (Rather, the latter have an impact on the *application* of moral norms.)

The maxim 'keep your human dignity' is, for example, not valid (and can never be rationally validated) with respect to a problem it 'solves' or a non-evaluated objective it achieves. However, the validation of laws and other social–political norms and regulations occurs precisely in conjunction with such objectives and problems, or at least this is what should happen if validation is supposed to be *rational*.

I shall give an example which covers all possible cases. In a particular community water is in short supply. If everyone in this community uses water according to his or her usual needs (beyond justice), the existing water reserves will rapidly decrease and in the foreseeable future it will prove impossible to satisfy elementary needs. So there is a problem, that of a water shortage, and there is an objective, to provide the amount of water needed for the culturally determined basic needs in the foreseeable future. The decision here is obvious. The use of water should be *regulated*. But what kind of regulation should be accepted? How should the rule (regulation) be established? In a society based on symmetric reciprocity, the *kind* of regulation must be decided in a *real discourse* in which everyone concerned can participate (if they wish). The fundamental principle of universalization (with my modification) informs the discourse. First, *life* should have priority. The use of water should be regulated so that drinking-water is available for all persons and animals, and for the survival of necessary vegetation. Secondly, the regulation should be formulated in such a way that the consequences and side effects that a rule of this kind exerts on the need satisfaction of every individual should be accepted by every individual. This second condition is met anyway if the rules emerge out of real discourse. The discourse cannot be conducted *about* needs (and interests). It must be conducted about values having affinity with those interests. One cannot discuss whether someone has the need to use the home swimming-pool (for all needs must be recognized equally), but even those who have such a need can resign *freely* the satisfaction of their needs if they accept other values (for example, the value of hygiene) as having a higher standing than the value 'pleasure'. Finally, a regulation will emerge which satisfies the criteria of the fundamental principle of universalization. And this rule (the law) is to be observed by every person. Failure to do so will result in just punishment (retribution).

'Everyone concerned' can be a group of people, a community, the citizenry of a state, 'every member of any given culture', 'every member of every culture' (that is to say, humankind). The problems or objectives encompass all problems or objectives which can be solved or achieved by social and/or political regulation, and by such regulation alone.

It follows that those laws (conventions, norms, rules) regulating the social–political intercourse between different cultures (in the pluralistic cultural universe) must be validated by all human beings in sequences of real discourse conducted within each culture (way of life). Yet laws (conventions, norms, rules) regulating the social and political intercourse *within* a cultural universe must be validated only by members of that universe (by all of them, in sequences of real discourse). Norms and rules regulating the social and political intercourse of a group of people (a single way of life) must, again, be validated only by the members of that group (in real discourse). Accordingly, the social and political norms validated within one culture, one state, one group, one way of life will differ from one another and from all others. If there are to exist several ways of life within one body politic, the laws of that body politic must be validated by each citizen of the body politic regardless of his/her own way of life. However, the regulations within a particular way of life are validated solely by the members of that way of life, and do not require the participation of citizens who are not members. But all discourse must be informed (guided) by the fundamental principle of universalization.

The above discussion calls for the reassessment, although not for the redefinition, of the fundamental principle of universalization. The term 'universal' cannot carry the same meaning in this context as it does in the composite 'universal maxim'. A maxim is universal if claimed to be valid for every human being. The fundamental principle of universalization, though, vouchsafes the validity of a socio-political norm even if the norm itself is not valid for every human being (but only for those whom the norm concerns). Only norms validated by every member of humankind, thus norms regulating socio-political intercourse among different cultures, are universally valid. Strictly speaking, the fundamental principle of universalization is not the principle of universalization at all, but the *universal* principle of the logic of argumentation for validating socio-political norms. There is an analogy here with moral maxims and moral norms. On the one hand we encounter moral maxims claiming universal validity (validity for every human person), and socio-political forms validated by every human being via real discourse under the guidance of the fundamental principle of universalization. On the other hand we encounter moral norms not claiming such universality, because they are binding only for those who resolve to observe them, and socio-political norms validated by every member of a culture, way of life, body politic, community or group, but binding only on the members of the group to which the norm relates. We test norms with universal maxims (moral norms should not contradict the observance of universal maxims). Similarly, the validation of any socio-political regulation is informed by the fundamental principle of universalization. I have also mentioned the fact that moral norms which do not contradict moral maxims are *recognized as valid* also by those uncommitted to them, who do not observe them. To formulate this more cautiously, these moral norms *should* be recognized as valid by everyone, since they would be recognized as valid if people were equally free and if the moral were rational. The same must be stated about all socio-political norms legitimized by discourse informed by the fundamental principle of universalization. Each culture or way of life must recognize as valid the socio-political norms and rules of any other culture or way of life, even if it has validated, and thus observes, different ones.

This analogy does not eliminate, or even diminish, the essential and crucial differences between moral norms and socio-political regulations (laws) in non-traditional societies. It is probably completely superfluous to add that a theory formulated with the intention of replacing theories of social contract cannot relapse into traditionalism of any kind. Universal maxims are both substantive and formal, whereas the fundamental principle of universalization is formal, even though I have added one substantive qualification to it (actualization of the universal values of life and freedom). No real discourse is needed in testing norms by maxims (though such a discourse could be conducted), whereas the validation of all socio-political norms should occur via real discourse. Notwithstanding the crucial differences, the analogy is still important. And, since the fundamental principle of universalization performs the function of guiding and testing, I shall term this principle the *universal maxim of dynamic justice*.

Let me briefly reiterate certain basic steps of my argumentation. I defined the formal concept of justice as follows: if the same norms and rules constitute a social cluster, these norms and rules apply to every member of that cluster. I termed this formal concept the 'maxim of justice' (all kinds of justice must meet this standard). Dynamic justice, on the other hand, has been defined as the procedure by which existing (valid) social and political norms and rules are tested, queried and devalidated, and, simultaneously, where alternative social–political norms and rules are validated. I have argued that those contesting existing norms and rules as *unjust* can have a moral right to do so (the moral right ensues from the observance of valid moral norms). Further, I have proved that the contestants normally have recourse to one interpretation of the value of 'freedom' or 'life' to back their claim. Finally, I have concluded that the 'contestation of justice' can be made by discourse, by negotiation and by force. Discourse, as the vehicle, the form of contestation, is possible if the contestants are both free and each other's equals.

A 'just society', a society *without* dynamic justice, is undesirable. What is desirable is the generalization and universalization of dynamic justice as a *just procedure*. The only just procedure for (generalized and universalized) dynamic justice is *discourse*. Discourse can be such a procedure if the contesting parties are free and equal. And they are free and equal in a society where the 'golden rule' is universalized and generalized – thus, in a society of symmetric reciprocity.

The universal principle of dynamic justice is but the symmetric counterpart of the maxim of justice. The norms and rules constituting a social cluster should be applied to every member of the cluster consistently and continuously. Every member of a cluster should reaffirm, consistently and continuously, the norms and rules of this cluster.

Do we have a *moral right* to claim that the universal principle of dynamic justice should be accepted as the principle of the just procedure for establishing and contesting socio-political norms and rules? Indeed we have, for the universal principle of dynamic justice is but a claim to observe a *universal moral maxim* in full. This maxim is the Kantian one that no human being should serve as a mere means for any other human being. The moral maxim stands higher than the universal principle of dynamic justice because the universal principle draws its 'moral right' from the moral maxim. This maxim is also the source of the 'sense of justice' which suggests (and insists) that people should not be subjected to socio-political regulations of which they are not authors. The fundamental principle of universalization cannot even be viewed as the 'sole moral principle', for the validation of its own claim rests on another (and higher) principle, an authentically universal and moral one.

The universal principle of dynamic justice universalizes one of the outstanding aspects of all types of dynamic justice – namely, the possibility of having recourse to the values of freedom and life. The universal principle of dynamic justice *explicitly includes* the injunction to actualize the values of life and freedom. The formula itself guarantees that only such interpretations of freedom and life can be actualized as do not involve the use of other people as mere means.

I have set forth my view that Habermas's 'fundamental principle of universalization' and 'discourse ethics' offer a sensible alternative to theories of social contract, but I have not yet elaborated on how and why this is so. I now turn to this matter. Since I have modified both Habermas's concepts, from now on I shall refer to these modified versions only, under the labels 'the universal maxim of dynamic justice' and 'value discourse'. In chapter 3 I mentioned that social-contract theories contain certain problems. I repeat them here, with certain modifications and additions.

1   The theory must presuppose a single Time One (the time of entering into the contract).

2 For this reason, it must presuppose a real (or imaginary) 'state of nature'. In other words, it must step 'outside history'.

3 The legitimation of the contract is to be based on the 'laws of nature'.

4 All contestations of injustice must have recourse to the same 'laws of nature' (a conjectured past which has never existed).

5 Although anchored in *our* historical consciousness and *our* claim to universality, this historical ubiety remains unreflected in theories of social contract.

6 Theories of social contract must (and do) design particular social and political systems (norms, laws, and the like) as *the* good and *the* just systems.

7 In theories of social contract, the 'good' and 'just' institutions cannot be modified. This follows from their definition as the good and just institutions *par excellence*. Unless it comes to a breach of contract (by the sovereign), all norms and rules set by the contract remain in full force.

8 *Real* consent of everyone is relegated to Time One. In Time Two, Time Three, and so on, 'consent' must be considered 'tacit'.

9 Whether or not the 'general will' originates from the 'will of all', the former is always alienated from the latter.

10 Accordingly, theories of social contract legitimize a kind of domination (Rousseau's included).

Rawls's theory of social contract has circumvented several traps of the traditional theory of social contract, but not all of them.

a The 'original position' is only a streamlined version of the 'state of nature'. It is impossible to choose, to legislate, to reason, under the 'veil of ignorance'. If the existence of a real Time One (in the past) is not assumed, it must be assumed that Time One is *always here*. In my view this is a very reasonable assumption. Yet, even if we *could* abstract completely from the position *we* occupy in a society (from our group affiliations and vested interests), we can never place our values, our 'concepts of good', our commitments, under the 'veil of ignorance'. If we inquire as to what people would choose *if* they were able to forget not only their group affiliations and vested interests, but also their values, commitments, and concepts of good, we can answer this question only by relying on *our* values, commitments, and concepts of good (which are not without affinity to our group affiliations and vested interests). Rawls is guilty of what we could term the 'substitutionalist fallacy', just like all traditionalist theorists of contract.

b   It follows from this point (which has been made frequently in this book) that Rawls must draw up the model of a just society (or of an approximately just society). To establish the priority of freedom (with which I wholeheartedly agree), there is no need for the makeshift 'original position' at all. Designing concrete social rules (in the main, the rules of distribution) is the result of the substitutionalist fallacy.

Constructing the normative foundation of the theory of justice via the universal maxim of dynamic justice and value discourse avoids all the pitfalls of the traditional theory of contract.

(1) What could 'Time One' possibly mean in this conception? One could answer in the following way: the ultimate (imaginary) Time One is the time when, in a pluralistic cultural universe, all ways of life will be connected by the bonds of symmetric reciprocity. For, in the pluralistic universe of the overarching cluster 'humankind', all ways of life can be connected by these bonds if the ties between different cultures (the common socio-political norms of 'humankind') are set via value discourse according to the universal principle of dynamic justice. However, we could also answer the question in this way: imaginary Time One is the particular time when in a single state (or culture) the citizens are connected to each other by the bonds of symmetric reciprocity. For all citizens (regardless of the way of life they are otherwise committed to) will set their common socio-political norms and rules (they will legislate) in terms of the universal principle of dynamic justice, via value discourse. We could even answer the question in this way: Time One is the particular time when the members of any group or community are connected to each other by the bonds of symmetric reciprocity. For all members of that group (community) set their common socio-political norms and rules in terms of the universal maxim of dynamic justice, via value discourse. Clearly there are *here and now* such communities and groups. Thus Time One is here and now. And Time One will be here tomorrow, and the day after tomorrow. Time One is a *continuum*. The universal Time One of the pluralistic universe when all ways of life are connected by the bonds of symmetric reciprocity is the *regulative idea of each and every Time One*. Yet the universal maxim of dynamic justice and value discourse are *constitutive ideas* of each and every Time One. Thus 'Time One' is both existent and imaginary.

(2) The theory does not even permit 'stepping outside history'.

Dynamic justice itself is seen as a relative latecomer to histories. The generalization of dynamic justice is attributed to modernity. Similarly, the universalization of the values of freedom and life (the values of 'higher-order consensus') is understood as a historical product.

(3) The legitimation of the theory is based on something that *does exist* (both empirically and as an idea): humankind. The different cultures of the pluralistic human universe are in fact already tied to each other, with the bonds of domination and violence, but also with the bonds of mutual dependence, and occasionally even those of co-operation and negotiation. This is the empirical fact. Humankind, as the overarching essential cluster, exists as an idea: this is the fact of reason.

(4) The contestation of laws (norms and rules) must involve recourse to the universal values of life and freedom. These values are not products of philosophical speculation. They are factually universally valid (freedom), or in the process of factual universalization (life). When I say 'factually universal' I mean 'transculturally universal'. Freedom has become first and foremost a 'value idea'. By 'value idea' I mean a value, the opposite of which cannot possibly be chosen as a value by anyone.[9] Since Hitler, not even the worst kind of tyrant can now publicly confess that he prefers unfreedom to freedom. He does in fact prefer the former to the latter (he infringes systematically the value he is publicly committed to), but the problem of validity and the problem of observing values are worlds apart. There is no culture today in which unfreedom could be publicly chosen as a value (whereas inequality can be).

(5) The theory understands the universal maxim of dynamic justice and value discourse as expressions and products of *our historical consciousness*.

(6) The incomplete ethico-political concept of justice does not design, propose or conjecture any particular social system as *the* good or *the* just one. It presupposes that there may be several good or just systems, each quite different in nature. For all possible laws, rules and socio-political norms and rules are good and just by definition, if they are legitimized by all concerned in a rational value discourse, under the guidance of the universal maxim of dynamic justice, at the time of legislation.

(7) The generalization and universalization of the 'golden rule' is

the generalization and universalization of 'just procedure'. Whenever and wherever, in any Time One, a group of people agree that social norms and rules (or laws) will be legitimized from that particular moment on via (value) discourse, discourse conducted under the guidance of the universal maxim of dynamic justice, they have already agreed to just procedure. Such an agreement does not include agreement on the acceptance of any single concrete norm, rule or law as just. Only this much is assumed: that if a group of people does legislate via just procedure, *and* the value discourse is terminated by real consensus (which may or may not occur), then the recommended norm, rule or law will be validated, and will be *just* at the time of validation. Everyone is the author of that norm (law), and as author will consider the law just. Authorship is tantamount to commitment.

Everyone is author of the law and thus everyone is committed to observing that particular law (social norm, rule and the like). However, the fact that a law (a social and political norm and rule) is considered just by everyone at the time of its validation does not mean that the same law will be considered just in Time Two, Time Three, and so on. First, unforeseen consequences and side effects may occur, and certain of those who have authorized the law (norm) may conclude, in view of these things, that the law is, in the end, unjust. They will then recommend alternative laws (rules, socio-political norms) in the traditional language of dynamic justice: 'This is not just, but this other would be just.' Similarly, in Time Two, Time Three, and so on, a generation which has not authorized the law (the socio-political norm or rule) can make the same delegitimizing statement. In this case the norm (law) will be retested in a new (value) discourse, since the just procedure for the contestation of justice is, and remains, discourse. Of course, in all forms of social intercourse a certain kind of stability is needed. The entire system of laws and socio-political norms cannot be changed every day. However, I doubt that the model of 'just procedure' runs the risk of becoming unstable. Acting according to already accepted norms is a matter of *Sittlichkeit*, and the latter has an affinity with 'steadiness'. One can assume that, once laws, socio-political norms and rules, have been legitimized in a completely just procedure (as authorized by everyone), small divergences and inconveniences will not trigger the delegitimizing statement.

Is it not a curtailment of dynamic justice if only one kind of procedure is considered just? To my mind this question must be overruled as immaterial, for the simple reason that just procedure rests on the universal maxim of dynamic justice. The 'golden rule' itself is not open to choice or agreement because it is but one formulation of the *definition* of justice (the maxim of justice) *and so it has been always understood*. Where there is symmetric reciprocity, the 'golden rule' applies anyway. What is open to choice (and to agreement) is the *matter* (the substance) 'given' to the 'golden rule'. I do unto you what I expect you to do unto me. *What* I do unto you and *what* I expect you to do unto me should be decided by you and me. No other just procedure can possibly be *imagined*, unless we believe in extrahuman, divine, legislation. In our world, some people believe in divine legislation, some do not. Furthermore, those believing in divine legislation believe in different forms of such legislation. Religious values (values intrinsic to religious beliefs) can enter the value discourse just like any other values, but they cannot provide the *authority* for socio-political legislation as such. If a group of people share the same belief and set (validate) their laws and socio-political norms in a just procedure, the consensus will accord with the values of that belief anyway. Even so, beliefs can change, as can values, and the laws accepted today as just will (or at least can) be devalidated tomorrow as unjust, with ours just as with any other human group and community.

(8) It follows from the aforementioned that *real* consent is not relegated to Time One. Since every law or socio-political norm and rule can be rediscussed (revalidated and devalidated) at any time, and they *must* be revalidated or devalidated every time there are members of the community (body politic, humankind) who believe them unjust, 'tacit consent' cannot be viewed as the source of legitimation. Nevertheless, the 'tacit consent' of single individuals is not excluded. Participation in value discourses is a *right*: more precisely, a *civil right*. Whether such a civil right should also be considered a *duty* is, again, a problem that must be left open in an *incomplete* ethico-political concept of justice. Members of communities (of groups, of the body politic) should reach agreement on this matter too. As a citizen of a group (or a community) I would vote in favour of the possibility of 'tacit consent', and against making the right of participation a citizen's duty. If someone could argue against my position from the standpoint of values I am ready to share, I would willingly listen to their arguments.

(9) In the theory I have proposed as an alternative to theories of

social contract, *the 'general will' is the result of the 'will of all'.* Any time that a divergence occurs between the general will and the will of all, the general will is to be re-established by the will of all. The will of all *authorizes* the law, the socio-political norm (the general will); in addition, it can withdraw authorization. If the will of all were to express the needs (and interests) of every person, the general will could not possibly be constituted by the will of all. But the constitution of the general will occurs via value discourse. Every person enters into this discourse, not in the form of a bundle of interests and needs, but as a bearer of cultural, social, political and moral values. (This is so even though, of course, people stand within institutions – which have already been established as the result of value discourse – for their own interests, and may consider the best result to be a compromise.) The discourse itself is about the cognitive justification of values. The latter can be conclusive because of the 'higher-order consensus' concerning the two universal values. True values accepted by rational insight determine the will as good will. It is precisely because of the rational justification of values (via discourse) that the will of all can engender and promote the general will.

(10) The normative foundation of an incomplete ethico-political concept of justice legitimizes (self-legitimizes) a society based on symmetric reciprocity. This, then, is a society *without super-ordination and subordination, without social hierarchy, without domination.* Regardless of whether a 'society' such as this is 'founded' in the form of a democratic family, a community, a group of friends, an association, a political or social organization, a body politic, a culture, many interrelated cultures, or the whole of humankind (as the overarching cluster), we are always in Time One.

I have suggested that Habermas's 'fundamental principle of universalization' and 'discourse ethics' provide us with an alternative to theories of contract, and a superior one. I have recommended slight modifications to the formulas of both, to make them suitable to the purpose of this chapter: the laying of the normative foundation of an (incomplete) ethico-political concept of justice.

Still, the substantive qualifications I have recommended to be introduced into the (otherwise too empty) formula of the fundamental principle of universalization have solved one problem only to create a new one. The new problem is novel only in this present context, for I discussed it earlier (in chapter 3).

I have placed two universal values in the 'higher-order consensus'. I have said that argumentation (in the value discourse) must have recourse to them. As is known, the socio-political norms and rules (laws) validated via just procedure are also *means* to solve a problem or continuously to maintain an objective (such as distribution and redistribution, education, the institutionalization of political decision-making and execution, retribution, the peaceful settlement of international conflicts). Sometimes the objective (the problem) itself is such that only one of the two universal values (the 'higher-order consensus') can prevail in the discourse. When both universal values have equal priority in the 'higher-order consensus' (with respect to the problem to be solved, the goal to be achieved), all members of the (value) discourse can have recourse to both freedom and life. And, if the value claims related to freedom and to life cannot be synthesized in a general will doing justice to both, no agreement, no consensus, can be achieved. Then the social rules, norms and laws will not be legitimized at all, or, alternatively, they will not embody the will of all (as rational good will). However, laws (social norms and rules) can still be set by *negotiation*; in other words, by *compromise*. To accept such a compromise in legislation is not tantamount to acting in awareness of the 'dilemma' of morality. If I must act in a concrete situation, and must choose between life and freedom in so acting, then I act in the awareness that, although the maxim of my action is universalizable, *my action is not* (I cannot recommend that everyone should choose the same!). But again, in the case of legislation, if I enter into a compromise concerning the 'higher-order consensus' and consent (against my rational will) – a compromise to the effect that freedom should be preferred against life, or *vice versa* – I do make a recommendation that should not be made.

If a conflict can appear within the 'higher-order consensus' (between freedom and life), this problem is insoluble. And such a conflict can occur at any Time One, *except Universal (ultimate) Time One*. Only if all cultures of the universal cluster of humankind were tied to each other by the bonds of symmetric reciprocity, and this were to happen within *all* cultures, groups, bodies politic, could both universal values be actualized consistently and continuously *without contradiction*. This is why I describe 'Universal Time One' as *the best possible socio-political world*. It is a world where there is no conflict between the universal value of freedom and the universal value of life.

At the beginning of this chapter, I defined the generalization and universalization of the 'golden rule' the *supreme political good*. And

I termed the plurality of cultures, the plurality of ways of life, where all of them meet the standards of the supreme political good, the *supreme social good*. I concluded that the actualization of both the supreme political good and the supreme social good is the *best possible socio-political world*. Now I have arrived at the same conclusion from a different point of departure. In any Time One bar Universal Time One it is possible to have a conflict between the universal values of freedom and life. But this should not be so, because Universal Time One is the regulative idea of each and every Time One. Yet the conflict between life and freedom simply cannot be eliminated from the horizon of our present (as has been discussed in the final section of chapter 4, on 'just' wars). This is why Universal Time One is also the *telos* inherent in every Time One. If we are forced to face a choice which should not be made, we gaze towards an imaginary *telos* where this choice is not to be made.

Creating a world around us (be it as small as it may) in which we are tied to our fellows by bonds of symmetric reciprocity; generating our social norms and rules in a value discourse by having recourse to universal values; observing the norms of which we are authors, applying them consistently and continuously to each and every co-author of these norms – this is also an end-in-itself. In short, to live up to the universal maxim of dynamic justice – this is also an end-in-itself. However, the *telos* of the best possible socio-political world is inherent in all actions in which people live up to the universal maxim of dynamic justice. And here the analogy between righteousness as an end-in-itself, and the best possible moral world inherent as an end in the act of the righteous, is more than mere analogy. The best possible socio-political world is the *condition* of the best possible moral world. To live up to the universal maxim of dynamic justice does not require righteousness. But, in our times, righteousness requires that we live up to the universal maxim of dynamic justice, though it requires something above and beyond this as well.

THE NORMATIVE FOUNDATION OF AN INCOMPLETE ETHICO-POLITICAL CONCEPT OF JUSTICE: THE ETHICAL ASPECT

The universal maxim of dynamic justice has turned out to be the simple reversal of the maxim of justice. The universal maxim enjoins that socio-political legislation should be the result of 'just procedure'. Value discourse (with its well-known specifications) has been characterized as such a just procedure.

Settling socio-political conflicts via discourse is not a novelty. In chapter 3 I mentioned situations in previous histories where certain types of conflicts were settled by discourse. It is only among equals (members of the same cluster) that they were settled in this manner, and usually only among members of the *highest* social cluster, if 'resolving socio-political conflicts via discourse' was the *procedural norm* of the (higher) social cluster. Such discourses were always guided by a set of traditional norms. Participants had to resort to these traditional and sometimes divine norms, but always norms taken for granted. Value discourse guided by the universal maxim of dynamic justice is but the universalization and generalization of the traditional value discourse. Naturally, in an environment where socio-political conflicts are settled either by violence or by negotiation, such a discourse is possible only within one group, one way of life, one community, but the *validity* of the procedure cannot be restricted to those single groups. As we know, the regulative idea of the value discourse is Universal Time One. That is why the *will* to universalization should be inherent in every value discourse, even if conducted in the smallest group. Of course, 'will' is more than a mere subjective wish, for the *rules* of value discourse entail that will, in so far as the 'higher-order consensus' concerns *universal values*. Given that the values of 'higher-order consensus' are universal, *any* community engaging in practical discourse can claim that *every* community should do likewise. What you should do, you can do. Each and every community *could* validate its norms and rules by resorting to universal values. That is why the claim that they *should* do so is a *valid* claim. It must be stressed again that the universal claim is raised for just procedure, and *not* for the *result* of a just procedure. In different communities different value claims are raised. Discourse can be conducted among different values, and the values accepted consensually as true, and actualized in the socio-political rules and norms of the community, will also be different in kind. The injunction that all values must be related without contradiction to the values of 'higher-order consensus', and that the universal values should be interpreted such that the actualization of one interpretation should not in principle exclude the actualization of any other interpretation of the same universal value, covers the *testing* of all values, but does not *define* the substance of those values.

The definition of justice holds that justice means applying the norms and rules constituting a social cluster to each and every member of that cluster consistently and continuously. People who in fact apply these norms consistently and continuously *are just*. We know that to be just is a *virtue*, and to be unjust is a vice. Failure to apply the common yardstick, or applying it inconsistently and intermittently, means being guilty of the vice of injustice. A single unjust action or judgement does not make a person unjust. The action is unjust, but the person is not. However, repeated acts of injustice do make a person unjust. We also know that an unjust act is a moral offence, and an unjust person is morally inferior, even if the norm or rule which has not been applied in the way it should have been is *not a moral norm*.

One can become just in practising justice. In respect of pure static justice, the norms and rules all persons must learn to apply consistently and continuously are the norms and rules of *Sittlichkeit* (moral ethical custom). Practical reason (the rational testing of the validity of norms) has not yet appeared. One cannot as yet infringe the norms and rules by *moral reason*, by listening to the voice of the 'internal authority' of moral conduct (conscience). In the case of dynamic justice we do test the norms and rules of *Sittlichkeit* by rationality of intellect. Rationality of intellect tests these norms and rules from the standpoint of values and (moral) norms, and so morality and *Sittlichkeit* do not coincide. People can choose not to apply the yardstick provided by *Sittlichkeit* in their actions and judgements. They can choose to be 'unjust' (in terms of *Sittlichkeit*) in order to be just (in terms of morality). Also, they can choose to observe an alternative set of norms.

If the *just procedure* of legislation takes root in any community, the *schism* between *Sittlichkeit* and morality (in justice) disappears again. To use a Hegelian term, this is the state of the negation of negation. Both static and dynamic justice are negated as well as preserved, and thus synthesized at a higher stage. Static justice is preserved, because no one can label the just procedure as unjust. Static justice is negated in that no socio-political norms and rules are to be taken for granted (only the procedure by which they are derived is to be taken for granted). Dynamic justice is preserved, because the maxim of the value discourse is the universal maxim of dynamic justice. For obvious reasons, dynamic justice is negated. It cannot be claimed that the application of the universal maxim of dynamic justice is unjust from the standpoint of dynamic justice. Both kinds of justice are elevated to a higher (maximum) stage. How does this happen? Why does it happen?

Habermas spoke of 'discourse *ethics*', and to my mind correctly so. In a society where just procedure is taking root, engaging in value discourse and observing the norms of discourse are both procedures which become *Sittlichkeit*. We must assume that value discourse has been institutionalized in the broadest meaning of the word: every member of the community of argumentation expects every other member to observe the rules of the value discourse. I have in mind not the institutionalization of *all* value discourses, only the institutionalization of procedures of just legislation. But, even so, socialization goes with 'acquiring the practice' of conducting value discourses. The virtue of all members of a community must share is that of 'observing the rules of the value discourse' and observing the socio-political norms of which they have been authors (for as long as they remain valid). Thus discourse ethics is seen as the strongest version of *Sittlichkeit*. By this I mean (a) that, as far as legislation is concerned, one cannot opt for alternative kinds of *Sittlichkeit*; (b) that moral customs are unconditionally binding; (c) that custom is a *moral authority*, and in socio-political matters the exclusive authority. The authority of just procedure is an *external* authority in that it embodies the *ethos* of the community. Failure to observe the rules of discourse entails the 'eye of others' bringing shame to the transgressor. Yet value discourse is the only external authority of socio-political decision-making which *cannot* become the authority of domination, for it is the authority *par excellence* which excludes domination. Thus internal authority (conscience) cannot query and test the validity of this authority (in socio-political legislation). *Moral conscience* cannot be other than the *full internalization* of the authority of socio-political decision-making. Of course, moral conscience not only pertains to matters of justice and injustice. It is invested in moral norms proper as well. But moral norms proper are either not constituted by discourse at all or are constituted by another type of discourse. I shall address this matter in chapter 6. Here it needs only to be stated that, since the 'best possible socio-political world' is the condition, though not the *sufficient* condition, of the 'best possible moral world', *no moral norm* can query the validity of just procedure. This being so, the conclusion lies at hand. If practical reason is about querying the authority of the universal maxim of dynamic justice and of value discourse in matters of socio-political legislation, such querying cannot be grounded in *moral reasons*. Such a query would constitute a *moral transgression* against the 'human bond' in general, and could only aim at a new form of *domination*.

The ethics of just procedure is the ethics of *optimum* freedom. It is *not* the ethics of *absolute* freedom. Absolute freedom, the deification of individuals *qua* individuals, is also the renunciation of all human bonds constituted by symmetric reciprocity. The idea of the *absolute autonomy* of the empirical person, the individual unrestricted in action and behaviour by any kind of authority, is not only a chimera, but also a dangerous chimera. *Relative* autonomy is the human condition.

It is appropriate now to return to the *virtue of justice*. The allegory of justice is the blindfolded woman, scales in one hand, sword in the other. The message of this allegory is clear: impartiality (objectivity) in judgement, retribution proportionate to the offence. The allegory is that of the formal concept of justice (as static justice). To what degree is this image relevant to the virtue of justice in our model?

I have stated above that, *if* just procedure has already taken root in a community, static justice is not only negated but also preserved. Nevertheless, action and judgement guided by the *idea* of just procedure cannot yet be subjected to the moral custom of procedure. In the latter case, *Sittlichkeit* (moral custom) is only *in statu nascendi*, and thus the observance of the norms of discourse ethics is still a matter of *morality* (informed by conscience and not by any kind of external authority). Yet this distinction is *relative* in character, far more so than where pure moral maxims are to be observed. It is only a *group* of people that can derive their social norms by just procedure. As individual human beings we can observe the maxim 'You should preserve your human dignity', even if no one else in our environment does so, but we cannot observe the norm that we should legislate via value discourse if we cannot find any possible participants in this discourse who are similarly committed to legislation via just procedure. If a person observes the norms of value discourse while those around him do not, this person does not partake of a just socio-political procedure, but rather observes a moral norm (or maxim). What is *Sittlichkeit* (moral custom) within the in-group is collective morality in relation to the out-group. Even so, in a hostile environment where there are several social and political constraints (the power of public opinion included), the *virtue of justice* cannot be 'cold', and a kind of *righteousness* will be the prerequisite of being just. If just procedure has already taken root, a person can be just without being righteous. If this is not yet the case (or if it is the case, yet admits hostility and constraint), certain additional virtues are required. This is especially so if there are no partners to the discourse, and the observance of norms of discourse is motivated by 'legislative conscience' alone.[10]

Thus we must analyse the virtue of justice in two consecutive steps: (1) *after* any given Time One, and (2) *before* and *during* any given Time One.

(1) In the process of (just) legislation justice need not be

blindfolded for the sake of impartiality (objectivity), for the simple reason that all needs should be *recognized* from the outset, and equally so. 'Impartiality' is tantamount to the recognition of *all* needs (except those the satisfaction of which would involve the use of other people as mere means). The requirement that all needs should be recognized is not based on a presupposition of ignorance about these needs, or ignorance about *who* has *what type* of needs. All needs make their appearance as *claims*. They are public (they are *made* public by the claimants), and thus known. Further, impartiality (objectivity) does not require that people who claim satisfaction of their needs must first reflect upon these needs and reject 'realistic' or 'unruly' ones. If we should recognize all needs equally, this must be true of *our own* needs too. The kind of allegory of justice relevant here is similar to that depicted by Giotto: it gazes towards the future, it looks ahead. And no wonder, as here we are dealing with *just socio-political procedure*. The virtue pertaining to justice in our 'original position' is thus the recognition of all needs. This is indeed the virtue of *impartiality* (as objectivity), for it is *forbidden* to recognize one need more than another. Here again, the virtue of justice is a 'cold' virtue. It is natural to *sympathize* with one set of needs more than with another. We sympathize with certain needs because we share them more than others, understand them more than others, find them more valuable, and so on. However, in just socio-political procedure we must abstract from such likes and dislikes. In all other human relationships (e.g. personal attachments) we can value certain needs over others. In all other human relationships we can *criticize* the needs of others. But we have *no right* to criticize the needs of anyone if these needs register a claim relating to just socio-political procedure (except if the satisfaction of these needs involves the use of other people as mere means), because the full and equal recognition of all personal needs is the *right of everyone* engaging in this procedure. (The act of infringing a right cannot be a right.)

Needs do not enter the discourse as *matters* of the discourse (and obviously so, if all needs are equally *recognized*). People do not argue *with* their needs, but state their *values* (which can have affinity to their own need satisfaction, and to the need satisfaction of others). We know now that the discourse centres upon values. The proposition that equal recognition is due to all needs is tantamount to the one that equal recognition is due to all values. In the abstract case of an absolute 'starting-point' (at which no single norm, rule or law has yet been validated), no value is recognized as *true*. All are equally recognized in their capacity of *making a truth claim*. (Of course, the two universal values are recognized as true by every person.) *Proportionate* recognition is accorded to the various values in the process of discourse: the more that some particular values are proved false, the more will they be 'phased out' of recognition; the more that some are proved true, the more will they gain recognition.

If the just procedure of value discourse is part and parcel of *Sittlichkeit*, and if newcomers to the community (society) are thus socialized through 'acquiring the practice' of the value discourse, then no special skill, training, professional knowledge or exceptional gift is needed to practise such a discourse. Everyone is familiar with the rules, everyone has learned how to observe them, everyone should observe them, everyone can observe them. The 'preservation' of static justice in the dialectical 'sublation' (*Aufhebung*) of the same is tantamount to the preservation of the attitude of *rationality of reason* (in the dialectical 'sublation' of the same). I have mentioned that the 'higher-order consensus' itself indicates the preservation of the attitude of rationality of reason. It should now be added that discourse ethics as *Sittlichkeit* keeps rationality of reason in force. Discourse ethics is, so to speak, 'taken for granted'. However, the maxim of discourse ethics is the *universal maxim of dynamic justice*, and dynamic justice presupposes, as well as activates, the attitude of *rationality of intellect*. Rationality of intellect (at least in its most sublime and adequate form) is argumentative reason. Thus, in discourse ethics rationality of intellect and rationality of reason *merge*. If 'minding the norms and rules of my own integration' is tantamount to making full use of the attitude of rationality of intellect, then this attitude is to be 'taken for granted'. I have argued elsewhere[11] that the attitude of rationality of intellect is usually suppressed in childhood, when questions such as 'Why should I do this or that?', 'Why is this so and not otherwise?' are rebuked by a sententious 'Just because, and don't ask silly questions.' I have added that it is *philosophy* that takes these childish questions seriously, by answering them properly. What I have called 'philosophical discourse' is the discourse conducted around such 'childish questions'.[12] If rationality of intellect is taken for granted, if the childish questions are not rebuked, but taken up and answered continuously, we enter into a 'philosophical discourse'. Nothing but our reason is required for participating in a philosophical discourse. We all have the capacity for logical thinking and judgement (both reflective and determinative judgement, as seen in chapter 3). The exercise of these abilities is all that is needed for philosophical discourse.

It seems odd, though it is true, that the way in which we exercise our mental abilities is also a *moral* matter, and an important one. In an environment where one should not ask 'silly questions', the use of rationality of intellect is regarded as a (moral) transgression. The decree of the Enlightenment that we *should* think for ourselves imposes a moral obligation on us. Kant referred to our 'self-incurred' tutelage, where the term 'self-incurred' entails a negative moral judgement. Discourse ethics obligates the members of the 'community of argumentation' to uphold the attitude of rationality of intellect, and this should be understood as a *moral* obligation. In short, practising rationality of intellect is seen here as a *virtue*: as the *public* virtue of any socio-political actor (legislator). The participant in the discourse is *obliged* to use the logic of argumentation in order to pass good judgements. This obligation entails mental discipline (self-discipline) on the part of the participants in the discourse. There is certainly no *generally required* moral virtue possible without discipline (self-discipline). As we are not all born with exactly the same degree of good moral sense, even if everyone is equally born with this good moral sense, the happiness ensuing from virtuous activity is not identical with the pleasure of drive reduction, and never can be. And there is nothing wrong with discipline (self-discipline) *if* it is not imposed by authorities of domination.

When legislation has already taken place, and a socio-political norm or rule (or law) has been validated, the formal concept of justice defines the *virtue* of justice. In other words, the norms and rules must be applied to every member of the community in question consistently and continuously. At this stage, good judgement as *phronesis* is the *cognitive virtue* of just action and judgement.

The cognitive virtue of *good judgement* appeared twice in my model of an incomplete ethico-political concept of justice: first, as inherent in the value discourse, and, secondly, as inherent in the application of already consensually accepted norms and rules. Although in both cases I referred to 'good judgement', I used the Aristotelian notion of *phronesis* only in the second case. It is easy to explain this difference. The type of judgement performed in value discourse is secondary judgement. We discuss values (value judgements, normative judgements, and the like), but we do not, and should not, discuss the needs (the motivations and the characters) of persons who claim the validity of values (norms).

However, if we apply the already validated norms and rules, our judgements will be primary (initial) judgements. When and where the norm should be applied, to whom and how, as well as whether or not it applies to the case in question at all, are matters that can only be answered if the judgement takes into consideration motivations, needs and characters as far as these things are *relevant* to the application of the norm. Since Aristotle introduced the category of *phronesis* in terms of initial judgement, I too restrict the use of this notion to judgements of this kind.

If one of the norms and rules (laws) established by consensus is regarded as *unjust* by anyone, a new value discourse must take place, and a new process of 'legislation application' must begin.

What, then, are the virtues which constitute the virtue of 'justice' following any Time One? They are, first, *impartiality* as *radical tolerance* (full recognition lent to all needs and thus to the ipseity of every person); secondly, the *cognitive virtue of argument* in having recourse to the universal values of the 'higher-order consensus' (rationality of intellect); thirdly, commitment to the values which have been proved true (acceptance of the *authority of truth*); and, fourthly, *phronesis* (the cognitive virtue of the application of norms and rules). With the exception of the virtue of impartiality as radical tolerance, all other constituents of the virtue of justice are cognitive in character.

I shall call the virtue of justice (with the above-enumerated constituents) 'citizen's virtue'. I shall call all those practising and displaying this virtue, in the Aristotelian manner, 'good citizens'.

For a moment, let us imagine 'Universal Time One', the pluralistic cultural universe where each culture is tied to every other culture by the bonds of symmetric reciprocity. In such an (imaginary) Universal Time One, all human beings would, to an equal degree, be good citizens. They would all share the virtue of justice (citizen's virtue). But in respect of all other virtues they would be different. And in this context the word 'different' involves two entirely distinct problems.

First, communities, groups, different forms of the body politic, and different cultures – all these entities, in a just procedure, engender not only different norms and rules (laws), but also norms, rules and laws with different widths of validity. The laws of a body politic are legitimized by all its citizens (all citizens participate in the value discourse), and this is why such laws apply to all citizens of that body politic. One particular community (within this body politic) legitimizes certain norms and rules as pertaining to that community, and these are valid for, and applied to, the members of that legitimizing community. Going to the other extreme, commonly shared rules relating to the essential cluster 'humankind' should be generated by all members of humankind, and so their validity applies to all human beings (as members of the overarching cluster). Only the norms, rules and laws which have been generated (validated) by all human beings are valid for, and should be applied to, all human beings. If all norms and rules are generated and validated by discourse, then all the norms and rules of any particular body politic, culture, group or community should be *unconditionally recognized* as just by the members of all other communities to whom the same norms do *not* apply. *Within* one particular community of argumentation, values are to be recognized *in proportion to* their truth. *Among* different communities of argumentation, such recognition should not be given in a proportionate manner, but, as I have said, should be given unconditionally, for it must be presupposed that the *result* of any value discourse is the establishment of norms and rules that actualize true values. The plurality of ways of life includes a commitment to the plurality of socio-political norms (rules). Mutual recognition should be lent to all of them. Clearly, any particular social norm or rule (law) can enjoin us to practise other virtues too, not just the commonly shared 'citizen's virtue'. It is possible that the 'good citizen' of a way of life may display virtues above and beyond the 'citizen's virtue', just as it is possible that he or she may not: this depends on the particular way of life. The 'citizen's virtue' is simply the virtue *all good citizens must share.*

Secondly, the virtue sufficient to keep the just procedure alive does not require great moral effort, self-sacrifice, or supererogation, nor does it require a sublime moral character. The virtue of justice is a 'minimal virtue'. A word populated with 'good citizens', without simultaneously being populated with good (righteous) persons, does not seem very attractive. At least, it does not seem attractive to me. However, since it has been assumed that the 'best possible socio-political world' is the *condition* of the 'best possible moral world', one can hold the rational belief that, *if* all members of the human race met the criterion of being good citizens, there would be far more righteous people than under any other circumstances. This conclusion has already been drawn in the analysis of value discourse. Let us suppose that at the end of the discussion a few values have proved to be true. Let us further suppose that each of these values supports a preference for the satisfaction of certain needs as against the satisfaction of other needs. Let us also suppose that the problem to be solved or the objective to be achieved is such that no norm or rule (law) can guarantee the simultaneous satisfaction of all needs that are backed by a true value claim, or at least not the equal and simultaneous satisfaction of all of them. In such a case, or so we may believe, consensus, as *true consensus*, is excluded. How then can any norm or rule be set? The answer could be that no norm or rule should be established at all, or that the matter should be settled by negotiation, and thus by compromise. But what if a lack of regulation impedes the achievement of a goal or the solution of a problem vital for the life and freedom of everyone concerned? Is it then essential to resort to negotiation and compromise? I do not think so. It can be rationally assumed that *some* of the participants in the discourse will be not merely just, but also righteous. If, for example, three sets of needs cannot be satisfied simultaneously, or not to the same extent, even though all three parties back their claim with equally true values, one party to the discourse can still say, 'Let us satisfy the needs of others first! Let us give them priority! We have a right to satisfaction equivalent to that of these other sets of needs, but we resign this right of our own *free will*.' It would be just if all three claims were equally met. However, it is not only injustice that overrules justice, but *goodness* as well. True enough, a rule legitimized in this way would not be completely just at the time of legitimization. It would not be solely the result of a just procedure but also the result of the *gesture of goodness*. But it would still be consensually accepted, and this consensus would still be a *true consensus*. Constraint and power would be absent. Only if the power of argument is complemented by the power of charity can just procedure work in all possible cases, and without fail.[13] But I do not think that such a proposal is guilty of excessive optimism concerning the reserves of human nature. The gesture of goodness is an everyday phenomenon, and, when an emergency arises in day-to-day life, many people, including some who are not even righteous, are ready to make such a gesture. The controversial case briefly discussed above concerns such a 'state of emergency'. And these things may be said before we even remember that respect is due to human goodness; that if people, in a state of emergency, resign one of their rights for the sake of charity, the respect bestowed upon them will compensate them for any loss. The vote of confidence granted the human race was thus neither excessive nor premature.

(2) The virtue of justice *before and during* any 'Time One' must encompass all elements of the virtue of justice after Time One. If the *idea* of just procedure regulates someone's actions and judgements, this person is committed to act and judge *as if* just procedure were already the case. This is so because we devalidate norms and rules, from the attitude of rationality of intellect, by observing the norm (value) we counterpose to those already existing. However, since just procedure is only an idea prior to at least a single Time One, and has not, during a single Time One, become *Sittlichkeit* (moral custom), the practice of the virtue of justice repudes the mobilization of certain additional *moral resources*. These resources consist of so many additional virtues. Thus we must attribute certain additional *virtues* to the constituents of citizen's virtue before and during Time One. More than a 'minimum morality' is required from a 'good citizen' before and during Time One. And yet the 'good citizen' is not identical with the good (righteous) person before and during Time One either. Only that degree of additional virtue is required from 'good citizens' the practice and display of which makes them act and judge *as if* just procedure were the case, when it is not.

It is the citizen's virtue to recognize all needs equally, except those the satisfaction of which involves the use of other people as mere means. If the citizen lives in a world where not even all needs are recognized (let alone equally), yet where those needs the satisfaction of which involves the use of other people as mere means are recognized, the virtue of the 'original position' cannot be a 'cold' virtue, and the cognitive aspect of the virtue must be very demanding.

Needs are not equally recognized because, first, owing to the norms and rules of a particular society, they receive unequal recognition, and, secondly, because certain needs are not expressed, or not expressed strongly enough. People may not be able to express needs owing to legal constraints, lack of education, lack of organization or lack of access to the public sphere. The good citizen can help such people by speaking on their behalf. But, if the good citizen does no more than this, he or she fails to demonstrate the citizen's virtue proper. One can display citizen's virtue by helping the needy speak, by entering into discourse with them, by discovering their needs, their values, by helping them engage the public sphere on their own. The good citizen does not substitute his or her values for those of persons and groups whose needs are in want of recognition, or are not fully recognized, but rather displays *solidarity* with them. The virtue of solidarity is indeed one of the (additional) virtues of the good citizen (before and during Time One). Solidarity is due all persons, and groups of persons, whose needs are not recognized, or not fully recognized. The virtue of solidarity is not the virtue of charity (of the righteous person). Solidarity does not entail the gesture 'Here I am, and I will satisfy your unrecognized need.' Solidarity has nothing to do with need *satisfaction*. It is the virtue invested in need *recognition* (and value recognition). But the virtue of solidarity is not simply a 'good wish' either, nor is it restricted to the recognition of needs and values on the part of those who display solidarity. It is an active virtue. The person who displays solidarity makes his or her best effort (everything which is in his or her power) to ensure that the needs and values in question are recognized by all. Solidarity is a *warm* virtue. *Enthusiasm* invested in the idea of just procedure is the precondition of such solidarity.

The good citizen must criticize all needs the satisfaction of which involves the use of other men and women as mere means. Such criticism is very demanding, and requires much circumspection. One must learn to distinguish between needs the satisfaction of which involves the use of others as mere means in principle, and those which do not necessarily imply such use in principle, but do so under contemporary social circumstances. This distinction is very important, for the latter cluster of needs must be recognized, even if their current mode of satisfaction should be rejected. In this case, bad judgement invites disaster, for it excludes the actualization of just procedure at the outset. The idea of dictatorship over needs, or, on a milder note, the idea of the paternalistic imputation of needs, will then be substituted for the idea of just procedure. Good judgement must be rooted in a *virtue*. I shall term this virtue *radical tolerance*. The recognition of all needs the satisfaction of which does not involve the use of others as mere means *in principle* must be practised. And it can be practised by the virtue (attitude) of radical tolerance. Only needs the satisfaction of which necessarily implies domination must be excluded from recognition. Not even the quantified needs for having or for fame should be excluded from recognition, though we must reject the idea of their satisfaction via domination. Of course, no citizen forgoes his or her right, as a private person, to sympathize with certain needs and to loathe others, just as no one forgoes the right to criticize needs he or she loathes in personal relationships. But as *citizens* we must recognize them all, and equally so.

The good citizen is committed to value discourse as the just procedure. She or he makes the claim that norms and rules should be validated by the authorization of everyone concerned, by consensus. But before Time One the good citizen must assume that *no* norm, rule or law has been validated by just procedure. It must therefore be assumed that *every consensus is false*, apart from the consensus about the validity of the universal values (freedom and life). In a further specification, if the citizen sides with the *opposition* to the social regime, he or she must also assume that the norms and rules guiding the actions of the *opposition* are also based on *false consensus*. The virtual starting-point for becoming a good citizen is the *Cartesian moment*. By this I mean that every citizen, as a single person, as a single *cogito*, clarifies all criteria of 'true consensus' for himself or herself with the resolution to check the 'preliminary consensus' by those criteria. This person must of course invite others to share the Cartesian moment, in order to devalidate the false consensus and begin formulating a true one via just procedure. These 'others' may be very few. It can even happen that there are no 'others' in sight. The good citizen can be a solitary person, even if she or he does not take pride in this solitude because of the fact that the citizen's idea is *value discourse*, and being a solitary person means to fall short of observing this idea. However, under no circumstances does a good citizen resign *autonomy* as a moral being by accepting false consensus in order to 'participate'. The good citizen is also a *dissenter*. Such dissent is practised for the sake of true consensus.

Steadfast criticism of all needs the satisfaction of which involves domination, and rejection of all kinds of false consensus, are two sides of the same coin. False consensus always entails domination, for it entails *constraint*. Whether there is awareness of it or not, constraint is present in all forms of false consensus. We are aware of the presence of domination if power restrains us from outside; we are generally unaware of such a presence if power is *internalized*. Power can be internalized in many ways. What I have called the 'Cartesian moment' is a process whereby we rid ourselves of internalized power.

To challenge external domination and internalized power, to reject all kinds of false consensus, to be a dissenter, requires two additional virtues. One is the oldest virtue of philosophy, the *Socratic practice in self-knowledge*. But introspection is not sufficient to achieve self-knowledge proper. People come to know themselves from their own deeds, and from looking into the 'mirror' of other selves. One learns, via the interplay of introspection and action, the extent to which one has internalized power, as well as the extent to which one can expel the 'power inside'. The second additional virtue is the old virtue of democracy: *civic courage*. It is civic courage that makes us speak our mind amidst false consensus, and act in harmony with our beliefs amidst hostility and discouragement. Civic courage is not a display of daring but the actualization of moral autonomy in the public domain.

At this point I reiterate the constituents of citizen's virtue after Time One: impartiality as radical tolerance; the cognitive virtue of arguing whilst having recourse to the universal values of the 'higher-order consensus'; acceptance of the authority of truth (true values); *phronesis*. As mentioned, all except the first are cognitive in character. Let me now turn to the constituents of citizen's virtue before and during Time One. The same virtues are required here, but all virtues except for the second (arguing whilst having recourse to the universal value of the 'higher-order consensus') are to be practised in different ways. Moreover, only this second virtue is merely cognitive in character. All the other virtues encompass enthusiasm as well. Thus the virtues I have referred to as 'additional' virtues turn out not to be 'additional' at all. They are necessary in order to practise citizen's virtue before and during Time One. In solidarity, we claim recognition for as yet unrecognized needs, and we act so that these needs can be and are voiced. In self-knowledge, we rid ourselves of the power 'within our soul', and by doing so prepare the ground for the practice of the second (cognitive) virtue. In civic courage, we challenge domination and all kinds of false consensus, for otherwise no true consensus could ever be achieved.

I did not conjure 'civic virtue' out of the model of the best possible moral world or the idea of just procedure. All the civic virtues which are part and parcel of the 'good citizen' are conspicuously present in the democratic imagination. They are 'popular virtues', at least in societies of strong democratic tradition.[14] Whether or not we practise them, these virtues always 'appeal' to us. The goodness of the citizen does not require commentary; everyone recognizes, hails, respects it. There are even some who imitate it.

At the beginning of this chapter I remarked that all ethico-political concepts of justice must be 'backed' by the actual ethics, morality and practices of people, even if these people are few in number. If the ethico-political concept of justice designs the utopia of the best possible moral world, the theory will be 'backed' by people who, even in the worst possible world, prefer to suffer injustice than to commit it. The incomplete ethico-political concept of justice under discussion is more modest. It makes a case not for the best possible moral world, nor even for a 'just society', but for the best possible socio-political world, which is not just but which operates by just procedure. By this I mean that norms and rules are validated as the result of value discourse guided by the universal maxim of dynamic justice. All the elements of just procedure have been related to, or deduced from, traditional and contemporary just procedures, such as the formal concept of justice, the 'golden rule' and dynamic justice, having recourse to the values of freedom and life, and discourse as the means of settling socio-political conflicts. The entire model is but the rearrangement of the above-mentioned traditional and contemporary practices, and, I hope, not an arbitrary rearrangement. It is the only possible rearrangement involving all the constituents of 'justice', *if* humankind is thought to be the essential (overarching) social cluster, and *if* human relations are relations of symmetric reciprocity.

These two qualifications embody my value commitments. In a way, these commitments are arbitrary, for I do not share them with everyone, yet they are also non-arbitrary, for I share them with many. Of course, if I performed the transcendental deduction, and presented my model as 'truth' *par excellence*, it would have a ring of greater plausibility. Yet my project of an *incomplete* ethico-political concept of justice, in which certain substantive values have the status of axioms (to avoid mere formalism), is a very different commitment. It is not possible for me to ignore empirical motivations. Empirical motivations can be needs, wants, desires, passions, insights, interests, and the like. *Radical needs* can be understood as motivating forces. However, they can only produce the commitment to an *objective* (the transcendence of the world of superordination and subordination, the world of domination), *not the procedure itself.* Just procedure cannot be motivated by radical needs, for these needs can be *blind* and can express themselves in irrational gestures. Just procedure is rational. But this procedure cannot be motivated by *rational insight* either, for there are different kinds of rational insight (attitude), and the decision to opt for a particular one (for example, rationality of intellect) must be motivated by something other than rationality. A commitment to the universal values cannot be termed an empirical motivating force either, because people must first be motivated in order to accept such a commitment. Who can be so motivated as to accept this commitment? Only the 'good citizen', whose main motive forces are the citizen's virtues. It is in these virtues that radical needs and rational insights merge. It is in citizen's virtues that radical needs and rationality of intellect *can* merge. Thus 'good citizens' are those people who 'back' the incomplete ethico-political concept of justice. The good citizen backs, but does not guarantee, the 'best possible socio-political world'. And because the good citizen does not guarantee, but only supports, the model of such a world, such a world is possible, but only possible. It is not probable. However, good citizens not only back, but also guarantee, the incomplete ethico-political concept of justice.

Michael Walzer writes, 'The self-respecting citizen is an autonomous person. I don't mean autonomous in the world; I don't know what that would involve. He is autonomous in his community, a free and responsible agent, a participating member. I think of him as the ideal subject of a theory of justice.'[15] And so do I.

6

The Good Life

As I have repeatedly argued, a just procedure is the *condition of the good life* – of all possible good lives – but it is *not sufficient* for the good life. Justice is the skeleton: the good life is the flesh and blood. The 'good life' consists of three elements: first, righteousness; secondly, the development of endowments into talents and the exercise of those talents; and, thirdly, emotional depth in personal attachments. Among these three elements, righteousness is the overarching one. All three elements of the good life are *beyond justice*. Neither the maxim of justice (the formal concept of justice) nor the universal maxim of dynamic justice applies to them in full, if at all.

All three issues to be discussed in this final chapter have a somewhat anachronistic flavour to them. The manner in which they will be discussed may be regarded by many as utterly outmoded. I must therefore state at the outset that I am taking this course quite deliberately. I apply the method that I recommended in the previous chapter, and have termed the 'Cartesian moment'. When confronted with a cultural consensus, one must first presume that the consensus is *false*, and go through the problems once again before either giving consent or restating dissent. In what follows I shall talk in a positive vein about the self, morality, ethics, emotions, creativity and reason. Is this anachronistic? I hope not. Together with several others, I am swimming against the tide. Let us hope that the tide will turn.[1]

THE RIGHTEOUS PERSON

In the previous chapter I made a case for an incomplete ethico-political concept of justice. I discussed both the socio-political and the ethical aspects, in separation as well as in their relationship of interdependence. The subject, the bearer of the ethical component, was identified as the 'good citizen' practising the 'citizen's virtue'. But I added that, although not everyone need be a 'good person', in order to make the model workable, *some* must be. The universal values to be actualized were identified as the values of freedom and life. However, I added that the actualization of these values is the indispensable and yet insufficient condition of the good life. The subject of the good life is the good (righteous) person.

The key concept here is the 'righteous person'. To discuss this concept we must leave behind all social utopias, and turn to the most general problems of moral philosophy. Even so, no detailed elaboration of a moral philosophy is intended here.[2] The objective of this section is far more modest: not the landscape, just a sketch, and in addition one in need of correction. It is a first attempt, far from completion. But the canvas cannot be left empty.

Morals comprise those human bonds which have been internalized. This proposition is not meant as a definition. In fact, the opposite applies. If all internalized human bonds are moral, or at least include a moral element simply by being internalized, then the concept 'morals' escapes all sensible definition. It is possible to define the various *constituents* of morals (norms, virtues, ideas, principles), but in so doing one does not define morals. Instead, one has given preference to one moral attitude as against another. It is also possible to distinguish between human bonds which in principle escape internalization, and all the bonds which are internalized and thus have a moral component.

If morals are the internalized bonds between humans, if social integration occurs via internalization, and all forms of social integration thus have a moral component, *morals do not constitute a sphere.* On the contrary, *every social sphere is moral* to the extent that the practices it includes require internalization. The greater the degree of internalization, and the more intensive the internalization that such practices require, the more manifest is the moral aspect. If we think in very abstract terms and disregard historical peculiarities, we can roughly state that, *if a sphere becomes increasingly differentiated* from all other spheres, one of two contrasting developments might occur: either the moral component becomes much larger, or it is substantially weakened. In modernity, the tendency of the latter to occur is easily observable.[3]

The theory of a 'moral sphere' has been invented against the 'marginalization' of morals. Despite my sympathy for this motive, I consider the theory false. It is based on the tacit presupposition that the very existence of *ideal objectivations* indicates the presence of a *sphere*. Abstract norms, terms of virtue, are indeed ideal objectivations, but they do not and cannot constitute a sphere. Let me express this in very simple terms. In writing a philosophical treatise, we enter into a specific sphere (the objectivation 'philosophy' is one of the sub-spheres of the sphere 'objectivation-for-itself'). We observe the norms and rules of that sphere and thus perform a *philosophical activity*: we 'do philosophy'. However, in observing norms or being virtuous we do not 'do morals'; we engage in other things, such as politics, work, love, or even philosophy. Nor do we 'do morals' in acting courageously, but act under the guidance of the virtue 'courage' (an ideal objectivation), as for instance in war; in a social institution, when we give our opinion against overwhelming odds; and when we rescue people from fire, and the like. We can be guided by the same norms in different spheres and, incidentally, by specific norms in one or another sphere. If I understand him correctly, Habermas needed the construct of the 'moral sphere' in order to *determine* this sphere, in the spirit of his theory, as *practical discourse*. The solution is ingenious and seems to overrule my most serious objections to positing a 'moral sphere': we can 'do practical discourse'. If 'doing practical discourse' is equivalent to 'doing morals', then we can 'do morals'. In 'doing practical discourse' we suspend, at least in principle, all other activities; thus *we do nothing else*. But the question remains: *why* do we enter into practical discourse? And what is the *intended* result of such a discourse? We enter into such a discourse *because* certain of our values have become shaky, certain of our norms problematic. The goal of a discourse is to establish consensually new norms and rules. Thus practical discourse is the procedure via which *ideal objectivations* are rationally constructed and substituted for previous, problematic ideal objectivations. However, the different ideal objectivations *themselves* do not constitute a sphere, even if they have derived from practical discourse. They guide us in actions or practices in one or another sphere, or in all of them. Practical discourse constitutes norms and rules for *something other* than discourse – namely, for action. Practical discourse is 'doing morals' in a sense completely different from that in which theoretical discourse about philosophical matters is 'doing philosophy'.

To this point it appears that I have accepted Habermas's view that *moral* norms are constituted by practical discourse, or at least that they should be constituted by such discourse. However, this is not my view. In chapter 5 I gave reasons for recommending that *sociopolitical* norms and rules alone should be legitimized via practical discourse. If the reader accepts my proposal, the entire edifice of the 'moral sphere', even its most sophisticated version, collapses. Practical discourse conducted consensually to establish socio-political norms and rules cannot be described as 'doing morals'. Such a discourse is political and social (socio-political activity), although this socio-political activity has a moral aspect (implication): the rules of discourse *should be observed*, and 'observing the rules of discourse' is a process that should be *internalized* as *Sittlichkeit* (moral custom).

This brief criticism of the 'theory of the moral sphere' opens the way to broader considerations. If moral philosophy concentrates on the problem of constituting norms, almost all the vital questions of ethics will be neglected: questions such as the moral content of actions, virtues, and moral character. Of course, we can leave this approach behind and fall back upon hackneyed attempts. Instead of taking as our point of departure the constitution of 'good norms', we can choose as a starting-point primary motivations such as attraction/repulsion, sympathy, self-preservation, and so on. We can also try to deduce morals from reason, interests, and the like. But, whatever explanatory or evaluative principle we choose, it will be impossible to deduce *all moral phenomena* from this principle. Such an attempt can be given away altogether, or moral phenomena can be distorted by putting the same straitjacket on all of them. Or – and this is by far the most attractive solution – one can complement the main principle with secondary principles (as Kant did). The gist of the matter is that, since morals is not a sphere, *no homogeneous medium of morals exists or can be theoretically constituted.* Each and every time we attempt to construct a homogeneous medium of morals by deducing moral phenomena from one principle (or one main principle), the complex and multifarious nature of moral-related phenomena escapes our grasp.

Although only spheres or sub-spheres are characterized by a homogeneous medium, one sphere stands out for its *heterogeneity*: this is the sphere of 'objectivation-in-itself', the *primary* social sphere, the *fundamental* sphere of everyday life.[4] There does not exist and cannot exist any single principle which can homogenize this sphere, nor can any theoretical principle be constituted to perform this task. However, all heterogeneous activities guided by this objectivation can still be connected by a shared *meaning*. These activities remain heterogeneous. They cannot be deduced from one another, and are not even directly related to one another, but together they constitute a 'meaning' called 'way of life'. Let us briefly imagine a society with a single sphere of objectivation, the sphere of 'objectivation-in-itself'. Activities having a moral component can be related only to this sphere. So how could we gain access to all the heterogeneous elements of the 'moral bond'? By examining the *way of life* itself. This procedure is not so perplexing as it appears: every practising anthropologist does precisely this. Let us now imagine a more complex model containing many spheres: the sphere of 'objectivation-in-itself', various socio-political institutions, and the sphere of 'objectivation-for-itself', which in turn contains a number of differentiated sub-spheres. Clearly, there are many possible ways of life in such a complex model, and some form of meaning is borne by every one of them. However, within this framework certain ways of life are considered *exemplary* compared to others. This is because it is assumed, first, that people engaging in one of these ways of life have internalized to the maximum degree the human bond and act accordingly; and, secondly, that these people have accorded the highest possible level of meaning to their lives. The homogenization of the most heterogeneous moral principles, norms, activities, attitudes and feelings is *performed within the way of life of the good person*. Accordingly, the category 'the good life' should not be *deduced* from one or another principle or idea of morality, nor should it be conjectured from one or another specific human motivation. The image of the good life is the absolute starting-point of moral philosophy, and in fact of *all* moral philosophies, with the exception of utilitarianism. Moral philosophers formulate a concept of the good life prior to embarking on the quest for principles and motivations. For Plato and Aristotle this was self-evident, as they were able to rely on a preliminary consensus on the hierarchy of values. Although at this time a measure of pluralism had already emerged, it was still possible to distinguish in a reflective manner the good or the better way of life from the bad or the undesirable way of life through reinterpreting the traditional hierarchy of values. In modern philosophy similar efforts become problematic. *Why* this particular way of life and not another is the 'good' one is a question simply unanswerable by reinterpreting traditional values in the spirit of their traditional hierarchy. Philosophers thus perform a handstand: they construct 'first principles' or 'natural' and 'elementary' motivations in order to conjure up the very good life they have already presupposed (*quod erat demonstrandum*, to speak with Spinoza). The future-directed attitude of modernity had to be curtailed in order to return, via a 'historical detour', to the ancient method. This is why Hegel's moral philosophy is a disappointment.

Briefly, the problem to be faced is as follows. The traditional starting-point of moral philosophy is the good life of the righteous person. The different (and in relation to each other quite hetero-geneous) components of morality are homogenized only in the good life of righteous persons. But, if different ways of life compete with each other, and one must be *chosen* from among several (the problem discussed by Weber), the traditional starting-point of moral philosophy becomes inaccessible, at least for those who treat the problem with all seriousness. To deduce one form of life as the 'good' from first principles of 'primary motivations' is to avoid the problem rather than face it.

What is called the 'formalism' of Kant can be viewed and appreciated from this approach. Like the ancient thinkers, Kant made no secret of the fact that he *ascended* to the formulation of his moral principles and ideas from the *image* of the righteous person. The righteous person was for him the *man of good will*. The *existence* of the righteous person is first noted, and only then is the question raised: how is the righteous person possible? The element of *formalism* appears in the *image* of the righteous person. All concrete constituents of the good life are absent. Since righteousness is defined by the good will, everything else is left undetermined. Thus the starting-point of moral philosophy is not a *form* of the good life but righteousness as the *static* and *constant* precondition of *all possible good lives*. And righteousness itself is not the sum total of virtues. If it were, we should already have a concrete image of the good life in the back of our minds, which we should not. If the good person is the person who wills the good, the concrete quality of the good can be left undetermined.

So far I have only referred to the *starting-point* of the Kantian moral philosophy, and this is as far as I intend to go. In the course of argumentation in *The Metaphysics of Morals* the good life is made fairly tangible, despite all formalism. However, Kant is no longer relevant to our inquiry at this point. Following his path, but not all his solutions, I offer the following recommendation for a moral philosophy. I shall start at the only point possible: the good life of the righteous person. Let us assume that we cannot say, and should not say, anything about the concrete properties of the good life. This follows from the conclusions of chapter 5. The incomplete ethico-political concept of justice relinquishes the intention of designing a model of the good life. It has been assumed all along that several forms of the good life exist, and that they are equally good. Thus a moral philosophy conceived within the framework of an incomplete ethico-political concept of justice *should not* comment on the concrete properties of the good life. It can even be stated that we *cannot* say anything about these properties, because we already live in a pluralistic cultural universe. Moreover, it is not the concern of moral philosophy to ask whether the good life as a *total* way of life is socially possible for everyone, for a number of people, or is possible at all. This question has already been raised and answered by the incomplete ethico-political concept of *justice*. As this concept deals with the examination of the *socio-political conditions* of the good life, moral philosophy must deal with the examination of the *moral condition* of the good life. And the moral condition of the good life is *righteousness*. Embarking on moral philosophy means accepting the fundamental tenet of all moral philosophies: that no good life exists without righteousness, and that only righteous people can live the good life. However, one is not at the same time compelled to accept the fundamental tenet of some moral philosophies that being righteous means living the good life. Rather, we define the 'good life' as the coalescence of the moral and the 'natural' good, and associate it (sometimes vaguely) with the notion of 'happiness'.

Thus the starting-point of my moral philosophy is not the good life, but the moral condition of the good life: righteousness. But, if we wish to abstract from all concrete elements of one or another good life, then 'righteousness' cannot be defined, following Aristotle, as the 'sum total of virtues'. Our definition must be abstract enough to encompass all righteous persons regardless of their way of life. The Kantian 'good will' appears to lend itself to such an abstract definition, but does not actually do so, and this is not because of its formalism but because it excludes *Sittlichkeit* (moral custom) and action itself from the fundamental 'image' of the righteous person. I believe that here it is best to return from Kant to the Platonian definition: that the righteous person is the person who prefers suffering injustice (being wronged) to committing injustice (doing wrong), where 'committing injustice' means infringing moral norms in *direct* relation to other people.

This definition of 'righteousness' I believe sufficiently abstract. The fact that a person prefers suffering wrong to committing it says nothing about this person's way of life. Just *what* is considered right or wrong has been left undecided. The empirical *motivation*, too, is left undecided. Also, the definition is not maximalist in nature. The requirement is not that *you should do good* to everyone, but that *you should not wrong* anyone. Nor is it required that you should continuously suffer wrong (in other words, martyrdom and self-sacrifice are not mandatory), only that you should suffer wrong *if* the only alternative is to commit wrong. Finally – and this follows from what has been said before – the definition of righteousness is *equally* valid in societies with very few norms and regulations and in societies with very dense normative systems. References to the present as well as to the utopia of symmetric reciprocity can illustrate the viability of this definition. Owing to the preponderance of functionalist rules, in contemporary institutions moral decisions proper are infrequent. But, when such decisions (or choices) do take place, 'basic righteousness' still concerns suffering or committing wrong, and we still pass judgements along these lines. In the utopia of symmetric reciprocity there is room for people who do not enter *any other* social relationships but 'civic ones'. In such cases, practising 'civic virtues' is tantamount to righteousness, because whoever does this does not wrong anyone. Of course, within ways of life having dense normative structures and multifarious human relationships, being righteous is more demanding.

Plato presented a particular definition of righteousness. He also attempted to prove in a rational manner the thesis 'It is better to suffer injustice than to commit it', and failed. Subsequently, several others have tried to do the same, and have also failed. In chapter 2 I discussed the hopelessness of this venture. Righteous people are in no need of proof *precisely because* they are righteous; for these people it is beyond doubt that suffering injustice is better than committing it. However, wicked people can rationally prove (as is shown in Plato's dialogues) that it is better to commit injustice than suffer it. But they are in no need of proof either, *precisely because* they are wicked. For these people it is beyond doubt that committing injustice is better than suffering it. Usually, people are neither righteous nor wicked. Hence the righteous person is able to convince people in a rational manner that it is better to suffer wrong than to commit it, and the wicked person can, in an equally rational manner, convince people of the exact opposite.

It is possible to prove that it *would* be good for everyone if everyone were good, but not that it *is* good for everyone to be good. One cannot even enjoin a particular person to be good by referring to the assumption 'it would be good for everyone if everyone were good.' Accordingly, I recommend the discarding of this approach altogether, and the adoption of another – namely, the Kantian.

It is clear that Kant, when speaking of his 'man of good will', does not even bother to prove that it is better to be guided by good will than not to be, where 'better' relates to the *material good*. He simply points to the 'man of good will', to the subject worthy of supreme respect. Good will shines as a jewel. The jewel shines, therefore the jewel is visible. Righteous people do exist, and we know this because we see them. In these steps I have substituted the Platonian definition of righteousness for the Kantian. For this reason, we can take as our point of departure the fact that there *are* people who prefer suffering wrong to committing it. Whether such people are few or many is irrelevant. Yet, wherever morals exist, and as long as they exist, there will always be people who prefer to suffer wrong rather than commit it. No matter where we look, we shall always find righteous people. *They exist.*

I would formulate the basic question of moral philosophy as follows: righteous persons exist, how are they possible?

If we begin our inquiry with the Platonian definition of the righteous person, we gain the following theoretical advantages:

a   We begin with the idea of the 'good life', but we can leave *the concrete patterns of the good life undetermined,* for we are concerned exclusively with the moral conditions of this good life.
b   The concept of righteousness is abstract enough to leave both the *content* and *density of moral norms* undetermined.
c   The question 'How are righteous persons possible?' can be answered by reflecting upon *all* the facets and elements of morals, for only in their entirety do they make the righteous person possible. There is no longer any need to connect *systematically* these facets and elements of the moral life, nor is there any need to deduce all of them from one or a number of principles or motivations. The actions, attitudes and motives of the righteous person comprise the *juncture* at which all these facets and elements *meet* and eventually *coalesce.* This coalescence occurs via the *homogenization* of all these components in and through the *righteous character.*

Righteous persons are possible because they exist. What makes them possible?

1   Good moral sense.
2   The existence of norms, provided that:
    i   these norms are conveyed by the society (group) of which the person is a member;
    ii   the three components of normative regulation (concrete norms, abstract norms, and values) have already been differentiated;
    iii certain norms or values are (or at least one of them is) consensually validated.
3   Relative autonomy of the individual, in so far as:
    i   he or she can *reinterpret* the content of norms, can reject

        some, accept others, prefer one value to another (can say both 'yes' and 'no');

  ii his or her deliberations concern not only the 'how' but also the 'what' of the action;

  iii there is a choice, if only occasional, between suffering and committing wrong in the person's world.

4 Self-consciousness, in so far as:

  i the regulation of conscience (internal authority) complements the regulation of shame (external authority);

  ii there is an awareness that *my* action brings about something in the world;

  iii there is personal responsibility (and the sense of this responsibility);

  iv there is self-reflection (the possibility of *knowing* the self).

5 Ethical discourse (on an everyday level and beyond), in so far as ethical choices and decisions can be problematized, criticized and credited.

6 A relative stability of the normative universe. At least some norms should be *continuously* valid (throughout the life of a generation).

7 A relative stability of the social universe. Certain consequences of actions must be foreseeable.

8 Good judgement in general, and phronesis in particular (both as primary and secondary judgement).

9 At least a minimum of rationality of intellect up to a maximum of rationality of intellect in order that:

  i commitment can be *partially* (not completely) guided by rational insight;

  ii the non-moral properties of the subject (viewed by the subject as 'nature') can also be shaped (though not exclusively) by rational insight.

10 Goodwill as the desire to be good transformed by the actor into the *cause* of his or her actions.

11 The possibility of *neutralizing* (and not only channelling) wrong or accidentally irrational impulses.

12 The possibility of transforming endowments into 'virtuous faculties' (as Lessing put it).

13 Rectification. Although all actions are irreversible, the majority of our actions must not be such that the moral component is irreversible.

The conditions which make righteous persons possible are in part objective, in part subjective. Some of these conditions are coextensive, certain others are not. Since righteousness is relative to social expectations, it is not necessary for every condition to be met for persons to be righteous. But the idea of the righteous person in modernity presupposes that all the above-enumerated conditions are met.

To sum up all these conditions of righteousness in one phrase, a person can be righteous if he/she has a *conscious and self-conscious relationship* to the norms and values of the community (society) of which he/she is a member, and if his/her actions are continuously and consistently guided by this relationship. Following Hegel, we can term the norms and values to which this person has a conscious relationship *Sittlichkeit* (moral custom), and the conscious relationship itself *morality*. Morality is the autonomous aspect, whereas *Sittlichkeit* relativizes autonomy (a situation where at least one *socially and intersubjectively* valid norm or value must be taken for granted, at least one value or norm must be accepted as a representation of 'external' authority). The states of absolute autonomy and of no autonomy at all are to an equal degree *negative* utopias. If, generally speaking, morality is the internalization of *human bonds*, then the rejection of all human bonds as a *project* (and only in the capacity of a project, for we simply *cannot* shed all human bonds) cannot be anything other than *immoral*. What we can legitimately call 'moral autonomy' is not the autonomy of the subject, not even that of our pure practical reason (a mere philosophical construct), but the *way of life of righteous persons*. The 'good person' has achieved the maximum degree of moral autonomy, not because this person is *completely* autonomous, which can never be, but because his or her moral character does not yield to social constraint.

The Platonian definition of righteousness is almost as abstract as the Kantian. It has, however, the advantage of being 'minimalist'. Righteousness is defined as the *forbearance* of an act (a wrong), and not as *doing good*. Of course, if we do not wrong anyone, we have performed the 'good' in a negative sense, but not yet in a positive sense. But when I stated above that 'righteous persons exist', I had in mind not only those people who never deliberately wrong anyone, but also people who perform good in a positive sense, who do good even through refraining from doing so is not tantamount to doing wrong. (For example, people who volunteer to help others would not wrong those others if they did not decide to volunteer.) Generosity, a readiness for self-sacrifice or to alleviate suffering for which one is not responsible – these and many other things of a similar nature pertain to a form of righteousness which involves more than the concept of righteousness defined by Plato. As I have repeated several times, people can be righteous to a greater or lesser degree. But everyone who suffers rather than commits wrong is righteous, even if not to the same extent. Supererogatory goodness is not the condition of righteousness. This is precisely why we can speak of 'supererogation' at all. In what follows, I shall term righteousness that is not of a supererogatory nature 'honesty', and the righteous person who suffers rather than commits wrong the 'honest' or 'good' person. The person of supererogatory goodness is always an honest person, but not all honest persons display supererogatory goodness. Those who exhibit the most sublime supererogatory goodness I shall term 'transculturally good persons', for this kind of goodness transcends all concrete and particular cultural determinations. Honest people are sometimes able to show supererogatory goodness, sometimes not. There is no fixed dividing-line between 'honest' and 'transculturally good' people. This is especially so considering that, if a person chooses to observe moral norms of a highly demanding type, he or she must stand by this commitment, and consequently must be exceptionally good in order to remain honest. At any rate, unless I indicate otherwise, when I refer in what follows to the 'righteous person' I have the 'honest person' in mind, and *vice versa*.

I have not made any attempt to prove that it is better to be righteous than not to be righteous. Instead, what I have tried to make a case for is the view that the righteous person has the highest degree of *moral autonomy*. However, it would be foolish to assume that everyone wants to be morally autonomous, even if this were possible. On the other hand, there are forms of relative autonomy *other than* the moral one (such as wielding great power). Of course, philosophers can prove that this kind of autonomy is 'not the real one'. Persons of great power, fame or wealth are still subject to vicissitudes – for instance, the hand of fate. Yet, because relative autonomy is 'borrowed' in such cases, it does not dwell in the self, and can be lost. Other philosophers point to the moment of 'reckoning': faced with death, those who are 'merely' powerful or wealthy stand to lose everything, whereas the righteous can rely steadfastly on their goodness.

In fact, all these arguments are shaky, and can in practice backfire. Indeed, viewed from one particularly crucial aspect, righteousness cannot be lost, for we do not lose our readiness to suffer wrong rather than commit it. But, again, we can in a sense lose our righteousness without really losing it (as the readiness to suffer rather than commit wrong), especially amidst great tribulations, when our sense of proportion is disturbed, when our preliminary knowledge and practice proves insufficient to tell wrong from right. This has occurred more frequently in modern times than ever before. There is an unmistakable element of 'good luck' in making good our own righteousness throughout our entire life. Moreover, wealth, power and rank were considered 'virtues' in every pre-modern society, and have increasingly been considered 'meritorious' in modern times. A person who has attained great power, wealth or fame can, in dying, look back with satisfaction on the achievements of his or her life. Not even the argument that such people are controlled by external factors can be used here: the term 'self-made man' tells the whole story. Achievement is self-made, success is self-made, and greatness can be as well, and each of these things may have little moral content, or none. And, as far as the Grim Reaper is concerned, and given that faith in the hereafter has largely disappeared, there is no evidence to suggest that the righteous will necessarily find peace in their final hour, and that the man of wealth, fame or power will be tormented by guilt. Rather, one could say that, if by some miracle humankind were granted immortality on earth, most people would prefer to suffer injustice rather than commit it, for there would be nothing to lose. One can be righteous precisely because one has something to lose in gaining something else. If there were nothing to lose, nothing could be gained either. But losing *something* means *losing* something, and what the righteous stand to lose is not a trifling thing. Thus people who choose what the righteous lose for the sake of their righteousness do not choose a trifling thing. The non-righteous prefer committing injustice in order *not* to suffer wrong.

Within the Jewish–Christian tradition, 'suffering wrong' has occasionally been elevated to a position of sublime distinction. However, the Platonian notion of righteousness has nothing whatsoever to do with this tradition. There is nothing sublime in suffering wrong. On the contrary, it is bad to suffer wrong, and we do not become righteous *by virtue of* so suffering. If we have no choice but to suffer wrong, we simply become miserable. And we can indeed both suffer and commit wrong, at which point we are non-righteous, even though we do suffer this wrong. In fact, we should not suffer wrong. No one should. We should not suffer wrong if we can do anything to prevent it, and we can do something to prevent it whenever we are not facing the choice of either suffering it or committing it. This is the choice we make, not the choice of suffering wrong.

I return to the basic question: righteous persons exist, but how are they possible? It is now appropriate further to concretize this question. Hence I ask: righteous persons exist today, but how are they possible *today*? Since this question can only be answered by a complete moral philosophy, discussion will be restricted to analysing certain new issues which have arisen in the latest period of Western modern development. Also, these issues will be raised solely from the viewpoint, and within the framework, of the incomplete ethico-political concept of justice. Put succinctly, the reference point of analysis is *Time One* (any Time One). This approach is determined by the objective of this book. I want to distinguish the good person (the righteous person) from the good citizen, the best possible moral world from the best possible socio-political world, the good life from just procedure. Since Time One is already *here*, I can refer solely to conditions (of righteousness) which are *here*. The analysis will be rooted in the absolute present. However, the method of both selecting and solving problems has the hallmark of a *theoretical position* which has crystallized around a social and evaluative position.

We live in a complex of pre-modern and modern normative patterns (modern to varying degrees). None the less, the trend towards a high degree of differentiation of moral norms, values and virtues is unmistakable. There is nothing novel in the differentiation itself, only in its extremity, owing to which the three constituents of normativity have completely separated. This means that the interplay among the three constituents is not socially reproduced as 'taken for granted'. However, there is no morality at all without such a pattern of interplay. Thus groups of people must *construct* and *reconstruct* such an interplay again and again. We live in a pluralistic normative universe *not* because of a lack in shared norms, but because of a lack of shared interplay between norms, values and virtues. Let us take a final look on the 'ancient situation'. The 'city' was at that time the supreme shared cultural value. The interplay between the 'good' of the city, moral norms and moral and cognitive virtues was shared and transparent. The interpretation was subject to change, but not the 'interplay'. Today this is no longer the case.

Indeed, values, virtues and norms are different elements of our normative universe. Values are *social–material* goods (*Güterwerte*), and are always utterly *concrete*. Even generalized or universalized values are 'constructed' from the building-blocks of concrete goods, or, alternatively, are analysed by referring to all the concrete goods of which they consist. This is exactly the procedure of the interpretation of universal values. But, the more generalized and universalized certain values become, the less consistent is their interpretation. There is no continuous relation established between concrete goods (values) and general and universal goods, and all concrete goods (values) split apart when considered separately as 'goods' (values), or as values for some persons and negative values (*Unwerte*) for others. Thus the supreme goods (values), life and freedom, exist in limbo, and do not provide any consensual hierarchy among values, not even a relative hierarchy. The assertion that social–material goods (values) are *concrete* means that they are *active* values in their concreteness. They are *active as values* if they are continuously validated by actions because they *motivate* action: people act such that these cultural values should exist, should flourish, or occasionally should be 'immortal'. These values include such things as the nation (*my* nation), the family, freedom of speech, progress, health, humankind, independence, welfare and culture (still!). And because they are concrete values they *can* in principle motivate human actions 'towards themselves'. However, they do not underlie the actions of every person who is committed to them (either to some of them or to all of them). From the viewpoint of most individuals they are passive rather than active values.

Terms of virtue do not refer to *anything concrete*; every such term is a *type*. These terms typify the *character traits* and *action patterns* that are *typically* required for the *actualization of* values. Virtues are defined and redefined from the viewpoint of the *active values* validated by the (virtuous) action. Virtues make no sense except in relation to 'material goods'.[5] If values change, virtues can be dethroned. (Spinoza remarked that humility is not a virtue, a statement that was echoed by Kant. This is self-evident if *hierarchy*, earthly or divine, is not a value.) Virtues are reinterpreted, if the (active) values they are related to change (loyalty – to whom, to what?). There is only one single type of virtue which can be related to *passive* values: the *cognitive*. Reflexivity, rationality of intellect, the readiness to conduct ethical discourse – these virtues, among others, have become extremely important in modern times (and they undoubtedly are cognitive virtues), partly because of the *passivity* of most contemporary values in this paramount reality of so many single individuals. The *only* action we can continuously perform that is related to these values (or is performed in conjunction with them) is the *speech act*. But, of course, certain values are 'active' or are frequently 'activated' in our lives, and we need to mobilize virtues (other than the cognitive one) to actualize them. If this were not so, we could not 'characterize' our fellow-creatures in terms of virtues, which we are always doing.

Norms can be concrete or abstract. Concrete norms demand (and occasionally also command) the observance of customs. These norms can be rules, or something very similar to rules. They can be optative as well as imperative. Abstract norms, as mentioned, are transcultural, and I have called them *moral norms proper*. Moral norms proper are also related to values. These values can be termed 'yardstick values': they are the values by which we evaluate social values and virtues, and we call them 'moral values'. Virtues necessary for the actualization of *all* values are always *moral virtues*, and are commanded by abstract moral norms. Moral norms proper can *prohibit* certain actions (such as murder or perjury) as wicked in themselves (these actions annul the value of a social institution or a character). They can also enjoin or recommend certain actions the practice of which *makes* the character virtuous and the institution valuable, regardless of whether or not they are regarded as such from the standpoint of concrete norms.

In traditional societies concrete norms change slowly. Such changes are hardly noticeable over a generation. Yet from time to time dramatic ruptures can occur. Very roughly, one could describe such changes as a process of *sedimentation* (concretization) whereby certain abstract (transclusteral) norms become new *clusteral* norms. Thus the new concrete norms will be functionally equivalent to the former ones: they are social customs and habits that are taken for granted and observed by the members of the social clusters to which they apply. At the dawn of modernity, however, this type of rupture was not followed by the process of sedimentation as I have just described it. Certain instances of the sedimentation of abstract norms into new and clusteral concrete norms did occur, but this sedimentation proved to be only momentary, whereas the rupture itself proved to be steady. When Tugendhat refers to concrete norms as norms which come about via the *application* of abstract norms (in action, decision and discourse), and describes this process as the *moral learning-process par excellence* he touches upon the most conspicuous feature of a *pluralistic moral universe*.[6] To avoid any misunderstanding on this matter, it must be emphasized that the application of norms has always been part of the moral learning-process of the individual, but that normally no new concrete norm is engendered in this process. *Pluralism* of the moral universe is to be attributed not to the coexistence of *different* groups of concrete norms, but to the fact that these different groups are *no longer clusteral*; that they no longer stratify society, that they are no longer taken for granted. Put simply, individuals choose one or another set of concrete norms and can establish new ones via the 'concretization' of abstract norms (in principle it is already possible for two people to activate this process). Of course, the 'traditional' concrete norm has not disappeared. The real social milieu into which we are thrown by the accident of birth still furnishes us with initial concrete norms, and throughout our lives we continue to take several of these norms for granted (to a greater or lesser degree). But only some of these norms are 'clusteral'. Moreover, since we can choose sets of concrete norms other than those we obtain by birth, we choose again and again our traditional norms in that we unwittingly stick by them.

It has become the creed of moral philosophy that morals in a pluralistic moral world are by definition more 'rationalistic' than morals in a pre-modern world. I should like to modify this thesis as follows: morals *can* become more rational in a pluralistic moral universe, but do not necessarily do so.

No morality can be *completely* rational. However, the *optimal* rationality of morals can be achieved if we *choose ourselves* as honest persons in a morally pluralistic universe. Every rational aspect of morality in modernity follows from the *existential choice*. My argument on behalf of this existential choice will be conducted in three consecutive steps. First, I shall briefly explain how and why moral rationality decreases in our modern universe, except for the existential choice of righteousness. Next, I shall explain my notion of the 'existential choice' and argue for the optimum rationality of such a choice. Finally, I shall discuss how the existential choice (of honesty) can be made good in a pluralistic moral universe.

Being rational is only possible through *rendering* meaning to one's actions, if meaning is created through one's actions. An action is morally rational if one acts in relation to a value (or several values) with the intention of maintaining this value via the observance of norms (abstract or concrete) or the display of virtues. If the value is passive (that is to say, one can neither maintain nor reject it by direct action), it is still possible to be morally rational by displaying *cognitive virtues* in conjunction with these values (for example, checking the value content of the institution in question in discourse). However, our modern world is not only a pluralistic moral universe, but simultaneously a *functional social universe*. Luhmann was on the mark when he insisted that within functionalist social institutions we do not act in a *morally meaningful way*. As he puts it, we can *attribute* meaning to institutions, but we cannot *constitute* such meaning, for observing the rules in rationalized institutions does not require (moral) *attitudes* but requires only certain *behavioural patterns*. Translating Luhmann's ideas into my theoretical language, it can be stated that if we enter into any rationalized institution, which we always do, we do not choose norms but become subject to rules. And we take these rules for granted. We never check them by moral standards. Also, because we do not constitute the meaning of the institutions in which we perform, as specialized human beings, one or another function, we do not relate to such institutions as to values either. We relate to them as to values only if we choose them. Rule conformity in rationalized institutions is not a moral matter at all (unless we have chosen the institution as a value or rejected it as a negative value). Large segments of our actions become morally indifferent, not morally rational.

Moreover, the very fact that different sets of norms are open to choice in a pluralistic moral universe means that moral rationality can be decreased even further. What is open to choice is not necessarily chosen. We can simply *enter into* a loose set of norms, not because we consider them to be good or better than another set for moral reasons, but simply because they suit our tastes, desires and interests. We can incidentally rationalize them as good, and even the process of rationalization can be cut short. And we can simultaneously enter into the rules of certain rationalized institutions. There is certainly a tendency here to live in a moral vacuum. We *could* give *moral* reasons for our actions, but unfortunately we usually do not do so. People are confronted less and less with the necessity to give moral reasons for their actions. Instead, they give *psychological* reasons if they give any reasons at all. This practice has become so predominant that the *choice of values* becomes replaced by the *choice of goals*. Of course, the same institution or project can be simultaneously a goal and a value. The difference lies in the actions oriented towards them. If the goal is a value, the actions are normative; if the goal is not a value, the action is instrumental. The practice of directly connecting individual psychology and a political exigency or objective, without the mediation of moral personality, moral norms or moral reasons, has become quite widespread.

In order to choose from amongst sets of norms (and not only enter into them) – in other words, in order to commit ourselves to norms and actions for *moral reasons* – we must first *choose* ourselves as the people who check norms and actions from a 'moral point of view', as the people who give the moral point of view preference over other (pragmatic) reasons. We must thus make an *existential choice*, by which I mean, with Kierkegaard, the choice of the choice between good and evil. The existential choice is introduced here not as an *ontological* but as a *historical* category. Of course, there has always been an existential element in the choice between good and evil. This follows from one of my fundamental assertions: that it is impossible to prove that it is better to suffer wrong than to commit it. If persons choose to be righteous, then they choose themselves as persons for whom the above statement is true, but this choice is *not* determined by the truth of the statement. However, even if there has always been a choice between good and evil, and in choosing the good one choses one's own self as a righteous person, making the choice itself was something not always *open* to choice. If norms and rules are reasonably coherent, the twin values of orientation of good and evil have priority over all other values of orientation ('good comes first'), and everyone knows *what* good is. Norms are external to the individual, and are normally embedded in meaningful world views of legitimation. There is no choice between norms, except in periods of crisis, even if they eventually become open to interpretation. To refer once again to Luhmann, *attitudes*, and not simply modes of behaviour, are required. It is only in modern times that the choice between good and evil has come to be seen not simply as a matter of course, and this is increasingly the case. This is why this choice itself must be chosen. In the main, if we make the existential choice, if we choose to choose between good and evil, then *we have chosen ourselves as honest persons*, as persons who give priority to moral reasons over other reasons.[7] Thus we have chosen ourselves as persons guided by practical reason.

The existential choice can be made in a single gesture, but this is not necessarily the case. As Schütz has pointed out, we cannot fathom the notion of choice using a spatial analogy. A person never stands at point O, confronted with two or three possible paths, and then decides to follow path A rather than path B. The existential choice, like all other choices, comes about via a series of intentional acts *in time*. And it can miscarry if the first intentional act is not followed by the second, the third, and so on, just as it can be successful if the person has already chosen himself or herself as an honest person, as someone guided by practical reason, as someone who suffers rather than commits wrong.

If a person has not made the existential choice, his or her moral rationality *decreases* in comparison to the moral rationality of a person of pre-modern times. If a person makes the existential choice, his or her moral rationality *increases* in comparison to the moral rationality of a person of pre-modern times. This is so for the following reasons. First, the choice between good and evil is not taken for granted: the choice itself is chosen. Secondly, since there is a choice between different values and different sets of norms, then values and norms, if chosen, are *not external* to the individual. Thirdly, the person is ready and able to give moral reasons for accepting one and rejecting another value or set of norms; indeed, making the existential choice involves a commitment to give such moral reasons. Fourthly, in every moral decision the honest person chooses himself or herself as the person making the existential choice. This is, in fact, the optimal possibility of moral rationality. However, no one can give reasons *why* he or she has made this existential choice. To put it another way, one can give as many reasons as one likes, but these reasons will not add up to 'reason as such'. Of course, it could be said that certain psychological tendencies make the existental choice *more likely* to occur than do other psychological tendencies. None the less, psychological tendencies do not determine the choice, or else one is no longer an autonomous person and hence cannot make a choice anyway. It could be further stated that under certain *personal* and *social* conditions such an existential choice is, again, *more likely* to occur than under different personal and social conditions. It might even be added – something of no minor importance – that in a society based on symmetric reciprocity the existential choice will be far more frequent that it is today. Without such a belief, it would be difficult to hold the view that the best possible social world is the condition of the good life. Yet, despite all this, social circumstances *do not determine* the existential choice, and for the same reasons as noted above. The Kantian distinction between theoretical and practical reason is relevant here. The existential choice is a free act. It cannot be grasped in terms of determination, not because it is irrational, but *because it is rational beyond the authority of theoretical reason.*

The existential choice is the root of all concrete choices, of all subsequent choices, but it *does not determine* these choices. The honest person has opted for the choice between good and evil, and has chosen himself or herself as an honest person. He or she is committed to choosing values and norms via moral reasons. But the type of concrete values and norms the honest person will choose is not determined by or inherent in the existential choice. Even if we are ready to give priority to practical reason in all our choices, we can still make mistakes, and sometimes grave ones. The existential choice cannot be wrong, because theoretical reason plays no part in it. But, every time we give priority to practical reason (the good) in our decisions, we must first determine whether the norms are good or otherwise, whether the action is good or otherwise. Thus we must pass judgement. Judgement is the act of theoretical reason, even if theoretical reason is subordinate to practical reason. Where theoretical reason is involved, we can be wrong as well as right. True enough, honest persons do not stop to 'check' and 'recheck' the norms already chosen. Rather, they withdraw their commitment to these norms once they are proved wrong by subsequent judgements. They can say, 'I was wrong', 'I was committed to the right, but I could not tell the right from the wrong in my judgement.' Without doubt, mistakes can be fatal. Sometimes they cannot be corrected or 'put right' at all. These are the tragic situations *par excellence*. Not making any mistakes at all in our choices can be matter of sheer good luck, as well as of employing good theoretical reason in our judgements.

This is why it has become so important in modern times to make concrete decisions under the guidance of moral maxims, and, in particular, to formulate certain moral maxims (those of the first order) which cannot be arrived at by intellectual intuition. The application of such maxims minimizes, though it does not wholly exclude, the likelihood of mistakes in judgement. Yet it does completely eliminate fatal mistakes. I shall return to this question shortly.

If two sets of moral norms are equally good, the choice between them is, by definition, *not* the choice between good and evil. The honest person commits himself or herself to choosing good norms, as well as to *not choosing* norms which enjoin, or even permit, the doing of wrong to others. Furthermore, the honest person commits himself or herself to observing this chosen set of norms, for infringing them would, by definition, mean doing injustice to all others committed to the same norms. However, the existential choice of honesty does not exclude the possibility of abiding by rules, if these rules are regarded as morally indifferent (neither good nor bad), as solely instrumental, pragmatic or aesthetic. Only those actions should be subjected to moral norms that are either good or bad, in the very relation, time, place or situation in which they are good or bad. Obviously, if an action has nothing to do with the choice between doing or suffering wrong, and if, therefore, I do not, or cannot, do wrong in a particular action, then this action is by definition not subject to moral appraisal.

A moral theory can present the proposition that people should *also* enter into a set of social norms and rules via the guidance of moral reasons. But a moral philosophy must not propose that people should enter into a set of social norms and rules *exclusively* on the grounds of moral reasons. Likewise, a moral philosophy can propose that norms and rules should be open to testing in practical discourse. But it must not propose that moral norms should always be validated in practical discourse (a problem to which I shall shortly return). Finally, a moral philosophy can propose that all norms and rules should be checked by universal maxims, but it should not propose that valid norms and rules should themselves be universal.

All these recommendations follow logically from the idea of a *limited cultural relativism*, and from the project of an incomplete ethico-political concept of justice. I have made a case for a pluralistic moral universe, one in which different sets of moral norms and rules coexist, and in which people are free to choose one or another of these sets. What is the 'limit' to this *moral* relativism? Obviously, all normative sets must have some norms or at least one norm in common. What they need to have in common is, however, not a *concrete* norm, but *moral maxims* concretized in different norms. Now, if people are free to choose any set of norms, then, provided that none of these sets of norms and rules contradicts moral maxims, they do not choose one over another for *moral reasons only*. They choose one set over another because one particular form of morality suits their personalities better than the others. Their decision is indeed a 'matter of taste', a 'matter of desire', a 'matter of interest'. In such a pluralistic universe, the *recognition of validity* of the sets of norms and the *act of validation* of the sets of norms do not coincide. For everyone recognizes the validity of all sets of moral norms and rules as long as they do not contradict moral maxims. But each person validates only the particular set of norms and rules she or he observes. Only those moral maxims validated by everybody are *factually universal*, or, at least, these are the moral maxims for which we can legitimately claim factual universality. Moral maxims are universalized through the observance of norms, which, for their part, do not claim universality.

Should moral norms be validated in practical discourse as socio-political norms (of justice)? Is rational discourse the sole procedure which makes moral norms rational?

We can make our normative commitments rational by attaining *consistency* in our value commitments. The clarification of our value commitment implies the elimination of contradictions between the various concrete sets of values we are committed to, and, first and foremost, the elimination of contradictions between the abstract moral ('yardstick') values, *alias* the moral norms and concrete values, we are committed to. Rationality is then tantamount to the

homogenization of heterogeneous sets of values. Such homogenization can be achieved via a step-by-step process: action–discourse–
action–discourse–action. Thus the homogenization of our value
(commitment) is never a monologic performance. Action cannot by
definition be monologic, and discourse, even though it can in
principle be conducted in thought acts, is in reality almost never
conducted via thought acts alone.

In my discussion of discourse ethics I concluded that, if everyone
were to accept life and freedom as supreme values (values beyond
testing and querying), the discussants could phase out all false values
and select the true ones. Since consensus concerning the truth of
certain values can be achieved, a consensus can also be achieved
concerning a *set of socio-political norms* within the framework of
which all true values can be actualized. However, consensus on
socio-political norms does not imply consensus on moral norms.
There is not just one true value. People can be committed to one
group of values rather than another. And commitment to values is
tantamount to commitment to a set of moral (concrete) norms. Thus
different persons committed to the same socio-political norms and
rules can still commit themselves to different sets of moral norms,
depending on their value choice, provided their values are true.
People can also be committed (or uncommitted) to certain virtues.
Now, the idea that all these moral norms should be established via
the 'discourse of everyone concerned' is, to my mind, misconceived.
In modernity, at least, we *become* concerned *because* we commit
ourselves to one norm and not another. 'Being concerned' is
equivalent to being committed. If we decide upon a communal or a
solitary life, if we opt for religion or atheism, monogamy or sexual
liberty, frankness or limited sincerity, it simply does not make sense,
it is not meaningful, to ask whether or not the norms to which we
are committing ourselves are rational. If different sets of norms can
be equally good, the only relevant question is whether they are good
for us, whether we can better homogenize the different aspects of
morals by choosing one or the other. No other question *should* be
raised. If all moral norms are good (although good in different ways
and good for different people), commitment to one or another of
them constitutes a *promise*. Once committed, I must keep this
promise. Of course, there are *elements of ethical discourse* even
within this model, and in two respects. First, people committed to
the *same* set of norms can conduct a discourse about changing
certain moral norms. Secondly, shifting allegiance from one set of
moral norms to another entails entering into discourse with people
directly concerned with this shift of allegiance, if such people exist.

Such a discourse cannot deal with the new set of norms chosen, but can determine only whether the new allegiance is a breach of a promise given to particular persons, not to everyone who shares the previous commitment.

Granted this, the crucial question still faces us. The existential choice of honesty (righteousness) is the only rational moral choice. It is tantamount to the choice between good and evil whilst resolving to choose the good. The choice constitutes a resolve to be what we are. But in a pluralistic moral universe *we must make ourselves into what we are.* We require a dependable yardstick to measure the goodness or badness (and, incidentally, the moral indifference) of norms and rules. This must be a *universal* yardstick, and moral maxims provide such a yardstick. In my view, there are two kinds of moral maxims. The first is *deduced* from the universal values of life and freedom. The second is related to these two values. We can provide a complete *catalogue* of the first kind, but we cannot do so for the second kind because we obtain these particular maxims by intellectual intuition. The first kind is not only universal but also general: all norms and actions are bad (evil) if they contradict the maxims of the first order. Maxims of the second kind are not general, as they cannot serve as yardsticks for testing all kinds of norms, rules and actions. However, they are still universal in so far as all norms and actions in harmony with those maxims (of the second order) are good if they do not contradict maxims of the first order.

Here I must refer back to certain ideas advanced in chapter 5. There the best possible socio-political world was said to be the condition of the good life, and righteousness the paramount constituent of the good life. Righteous is the person who suffers wrong rather than commits it. Righteous persons exist. They exist everywhere. There are righteous persons in every way of life and in every normative system. But all patterns of the good life, the condition of which is the best possible socio-political world, are, for their part, conditions of the best possible moral world. Not *all* righteous persons carry the promise of the best socio-political world, only those who make the existential choice and who subordinate all their subsequent choices to moral maxims. *Thus we have introduced a substantive qualification into the notion of righteousness.*

Maxims of the first order are (1) of a prohibitive nature or (2) of an imperative nature.

1   *Prohibitive maxims*
    i   Do not choose norms which cannot be made public.

    ii Do not choose norms the observance of which involves – in principle – the use of other people as mere means.

    iii Do not choose norms which not everyone is free to choose.

    iv Do not choose norms as *moral norms* (binding norms) the observance of which is not a goal-in-itself.

2   *Imperative maxims*

    i Give equal recognition to all persons as to free and rational beings.

    ii Recognize all human needs, except those the satisfaction of which involves the use of other persons as mere means for reasons of principle.

    iii Respect people solely according to their virtues and (moral) merits.

    iv Maintain your human dignity in all your actions.

All these maxims logically follow from the process of actualizing the two universal values, for neither 'equal life-chances for all' nor 'equal freedom for all' could be the case if *any norms* which contradict the 'first order maxims' could be chosen.

Maxims of the second order cannot be enumerated. Whenever we perform an act under the guidance of a norm for which we claim universal validity, we make this norm the maxim of our action. This definition of the moral maxim, though close to the Kantian, is not identical with it, as I reject the logical argument of 'non-contradiction'. I cannot prove *logically* the maxim character of my maxim by referring to the logical contradiction which would occur if I did not observe it. The argument of 'logical contradiction' is too narrow. If I choose as the maxim of my action 'Help everyone in need', I will that all those in need should be helped. But there is absolutely no logical contradiction involved if I do *not* act under the guidance of this maxim, but instead act under the guidance of the maxim 'Help everyone who deserves help.' In the latter case I do not make the claim that everyone should help everyone else in need: I instead claim, 'Everyone should help everyone else who deserves it', and this difference is not logical in nature. For this reason the principle is too narrow.

Indeed – and this is the Kantian aspect of my theory – no one should act under the guidance of a supreme norm if he or she cannot wish that everyone should be guided by this norm. Such supreme norms, because they are maxims, serve to verify a set (all sets) of norms. The concrete norms we choose or observe must not contradict the supreme norms (maxims) we should like everyone to be guided by. There is only one limitation to this 'intellectual intuition'. We cannot choose for our actions (and for the purpose of checking normative systems) supreme norms (maxims) which *contradict* first-order moral maxims. For example, we cannot choose 'self-sacrifice' as a universal maxim, or the celebrated 'turn the other cheek'. Clearly, in concrete moral worlds we can live according to the norm 'turn the other cheek'. If everyone chooses this norm, and if everyone is free to choose it, we have not infringed any first-order maxim; moreover, our personality, moral system, and needs should be recognized by everyone. But we cannot possibly will that everyone should observe this concrete norm, and that is why we cannot elevate it to the level of a maxim.

This is not the point at which moral philosophy ends, but that at which it begins. If only we had a (by and large) consensually accepted normative system, the whole painstaking effort of determining how to validate norms and what should provide the yardstick of such validation would be completely superfluous. We could then start at the beginning, at the 'how' of observing and infringing moral norms, at the application of such norms to action (speech act included), to the moral learning-process, to the moral character.

Choosing a norm means being committed to observing that norm. To infringe a norm we are committed to is an offence. We can commit an offence for two reasons: an amoral reason and a moral reason ('in-order-to motives', as Schütz put it). Further, we can commit an offence for a false reason, or no reason at all (because of ignorance, or because of impulses). We are *dishonest* (bad) only if we infringe norms for amoral reasons (in order to serve best our non-moral interests). Honesty (goodness) is by no means diminished if we occasionally infringe norms for moral reasons. This applies to all moral conflicts. If I act in a situation where two equally good norms apply, yet I cannot act so as to observe both. I must infringe either one or the other in order to act at all. This is one reason why the 'generalization principle' of Marcus Singer is false. In the example just given, I cannot wish that another person who chooses between the same two norms should act as I would act: this person can give priority to the norm I would not choose, but his or her choice will still be as good as mine. If we infringe a norm for false reasons, or for no reason at all, we are only dishonest if we rationalize our actions as good or persevere in infringing this norm.

The observance of any norm (but not of rules) is a constant task, in that it needs to be applied with good judgement to every concrete situation and concrete person, and the character of the person applying the norm has a bearing on the situation. Only norms and maxims can be generalized, not actions. This is the other reason why the 'generalization principle' is false. I am not entitled to say, 'I act such and I wish that everyone in this situation should act likewise', for situations are always unique and concrete. If it is possible, ethical discourse should here be used. Such discourse provides a better guideline than the 'generalization principle', because I can discuss with everyone directly concerned with my action whether to apply the norm in this way or that.

So where do we stand at this point? I have sought an answer to the question 'How is the righteous person possible today?', and the following conclusions have been reached.

Morals can be, but are not necessarily, more rational now than they used to be. Optimal rationality in morality is determined by the existential choice: we can choose ourselves as persons who choose between good and evil and who have resolved to choose the good (to suffer rather than commit wrong). We make ourselves into what we are by choosing the good (the permitted) set of norms, though we can make mistakes. We have guidelines for checking the norms: the first-order maxims which we can deduce from the universal values of life and freedom, and the second-order maxims which we can relate to the supreme values and which we discover by intellectual intuition. The chosen norms can be observed, as can all other norms. Observing chosen norms means keeping our promise. We can deliberately infringe our norms for moral reasons (because we realize that we have made a mistake or because we cannot simultaneously observe two or more equally valid and good norms). The observance of norms and their application to specific actions requires good judgement. The honest person exercises himself or herself in forming good judgements. He or she learns to problematize decisions and actions in moral terms, and enters into ethical discourse with everyone *directly* concerned with those actions and their consequences. The honest person never generalizes his or her *concrete* actions and decisions as actions and decisions, but only generalizes the *maxims* of those actions and claims general validity for the procedure of applying norms to a particular situation as a problematization of the act, good judgement, and ethical discourse with those directly concerned.

Everything hitherto said of the honest person has still left the 'image' of that person vague and abstract. Our righteous person does not yet possess much flesh and blood. We do not know much about this person other than that he or she prefers to suffer wrong than to commit it, and homogenizes, both in action and in life in general, all the heterogeneous elements we sum up in the term 'morality'. And in fact we do not really need to know more about the honest person. What has been said covers everything we need to know.

I wish to return now to the point of any given Time One. It has been assumed that in a society based on symmetric reciprocity everyone participates in the value discourse with the aim of establishing socio-political norms and rules. Even here it is still possible that some people may decide not to participate at all and simply give their tacit consent. We have also assumed that citizen's virtue forms around the new (discursive) *Sittlichkeit,* and that citizen's virtue suffices, that no other kind of virtue is needed to keep the just socio-political procedure in operation. Participation in the public debate means already having chosen a norm in accordance with all first-order maxims. Yet it is equally possible to choose a solitary life and not to establish any internalized bonds (such as community, love, friendship) with other human beings, but to engage in certain pragmatic functions to which no value is attributed. This is an extreme case, but not an impossible one. Such a person can be honest (good) by simply being a good citizen, even in the absence of all other commitments. But what of some other person who has chosen to live in a community, and to participate in associations, political, cultural, and so on, and who has made a commitment to the bonds of love and friendship and to many norms, both abstract and concrete. Such a person cannot be an honest person simply by being a good citizen. This person must observe not only all the norms to which she or he is generally committed, but also the promises that only a small group of people have given to one another, and forms of solidarity pledged only between particular members of a small group. By choosing ourselves as honest persons we make ourselves into 'such and such' honest persons, honest persons committed to 'such and such' a way of life.

All the same, the expression 'choosing ourselves as honest persons' is not an empty one. I have already mentioned that in a pluralistic moral universe sets of norms can be changed. And I added that, if all norms are good, a shift in allegiance from one set to another is really a matter of personal preference, desire and taste. If a person chooses only those norms in accordance with moral maxims, and if he or she shifts allegiance to norms which are also in accordance with maxims, and does so by establishing new human bonds as well as by breaking old ones, this person remains honest, provided that he or she does not rationalize this change of allegiance, but rather says something like 'The burden was too heavy for me', or 'My life was too empty': that is, refers exclusively to his or her needs. Those querying the honesty of such a person do not live up to the maxim 'Lend recognition to all persons and recognize all human needs.'

The reader may recall that Time One is not a point of rupture, but a process, and that we can live simultaneously before, during and after Time One. (For example, in a democratic family we live during or after Time One, whereas in the society in general in which the particular democratic family is located we live *before* Time One.) We do not have a great range of options in relation to changing one good way of life for another. We live amidst norms and rules of domination, as do all honest people. As we know, honest people only choose norms which do not contradict moral maxims, and they observe those norms consistently and continuously. However, there are other people who, for non-moral reasons, do not observe the same norms, or at least infringe them whenever non-moral reasons so dictate. And there are yet other people who observe bad and evil maxims. Wrong is always done to honest persons. To suffer wrong rather than commit it is what righteousness is all about.

I have stated several times that in a pluralistic moral universe sets of norms can be changed. The honest person can legitimately shift his or her allegiance in this way if none of the new norms contradicts moral maxims and if the person refers to his or her needs in choosing these new norms. But acts of righteousness are not only goals-in-themselves. Honest and good (righteous) persons act with a view to creating the best possible moral world. The condition of the best possible moral world is the best possible socio-political world. That is why, regardless of the set of norms they choose, honest persons today should, in addition to all the other virtues they practise, choose value discourse as the procedure of justice, and develop citizen's virtues. They must wish that norms which contradict moral maxims should not be valid for anyone. In order to be good, it is not sufficient to choose only those norms not contradiction moral maxims. Honest persons should do everything possible to eliminate norms which contradict moral maxims. That is why the choice of sets of norms is not completely adequate to needs. It is not enough to say, 'I have chosen a number of norms the observance of which results in the exclusion of domination, and these are the norms adequate to my needs, and establishing other human bonds would be alien to my needs.' Today, an honest person must respond to the 'call of duty' by entering into human bonds to which she or he may feel no particular inclination. I do not recommend a self-conscious and general repression of our needs for the sake of the good. I only suggest that sometimes we should do things we do not like doing, and that we should sometimes form human bonds we should not be likely to form in a world free of domination. It belongs to the *quality* of goodness today, for it belongs to the capacity of *good judgement*, to know exactly when duty calls. A person who has chosen to live in the 'small world' of family and friends, who never uses anyone as a mere means, who is prepared to engage in value discourse, who helps the needy and who carries out his or her duties, is good. Yet, in addition to all this, she or he must respond to the 'call of duty', if it becomes clear that some evil power of the broader world must be resisted. There are also those who have no inclination to observe the norms of elementary goodness. These people can still be good and honest in the public world, but, when duty calls them to observe the elementary norms of the human bond (and this call of duty can occur), they should observe those norms despite this disinclination. In a world of domination it is not possible to observe exclusively sets of norms which suit our own needs best. But those who have chosen the existential choice of being honest will not experience the call of duty as a mere constraint.

DEVELOPMENT OF ENDOWMENTS INTO TALENTS, OR CONSTRUCTION OF THE SELF

Norms are undoubtedly authorities, and observing norms undoubtedly entails subjecting oneself to them. To talk of the *power* of norms is to do more than use a figure of speech. The devalidation of norms, a process under continuous acceleration since the dawn of modernity, has given rise to certain typical attitudes in the face of the new human condition: the classicist, the liberal, the romantic, the tragic, the existentialist, the post-romantic, the fundamentalist, the neo-fundamentalist, the communicative–rationalist, and every combination of these types. This list is not in any strict historical order, for the simple reason that all these attitudes are continuously *recycled*. Freud recycled the tragic dimensions of Kant (in the sense that Goldmann understood the latter); Lukács, the classical–classicist; post-modernism, the post-romanticism of the *fin-de-siècle*. Foucault gave anarcho-liberalism a tragic twist, whilst Rousseau, in *The Social Contract*, had already introduced neo-fundamentalism. And so on and so forth. The story is one that cannot be told simply and succinctly, yet the directions in which answers have been sought can be roughly pointed out.

(1) Moral norms are by definition oppressive. They repress instincts and desires; they weaken the personality; they rob people of autonomy; they are agents of domination (political, economic, sexual); they enslave us, making us unhappy, miserable, ravaged by guilt. Hence the following conclusions.

i   The person is free if guided by his or her interests. There is no higher agency than the rational interest of the single person. If desires are kept in check by rational interests, the self can be constructed without being subject to an external power (authority).

ii The alternative to subjection to moral norms is *creativity*. Art, science and philosophy are the superior substitutes for these norms. The creative self constituted by creative activities is harmonious. Desires, feelings and emotions are not constrained, but merge with reason. Moral norms are irrational. Creativity leads to the coalescence of the rational and the non-rational.

iii Moral norms are repressive, as is the constitution of the self via the 'reality principle'. It is our tragic human condition to live with repression. The consciousness of repression, if freely self-imposed, is our optimal freedom. Without moral norms *and* repression there is no human life, for there is no self.

iv All things 'external' to the individual are representations of domination and power, including moral norms, objectivations of creativity, and the necessity to cope with reality. The deconstruction of the self, the 'unmaking' of the self, is equivalent to the deconstruction and unmaking of power.

v   The self, as constituted by norms, objectivations and spheres of 'reality', is inauthentic. A radical break with externality and temporality, and the choice of ourselves in the gesture of resolve *vis-à-vis* nothingness, is the choice of the authentic self.

(2) All moral norms are repressive, because socio-political norms and rules are oppressive. Hence the following conclusions.

i   It is necessary to go beyond all socio-political normation, and thus moral normation. This means to go beyond justice (in the future).

ii It is necessary to construct socio-political institutions within the framework of which *all* human instincts and desires can be 'lived and acted out'. This means to go beyond repression (in the future).

    iii   Everyone participates in *creating* social, political and moral norms – the self is constituted primarily through communicative rationality, both in the present and in the future.

    iv   A way of life is needed which is to be constituted by non-social, non-political and non-moral norms; in other words, by norms of 'beauty' or 'nature'.

    v   A way of life is to be constituted, in small communities, by *alternative* social, political and moral norms, norms which ensure the construction of the self amidst the ties of love and friendship. This is the model of the 'island'.

This outline of alternatives must necessarily be sketchy, for there are several unique and idiosyncratic combinations. My own 'combination', which I present below, is also idiosyncratic. I combine 1(ii) and (iii) with 2(iii) and (iv), without fully accepting any of them.

A brief remark first. Even though it is true that all norms, be they social, political or moral, *can*, though not necessarily do, repress desires and wants, that they are *powers* we must learn to cope with, that the construction of the personality is not a journey of pleasure but a kind of labour, and a labour which involves some suffering, *our self is our freedom. Relative autonomy is the human condition.* To ask for more than this is to end up with something less. The more we 'liberate' ourselves from all norms, the more we proceed with the unmaking of the self, the more we become unfree. The self is the only rock on which the forces of power can be broken. Indeed, any undesirable power can be internalized for the wrong reasons (or for no reason at all). But we unbutton the badly buttoned waistcoat in order to fasten it properly, not to leave it unfastened. The unmade self is by definition unfit for self-defence. Spinoza, so utterly modern a thinker, was more aware of this than anyone. He insisted that it is an illusion, and a fairly dangerous one, to believe that energies and impulses spring from the 'inside'. These things are always defined by external 'stimuli'. Any random object can be such a stimulus. Energies and impulses are *passive*. They are passions in Spinoza's own definition of the term. The person left without norms, without authorities, is indeed the slave of external stimuli, the unhappiest of creatures. If nothing is temporal, nothing is timeless. Kierkegaard referred to the life of people who 'unmake' their self as a life of *boredom* and *repetition*. The story of O is a story about the unmaking of the self. If the self is completely unmade, everyone can rape us, and we shall not even know that we have been raped (for in this state rape cannot exist). The unmade self is the raw material of totalitarianism.

One can speak out against the 'terror' of norms, *alias* the 'totalitarianism' of norms. However, if the norm which forbids us to rape children, the norm which orders us to murder children on the command of any Führer, the norm 'Love your neighbour' and the command 'Denounce your neighbour' are all equalized and homogenized via the criterion 'terroristic' or 'totalitarian', *what then* will save us from totalitarianism?

The unmade self can be raped because it does not know that it is being raped (there is no rape for it). That is why the unmade self is ready to rape: it does not know that it is committing rape; it only knows that it gets a kick out of it (because it is not subject to the 'terror' of norms).

The unmade self is not the only raw material of totalitarianism. The person who follows only 'rational' interests falls into the same category. So does the person of the 'aesthetic way of life'. So too does the person who contends that 'creativity' as such can be substituted for social and moral norms. The cult of unreason meets the cult of calculative reason midway. The common creed of the cult of unreason and the cult of calculative reason both hold that there is *no human bond* binding us all together *in the name of which you should say 'no'*. However, *if you are going to say 'no' to the human bond*, as Don Giovanni did thrice, you can say 'yes' to every power on earth.

If socio-political norms are established via just procedure, where every participant in the value debate has recourse to the supreme values of life and freedom; if everyone can once more start from the beginning upon finding a particular rule or norm to be unjust – *then* socio-political norms and rules are completely rational. And they can all be rational, not because every value has been tested, but because the ultimate ones have not been tested. Just (rational) procedure involves a 'no' in the following sense: you should *not* query and test the validity of ultimate values. In the value debate *all needs are recognized except those the satisfaction of which involves the use of other people as mere means for reasons of principle*. This is again a 'no'. One does *not* recognize such needs. Finally, one cannot establish norms and rules which would ensure (in a situation of distribution) the simultaneous satisfaction of all recognized needs. There is again a 'no' here; not a 'no' for reasons of principle, but because of circumstances: there are certain needs which simply *cannot* be satisfied at the same time or to the same degree as others. The two forms of 'no' uttered for reasons of principle are *taboos*. They are taboos of *Sittlichkeit* (moral custom), and are accepted by everyone who enters into a value debate. Even if someone does not engage in value debate, and hence gives only tacit consent, this person is still subject to the same taboos.

Norms and rules set by just procedure do not embody *social* or *political* oppression (domination); nor does just procedure itself. However, just procedure *and* the norms and rules set by it incorporate *power*. Even if such a power is legitimized by each and every person, and thus by all, even if it 'incorporates' the joint power of each and every person, it can still be *repressive* in that it imposes *obligations*. Those who legitimize a socio-political norm commit themselves to 'being just'; they commit themselves to applying the same norms and rules to everyone consistently and continuously, themselves included. Of course, we can show reluctance to observe norms consistently and continuously, even if we recognize them as fair and just. It is not theoretically impossible that certain people may desire to test and query the validity of supreme values they should unhesitatingly accept. Nor is it theoretically impossible that certain people may develop wants which cannot be satisfied except by using other persons as mere means. Moreover, since not every *recognized* need is to be satisfied at the same time, at least not in respect of every type of normative regulation, people who freely consent to satisfy the needs of others before they satisfy their own needs can still experience the observance of such (just) norms as repressive towards those personal needs. Put succinctly, norms and rules which do not embody *any* social or political repression or domination can still be repressive as *moral* powers. I believe, however, that moral repression of this type can be minimized. Our innate impulses, drives and affects are cognitively and socially codetermined and overdetermined. If socio-political norms and rules are not oppressive, if just procedure becomes a matter of *Sittlichkeit* and maturity involves practice in rational value debate, it seems quite unlikely that people need to be heavily self-repressive in observing norms which *do not determine* their concrete way of life, but provide only the broadest socio-political framework of human co-operation.

Since ways of life are different, there can exist communities (societies) in which there are set socio-political norms of a type which encompass great segments of human life. Yet people are still *free* to choose their way of life. If they experience the observance of such norms as repressive, they can relinquish one way of life and take up another. Conversely, if people desire more stringent socio-political regulation, they can relinquish those ways of life not characterized by such norms and take up a way of life with a greater normative density.

There can exist *one single* socio-political body encompassing different ways of life. The socio-political norms and rules of such a body are identical (set by all), but the *moral norms* can still differ. Some people can choose one set, others another. Everyone must observe the common socio-political norms, but persons observe only those moral norms *chosen by themselves*. There can exist different socio-political bodies having the *same* set of moral norms, and socio-political bodies with their own intrinsic moral norms. Moral norms themselves can be loosely organized or tight-knit; they may be scarce or they may be plentiful. The sole requirement is that no moral norms, loosely knit or tight-knit, scarce or plentiful, *should contradict* moral maxims, and that all actions contradicting moral maxims should be prohibited (by norms). Certain ways of life are commensurate with moral norms that possess a more prohibitive nature, or demand action and behaviour of a type the *lack of which* does not contradict moral maxims. Even so, the latter is not a requirement: people are morally entitled to choose norms the lack of which does not contradict moral maxims, if they so will and if they feel the need for such a choice. If someone cares for ways of life based on mutual support, that person will avoid or relinquish ways of life where people keep each other at a distance, and *vice versa*. If someone experiences the sexual mores of a particular way of life as oppressive, that person can choose the most lax sexual normation possible, but one which still excludes the use of other persons as mere means (sadism, rape, sexual acts with minors), and *vice versa*. Moreover, *vice versa* is not a casual or incidental qualification here. Although I have emphasized that relative autonomy, our human condition, is always accompanied by a measure of repression, I do not believe that, if we were free to choose among different sets of good moral norms whilst being guided solely by our tastes, desires, inclinations and needs, we should necessarily prefer the most lax sets of norms. Just as many people, I believe, would choose the opposite. Norms can be in perfect harmony with our needs and desires (and therefore not repressive at all). Of course, we must allow for the usual human frailty. We should like to have the rose without the thorn; *we* should like to live in a world of loosely organized norms where *others* should act towards us guided by a heavy normative structure. However, when we choose moral norms (in the model under discussion), we choose a way of life: we choose the community of people with the same norms as ours. One cannot have the rose without the thorn.

The best possible socio-political world is the condition of the good life for all. Every socio-political relationship based on symmetric reciprocity, every socio-political integration where just procedure is practised, is a *microcosm* of the best possible socio-political world. To be born into such a microcosm is a piece of good luck: the newcomer will have better conditions for the good life than others. As I have already stated, the existential choice is not 'determined', either by the social environment or by genetic endowments. Thus the best possible socio-political world, or a microcosm containing all the important features of such a world, is not the *cause* of the existential choice. The term 'good luck' refers to the optimal condition, but not the cause, of this choice. The microcosm of the best possible moral world provides the best possible social conditions for goodness, by virtue of the fact that social and political rules do not involve domination. However, even if it were not assumed that the microcosm of the best possible social and political world provides the conditions for goodness, it would still be certain that such a world provides the best possible social conditions of the good life. Goodness (honesty, righteousness) is the fundamental and overarching constituent of the good life, but is not the good life itself. *This thesis is one of the basic tenets of all moral philosophies.*

The good life entails the development of our endowments into talents. If no endowments but the moral ones are developed into talents, we shall not live a good life unless we are moral virtuosi. If an honest life is lacking in all other positive satisfactions bar that of being honest, if the honest person cannot establish relative autonomy via non-moral accomplishments, a certain element of *negativity* is inherent in being good. This person is then honest by virtue of *not* doing something, and not by doing something (not committing wrong, never committing wrong). Moral virtuosity is *full satisfaction*: the transculturally good person has not only chosen himself or herself, and thus chosen to develop his or her moral endowments into talents: these moral endowments *are*, in fact, his or her best endowments; it is in fact the best endowments that a moral virtuoso develops into talents. Moral virtuosi not only have a meaningful life; they are also happy in a positive sense, precisely because they are virtuosi. Of course, as I have mentioned several times, people can be righteous to varying degrees. Even though in the existential choice of honesty there can be no 'less' and 'more', there is still a continuum, rather than a gap, between the honest and the transculturally good person. If someone has chosen himself or herself as an honest person, this is the choice of the self as a person who suffers rather than commits wrong. Yet people can also be committed to perform good deeds to varying degres, and to develop several kinds of virtue to varying degrees of perfection, in addition to 'not committing wrong'. It is only for the sake of brevity that I juxtapose these ideal types. At any rate, the life of a good (honest) person can be the good life only under the condition that this person develops talents other than moral ones. A person can do this given that the development of certain of his or her other talents is in harmony with moral goodness. In such a person, the exercise of any talent does no wrong to any other person. But this is not yet the sufficient condition of the good life. It is possible to develop certain talents the exercise of which is very much in harmony with one's intrinsic honesty, and still be unable to develop other endowments – endowments one is, or can be, conscious of – into talents, because of experiencing the constraints of the social division of labour. In this respect, the lot of women (in all classes, ranks and strata) has been amongst both the best and the worst. It has been the best in the sense that the talents allocated to women by the social division of labour were mainly those which in practice did not require doing wrong to others. It has been the worst in the sense that the social division of labour has always restricted to a far greater degree the development by women of their endowments into talents than it has such development by men.

In our modern (functionalist) society, the constraints that the social division of labour place on the development of endowments into talents have dramatically decreased, though they have not disappeared. This has proved to be a mixed blessing. Here I shall only recap on the results of an earlier discussion. There is a dominant way of life, that exemplified in the 'triad' model. This dominant way of life puts a premium on the development of the talents needed for making money, or for manoeuvring well within rationalized institutions, irrespective of whatever further endowments people develop into talents. In exercising these talents skilfully, we do commit wrong to others, as well as infringe one of the first-order moral maxims.

The process of developing endowments into talents constitutes the 'construction of the self'. Every person is a self-made person, for every person is a self-making person. The world is 'given' to us, and in it we make our choices. All choices (similar to the existential choice) are results of a series of intentional acts. The existential choice (the decision to develop moral endowments into talents) is the choice of *my self*.[8] In all other possible choices *I construe* my self as the self-of-the-choice, but I do not choose my self. This is true even if the endowments I develop into talents heavily influence my choice (they call for development). I can make myself a writer, but *I am not* a writer in the same sense that *I am* a 'good person'. A writer can say, 'Look at me as a person, not as a writer', and this makes perfect sense. But to say, 'Look at me as a person, and not as a good person', does not make sense. There exists a *social constraint* to the effect that everyone *must* develop certain endowments into talents *in order to survive*, although just what particular endowments these should be is not a predetermined matter. There is no social constraint to the effect that we must choose ourselves (as honest persons), only the constraint that we must develop the capacity to conform to rules, and certainly some capacity to conform to norms. The self can be almost entirely constructed of panels, but constructed it must be. Goffmann described in an ingenious manner *how* the self can be constructed solely of panels, though in my view he went too far in this, for the different panels must be kept together somehow, and hence the self cannot be just an 'empty peg'. Yet, if we construe our selves as mainly consisting of 'panels', we construe the self as being the 'co-ordinator' of the panels, but never a *homogenizing* self. None the less, it would be incorrect to state that the development of non-moral endowments into talents and the construction of the self in practising such talents cannot possibly result in a *homogenized* self. The classicist, and incidentally the early romantic, schools were not completely mistaken in emphasizing that 'art' or 'science' – that is, the creative development of artistic and scientific (or, we may add, philosophical or political) talents – can indeed homogenize the self into *personality.*[9] However, there are two serious flaws in the original idea. First, it has outright *elitist* connotations. Secondly, the *homogenizing* and the *homogenized* components are reversed. In the case of the existential choice (of the honest person) the self homogenizes the heterogeneous activities; in the case of the creative personality the creative activity homogenizes the heterogeneous self. Yet this elitism and the reversal of the homogenized and homogenizing elements are but two sides of the same coin. Very few talents can be practised throughout the whole of life, and practised to such a degree as completely to *absorb* the self and thus homogenize it. People can occasionally encounter an uplifting experience by creating a thing of beauty, or be absorbed in enjoying it, without their selves being completely absorbed and thus homogenized by such an activity or such enjoyment. This is also true of science, philosophy, politics and religion.

The most representative thinkers of the 'classical' Enlightenment were very aware of the fact that the homogenization of the self via complete absorption in an objectivation or an activity not only differs from the choice of one's self (the existential choice of honesty), but can also be at odds with it (in other words, immoral or outright devilish). Instead, they wanted to argue for 'combining' the existential choice of honesty with the construction of the self via creativity. This project seems to have lost all relevance. The great spheres of objectivation (art, science, philosophy and religion) have themselves become problematic. More recently, all of them have become regarded as agencies of domination, constraint and power, and thus the homogenization of the self by them is seen as either impossible or as the process of the internalization of power. Two very different conclusions can be drawn from this: either we can make a case for the deconstruction of the self (a suggestion the dangers of which I have already pointed out), or we can return, via a detour, to a modified version of the apparently outdated classicist or early romantic tradition.

The more problematic the great spheres of homogeneous objec-tivations become, the more the homogeneous self can only be created via the existential choice. The good life becomes more improbable today than it has ever been since the dawn of modernity if one does not choose oneself as an honest person. Whether the development of endowments into talents occurs via 'making use of panels', a process in which the self is nothing more than the 'co-ordinator' of such panels, or whether the development of endow-ments into talents will have a homogenizing–homogenized core, depends on the presence or absence of the existential choice. The problematization of the great spheres of objectivation is twofold in nature: we relativize the *truth content* of these spheres and query the *certainty* they claim (in hermeneutics and other language games of relativism), and, as mentioned, we regard them as agencies of domination and power. These two tendencies can merge. In choosing ourselves as honest persons, both components of the rationality crisis can be balanced without being declared invalid. If we choose ourselves as honest persons, we obtain a yardstick of certainty *without* relapsing into 'cultural absolutes'. We can still recognize different truths as truths, different goods as goods, by checking all cultural values (and the norms related to them) by moral maxims. And, if we choose only those norms and values that do not contradict moral maxims, and develop into talents only those endowments which in practice do not involve doing wrong to others, then even our relativism will have its fixed point of reference (the good self), and our creativity in any sphere of objectivation will exclude the exercise of power and domination. It is not the spheres of objectivations that 'embody' power or domination, but the way in which people appropriate them. Discourse is not the discourse of domination if the attitude of the participants involves the resolution 'never to commit wrong'. It cannot be overemphasized that morality *is not a sphere.* All spheres have their own particular norms and rules, some of them fairly static, others changing and fluctuating. Practical reason does not provide norms and rules to these spheres, at least not in modernity. Its primacy is inherent in our *attitude* towards the spheres and within these spheres.

I have referred to the process of the development of endowments into talents as the 'construction of the self'. I have voiced my doubts concerning the contemporary relevance of the classic project of the homogenization of self by any of the great objectivations, the Weberian project of 'vocation' included. I have concluded that, owing to the increasing 'functionalization' of the exercise of talents, the self cannot be homogenized only if it homogenizes, and also that the homogenizing self is the self of the honest person. Today, even more than yesterday, only the honest person is likely to construct his or her own self by developing endowments into talents. The selves of others will in all probability be only 'organizing centres' of panels. However, that which is likely is not yet a certainty. Citizen's virtues as virtuous abilities spring from value commitments. People who choose values, and do not simply enter into functionalist rules, can still homogenize their selves to varying degrees without having made the existential choice of the honest self. On the other hand, the existential choice does not guarantee the development of our best endowments into talents. Good fortune is also needed for this to happen. What is certain is only that, if honest persons are 'lucky', they will fully construct their selves by developing their best endowments into talents.

The notion 'construction of the self' has the flavour of something 'inorganic', whereas the notion 'homogenization' has the flavour of something 'organic'. Even if talents are not identified with 'being good at work', 'being good at this or that profession', they undoubtedly stand for 'being good at something', for 'excelling in something'. It is indeed part of the good life to excel in one area, or in several areas. However, the merger of homogenization and the construction of the self creates the 'aura' we normally refer to as 'personality', and this is different from, and more than, the mere combination of the homogenizing and the constructed self. Such an aura involves certain non-rational propensities, such as a sensitivity to mystical experience, the ability of self-abandon, a sense of humour, creative energies, and so on. These non-rational propensities can also be termed 'talents', and, although they are not 'skills', they can be cultivated to the same extent as skills. When I emphasized that the development of our endowments into talents is part of good life, I also had these non-rational propensities in mind.[10]

The model of a pluralistic cultural universe in which all cultures (and persons) are tied together by the bonds of symmetric reciprocity now appears in a new light.

The best possible socio-political world provides the best chance for the good life because it offers the *optimal possibility* of developing our endowments into talents. This is so, first, because different ways of life enhance different talents, and a person is free to relinquish one way of life and take up another, depending on his or her needs. Secondly, since in this universe no way of life involves domination, and social intercourse between ways of life does not involve domination either, there cannot exist any endowment the development of which into a talent would not be permitted. Honest people can develop, and practise, any talent they have. Thirdly, every environment enhances the development of *intellectual virtues*, and, simultaneously, the intellectual element of 'observing honesty' will be less demanding, and will, in the main, be restricted to the readiness for practical discourse and good *phronesis*.

EMOTIONAL INTENSITY IN PERSONAL ATTACHMENTS

Just procedure is the pursuit of public happiness. The actualization of the supreme values as 'equal freedom for all', 'equal life chances for all', is *public happiness*. The readiness to engage in just procedure is shown by acting and arguing *as if the procedure were just. If someone acts and argues as if the procedure were just, she or he pursues public happiness*. The honest person as a *participating member* of the political sphere pursues public happiness. However, the latter is not sufficient for the good life – at least, not in general.

The existential choice (of choosing the choice between good and evil) and the resolve to suffer rather than commit wrong cannot be referred to in terms of the 'pursuit of happiness'. We can follow Aristotle, and say that only good persons can be happy, or Kant, and say that only good people are worthy of happiness, but in either case we do not refer to any 'pursuit'. The honest person too pursues happiness, but she or he does not pursue honesty. The person who does pursue honesty has not resolved to be honest ('self-righteousness', 'false repentance' and 'rationalization' are the terms we most frequently use in referring to such a pursuit). The pursuit of private happiness by the honest person consists of the effort to develop his or her endowments into talents and the pursuit of satisfying personal attachments.[11] In the main, the same goods are seen as the sources of happiness by *all persons*. The point is that the honest person defines these goods, and his or her relation to them, in a particular way. Ask a number of people what their happiness would consist of, and you will always get roughly the same answer: 'The world (society) should be fine (for me)'; 'I should be able to do what I like best, as well as excel in it'; and, finally, 'People should love me.' The pursuit of private happiness is the pursuit of the last two things.

As we are still searching for the constituents of the good life, and as it has already been presupposed that only the honest person can live a good life, in what follows I shall refer to the 'pursuit of private happiness' solely within this framework.

What I have in mind is a person of autonomous moral self who *homogenizes* all moral aspects of every social sphere or institution, and all action patterns of moral relevance (the homogenizing self). It is part of the good life of this person to develop some of his or her endowments (in addition to the moral ones) into talents and to practise these talents, constructing himself or herself as a *creative self*. It is not necessary for the good life, although it is a possibility, that the exercise of one talent homogenizes the self. The more autonomous the creative self becomes, the greater the chance of the good life. Of course, the creative self is always *only relatively autonomous*, for the mere apprehension of an endowment is guided by a social matrix of understanding. If any endowment apprehended by the guidance of the matrix of social understanding can be developed into a talent, and if no social constraint, overt or covert, codetermines the selection of endowments one does develop into talents, then relative autonomy is involved.

Private happiness is pursued in emotional ties and attachments. In entering into personal attachments one chooses one's *relative heteronomy*.

In introducing the category 'moral autonomy', I made the preliminary remark that moral autonomy is *not* the autonomy of the person. And, since I do not accept the Kantian distinction between 'person' and 'personality', I must add that moral autonomy is not tantamount to the complete autonomy of the personality. After Time One, social and political norms and rules do not entail domination. Persons are subjected to norms and rules created by themselves. Thus the *power* of norms is *moral* power (even if the norms are not moral norms, and even if they institutionalize a kind of social or political power). Moral autonomy is our determination to subject ourselves only to *moral power*. The development of endowments into talents and the exercise of these talents as the domain of private happiness is *homologous* to public happiness amidst *self-created* social norms and laws. In both cases, the emphasis is on self-creation. Endowments can best be developed into talents when a person is not under social or political constraints. The choice of the degree of emotional intensity in personal attachments – the essential aspect of the good life I shall discuss shortly – is homologous to our subjection to moral maxims. In both cases, we subject ourselves to the *human bond*. Although there is an element of heteronomy even in our moral autonomy, this heteronomy is not simply *present*, but is rather *chosen as heteronomy* in our personal attachment to our fellow humans. Dependence is not anonymous: it has a face; it is *personal*.

The personal attachments of an honest person do not contradict moral maxims. In this respect moral autonomy co-constitutes the choice of heteronomy, but a choice of heteronomy it remains.

Maslow has found a telling phrase for this in his characterization of love: he terms it *self-abandon*. That an honest person does not lose his or her self in self-abandon is a matter of course. Yet self-abandon remains the abandon of the self. I am not the source of my happiness, but the other is. My face shines not because of being illuminated by an insight, but because another face turns towards it.

An objection to this can be that personal attachments of emotional intensity are heteronomous only if (a) the relation is one of *social* subordination–superordination, and/or (b) the relation is one of *psychological* subordination–superordination. Indeed, either if (a) or (b) is the case, or both are, attachments are always heteronomous. But attachments of this kind do not make life a good life. If we think in terms of the model of symmetric reciprocity, we have already eliminated social superordination and subordination from all personal attachments. Yet psychological superordination and subordination cannot be completely eliminated from any social model. The most that can be said is that the less that psychological superordination–subordination is involved in a personal attachment, the more such an attachment makes life 'good', if all other conditions are met. However, even in the complete absence of both psychological and social superordination–subordination, we find *relative heteronomy* present in such attachments, but relative heteronomy which is *chosen*. Moreover, it is only in the absence of social and psychological constraints that relative heteronomy can be *freely chosen*. This explains the term '*relative* heteronomy'. Heteronomy is relative *because* it is freely chosen; it is relative to the extent that it is freely chosen.

Let us return to the social model of symmetric reciprocity. This model *appears* to have its counterpart in personal attachments, in *mutuality*, but appearance is all this really is. In a society based on symmetric reciprocity, everyone participates in 'legislation', and laws, norms and rules are set by consensus. In any personal *relationship* (although not in any attachment) there are norms which can be set by consensus, but emotions themselves cannot be 'set' in this way. 'Mutuality' in personal attachments cannot be sustained in the same way as symmetric reciprocity in social interactions can be. In self-abandon, everyone takes the risk that the attachment will not be mutual. Self-abandon accompanied by a 'guarantee' is not self-abandon at all. And, even if the attachment is mutual, the quality and quantity of emotional involvement can be disproportionate. There is not much of an objective nature in this type of 'proportionality' – the quality and quantity of emotional intensity cannot be 'measured'. Only if all the needs of the persons attached to each other are satisfied through this attachment are we entitled to speak of 'pure' mutuality. However, pure mutuality is essentially different from symmetric reciprocity. The former is the only relationship where the Marxian idea of distribution can serve as *the* regulative idea ('to each according to his or her needs *for the other*'), *because not distribution is involved*. 'Pure mutuality' is indeed the regulative idea of all personal attachments, and, as a regulative idea, it is usually counterfactual. The tension between the regulative idea and the factual nature of the relationship gives rise to the reactive and reflective feelings of sorrow and joy. Reflective feelings belong to the most common feelings of human experience, but they manifest themselves to a heightened degree if triggered by the 'tension' of attachments, and they are less controlled by the self in this situation than in any other, precisely because the self has been abandoned through self-abandon.

Pure mutuality is normally counterfactual in terms of temporality. But in terms of timelessness, in the eternity of the moment, it is not. It was in these moments that Plato detected the experience of absolute and complete *happiness*. The latter is the unity of heteronomy and autonomy. The two are one, while still remaining two.

There has been a constant tendency in philosophy to eliminate heteronomy from the human condition, or to degrade it. The complete curbing of emotions, even to the point of utter indifference (*apathia*), has offered itself as a solution. A further solution has been that of degrading love, and thus self-abandon, and ushering them out of the good life (one of the people for whom this was an option was Kant). However, the most frequent solution has been to make an absolute the sole, or supreme, object of love. In this situation mutuality is irrelevant, as is temporality. Self-abandonment becomes autonomous, in so far as autonomy and heteronomy *always* (by definition) coalesce. The absolute is not *a* choice: it is *the* choice *par excellence*. Here, attachment does not create a human bond, and happines does not depend on human creatures. As there is no risk involved, there exists a 'guarantee'. From these great – although to my mind misconceived – pleas for total autonomy, we have slowly descended to the level of the unmaking of the emotional self. All emotional ties are regarded as so many power relationships, and therefore traps.

For all of this, historical diagnoses are almost completely irrelevant for the problem under discussion. I have proposed that emotional intensity in personal attachments is a necessary constituent of the good life. I have also pointed to the paradox hidden behind the proposal: that the choice of emotional attachments is the choice of relative heteronomy. But the fact still remains that heteronomy is power. Even if we have in mind only those personal attachments which do not involve social power or psychological constraint, we must still say, 'If I abandon my self to any other human being, I freely choose relative unfreedom.' (If psychological constraints are strong, the choice is no longer free, and the unfreedom chosen is not a relative type of unfreedom, but for the sake of simplicity I shall disregard this possibility.)

The reader may remember that in the discussion of Habermas's fundamental principle of universalization I excluded the free choice of unfreedom from the possible results of just procedure. This is exactly why, in discourse, we should also relate our values to the universal value of freedom or the universal value of life. The free choice of unfreedom cannot be part of the pursuit of public happiness, because in this pursuit I make a choice not only for myself but also for others (happiness is *public*). Nevertheless, a free choice of relative unfreedom can still be part of the pursuit of *private* happiness where I make a choice only for myself. There are two reasons why the unfreedom I choose is relative. First, the object of self-abandon cannot be endowed with social power. Secondly, it is not permissible to resign one's *moral autonomy* in the gesture of self-abandon; in other words, my relation to the subject–object of self-abandon should not contradict moral maxims. But even relative unfreedom is unfreedom, and it has been chosen freely. And it is relevant to ask such questions as 'Why has it been chosen?' and 'Why do I expose myself to a *power* outside or above myself in addition to the power of moral maxims?'

Of course, everyone is familiar with the answer to this matter. Heteronomy created by the investment of emotions is experienced as something *intrinsically good* rather than as a curse. Even if, in moments of unhappiness and sorrow, men and women experience *one* particular emotion invested in *one* particular person as a curse, and even if, in the same moment, they accidentally generalize this experience, in the main everyone knows that a life without any emotional intensity in personal attachments cannot be good, and is not worth living. The most hackneyed phrases, so frequently used to describe the intrinsic goods of such attachments, express a truth beyond all clichés.

I have not yet mentioned the *need to be loved*. No amount of respect, no amount of recognition, is a substitute for the satisfaction of this need. I have only mentioned the *need to love*, but, of course, if people did not abandon themselves to others, no one would be loved.

I have defined morality as an internalized human bond. It would be ridiculous also to refer to love as an internalized human bond: what is 'internal' cannot be 'internalized', and it is only the *object* of love that is external. Of course, we love not only persons (God included), but also all kinds of goods (values), yet it is only the love of persons that satisfies the need for love (to love and be loved), and this is why only the love of persons establishes and re-establishes the human bond. By 'human bond' I mean the bond described by Lessing as *that which transcends social determination*. To formulate this more cautiously, the 'human bond' is the bond which *can* transcend social determination, though it does not usually do so.

In all other social ties we relate to each other as 'this kind' or 'that kind' of person, where our 'kind' is defined in particular social terms. I am a member of this culture, you are a member of that culture; I do this kind of work, you do that kind of work; I perform in this office, you perform in that office; I have this set of needs, you have that set of needs; and so on and so forth. However, those who have chosen themselves as honest persons are bound together by other ties additional to those of symmetric reciprocity. Honest persons are paragons for the 'good persons' in one or another way of life, for, under the guidance of the particular set of norms chosen by them, they prefer to suffer rather than commit wrong. At the same time, all honest persons are models for the 'good person' as such, for respect is due to goodness irrespective of whether or not one chooses as binding the same norms as does the subject–object of one's respect.[12] This respect is a tribute to the internalized human bond. Consequently, even if goodness is not transcultural in content, it is *transcultural in form*. Everyone who suffers rather than commits wrong is bound by the form of his or her action (although not by his or her form of life) to all human persons – contemporaries, predecessors and successors alike. Kant spoke of the 'invisible Church' of persons of good will. The expression is beautiful but it can be misleading. In a church the *members* of that church are bound to each other. Yet the human bond is not that which ties honest persons to each other, but that which ties *all* human persons to each other. Honest persons take upon themselves the human bond, the bond of *universal solidarity*, under the aegis of goodness. To be honest is to offer one's hand to every human being except to the evil, in brotherly and sisterly solidarity. Only the evil person, the person ex-communicated from the human race, is excluded from this solidarity. If it were otherwise, 'goodness' or 'honesty' would make no sense at all, for it would be only in relation to honest people that we should prefer to suffer rather than commit wrong. And this remains the rule even if the honest person accidentally commits wrong (owing to a mistake in judging norms or a mistake in judging situations), as he or she does not cease to be honest as long as the mistake can be set right. Setting right a mistake either by action or by asking for forgiveness is to reinforce this brotherly and sisterly solidarity with every member of the human race (again, with the exception of the evil).

In intense personal attachments one also enters into the human bond. The less the attachment involves social domination, the more one enters into this bond. One can form emotionally intense attachments with only a few people. But, even if only *one* person is the subject–object of our attachment, in forming this attachment we form the human bond. Making my happiness dependent on the happiness, well-being or mere existence of another person, makes me a full member of the human race. By being bound to one human being, I am fully bound to the human race. The bond of personal attachment is the *microcosm* of the human bond, whereas honesty is its *macrocosm*.

In our contemporary Western world, moral autonomy is the resolution to subject ourselves to moral maxims, to moral power. After any Time One the *power* of social and political norms and rules of *justice* also embodies *moral power* (or embodies moral power alone). This is our optimal freedom, and freer than this we should not be. In the same world, we freely choose our heteronomy in personal attachments. Thus we subject ourselves to the *power of love*. We can be freer than that, and one cannot say that we should not be, for not to enter into the bonds of love is not a moral transgression; but, even if we can be freer, we cannot be more humane.

Indeed, there is power everywhere, and, by definition, all forms of power restrict the self. But to rid ourselves of every form of power is equivalent to ridding ourselves of our own self. The power of the 'moral law' homogenizes the self; the power of love makes it a humane and full self. Power is crippling if it is of a dominating nature. But not even social and political power is automatically equivalent to domination.

One element of the project of the Enlightenment was indeed misconceived. This was the idea of absolute freedom, absolute autonomy, of the 'deification of man'. We cannot step beyond the human condition. Humanness is the human bond. We are in duty bound; we are in love bound. By trying to discard these bonds we can only become devils or worms. But there is another element of the project which was well conceived. This was the idea of the free and conscious construction of the human bond, of the proper distinction between the powers of domination and humane powers (and I mean humane, not human), of human solidarity. The incomplete ethico-political concept of justice, with all its connotations, moral and personal, was a product of the Enlightenment, conceived in the first volume of *La Nouvelle Héloïse* (*fuite en avant*), in Diderot's quest for a new meaning, and in Lessing's utopia of the 'humanization of power' in *The Wise Nathan*. Whether this well-conceived project will fail no one can know, but it has not yet done so. Every incomplete ethico-political concept of justice is a proof of its living presence.

BEYOND JUSTICE

Goodness is beyond justice. However, since justice always has a *moral component*, the goodness of a person involves the virtue of justice and the exercise of this virtue. The development of endowments into talents (except for the development of moral endowments) has nothing to do with justice – at least, not in my model of an incomplete ethico-political justice. The same holds true of personal attachments. This restriction, 'at least, not in my model of an incomplete ethico-political justice', is important. In pre-modern societies, both the development of endowments into talents and personal attachments were *socially regulated* and thus imputed to members of different clusters by the norms and rules of superordination and subordination. Accordingly, both these things had something to do with (formal) justice, though to a different degree. Our modern sense of justice suggests that this should not be so, and modern men and women, in the main, agree with the devalidating judgement 'The application of clusteral socio-political norms to personal attachments and to the development of endowments into talents is unjust.' Put plainly, this means that being attached to one person rather than to another, or developing one endowment rather than another, should be regarded as a completely personal and individual matter. Acts, decisions, attitudes, if not regulated by socio-political norms, are not matters of justice.

The paramount reality of modernity, depicted in the 'triad' model, is characterized by the increase in, and expansion of, social deregulation of the development of endowments into talents and of personal attachments (of emotional intensity). However, social deregulation does not bring with it the slackening of social constraints, or, if it does, the latter is not in proportion to the former. In discussing 'distributive justice' I have already pointed out that, if 'equal opportunity' were the case (as it is not), the paramount reality would still place pressure on our options as far as the development of endowments into talents is concerned. This pressure is *not normative* but *pragmatic–instrumental*. None the less, it is pressure, and heavy pressure at that. The same holds true of personal attachments, with one modification: here, social pressure, although also of a pragmatic–instrumental nature, takes on a pseudonormative character. There are 'fashionable' personal attachments and 'unfashionable' ones, and the pressure to keep pace with 'fashion' (which of course is changing all the time) is fairly powerful. Owing to this increasing deregulation, the choice, in both cases, is considered merely personal, but it is not considerably more personal than it used to be, only somewhat more so. Nevertheless, because of social deregulation, all maladjustments, mishaps, discontentment and failures ensuing from the choice of talents and attachments are imputed to *individual persons*. The ideology of our paramount reality suggests that our own life is our own making, and that consequently our disasters are also of our own making, or, alternatively, of the making of other persons. If we realize that the endowments we have developed into talents were not our best, that our emotions were or are invested in the wrong person and in the wrong way, we usually blame individual choices, either our own or those of other persons, and we vacillate between self-reproach and reproaching those others. The more we are aware of social constraints, and the more we are resolved not to comply with them, the more the development of our endowments into talents, and the choice of our personal attachments, can be genuinely personal and individual. We then have a better chance of avoiding despair, neurosis and crises of personality, and also a better chance of attaining the good life.

I have enumerated the three major facets of the good life: being an honest person, developing certain endowments into talents (the best ones were are aware of) and forming strong personal attachments. I have emphasized the individual and personal character of our choices in the realm beyond justice. This calls for further clarification.

The emphasis on the personal character of the choice does not contradict the theoretical axiom of the intersubjective constitution of the world. We can only choose between those options, values and action patterns *which in fact exist*, which are socially 'given', though it is possible to modify them by making our choices. Every single person can make the existential choice (choosing the choice between good and evil), because, since honest people do exist today, the distinction between good and evil still remains. We can only be aware of those endowments the development of which into talents is already apparent on the cognitive or practical horizon of at least one single form of life with which we are familiar.

In discussing justice, I have mentioned the 'Cartesian moment'. If we go beyond justice, the 'Cartesian moment' is not a theoretical attitude (that of general doubt), but an act of volition: it is the moment of the fundamental intentional act. There is not just one fundamental intentional act in a life; rather, there are several such acts, although the number is small. If we choose to develop a certain endowment into a talent, and later revoke this particular choice by making another choice, we have performed two fundamental acts, but, if we do this too frequently, our acts will no longer be fundamental, and the moment of the act will not be 'Cartesian'. In respect of personal attachments, it is not the choice of one or another subject–object of our attachment which is referred to as the 'Cartesian moment'. Sometimes we do not even choose in the proper meaning of the word, but are simply 'carried away'. The Cartesian moment (the fundamental intentional act) is the choice of the *character* of the personal relationships in which we invest. Such a Cartesian moment cannot be repeated too many times either. The paradigms of the intersubjective constitution of the world must not degrade the individual person to the realm of mere epiphenomena, and, if there is no Cartesian moment left, the person is indeed in the realm of mere epiphenomena.

Since honesty is the overarching element of the good life, the existential choice is the ultimate root of all Cartesian moments, of all fundamental choices. Fundamental choices are *not determined* by the existential choice (if this were so, they would not be fundamental, and the 'Cartesian moment' would be a fake). The notion 'root' involves both a limitation and a motivation. Choosing oneself as an honest person means not choosing sets of maxims in the knowledge that to act according to these sets of maxims will involve doing harm to others, just as it means not choosing to develop into talents those endowments the exercise of which will harm others for reasons of principle, and not forming social attachments of the type where the other party will be wronged for reasons of principle. Choosing ourselves as honest persons can motivate us to choose sets of norms which enjoin us to help others and to alleviate their suffering, to choose to develop into talents those endowments that are needed most by others, and which result in the greatest good, and to choose personal attachments based on generous goodness. The existential choice of every honest person delimits all fundamental choices in these ways. But not every honest person makes existential choices that motivate all the fundamental choices in the ways just described. If the existental choice of honesty motivates us simultaneously in all our fundamental choices, we are righteous to a higher degree: ours is then a supererogatory and transcultural righteousness.

The good life is beyond justice. This is a basic tenet of the incomplete ethico-political concept of justice that I have argued for in this book. My ethico-political concept of justice follows in the footsteps of *one* tendency of the Enlightenment. It reflects on the specific human condition of modernity whilst being aware of the possibilities and limits of the human condition in general. It is normatively founded upon the generalization of the 'golden rule', upon the universal maxim of dynamic justice, and upon the universal values of life and freedom. The normative foundation of the theory is the normative foundation of the best possible socio-political world, of a pluralistic cultural universe in which each culture is tied to every other culture by the bonds of symmetric reciprocity. The best possible socio-political world, where socio-political norms and rules (laws) are set by just procedure (value discourse), was said to be the *condition* of the good life of all. But the good life itself is beyond justice.

In the framework of my incomplete ethico-political concept of justice, the 'good lives' must be viewed in the plural. Different ways of life can be good, and can be equally good. Yet a lifestyle good for one person may not be good for another person. The authentic plurality of ways of life is the condition under which the life of each and every person can be good. *In the best possible socio-political world, the good life depends exclusively on the existential choice and the fundamental choices of the individual.* But, even if everyone's good life is unique, even if the good life depends on the existential choice and the fundamental choice, it is not a 'solitary enterprise', and cannot be. All three elements of the good life are rooted in '*togetherness*'. The existential choice and the choice of types of personal attachments are the choices of the *human bond*. We cannot develop our endowments into talents except through co-operation with others. Choosing ourselves means to choose the human bond and human co-operation; it is the choice of others. By choosing a form of the good life, we choose a form of togetherness. And the form of togetherness we practise lives in the concrete norms, in the customs, in the forms of intercourse of a community, a society, a group. The good life is always shared. The choice of a way of life is a choice of a human community with which we share our lives. Although the good life of each and every person is unique, it is simultaneously shared by the members of a community, a group, a society. However, in the model of the incomplete ethico-political concept of justice, all these shared ways of life are again unique: they cannot be ranked and compared. They are equally good, in so far as they can equally provide the good life for their members. And, again, something is shared by all ways of life, groups, societies and communities – namely, the readiness to participate in value discourse. That is why the goodness of every person includes the virtue of justice and the exercise of this virtue in the *public sphere*, in the pursuit of public happiness. And that the good person can also go beyond justice in the public sphere in all ways of life does not overrule the injunction that *the good person must be just*.

Owing to the abstract nature of the model of an incomplete ethico-political concept of justice, we cannot give a *general* answer to the question of the extent to which 'honesty' goes beyond justice. This depends very much on the particular way of life of the honest person. Active and generous goodness is always beyond justice. Empathy, sympathy, magnanimity, forgiveness, the readiness to help, to console, to give advice – all these are virtuous attitudes and acts beyond justice. However, as mentioned, in a best possible socio-political world a person who is 'only' a good citizen can be a good (honest) person as well. Such a person will not go beyond justice in his or her goodness. Such a person will never commit injustice, but might suffer injustice, something which can always happen even in the best possible socio-political world (though, by definition, not as a rule).

Denizens of our present world, we come to the conclusion that it is not possible to be honest without sometimes going beyond justice. A person who suffers slander in order not to betray the confidence of a friend goes beyond justice. A person who does not turn his back upon the unjustly persecuted person who seeks shelter, but risks freedom, risks life, to help this person, goes beyond justice. A person who speaks his mind and knows that doing so jeopardises job or social position goes beyond justice. A person who gives good advice in a family dispute and risks being hated by all parties concerned goes beyond justice.

One could say that, if some form of injustice is done to another, and we outweigh it by offering our hand to the victim, we do not go beyond justice, but rather restore justice. One could say that this is precisely what an honest person does, whereas a righteous person of the same ilk (up to the level of being a transculturally good person) does something above and beyond this. Those who are 'more righteous' (up to the level of being a transculturally good person) are 'supererogatory' in their goodness, precisely because active goodness involves more than 'rectifying injustice'. This statement is approximately correct. On the other hand, the honest person does more than 'rectify injustice'. This person can be guided by transclusteral moral norms (as in example 1). She or he can also resort to transclusteral moral norms and thereby devalidate existing socio-political rules. This is the case in our second example. Very often, a form of persecution may not be unjust in terms of the law of the relevant country (as with the 'legal' persecution of Jews in Nazi Germany), but is unjust from the perspective of the moral and (alternative) social norms to which the person is committed. In a way, 'rectifying injustice' (in the second example) is unjust in terms of the formal concept of justice (the maxim of justice). Sometimes the honest person can rectify injustices which occur through the incorrect application of valid social and political rules. This can be, although it is not necessarily, the case in our fourth example. Yet, if it is the case, the honest person does not go beyond justice. At all events, we cannot be honest today unless we occasionally go beyond justice.

However, 'going beyond justice' is not simply a matter of single acts or choices. The exercise of goodness becomes *character*. The characters of honest persons are different in kind, since the self which is homogenized is unique. But all honest persons have an 'aura' of their own. This aura calls for trust. It calls for trust in all facets of life regulated by the norms the honest person has chosen. The just person can also be trusted, but on a narrower basis. We know that she or he will apply the valid socio-political norms and rules properly. It is the 'aura' of the honest person, his or her character, which takes this person beyond justice.

The idea that the honest person is beyond justice had to be argued for, even though this could only be done briefly. No similar argument is necessary in order to prove that the development of our endowments into talents and the emotional intensity of our personal attachments cannot be referred to in terms of justice. Since both the development of our endowments into talents and our forming of personal attachments are already socially deregulated, at least in the modern Western world, we take these truths as self-evident. Social constraints, though still strong, are not rules. We no longer make the evaluative statement that the development of one endowment is just or more just compared with the development of another endow-ment, and we accept as a 'matter of course' that there is no justice in love.

Honesty (goodness, righteousness) is beyond justice. But 'beyond' has the connotation of 'higher', and not only of 'being different'. The development of our endowments into talents, and the character of our personal attachments, have nothing to do with justice. 'Nothing to do' has the connotation of 'being different', not that of 'higher'.

The good life has three constituents: honesty, the development of our best endowments into talents, and the strength of our personal attachments; and of these three *honesty* (goodness) is the over-arching element. Taking all three together, *the good life, as an undivided and indivisible whole, is beyond justice*.

Equal life chances for all, equal freedom for all, the regulative idea of the best possible socio-political world, can also be conceived of as a goal. Yet this goal is still a means. The goal of the best possible socio-political world is worthy of pursuit because it is the condition of the possibility of the good life for all. The only goal which is not also a means is the good life for all. *The goal of justice is beyond justice*.

And, indeed, this has always been so. Whenever people have raised their voice against particular injustices and have made a claim for justice, they have simultaneously made a claim *for a better life for some*. They have based this claim on a *moral right* (the observance of interclusteral moral norms), and have resorted to a particular interpretation of the values of freedom and life. Freedom and life carry, in any interpretation, not only the connotation 'for whom', but also the connotation 'for what'.

True enough, definitions of the 'good life' vary. Nevertheless, they all involve, though with different content and different orchestration, the three constituents of the good life enumerated above. Thus, by discussing these three constituents, I have not invented or said anything novel. The only thing I have done is to offer an answer to the question of how an honest person is possible today, and reaffirm the deregulation of the two other facets of the good life. In so doing I have simply redefined the good life as the adequate goal of a universally just procedure. The good life so defined is the goal of a just procedure: it is beyond just procedure.

The universalization of a just procedure has been posited in universal (ultimate) Time One. Time One is *here* in *any* Time One. But the universal (ultimate) Time One is still in the future. The bearer of the future is determined: it cannot be other than humankind. The locality of the future is also determined: the earth must be its centre. But the time of the future – this remains undetermined. In a practical sense, it is the infinite, an infinite which cannot be grasped in terms of 'infinite progression'. Our own culture may be doomed. We accept this possibility too in the 'bargain' we strike with life. Every particular Time One may go down with us. So may the dynamic concept of justice. So may rationality of intellect.

Granted all of this, the incomplete ethico-political concept of justice stands by the promise of the Enlightenment, which has not failed, although it can fail. There are only two alternatives to this stand: the prophecy of Doomsday, and the prophecy of Salvation, and both are frivolous. Frivolity and philosophy do not mix. Perhaps it is old-fashioned to make a case for the honest person. But at least no wrong is committed in doing so.

Notes

Chapter 1   The Formal Concept of Justice

1 Chaim Perelman, *The Idea of Justice and the Problem of Argument* (London: Routledge and Kegan Paul, 1963), pp. 16, 38, 40.
2 M. G. Singer, *Generalization in Ethics* (London: Eyre and Spottiswoode, 1963).
3 Of course, virtues can sometimes turn into vices; the slavish following of norms and rules which require the committal of crimes cannot be considered virtuous.
4 On the problem of 'asking for forgiveness' see Hannah Arendt, *The Human Condition* (Chicago, University of Chicago Press, 1958), p. 236ff.
5 Quoted in H. H. Rowley, *Prophecy and Religion in Ancient China and Israel* (London: Athlone Press, 1956), p. 64.
6 N. Rescher, *Distributive Justice* (Indianapolis: Bobbs-Merrill, 1966).
7 Perelman, *The Idea of Justice*, p. 7.
8 I prefer this formulation to Perelman's 'to each according to his works', since 'works' seems an odd description if applied to swordsmanship, playing an instrument, or running, for instance.
9 For details see Singer, *Generalization in Ethics*.
10 The Soviet judge at the trial was the 'judge' at the Bukharim show trial, a spirit akin to Roland Freisler, the presiding judge at the 'trial' of the 20 June anti-Hitler conspirators, who would have undoubtedly been hanged by the victorious Allies had he lived through the Allied victory. For documentation see R. Conquest, *The Great Terror* (London/Melbourne: Macmillan, 1968).

Chapter 2   The Ethico-Political Concept of Justice

1 According to Le Goff, *conscience* developed in the Middle Ages, in the twelfth century. Le Goff mentions the 'Christian Socratism' of Abelard, Saint-Bernard and others, which expressed and at the same time

accelerated this tendency. The *institutionalization of confession* informs us about the *sinner* and the *sin*. He mentions John of Freiburg's *Summa confessorum* and adds, 'The first section of this handbook, devoted to sins found generally in all sinners, is followed by a second section which treats the sins of the various socioprofessional categories: (1) bishops and other prelates; (2) clerics and holders of benefices; (3) curates and their vicars and confessors; (4) friars and monks; (5) judges; (6) attorneys and solicitors; (7) physicians; (8) professors and academics; (9) princes and other nobles; (10) married laymen; (11) merchants and bourgeois; (12) craftsmen and workers; (13) peasants and farmers; (14) manual labourers. The distinction between clusteral and transclusteral norms is thus accomplished.' See Jacques Le Goff, *Time, Work and Culture in the Middle Ages* (Chicago: University of Chicago Press, 1980), p. 119.

2 A. J. Heschel, *The Prophets* (New York: Harper and Row, 1969) I, 200–2.

3 Quoted from Heschel, ibid., p. 201 (emphasis added).

4 Quoted from Heschel, ibid., p. 205.

5 Quoted from Heschel, ibid., p. 215.

6 Martin Buber, *On the Bible* (New York: Schocken Books, 1968), p. 192.

7 Ibid., p. 195.

8 *Alfarabi's Philosophy of Plato and Aristotle*, tr. with an intro. by Aluhsin Mahdi (Ithaca, NY: Cornell University Press, 1969), VIII.31 (p. 65).

9 Plato, *Gorgias*, tr. Terence Irwin (London: Oxford University Press, 1979), 526d.

10 See the discussion of Greek historical consciousness in my *A Theory of History* (London: Routledge and Kegan Paul, 1982).

11 Plato, *Gorgias*, 483a–484b.

12 Plato, *The Republic*, tr. by Benjamin Jowett, ed. Scott Buchanan (Harmondsworth, Middx: Penguin, 1977), 343b–344c.

13 Ibid., 354c.

14 Ibid., 357a.

15 Ibid., 369a.

16 Ibid., 434c.

17 Ibid., 443d.

18 Ibid., 611b.

19 Ibid., 538c–e.

20 See Alasdair MacIntyre, *After Virtue* (Notre Dame, Ind.: University of Notre Dame Press, 1981).

21 G. W. F. Hegel, *Phenomenology of Spirit* (London: Oxford University Press, 1977), ★390.

22 For an elaboration of this, see the title essay in my study of rationality, *The Power of Shame: a rational perspective* (London: Routledge and Kegan Paul, 1985).

23 Thomas Hobbes, *Leviathan*, ed. C. B. Macpherson (Harmondsworth, Middx, 1968), pp. 202–7.

24 Ibid., p. 212.

25 Jean-Jacques Rousseau, 'The general society of the human race', in *The Social Contract and Discourses*, tr. G. D. H. Cole (London: Dent, 1973), p. 160.

26 Ibid., pp. 159–60.

27 P. F. Strawson, *Freedom and Resentment* (London: Methuen, 1974).

28 Rousseau, *The Social Contract*, ibid., p. 193.

29 G. W. F. Hegel, *The Philosophy of Right*, tr. T. M. Knox (Oxford: Clarendon Press, 1952), ★129.

30 Ibid., Preface, p. 10.

31 G. W. F. Hegel, *Grundlinien der Philosophie des Rechts*, ★277, in *Werke* (Frankfurt: Suhrkamp, 1978), VII.

32 Hegel, *Philosophy of Right*, ★150.

33 F. Hutcheson, 'An inquiry concerning moral good and evil', in *British Moralists*, ed. L. A. Selby-Bigge (Indianapolis: Bobbs-Merrill, 1964), p. 153. This point was later strongly emphasized by Hegel. However, I suspect that Hegel never read Hutcheson. In his lectures on the history of philosophy, Hegel mentions Hutcheson's name in passing, amongst 'further Scot philosophers'. At any rate, Hegel had a very low opinion of British philosophy after Locke; he treated it as 'mere philosophizing'. Because of this dismissal, his philosophy has been unduly neglected in Britain up to the present day.

34 Ibid., p. 107.

35 Ibid., p. 121.

36 Ibid., p. 122.

37 Ibid., p. 148.

38 I. Kant, *Critique of Practical Reason*, in *Critique of Practical Reason and Other Writings in Moral Philosophy*, tr. and ed. Lewis White Beck (Chicago: University of Chicago Press, 1949), pp. 184–5.

39 After Hutcheson, utilitarianism became more conclusive and more refined, but also more problematic. Since the moral (or rather, immoral) consequences of the utilitarian persuasion have been discussed recently by celebrated authors with whom on this point I am in full agreement – for example, Rawls in his *Theory of Justice* (London: Oxford University Press, 1972) – I feel free to dismiss the issue. By contrast, Kantianism has become less sophisticated and less refined since Kant.

40 Kant, *Critique of Practical Reason*, p. 156.

41 I. Kant, *The Doctrine of Virtue* (pt II of *The Metaphysic of Morals*), tr. Mary J. Gregor (Philadelphia: University of Pennsylvania Press, 1964), p. 92ff.

42 Kant, *Critique of Practical Reason*, p. 228 (emphasis added).

43 Ibid., p. 229 (emphasis added).

44 'We have good reason to say, however, that "the Kingdom of God is come unto us" once the principle of the gradual transition of ecclesiastical faith to the universal religion of reason, and so to a

(divine) ethical state on earth, has become general and has also gained somewhere a *public* foothold, even though the actual establishment of this state is still infinitely removed from us' – I. Kant, *Religion within the Limits of Reason Alone*, tr. Theodore M. Greene and Hoyt H. Hudson (New York: Harper, 1960).

45 Ibid., pp. 42–3.

46 In the description of the righteous person Kant follows ancient Greek philosophy. The more that someone acts only by maxims which qualify for the categorical imperative, the more moral his intentions (*Gesinnung*) become. If this person eliminates his conceit at the outset, the attainment of righteousness becomes easier and easier, will cause less and less pain. Finally, the righteous man cannot act except under the guidance of maxims which qualify for the categorical imperative. One may say that in every individual case when someone becomes righteous, an anthropological (moral) revolution has taken place. But even the best of men with the best possible intentions can err in choosing a maxim, or can choose it hastily. In less maximalist ethics, such as the Aristotelian, the occasional moral blunder does not alter the goodness of a man. This was not acceptable to Kant, at least after the 'moral revolution' had taken place. The blunder, then, is always due to the senses, never to the maxim.

47 I have analysed this problem in detail in the following essays: 'Marx and the liberation of humankind', *Philosophy and Social Criticism*, 9.3–4 (1982); 'The legacy of Marxian ethics today', *Praxis International*, 1. 4 (1982); and 'Marx, freedom, justice: the libertarian prophet', *Philosophica*, 33.1 (1984).

48 In my paper 'Marx and the liberation of humankind' I have sought to show the way in which this concept, as it is elaborated by Marx in *The Critique of the Gotha Programme*, is self-contradictory.

49 D. Diderot, *Refutation suivie de l'ouvrage d'Helvétius intitulée L'Homme*, in *Oeuvres philosophiques* (Paris: Editions Garnier Frères, 1964), pp. 594–6.

50 On Lessing see my 'Enlightenment versus fundamentalism: the example of Lessing', *New German Critique*, 23 (Spring–Summer 1981).

51 D. Diderot, *Rameau's Nephew*, in *Rameau's Nephew and D'Alembert's Dream*, tr. Leonard Tancock (Harmondsworth, Middx: Penguin, 1966), p. 112.

52 Ibid., p. 93.

53 Ibid., p. 122.

54 Ibid., p. 125.

55 Ibid., p. 39.

Chapter 3   The Concept of Dynamic Justice

1 For examples of the deduction of 'ought' sentences from 'is' sentences of this kind, see Kurt Baier, *The Moral Point of View* (Ithaca, NY: Cornell University Press, 1958); and MacIntyre, *After Virtue*.

2 This is by no means always the case when the judgement 'These norms and rules are unjust' took place in the past, and when the rejected norms no longer exist in the present in any form. *We*, in the present, can agree that the statement 'Those norms and rules *were* unjust' is true. No one will doubt *now* that slavery is unjust and that the very fact of the existence of slavery calls for its abolition. When *The Women of Troy* and *Uncle Tom's Cabin* were written, the rule of keeping humans as slaves and the norms and rules concerning the treatment of slaves were believed to be just by, in the first case, almost everyone, and, in the second case, by many. Thus the 'ought' sentence 'Slavery should be abolished because it is unjust' would not have been accepted to any degree, let alone consensually.

3 See Baier, *The Moral Point of View*.

4 Not *any* given devaluation of *any* group of norms and rules can be, or indeed is, formulated in the form of the evaluative statement 'These norms and rules are unjust.' We can reject norms and rules on the grounds of value criteria and insist that they are bad, inhumane, and so on, without stating simultaneously that they are 'unjust'. If, for example, premarital chastity is the norm for both sexes in a culture, one can denounce this norm as 'inhumane' but not as 'unjust'. One can reject rules (though not norms) on a purely pragmatic ground as 'bad' by having recourse to pragmatic criteria (such as efficiency) where the negative evaluation 'bad' is not tantamount to 'unjust'.

5 If a person does not advocate substituting for the existing norms and rules alternative norms and rules that are considered just, he or she can reject the existing norms and rules as bad, inhumane, irrational and the like, but cannot reject them as unjust. If someone believes that an anthropological revolution of a certain kind will dispense with all external normative authorities (as, we have seen, Kant and Marx did), or if someone asserts that every individual is capable of making a rational choice in every circumstance without recourse to any norm and rule (without positing an anthropological revolution), the judgement 'This or that norm or rule is unjust' cannot make sense, because all norms and rules should be considered as unjust (or none of them should be).

6 See the title essay in my book *The Power of Shame*.

7 For the elaboration of this problem, see F. Fehér and A. Heller, 'Forms of equality', in E. Kamenka and A. E. Tay (eds), *Justice* (London: Edward Arnold, 1979).

8 On the problem of 'equal possibility' *alias* 'equality in life chances', see the discussion of distributive justice in chapter 4 below.

9 See my essay 'Everyday life, rationality of reason, rationality of intellect', ibid.

10 They can only be settled if the interpretation of freedom or life does not include the interpretation of the other value, relegating it to a subordinate position. The discourse concerning the freedom of everyone to choose his or her vocation and the freedom of parents to decide the

vocation of their children can obviously be settled here and now (life chances are equal: every child is, in principle, going to become a parent, and every parent was a child). Discussions such as those above are normally conducted in the case of a 'cultural gap', and are guided by particular principles. However, if the interpretation of one value includes the other, while relegating it to a subordinate position (decreasing equality in life chances or in freedom), the final conflict takes place between freedom and life.

11 I discuss the sphere of objectivations-for-itself in *The Power of Shame*.

12 Roberto Mangabeira Unger, *Law in Modern Society* (New York: Free Press, 1976), p. 107.

13 In *The Power of Shame* I termed this set of primary norms and rules the 'sphere of objectivation-in-itself'.

14 The legal category *mens rea*, central to Hart's arguments, only makes sense because this is in fact so.

15 See in detail my study 'Rationality and democracy' in *The Power of Shame*.

16 A. Heller, *A Theory of Feelings* (Assen: Van Gorcum, 1977).

17 See the title essay in Heller, *The Power of Shame*.

18 It is easy to illustrate this fairly abstract proposal in relation to any set of norms and rules. For example, let us compare the following set of norms and rules: men and women can only live together in a marriage settled by their parents; men and women can only live together in marriage after choosing their partners freely; men and women can live together regardless of whether they are married or not. Or let us compare the following set of norms and rules: working people are the property of their masters; working people are the property of no one, but they cannot choose either their type of place of work; working people can choose their workplace but not the type of work they perform; working people can choose both, but must work in the service of an authority; working people can choose both and can also choose not to work in the service of an authority. Now, a woman who rejects the norm of the arranged marriage as wrong *is not morally obliged not* to marry the man chosen by her parents; the slave who rejects slavery as unjust is *not morally bound* to incite rebellion or to escape.

19 The distinction between civil disobedience and conscientious objection, discussed at length both by Arendt and Rawls, can stand here for any other examples. Civil disobedience is a social–political conflict; conscientious objection is the result of a moral conflict. In the first case, people devalidate certain norms and rules; in the second, one must decide whether it is right to fight even in a 'just war' or whether fully to observe the interclusteral commandment 'Thou should not murder.'

20 Social needs can, of course, be the motivating forces in conflicts other than socio-political.

21 And this is an important question, because, whenever the idea of justice is not among the motivating forces (in our judgement), we can be sure that the norms and rules defended are no longer legitimized, or that the

alternative norms and rules suggested by the contesting actor(s) are unjust. But this can be the case even when the word 'justice' is on every lip. In this event we are facing deception or 'false consciousness'.

22 Most riots belong to this category. However, riots, in contrast to rebellions, end in a search for *scapegoats*, not in a search for those responsible for the committed injustices. This is why the latter often incite riots: they do so to prevent rebellions or to defuse tensions.

23 How procedural justice is modified in the case of war between sovereign states is a matter I shall discuss in the final section of chapter 4.

24 It is quite traditional to settle certain intraclusteral conflicts by violence. In a situation of equality, both parties have the right to use force, and an equal right. Sometimes the use of force is also acknowledged as just, and equally just, by both parties to an interclusteral conflict.

25 We can agree with the French pig-farmers that EEC regulations do them injustice, and at the same time strongly disagree with their violent actions.

26 Norms and rules of Western democratic societies are sometimes rejected on the grounds that they harbour too much freedom. Social movements can, and do, carry the claim that personal freedoms should be decreased for all; that alternative (stricter) norms should be introduced and enforced by severe legislation; that amorality and decadence, which follows from too much freedom, are the hotbed of injustice.

27 If it is a binding custom that women *should* say 'no' when they mean 'yes', women can still refuse to follow this norm, because it is also a norm that under no circumstances should one lie; some other women may reject this norm as unjust, as being superimposed on them by the male world. In the first case we have a moral, in the second case a social, conflict.

Chapter 4 *The Socio-Political Concept of Justice*

1 Walter Kaufmann, *Without Guilt and Justice* (New York: Peter H. Wyden, 1973), pp. 56 and 67.

2 Karl Menninger, *The Crime of Punishment* (New York: Viking, 1968).

3 Anthony Flew, 'Justice: real or social', *Social Philosophy and Policy*, 1.1 (1983), p. 163.

4 Indeed, the notion 'modern concept' stands here for 'enlightened concept'. Revenge as a form of retribution is still widespread in certain non-Western cultures, and even in some Western sub-cultures. Collective retribution is the rule rather than the exception in totalitarian societies.

5 As I am not going to discuss legal theory, I mention only in passing that it is just as possible for private litigation to aim at retribution as it is for it to not involve retribution at all. For example, compensation paid for defamation of character is retributive.

6 John Austin, *The Province of Jurisprudence Determined* (New York: Humanities Press, 1965), p. 15.

7 John Locke, 'Second treatise', II.ii.8, 12, 13, in *Two Treatises of Government*, ed. with an intro. by Peter Laslett (New York: Mentor, 1965).

8 Cesare Beccaria: *On Crimes and Punishments* (Indianapolis: Bobbs-Merrill, 1963), pp. 42, 43.

9 In his brilliant book *Discipline and Punish* (Harmondsworth, Middx: Penguin, 1977), Michel Foucault has reconstructed this story.

10 Beccaria, *On Crimes and Punishments*, p. 90.

11 Ibid., p. 11.

12 I. Kant, *The Metaphysical Elements of Justice* (pt I of *The Metaphysic of Morals*) tr. John Ladd (Indianapolis: Bobbs-Merrill, 1965), p. 105.

13 Ibid., p. 103.

14 Kant also makes an exception of infanticide committed by fallen women, a crime which, he argues, should be punishable, though not by the death penalty. See ibid., p. 106.

15 Hegel, *Grundlinien der Philosophie des Rechts*, ★97, in *Werke*, VII.

16 Ibid., ★79.

17 Hegel, *Philosophy of Right*, ★100.

18 R. J. Bonner and G. Smith, *The Administration of Justice from Homer to Aristotle* (New York: Greenwood Press, 1968), II, 275.

19 Eichmann was in fact a law-abiding citizen in Argentina; and one now observes that these arguments are rampant concerning the only surviving Nuremberg defendant in prison, Rudolf Hess.

20 Hart asserts that to inflict less pain upon a person of no 'wicked mind' is based on utilitarian considerations, I believe, however, that this is precisely the outcome of just retribution. The person who unwittingly or carelessly causes harm suffers from shame and pangs of conscience. This is an additional pain not felt by the person of 'wicked mind'. The amount of pain inflicted by the sentence must be less, if a large degree of pain is self-inflicted. See H. L. A. Hart, *Punishment and Responsibility* (London: Oxford University Press, 1968).

21 This is the principle of consequences as suggested by Marcus Singer in his *Generalization in Ethics*.

22 Aritotle, *The Politics*, tr. T. A. Sinclair (Harmondsworth, Middx: Penguin, 1977), p. 75 (1267a14.).

23 One of the few exceptions is the area of anti-discrimination law.

24 See R. Dworkin, *Taking Rights Seriously* (London: Duckworth, 1977); and R. Dworkin (ed.), *The Philosophy of Law* (London: Oxford University Press, 1977).

25 See H. L. A. Hart, 'Separation of law and morals', in Dworkin, *The Philosophy of Law*, p. 31.

26 Istvan Bibo, 'A Zsidokerdes Magyarorszagon' ('The Jewish question in Hungary'), in *A Harmadik Ut* (The Third Way), Geneva: Magyar Konyves Ceh, 1973.

27 Hannah Arendt has pointed out that Nazi law was only the formalized expression of the Führer's will.

28 D. Hume, 'An enquiry concerning the principles of morals', II.i, in

Enquiries, ed. L. A. Selby-Bigge (London: Oxford University Press, 1966), p. 187.

29 Ibid., III.ii (pp. 193–4).

30 Ibid., III.ii (p. 194).

31 The most important contemporary contributions here are Rawls, *A Theory of Justice*; Nozick, *Anarchy, State and Utopia* (Oxford: Basil Blackwell, 1974); B. A. Ackerman, *Social Justice in the Liberal State* (New Haven, Conn.: Yale University Press, 1980); Dworkin, *Taking Rights Seriously*, and 'What is equality?', *Philosophy and Public Affairs*, Summer–Fall 1981. See also J. Narvenson 'On Dworkinian equality'; R. Dworkin, 'In defence of equality'; J. Narvenson, 'Reply to Dworkin'; C. Fried, 'Distributive justice'; and E. Mack, 'Distributive justice and the tension of Lockeanism': all in *Social Philosophy and Policy*, 1.1 (1983).

32 See the analysis of the Soviet societies as instances of the 'dictatorship over needs' in F. Fehér, A. Heller and G. Markus, *Dictatorship over Needs* (Oxford: Basil Blackwell, 1983).

33 See the analysis of 'dynamic justice' in the opening section of chapter 3, above.

34 See in detail my essay 'Can true and false needs be posited?', in *The Power of Shame*.

35 The democratic family is to the authoritarian family as a society based on equality in freedom and life chances is to a society of domination. In a democratic family the needs of all members are equally recognized, for the personality of every member is equally recognized. The need to develop endowments into talents always has first priority, and it has this independently of 'deserts'. The traditional custom of authoritarian families, that the bread-winner – the husband and father – has a greater claim to need satisfaction (the largest share of the food, the best clothing, etc.) than the other family-members, is gone. Nevertheless, the child who wants to study will have sacrifices made on his or her behalf – will get the 'biggest' initial share – and the wife or husband will experience the same thing in a similar situation. Thus *equality* in investing in the development of endowments, equality in satisfying all other needs (housing, clothing, food, etc.) and 'participatory' democracy when it comes to the use of the common financial pool (the sum total of all earnings) are the conspicuous 'distributive' features of a democratic family. Every democratic family is a kibbutz.

36 M. Rosner, 'Theories of participatory democracy and the kibbutz' (unpublished manuscript), p. 17.

37 Ackermann, *Social Justice in the Liberal State*, p. 202.

38 In the present state of general social insecurity in almost all places, an inheritance may even save the *lives* of our children or friends.

39 The same holds true about patterns of redistribution among different units of an identical way of life. Rosner, in 'Theories of participatory democracy and the kibbutz', describes how the kibbutz federation redistributes by means of participatory representative democracy.

40 This occurred during the Crusades, when all restrictions normally applying to conduct in war were waived.

41 J. Turner Johnson, *Just War Tradition and Restraint of War* (Princeton, NJ: Princeton University Press, 1981), p. 23; and M. Walzer, *Just and Unjust Wars* (New York: Basic Books, 1977).

42 For the best description of the Hegelian theory of war see S. Avineri, *Hegel's Theory of the Modern State* (Cambridge: Cambridge University Press, 1972). For the most comprehensive and profound recent analysis of Clausewitz see R. Aron, *Clausewitz: the philosopher of war* (London: Routledge and Kegan Paul, 1982).

43 Machiavelli had already discussed this principle in *The Art of War*. An analysis can be found in J. G. A. Pocock, *The Machiavellian Moment* (Princeton, NJ: Princeton University Press, 1975), esp. ch. 7.

44 Walzer's book is exemplary precisely because of the profound seriousness and conscientiousness of the author in passing judgement on contemporary wars without allowing his own sympathies for certain substantive criteria to 'bend' the principles of justice and injustice in war or to relegate them to the background.

45 I. Kant, 'Perpetual peace', in *On History*, tr. and ed. Lewis White Beck (Indianapolis: Bobbs-Merrill, 1963), p. 83. Translation slightly modified.

46 As Walzer has pointed out, far too much is left to 'free interpretation'. Siege or blockade is not considered a matter of unjust conduct of war, at least not as a general–formal principle, although siege and blockade always subject non-combatants to suffering and expose them to the threat of death.

47 Nuclear war, in my view, would significantly alter the just-war theory. For an elaboration of this see Ferenc Fehér and Agnes Heller, *Doomsday or Deterrence?* (New York: Sharpe, 1986).

Chapter 5   Towards an Incomplete Ethico-Political Concept of Justice

1 They may reflect upon it. Richardson's heroine Clarissa explicitly formulates the categorical imperative, and lives up to it.

2 I discuss this in 'The great republic', *Praxis International*, 5.1 (1985).

3 J. Habermas, 'Diskursethik – Notizen zu einem Begründungs-programm', *Moralbewusstsein und kommunikatives Handeln* (Frankfurt: Suhrkamp, 1983), pp. 75–6.

4 Ibid., p. 76.

5 Ibid., p. 103.

6 Ibid., p. 76.

7 K.-O. Apel, 'The *a priori* of the communication community and the foundations of ethics: the problem of a rational foundation of ethics in the scientific age', in *Towards a Transformation of Philosophy*, tr. Glyn Adey and David Frisby (London: Routledge and Kegan Paul, 1980).

8 Saint-Exupéry described a similar 'consensus' in a desert community in North Africa. Whether or not his observation is completely accurate, I must conclude that the possibility of a similar consensus cannot be excluded.

9 I have elaborated this problem in full, in conjunction with an analysis of value discourse, in my book *A Radical Philosophy* (Oxford: Basil Blackwell, 1984).

10 On legislative conscience see the title essay of my book *The Power of Shame*.

11 A. Heller, 'Everyday life, rationality of reason, rationality of intellect', in *The Power of Shame*.

12 See my study *A Radical Philosophy*.

13 This combination can be found, of course, in Robert Owen.

14 This question has been analyzed in some detail in F. Fehér and A. Heller, 'The West and the Left' (unpublished manuscript).

15 M. Walzer, *Spheres of Justice* (Oxford: Martin Robertson, 1983), p. 279.

Chapter 6   The Good Life

1 In *A Theory of History* I spoke of the *confusion* of historical consciousness. I insisted that a new kind of constructive consciousness, which I termed the 'consciousness of reflected generality', has already emerged from this confusion. Obviously, I did not have in mind a merely *chronological* progression. The wholesale post-modernist rejection of the Enlightenment project gained momentum in the second half of the 1960s, and not without antecedent influences. The philosophies of Apel, Habermas, Wellmer and others, although conceived earlier, have been further developed and have acquired new dimensions. The elderly Sartre also committed himself to this alternative project in making a case for a new ethics of solidarity. Castoriadis, far from being ultra-rationalist, like some of his German counterparts, stands in all of his writings for the *construction*, as against the 'unmaking', of the self. The liberal tradition continues to flourish. As Rorty writes in *Consequences of Pragmatism* (Brighton, Sussex: Harvester Press, 1982), p. 158, supporting the preference for the 'sense of our human lot' 'would involve a full-scale discussion of the possibility of combining private fulfilment, self-realisation, with public morality, a concern for justice'. I shall not mention here various fundamentalist projects with which I have no sympathy.

2 My next project is a study to be entitled *A Theory of Morals* (in the series already comprising *A Theory of Feelings* and *A Theory of History*).

3 Weber never supported the idea of a specific 'moral sphere'. Rather, he insisted that the political sphere must have its own morals, different from the morality of private life (and religion). Our *tragic* choice

between spheres is also a choice between morals, but not a choice between a 'moral sphere' and other, non-moral ones. Luhmann, in his work on the sociology of ethics, contends that morals resist complete sphere differentiation. See his *Soziologie der Moral* (Frankfurt: Suhrkamp, 1979).

4 I analysed the characteristics of this sphere in 'Everyday life, rationality of reason, rationality of intellect', in *The Power of Shame*.

5 The courage of a stuntman, for instance, is not a virtue but 'excellence'.

6 See Ernst Tugendhat, 'Kann man aus der Erfahrung moralisch lernen?', *Probleme der Ethik* (Stuttgart: Reclam, 1984).

7 In exceptional circumstances a person could choose the choice between good and evil *and* choose the evil thereby. This is the case of 'radical evil' — the Richard III syndrome.

8 This is why philosophers have insisted that the result of this resolution cannot be 'expropriated', cannot be lost. Unfortunately, this is less true in modern times than it used to be. We can make mistakes in choosing our set of norms, and, if such a mistake cannot be rectified, we may even lose our selves.

9 Max Weber was still under the spell of this school, although he gave the idea of a tragic twist. In his view, we can homogenize our personality *either* by science *or* by politics *or* by art *or* by religion, but choose we must, the classic ideal of the many-sided personality being an illusion.

10 I have analysed these propensities in detail in 'Everyday life, rationality of reason, rationality of intellect', *The Power of Shame*.

11 Indeed, the distinction must not be sharp. Some of our propensities, including non-rational ones, are developed precisely through personal attachments.

12 This happens whenever we pay our respects to honest persons of bygone days. Their norms are not ours, or their supreme norms are not supreme for us, but this does not prevent us from paying tribute to their goodness.

Bibliography

Ackerman, Bruce, *Social Justice in the Liberal State*, New Haven, Conn.: Yale University Press, 1980.

Alfarabi, *Alfarabi's Philosophy of Plato and Aristotle*, tr. with intro. by Aluhsin Mahdi. Ithaca, NY: Cornell University Press, 1969.

Apel, Karl-Otto, 'the *a priori* of the communication community and the foundation of ethics; the problem of a rational foundation of ethics in the scientific age', in *Towards a Transformation of Philosophy*, tr. Glyn Adey and David Frisby. London: Routledge and Kegan Paul, 1980.

Arendt, Hannah, *The Human Condition*. Chicago: University of Chicago Press, 1958.

——, *Eichmann in Jerusalem: a report on the banality of evil*. Harmondsworth, Middx: Penguin, 1977.

Aristotle, *The Politics*, tr. T. A. Sinclair. Harmondsworth, Middx: Penguin, 1977.

Aron, Raymond, *Clausewitz: the philosopher of war*. London: Routledge and Kegan Paul, 1982.

Austin, John, *The Province of Jurisprudence Determined*. New York: Humanities Press, 1965.

Avineri, Shlomo, *Hegel's Theory of the Modern State*. Cambridge: Cambridge University Press, 1972.

Baier, Kurt, *The Moral Point of View*. Ithaca, NY: Cornell University Press, 1958.

Beccaria, Cesare, *On Crimes and Punishments*. Indianapolis: Bobbs-Merrill, 1963.

Bibo, Istvan, 'A Zsidokerdes Magyarorszagon', in *A Harmadik Ut* (*The Third Road*). Geneva: Magyar Konyves Ceh, 1977.

Bonner, R. J. and Smith, G., *The Administration of Justice from Homer to Aristotle*. New York: Greenwood Press, 1968.

Buber, Martin, *On the Bible*. New York: Schocken Books, 1968.

Conquest, Robert, *The Great Terror*. New York: 1956.

Diderot, Denis, *Réfutation suivie de l'ouvrage d'Helvétius intitulée L'Homme*, in *Oeuvres Philosophiques*. Paris: Éditions Garnier Frères, 1964.

——, *Rameau's Nephew and D'Alembert's Dream*, tr. Leonard Tancock. Harmondsworth, Middx: Penguin, 1966.

Dworkin, Ronald, *Taking Rights Seriously*. London: Duckworth, 1977.

—— (ed.), *The Philosophy of Law*. London: Oxford University Press, 1977.

——, 'In defence of equality'. *Social Philosophy and Policy*, 1.1 (1983).

Fehér, Ferenc and Heller, Agnes, 'Forms of equality', in E. Kamenka and A. E. Tay (eds), *Justice*. London: Edward Arnold, 1979.

——, 'The West the and Left' (unpublished manuscript).

——, *Doomsday or Deterrence?* New York: Sharpe, 1986.

——, 'Equality reconsidered'. *Thesis Eleven*, no. 3 (1981).

Fehér, Ferenc with Heller, Agnes and Markus, György, *Dictatorship over Needs*. Oxford: Basil Blackwell, 1983.

Flew, Anthony, 'Justice: real or social'. *Social Philosophy and Policy*, 1.1 (1983).

Foucault, Michel, *Discipline and Punish*. Harmondsworth, Middx: Penguin, 1977.

Fried, C., 'Distributive justice'. *Social Philosophy and Policy*, 1.1 (1983).

Habermas, Jürgen, *Theorie des kommunikativen Handelns*. Frankfurt: Suhrkamp, 1981.

——, *Moralbewusstsein und kommunikatives Handeln*. Frankfurt: Suhrkamp, 1983.

Hart, H. L. A., *Punishment and Responsibility*. London: Oxford University Press, 1968.

——, 'Separation of law and morals', in Dworkin (ed.), *The Philosophy of Law*.

Hegel, G. W. F., *Grundlinien der Philosophie des Rechts*, *Werke*, VII. Frankfurt: Suhrkamp, 1970.

——, *Philosophy of Right*, tr. T. M. Knox. Oxford: Clarendon Press, 1952.

——, *Phenomenology of Spirit*, tr. A. V. Miller. London: Oxford University Press, 1977.

Heller, Agnes, *A Theory of Feelings*. Assen: Van Gorcum, 1979.

——, *Renaissance Man*. London: Routledge and Kegan Paul, 1978.

——, *A Theory of History*. London: Routledge and Kegan Paul, 1982.

——, *Aristóteles y el Mundo Antiguo*. Barcelona: Ediciones Península, 1983.

——, *A Radical Philosophy*. Oxford: Basil Blackwell, 1984.

——, *The Power of Shame: a rational perspective*. London: Routledge and Kegan Paul, 1985.

——, 'Enlightenment versus fundamentalism: the example of Lessing'. *New German Critique*, no. 23 (Spring–Summer 1981).

——, 'Marx and the liberation of humankind'. *Philosophy and Social Criticism*, 9.3–4 (1982).

——, 'The legacy of Marxian ethics today'. *Praxis International*, 1.4 (1982).

——, 'Marx, freedom, justice: the libertarian prophet'. *Philosophica*, 33.1 (1984).

——, 'The great republic'. *Praxis International*, 5.1 (1985).

Heschel, A. J., *The Prophets*, 2 vols. New York: Harper and Row, 1969.

Hobbes, Thomas, *Leviathan*, ed. C. B. Macpherson. Harmondsworth, Middx: Penguin, 1968.

Hume, David, 'An enquiry concerning the principles of morals', in *Enquiries*, ed. L. A. Selby-Bigge. London: Oxford University Press, 1966.

Hutcheson, Francis, 'An inquiry concerning moral good and evil', in *British Moralists*, ed. L. A. Selby-Bigge. Indianapolis: Bobbs-Merrill, 1964.

Johnson, J. Turner, *Just War Tradition and Restraint of War*. Princeton, NJ: Princeton University Press, 1981.

Kant, I., *Critique of Practical Reason and Other Writings in Moral Philosophy*, tr. and ed. Lewis White Beck. Chicago: University of Chicago Press, 1949.

——, *The Metaphysical Elements of Justice* (pt I of *The Metaphysic of Morals*), tr. John Ladd. Indianapolis: Bobbs-Merrill, 1965.

——, *The Doctrine of Virtue* (pt II of *The Metaphysic of Morals*), tr. Mary J. Gregor. Philadelphia: University of Pennsylvania Press, 1964.

——, 'Perpetual peace', in *On History*, tr. and ed. Lewis White Beck. Indianapolis: Bobbs-Merrill, 1963.

——, *Religion within the Limits of Reason Alone*, tr. Theodore M. Greene and Hoyt H. Hudson. New York: Harper and Brothers, 1960.

Kaufmann, Walter, *Without Guilt and Justice*. New York: Peter H. Wynden, 1973.

Kierkegaard, S., *Either/Or*, 2 vols. Walter Lowrie. New York: Doubleday, 1959.

——, *The Sickness unto Death*, tr. Walter Lowrie. Princeton, NJ: Princeton University Press, 1980.

Le Goff, Jacques, *Time, Work and Culture in the Middle Ages*. Chicago: University of Chicago Press, 1980.

Locke, John, *Two Treatises of Government*, ed. with intro. by Peter Laslett. New York: Mentor, 1965.

MacIntyre, Alasdair, *After Virtue: a study in moral theory*. Notre Dame, Ind.: University of Notre Dame Press, 1981.

Marx, Karl, *Economic and Philosophical Manuscripts*, in *Early Writings*, tr. Rodney Livingstone and Gregor Benton. Harmondsworth, Middx: Penguin, 1975.

——, *Critique of the Gotha Programme*. New York: International Publishers, 1938.

Mack, E., 'Distributive justice and the tension of Lockeanism', *Social Philosophy and Policy*, 1.1 (1983).

Menninger, Karl, *The Crime of Punishment*. New York: Viking Press, 1980.

Narvenson, Jan, 'On Dworkinian equality'. *Social Philosophy and Policy*, 1.1 (1983).

Nozick, Robert, *Anarchy, State and Utopia*. Oxford: Basil Blackwell, 1974.

Perelman, Chaim, *The Idea of Justice and the Problem of Argument*. London: Routledge and Kegan Paul, 1963.

Plato, *The Republic*, tr. Benjamin Jowett, ed. Scott Buchanan. Harmondsworth, Middx: Penguin, 1977.

——, *Gorgias*, tr. Terence Irwin. London: Oxford University Press, 1979.

Pocock, J. G. A., *The Machiavellian Moment*. Princeton University Press, 1979.

Rawls, John, *A Theory of Justice*. London: Oxford University Press, 1972.

Rescher, Nicholas, *Distributive Justice*. Indianapolis: Bobbs-Merrill, 1966.

Rosner, M., 'Theories of participatory democracy and the kibbutz' (unpublished manuscript).

Rousseau, Jean-Jacques, *The Social Contract and Discourses*, tr. G. D. H. Cole. London: Dent, 1973.

——, *Julie ou La Nouvelle Héloïse*. Paris: Flammarion, 1967.

——, *Emile*, tr. Barbara Foxley. London: Dent, 1977.

Rorty, Richard, *Consequences of Pragmatism*. Brighton, Sussex: Harvester Press, 1982.

Rowley, H. H., *Prophecy and Religion in Ancient China and Israel*. London: Athlone Press, 1956.

Singer, M. G., *Generalization in Ethics*. London: Eyre and Spottiswoode, 1963.

Strawson, P. F., *Freedom and Resentment*. London: Methuen, 1974.

Tugendhat, Ernst, *Problem der Ethik*. Reclam, 1984.

Unger, Roberto Mangabeira, *Law in Modern Society*. New York: Free Press, 1976.

Walzer, Michael, *Just and Unjust Wars*. New York: Basic Books, 1977.

——, *Spheres of Justice*. Oxford: Martin Robertson, 1983.

Weber, Max, *From Max Weber: Essays in Sociology*, tr. and ed. H. Gerth and C. W. Mills. London: Routledge and Kegan Paul, 1956.

Index